ELIZABETHAN THEATRE HISTORY

An Annotated Bibliography of Scholarship, 1664-1979

Formerly: *English Renaissance Theatre History: A Reference Guide*

DAVID STEVENS

James L. Harner

Editor

Lulu Press, Inc.
Lulu.com

Cover design by David Stevens.

DeWitt/Van Buchell drawing of the Swan Playhouse, University of Utrecht Ms. 842, f.132r., *Courtesy of the University of Utrecht Library.*

Library of Congress Cataloging in Publication Data

Stevens, David, 1947-
Elizabethan theatre history.

Includes index.

1. Theater--England--History--16th century--bibliography. 2. Theater--England--History-17th century--Bibliography. I. Title.
22014.D7S78 [PN2589]   016.792'0942 82-2965
ISBN 978-1-105-17521-3

Contents

The Author

David Stevens was associate professor of theatre and chairman of the Department of Theatre and Dance at Oakland University, and Chair of the Department of Theater at Southern Illinois University at Carbondale before his retirement from teaching in 1993. His articles and reviews have appeared in *Theatre Journal, Extrapolation, The Scope of the Fantastic, Survey of Science Fiction Literature, The Journal of Legal Medicine, The Illinois Bar Journal,* and *Choice.* He has delivered papers at the annual conferences of the American Theatre Association, the Speech Communication Association, the Popular Culture Association, and the Association for the Fantastic in the Arts. His books on fantasy writers J.R.R. Tolkien and Peter S. Beagle have been published by Borgo Press. In 1972 he was awarded a Woodrow Wilson Fellowship while completing the Ph.D. at Bowling Green University; and he has participated in the National Endowment for the Humanities Summer Seminars at the University of Iowa in 1981 and at Northwestern University in 1987. He practiced law in Illinois from 1993 until 2009, and published his legal memoir in 2010. An avid bridge player, he published an instructional book for beginning and advancing bridge players in 2010.

Preface

This reference guide provides an annotated, chronological list of the scholarship from 1664 through 1979 on Elizabethan theatrical history. My intention was to compile a comprehensive guide, with brief annotations to aid the researcher in determining whether a specific item might be helpful. I quickly discovered that the enumerative bibliographer is far more dependent than I had thought on the works of his or her predecessors. Consequently, the term "comprehensive" must be applied with caution. I began with existing bibliographies (silently correcting their errors as I expect to be corrected), adding all other scholarship that I could find. I was, however, dependent upon indexes for many of my additions--I could not page through each volume of every journal that might have a relevant item in it. Therefore, it is probably safe to assume that I have missed some, especially short notes that are frequently not indexed. While I have found many of these brief notes (especially in the *Times Literary Supplement* and *Notes and Queries*), I look forward to filling in the gaps at some future time. For now, I am reasonably sure that I have not missed many major items.

Since the field the guide covers is theatre history, I have eliminated almost all items whose scope is purely literary. The exceptions are those whose titles might lead a reader to believe they deal with the theatrical, and those that were listed in one or more of the bibliographies usually consulted for theatrical history, particularly volume 1 of the *New Cambridge Bibliography of English Literature*. I have also arbitrarily excluded almost all editions of Shakespeare (even though many contain basic discussions of the Elizabethan stage), as well as almost all general histories of the theatre.

I have chosen a chronological organization simply because my other alternative--a topical organization--would have yielded too many cross-references, since many of these items would fit under two or more categories. As a partial remedy I offer the Index, which includes both authors and subjects, with frequent cross-references to the Index in the text. (The note "See Index . . ." in an annotation refers to the Index in the present volume, not that in the work cited.)

The annotations are in all but two or three cases my own; the only exceptions are quotations from English abstracts of foreign-language articles, always credited. I have attempted to be descriptive rather than evaluative in my comments, although at times my biases may be apparent. I have also severely limited my comments, with the result that at times I devote more space to a brief article than to a major book. The amount of space taken up by an annotation should not be read as an indication of comparative value; my intention is to provide a guide to purpose, scope, and method so that the scholar can decide if seeing an item might be valuable.

Many of the American and Canadian dissertations listed were annotated from authors' abstracts published in *Dissertation Abstracts* and *Dissertation Abstracts International*. Those dissertations for which abstracts were not so available were annotated from the complete dissertation or from photocopies of selected pages from the library of the degree-granting institution. In one case the author graciously provided me with photocopies from his Australian dissertation.

An asterisk (*) preceding an entry number indicates that I have not personally seen the item. For each such entry I have provided my source for the reference.

Preface to the Reprint, 2012

When it was suggested that I prepare the text of this book for a reprint, perhaps online, I was initially skeptical. It was part of a series intended almost exclusively for libraries, where scholars and students could access it when needed. Very few, if any, theatre historians or students of theatre history would require an individual copy. Further, it has never been updated, and some thirty years have passed since its initial publication.

Nonetheless, interest if not demand for copies has been steady over the years, and it has now been long enough since publication that some non-research libraries have recycled their copies. There are, in fact, a few lightly used copies available on Amazon.com and other such websites, at prices ranging from reasonable to exorbitant.

I therefore agreed to prepare the text for reprinting or posting. Unfortunately, I did not think through what that task would entail; the text had to be scanned and run through an OCR program to put it into editable format (I rejected the other option, retyping the entire text, *ex hypothesi*). Unfortunately, the OCR programs we used for this project left the text in deplorable condition. It had to be reworked line by line, and in that process inevitably some additional errors have crept in. I say "additional errors" because I am well aware that the original text contained errors. I have corrected the most egregious of those of which I am aware, but I urge users of this reprinting, which is not really a new edition, to check with the original printed version wherever possible.

Users will notice two major changes in this volume. First, I have changed the title. The original title, *English Renaissance Theatre History: A Reference Guide*, was used because of the G. K. Hall series in which it appeared (Reference Guides to Literature). The new title, *Elizabethan Theatre History: An Annotated Bibliography of Scholarship,1664-1979*, was chosen as more descriptive and more useful to the primary users, students and scholars of theatre history. The second change involves the numbering scheme. Each entry is now explicitly numbered with both year and item number, in order to make searching the volume easier, both by hand and electronically (an e-book download is to be available through Amazon.com and elsewhere). There is also one minor change: I have used *italics* for titles where appropriate rather than underlining as in the 1982 version. I retain the use of <u>underlining</u> for empasis, as in <u>see also</u>.

What is really needed is a new edition, filling in whatever gaps there may be in the text and bringing the whole thing up to date. In the past thirty years there have been truly astonishing strides made in the field. Such an update needs, however, another, and younger, eye than mine. I hereby give my permission for anyone who wishes to do so to update, correct, or enhance this work in any way they wish. I would be happy to cooperate with an updating effort.

David Stevens
25 October 2011

Acknowledgments

One of the greatest joys of completing a project such as this one lies in the contemplation of all those who provided substantial assistance. While this list is necessarily incomplete (if for no other reason than the fact that so many librarians do their yeoman's work anonymously), I owe a large debt to each of the individuals and groups named below, To all, my profound thanks.

-The Oakland University Research Committee, who provided two small grants for the purchase of materials and a Faculty Research Fellowship for the summer of 1980. Without this material assistance, this Reference Guide would have ended somewhere around 1910.

-The Interlibrary Loan Department of the Oakland University Library, especially Mary Wright before her departure and Linda Guyotte, who cheerfully processed literally hundreds of requests for obscure, foreign, or sometimes handwritten items. Their success rate was remarkable.

-Tamara McIntyre, Beth Grafe, and Kathy Bradley, present and former Oakland University students, who provided valuable translation services for many items in French and German.

-Professor Jane Eberwein, my colleague in English at Oakland University, who interrupted a vacation to gather material for me in the Cornell University Library.

-The staffs of the Reference Department and the Rare Books Room of the University of Michigan Library, where I lived for what seemed months at a time.

-Professor Adeline Hirschfeld-Medalia, my colleague in Communication Arts and Director of the Theatre Arts Program at Oakland University, who helped arrange my teaching schedule for two years to provide the maximum amount of time far research and writing.

-Professor James L. Harner, friend and colleague, mentor and editor, who was willing to take a chance, and who has provided advice and encouragement every step of the way.

-Professor Frank Hildy, eminent theatre historian, who first suggested there could be a use for a new edition.

-Professor Carol D. Stevens, my colleague, friend, and spouse, who alone knows the extent to which this work is hers as well as mine.

To all of you, and to all the others who have helped in this project, thanks, thanks, and ever thanks. What virtues it may have are due to your assistance; its vices, of course, are mine own.

Introduction

The English theatre during the reigns of Elizabeth I, James I, and Charles I (1558-1642) developed into one of the finest flowerings of the player's art that the world has yet seen. William Shakespeare, of course, stands head and shoulders above the rest of the theatre artists of the period, but this was also the time of great actors such as Richard Burbage and Edward Alleyn, the influential designer and architect Inigo Jones, and other great playwrights such as Ben Jonson and Christopher Marlowe. Standing in the shadow of these giants were many theatre artists who would themselves have been considered among the best of their age had they lived at any other time--actor Nathan Field, playwrights John Fletcher and James Shirley, to name but a few. But because there are so few written records, only a half-dozen or so murky drawings, and a few tantalizingly vague eyewitness accounts, we actually know very little about one of the greatest periods of theatrical history. What we do know we owe to the efforts of the theatre historians whose work is the subject of this volume.

What is a theatre historian? He or she is a scholar whose particular interest is the description and explanation of the art form of the theatre as it has existed in the past and developed into the present.[1] I say *the theatre* very specifically as opposed to *the drama*, because the two are not synonymous. Drama is a separate art form, a variety of literature. Theatre is concerned with the physical aspects of play production: the playhouses, actors and acting, costumes, stage lighting, music, and so on. Theatre history is also concerned with what might be termed the sociological and political aspects of production: the nature of the audience and the actor-audience relationship, government control, debates about propriety and decorum. Economics, too, interests the theatre historian: how productions are financed is often a crucial question.

As is the case with other historians, the discovery and interpretation of evidence is crucial to the theatre historian's task. Objectivity is the ideal, and the ultimate goal is the determination of the historical facts. Unfortunately, in this as in other areas of human endeavor, "historical facts" are elusive creatures, apparently changing as our society (and hence our point of view) changes. Perhaps the best that can be hoped for is an interpretation of whatever evidence may be unearthed consonant with our current view of history and our best effort at objectivity.

This is at least part of the reason, I think, that scholarship in the field of Elizabethan theatre history (as this field is conventionally called, despite the fact that part of it is Jacobean and Caroline rather than Elizabethan) is cyclical. Herbert Berry has discussed this cycle,[2] dividing the scholarship to date into three periods, breaking at the publication dates of the two major reference works in the field: Chambers's *The Elizabethan Stage* (1923.2), and Bentley's final volumes of *The Jacobean and Caroline Stage* (1968.2). Berry sees the earliest period as dominated by the Germans and focusing on the alternation theory; the middle period as dominated by J. C. Adams and focusing on the debate on the inner stage; and the present period as focusing on single-playhouse studies and what we consider to be tight control of acceptable evidence. The evidence has not changed (or at least, not very much); what we make of it (our vision of "the historical facts") has.

Within Berry's useful framework, I would like to distinguish a few of the more than 1600 works that follow as landmarks of the history of Elizabethan theatre history.

Heading the list would be Edmond Malone, the first important Elizabethan theatre historian. In his seminal *Historical Account of the Rise and Progress of the English Stage* (1790.1) and Boswell's later edition of it (1823.1), Malone revealed the fruits of his labors among the many documents he discovered. Some of these documents have since been lost, and we have only Malone's transcriptions to go on. All theatre historians working in this field owe a major debt to this pioneering scholar.

The nineteenth century was virtually dominated by two giants in the field: James Orchard Halliwell-Phillipps and John Payne Collier. Both worked extensively with documents, producing many important works of interpretation. Unfortunately, some of the documents that Collier "discovered" were in fact his forgeries, creating a controversy that echoes into our own time. Nonetheless, we would do the man's memory a disservice if we did not acknowledge his many important contributions.

Perhaps the single most important discovery in the history of the field was made in 1888 by Karl Theodor Gaedertz. In the University of Utrecht library Gaedertz found a copy of a contemporary sketch of the Swan Playhouse--the now famous and widely reproduced DeWitt-VanBuchell drawing. From that day to this, no historian can afford to ignore the Swan drawing. It may be rejected, it may be accepted as flawed, or it may be accepted as it stands, but it must be considered. Our current understanding of the physical features of the playhouse stages of the period owes a great deal to this single sketch. It has achieved such iconic status that I have used a copy of it on the cover and title page of this reprint.

Another important document that much of our present knowledge of the Elizabethan theatre is based on was published by W. W. Greg in 1904, 1907, and 1908: Philip Henslowe's diary and account books. Henslowe was an entrepeneur, investor, and theatre owner, and his meticulous accounts are an invaluable resource. Collier had earlier published an edition, but Greg's stood as a landmark in the field for many years.

Probably the most diligent document-finder the field has known, Charles William Wallace, was active from about 1905 to about 1915. Wallace combed the Public Record Office with his wife during those years, trumpeting each new discovery (especially about Shakespeare) in the popular press. The Wallaces engaged in spirited competition with another, less well-known, document searcher, Mrs. Charlotte Carmichael Stopes, who published alternate interpretations of many of the same documents.

Mrs. Stopes was involved in the two major controversies in the field during the second decade of the twentieth century, over the authenticity of the seventeenth-century Revels Accounts, and over the site of the Globe Playhouse. The debates were fascinating, if somewhat repetitive, and both can be followed through the years with the use of the Index to this reference guide.

The scholar whose name appears mast frequently in these pages is W. J. Lawrence. It has been said that wherever the theatre historian ventures, he will find the footprints of this man. Certainly this is the case in the field of Elizabethan theatre history. His many articles and collections must be consulted by the contemporary scholar, and frequently we find that, even after fifty years, we can add nothing to Lawrence's conclusions. His lack of an academic appointment or a private income forced him to write for popular consumption, but popularization did not diminish the quality of his scholarship.

Joseph Quincy Adams published two remarkable books in 1917, *Shakespearean Playhouses* and *The Dramatic Records of Sir Henry Herbert, Master of the Revels*. The former was concerned exclusively with the exteriors and locations of the various playhouses, and is still valuable, and the latter is indispensable for tracing the repertories and production patterns of the various playhouses and companies in the latter part of the period.

As previously mentioned, E. K. Chambers's *The Elizabethan Stage* stands preeminent among the early studies. While somewhat in need of revision in light of more than fifty years of subsequent scholarship, it still ranks as one of the two most valuable works yet produced in the field. Leslie Hotson attempted the same task for a later period in his *Commonwealth and Restoration Stage* (1928), and many of the documents he prints concern the earlier time.

A slim volume that received little critical attention at the time was published by George F. Reynolds in 1940. *The Staging of Elizabethan Plays at the Red Bull Theatre, 1605-1625,* however, has since become one of the most influential works in the field. Almost all studies of staging since use some variation on the method that Reynolds pioneered.

John Cranford Adams made a much greater immediate impact with his *The Globe Playhouse: Its Design and Equipment* in 1942. Unlike Reynolds's, however, Adams's theories have been in constant decline since the middle fifties. To this day, however, it is Adams's reconstruction of the Globe that most people think of in connection with the Elizabethan theatre. Despite being discredited by two generations of scholarship, it remains perhaps the most influential single work yet produced.

Hotson, J. C. Adams, and Reynolds all first entered the field through their work on doctoral dissertations. In 1941 G. E. Bentley published a revised and expanded version of his dissertation that has developed into one of the two most important works in the field. *The Jacobean and Caroline Stage,* continued in 1956 and 1968, ranks with Chambers's great work as part of the backbone of all Elizabethan theatre history studies.

As we come closer to our own time it is more difficult to pick out the landmarks, probably because we are too close to them yet. Certainly among the most important recent scholars in the field I would list Richard Hosley, C. Walter Hodges, Glynne Wickham, Herbert Berry, John Orrell, T. J. King, and David Bergeron. And there are so many others who could easily be added to such a list. Rather than try to be *comprehensive* and offend anyone, I invite renders to examine the scholarship and decide for themselves its value.

NOTES

[1]Oscar J. Brockett, "Research in Theatre History," *Educational Theatre Journal* 19, no. 2A (June 1967): 267-75.

[2]Herbert Berry, "Americans in the Playhouses," *Shakespeare Studies* 9 (1976): 31-44.

Abbreviations

ADDT	*American Dissertations in Drama and Theatre*
AnRS	*Annual Report of Studies (Kyoto, Japan)*
Archiv	*Archiv für das Studium der Neueren Sprachen und Literature*
ArchivL	*Archiv für Litteraturgeschichte*
ArchR	*Architectural Review*
ArtJ	*Art Journal*
BLR	*Bodleian Library Record*
BMg	*Burlington Magazine*
BNYPL	*Bulletin of the New York Public Library*
CBEL	*Cambridge Bibliography of English Literature*
CE	*College English*
Century	*Century Monthly Magazine*
CHEL	*Cambridge History of English Literature*
CM	*Current Musicology*
ColQ	*Colorado Quarterly*
CompD	*Comparative Drama*
ContempR	*Contemporary Review*
CUS	*Colorado University Studies*
DEAL	*Dissertations in English and American Literature*
DuF	*Dichtung und Volkstum*

EA	*Etudes Anglaises: Grande-Bretagne, Etats-Unis*
E&S	*Essays and Studies (London)*
HER	*English Historical Review*
EIE	*English Institute Essays*
ELH	*ELH [formerly Journal of English Literary History]*
ELR	*English Literary Renaissance*
ES	*English Studies: A Journal of English Language and Literature*
ESRS	*Emporia State Research Studies (Kansas)*
EStudien	*Englische Studien*
ETJ	*Educational Theatre Journal*
FortR	*Fortnightly Review*
GMg	*Gentlemen's Magazine*
GRM	*Germanisch-Romanische Monatsschrift*
GuildMisc	*Guildhall Miscellany*
Harper's	*Harper's Monthly Magazine*
HLB	*Harvard Library Bulletin*
HLQ	*Huntington Library Quarterly*
ISLL	*Illinois Studies in Language and Literature*
JBArA	*Journal of the British Archaeological Association*
JDSG	*Jahrbuch der Deutschen Shakespeare-Gesellschaft*

JDSh	*Jahrbuch der Deutschen Shakespeare-Gessellschaft West (Heidelberg)*
JEGP	*Journal of English and Germanic Philology*
JHI	*Journal of the History of Ideas*
JMRS	*Journal of Medieval and Renaissance Studies*
JRIBI	*Journal of the Royal Institute of British Architects*
JWCI	*Journal of the Warburg and Courtland Institutes*
L&LT	*Life and Letters Today*
Lippincott's	*Lippincott's Monthly Magazine*
LQHR	*London Quarterly and Holborn Review*
M&L	*Music and Letters*
MLN	*MLN [formerly Modern Language Notes]*
MLQ	*Modern Language Quarterly*
MLR	*Modern Language Review*
MP	*Modern Philology: A Journal Devoted to Research in Medieval and Modern Literature*
MSC	*Malone Society Collections*
MuK	*Maske und Kothurn: Internationale Beitrage zur Theaterwissenschaft*
MusAnt	*Musical Antiquary*
MusQ	*Musical Quarterly*
N&Q	*Notes and Queries*
N&QSD	*Notes and Queries for Somerset and Dorset*

NCBEL	*New Cambridge Bibliography of English Literature*
Neophil	*Neophilologus (Netherlands)*
NS	*Die Neueren Sprachen*
NTM	*New Theatre Magazine*
NYCROJ	*North Yorkshire County Record Office Journal*
NYRB	*New York Review of Books*
ORRD	*Opportunities for Research in Renaissance Drama [later RORD]*
PAPS	*Proceedings of the American Philosophical Society*
PBA	*Proceedings of the British Academy*
PMLA	*PMLA: Publications of the Modern Language Association*
PMPA	*Publications of the Missouri Philological Association*
PMusA	*Proceedings of the Musical Association*
PP	*Philologica Pragensia*
PQ	*Philological Quarterly*
PRMA	*Proceedings of the Royal Musical Association*
PRPSG	*Proceedings of the Royal Philosophical Society of Glasgow*
QJS	*Quarterly Journal of Speech*
QQ	*Queen's Quarterly*
QR	*Quarterly Review*

REEDN	*Records of Early English Drama Newsletter*
RenD	*Renaissance Drama*
RenN	*Renaissance News*
RenP	*Renaissance Papers*
RES	*Review of English Studies: A Quarterly Journal of English Literature and the English Language*
RHT	*Revue d'Histoire du Théâtre*
RLC	*Revue de Littérature Camparée*
RORD	*Research Opportunities in Renaissance Drama*
RTh	*Revue Théatral*
SAQ	*South Atlantic Quarterly*
SCJ	*Sixteenth Century Journal*
Scribner's	*Scribner's Monthly Magazine*
SCSML	*Smith College Studies in Modern Language*
SEL	*Studies in English Literature, 1500-1900*
SFQ	*Southern Folklore Quarterly*
ShAB	*Shakespeare Association Bulletin*
ShFQ	*Shakespeare Fellowship Quarterly*
ShN	*Shakespeare Newsletter*
ShS	*Shakespeare Survey: An Annual Survey of Shakepearian Study and Production*
ShSP	*Shakespeare Society Papers*
ShSt	*Shakespeare Studies*

ShStage	*Shakespeare Stage*
ShStudies	*Shakespeare Studies (Tokyo)*
SIMG	*Sammelbände der Internationalen Musik-Gesellschaft*
SMC	*Studies in Medieval Culture*
SMNN	*Selborne Magazine and Nature Notes*
SP	*Studies in Philology*
SpMon	*Speech Monographs*
SQ	*Shakespeare Quarterly*
SR	*Sewanee Review*
SRO	*Shakespearean Research and Opportunities: The Report of the MLA Conference*
TDR	*The Drama Review [formerly Tulane Drama Review]*
ThArts	*Theatre Arts Monthly*
ThR	*Theatre Research International*
ThS	*Theatre Survey: The American Journal of Theatre History*
ThW	*Theatre Workshop*
TJ	*Theatre Journal [formerly ETJ]*
TLS	*Times Literary Supplement (London)*
TN	*Theatre Notebook: A Journal of the History and Technique of the British Theatre*
TQ	*Texas Quarterly*
TR	*Texas Review*

TrLeLPS	*Transactions of the Leicester Literary and Philosophical Society*
TrLMArchS	*Transactions of the London and Middlesex Archaeological Society*
TrNShS	*Transactions of the New Shakspere Society*
TrRHS	*Transactions of the Royal Historical Society*
TrRSL	*Transactions of the Royal Society of Literature*
TrWASAL	*Transactions of the Wisconsin Academy of Science, Art, and Literature*
TSL	*Tennessee Studies in Literature*
TSLL	*Texas Studies in Literature and Language: A Journal of the Humanities*
UNS	*University of Nebraska Studies*
UR	*Universal Review*
WRUB	*Bulletin of Western Reserve University*
YR	*Yale Review: A National Quarterly*
ZDP	*Zeitschrift für Deutsche Philologie*
ZFEU	*Zeitschrift für Französichen und Englischen Unterricht*

Elizabethan Theatre History

<u>1664</u>

1664.1   FLECKNOE, RICHARD. "A Short Discourse of the English Stage." In *Love's Kingdom*. London: Printed by R. Wood, sigs. G4^r-G8^r.
      The earliest extant attempt at a history of the Elizabethan stage. Flecknoe notes companies using inns, praises Burbage and Field for their acting ability, and lists Shakespeare, Jonson, and Fletcher as the best playwrights. He refers to the stages as "simple," with old tapestry and rushes. Reprinted: 1909.11; 1957.7; 1963.3; 1972.33; 1973.5.

<u>1699</u>

1699.1   WRIGHT, JAMES. *Historia Histrionica: An Historical Account of the English Stage.* London: printed by G. Groom, for W. Hawes, 36 pp.
      Set up as "A Dialogue of Plays and Players," this is the second attempt at a history and the first important one. Wright emphasizes the medieval origins in discussing both acting and playhouses. Much of the information presented has since been verified from historical records. <u>See</u> 1845.1. Reprinted: 1872.2; 1874.3; 1876.2; 1972.33.

<u>1788</u>

1788.1   NICHOLS, JOHN. *The Progresses and Public Processions of Queen Elizabeth.* Vols. 1 and 2. London: 3. Nichols, 1230 pp.
      Comprehensive compilation of works presented during the queen's progresses and on other occasions. For vol. 3, <u>see</u> 1805.1. Reprinted: 1823.1.

<u>1790</u>

1790.1   MALONE, EDMOND, ed. "An Historical Account of the Rise and Progress of the English Stage, and of the Economy and Usages of Our Ancient Theatres." In *Plays and Poems of William Shakespeare*. Vol. 1, pt. 2. London: J. Rivington & Sons, 294 pp.
      The earliest scholarly history; based on documentary sources, some of which have since been lost. Although Malone carries his history to roughly 1740, he concentrates on the pre-Restoration stage. <u>See</u> 1842.1. Reprinted: 1790.2; 1794.1; 1799.2; 1800.1; 1813.4; 1821.1; 1839.1; 1901.3.

1790.2   _____. *An Historical Account of the Rise and Progress of the English Stage, and of the Economy and Usages of Our Ancient Theatres.* London: H. Baldwin, 294 pp.
      Reprint of 1790.1.

1797.1　CHALMERS, GEORGE. "Of the History of the Stage." In *An Apology for the Believers in the Shakespeare Papers, Which Were Exhibited in Norfolk-Street.* London: Thomas Egerton, pp. 339-471.

　　　　An attempt at a comprehensive history of the stage in England, chiefly composed of additions and corrections to 1790.1. Chalmers begins his treatment of the Elizabethan period with a discussion of the boy companies, then goes on to the adult companies, governmental regulation, the playhouses, and the actors. Reprinted: 1799.1; 1811.4; 1821.1.

1798

1798.1　ELLIS, HENRY. *The History and Antiquities of the Parish of St. Leonard Shoreditch and Liberty of Norton Folgate in the Suburbs of London.* London: J. Nichols, pp. 208-12.

　　　　The relevant section includes information about the Theatre and the Curtain, both of which were built in Shoreditch, and on actors and playwrights associated with the parish. Lists entries related to the Curtain in the parish register from 1580 to 1639.

1799

1799.1　CHALMERS, GEORGE. "Of the History of the Stage." In *A Supplemental Apology for the Believers in the Shakespeare Papers. Being a Reply to Mr. Malone's Answer, Which Was Early Announced but Never Published.* London: Thomas Egerton, pp. 147-92,

　　　　Reprint of 1797.1.

1799.2　MALONE, EDMOND. "An Historical Account of the Rise and Progress of the English Stage, and of the Economy and Usages of Our Ancient Theatres." In *The Plays of William Shakespeare.* Vol. 3. Basil: J. J. Tourneisen, 430 pp.

　　　　Reprint of 1790.1.

1800

1800.1　MALONE, EDMOND. *An Historical Account of the Rise and Progress of the English Stage, and of the Economy and Usages of Our Ancient Theatres.* Basil: J. J. Tourneisen, 423 pp.

　　　　Reprint of 1790.1.

1805

1805.1　NICHOLS, JOHN. *The Progresses and Public Processions of Queen Elizabeth.* Vol. 3. London: J. Nichols, 482 pp.

　　　　Continuation of 1788.1. Reprinted: 1823.1.

1813.1   HASLEWOOD, JOSEPH. "Of the London Theatres. No. 1." *GMg* 83, pt. 2 (August):121-23.

        Presents information on the Fortune, from the contract and other contemporary sources. This is the first of a series on theatres of the period. See also 1813.2; 1813.3; 1814.1. Reprinted: 1837.1.

1813.2   _____. "Of the London Theatres, No. 11." *GMg* 83, pt. 2 (September): 217-8.

        Examines the Whitefriars, supposedly pulled down in 1580, and the Salisbury Court. Part of a series. See also1813.1; 1813.3; 1814.1. Reprinted: 1 837.1.

1813.3   _____. "Of the London Theatres. No. IV." *GMg* 83, pt. 2 (November): 437.

        Brief discussion of the Rose, the Hope, and the Swan. Part of a series. See also1813.1; 1813.2; 1814.1. Reprinted: 1837.1.

1813.4   MALONE, EDMOND. "An Historical Account of the Rise and Progress of the English Stage, and of the Economy and Usages of Our Ancient Theatres." In *The Plays and Poems of William Shakespeare*. Vol. I. Edited by James Boswell the younger. London: F. C. and J. Rivington, 522 pp. [Boswell's Malone.]

        Reprint of 1790.1, with additions related to the Henslowe papers and Chalmers (1797.1). See also 1821.1.

1814

1814.1   HASLEWOOD, JOSEPH. "Of the London Theatres. No. VI." *GMg* 84, pt. 1 (April): 337-39.

        Discusses Paul's Boys and their playhouses. Part of a series; see also 1813.1; 1813.2; 1813.3. Reprinted: 1837.1.

1821

1821.1   MALONE, EDMOND. "Mr. Malone's Historical Account of the Rise and Progress of the English Stage, and of the Economy and Usages of Our Ancient Theatres." In *The Plays and Poems of William Shakespeare*. Vol. 1. Edited by James Boswell the younger. London: F. C. and J. Rivington, 522 pp. [Boswell's Malone.]

        Reprint of 1790.1, with additions from 1813.1, including Chalmers (1797.1) and a new appendix by Malone.

1823

1823.1   NICHOLS, JOHN. *The Progresses and Public Processions of Queen Elizabeth.* 3 vols. London: J. Nichols, 1912 pp.

        Reprint of 1788.1 and 1805.1.

1925.1   WILKINSON, ROBERT. *Londina Illustrata.* Vol. 2, *Theatrum Illustrata: Graphic and Historic Memorials of Ancient Playhouses, Modern Theatres, and Other Places of Amusement in the Cities and Suburbs of London and Westminster.*   London: R. Wilkinson, plates 165-73.

    Contains reproductions of nine engravings and woodcuts showing London theatres, including the baiting houses, the Globe and the Rose (transposed), two other views of the Globe, the Swan (the Antwerp view), the Red Bull, and the second Fortune. Wilkinson provides brief descriptions.

1826

*1826.1   BRAYLEY, EDWARD WEDLAKE. *Historical and Descriptive Accounts of the Theatres of London.* Illustrated by Daniel Havell. London: J. Taylor, 92 pp. Cited in *NUC Pre-1956 Imprints* 73:310. Reprinted:

1828

1828.1   NICHOLS, JOHN. *The Progresses, Processions, and Magnificent Festivities of King James the First, his Royal Consort, Family and Court.* 4 vols. I.ondon: J. B. Nichols, 2552 pp.

    Comprehensive compilation of "poetical panegyrics; descriptions of various solemnities and festivities; or dramatic performances" including forty masques and ten civic pageants, arranged chronologically.

1829

1829.1   COLLIER, JOHN PAYNE. *The History of English Dramatic Poetry to the Time of Shakespeare; and Annals of the Stage to the Restoration.* 3 vols. London: J. Murray, 1450 pp.

    An ambitious early work, preceded only by Malone (1790.1). The first volume begins with the "Annals of the Stage," a lengthy recitation of documentary evidence related to play production. This is completed in the second volume, which also begins "The History of Dramatic Poetry." The third volume completes this section and also contains "An Account of the Old Theatres of London," "Details Connected with the Performance of Plays," and an index. See 1844.5; 1861.1; and 1886.4. See also the much revised second edition, 1879.2.

1833

1833.1   BRAYLEY, EDWARD WEDLAKE. *Historical and Descriptive Accounts of the Theatres of London.* Illustrated by Daniel Havell. London: J. Yates, 92 pp.

    The first chapter mentions the Phoenix in passing as preparation for a discussion of Restoration playhouses.

1836.1   KEMPE, ALFRED JOHN, ed. *The Loseley Manuscripts*. London: J. Murray,
pp.   15-117.
      An edition of the well-known manuscripts containing a good deal of
documentary evidence concerning the Elizabethan theatre. The relevant section
contains a brief discussion of the career of Sir Thomas Carwarden, Master
the Revels, and various documents related to his office.

1837

1837.1   HASLEWOOD, JOSEPH. "Account of the Old London Theatres." In
Roxburghe Revels, and Other Related Papers. Edited by James Maidment.
Edinburgh: Roxburghe Club, pp. 85-128.
      Reprint of 1813.1-3; 1814.1.

1837.2   NICHOLS, JOHN. *London Pageants*. London: J. B. Nichols and Son,   125 pp.
      Contains accounts of fifty-five royal processions and entertainments in
London from 1236 to 1831 and a bibliographical list of Lord Mayor's Pageants
from 1585 to 1831. The accounts are taken from contemporary writers. See Index,
under Lord Mayor's Pageants, Royal Processions, and Royal Progresses, for other
references.

1839

1839.1   MALONE, EDMOND. "An Historical Account of the English Stage." In
*Historical and Explanatory Notes with Various Readings Illustrative of the Works
of W. Shakspeare*. Paris: Baudry's European Library, pp. liii-lxxxiv.
      Reprint of 1790.1, with additions from 1813.1 and 1821.1.

1841

1841.1   COLLIER, JOHN PAYNE. *Memoirs of Edward Alleyn, Founder of Dulwich
College: Including Some New Particulars Respecting Shakespeare, Ben Jonson,
Massinger, Dekker, &c. London*: Shakespeare Society, 219 pp.
      A biography of the important actor, based on manuscripts held at Dulwich
College. Included in an appendix is Alleyn's part for *Orlando Furioso*, one of the
most important extant documents from this period. Collier cites documents freely,
and many are in Alleyn's own hand. Henslowe's relationship with Alleyn and the
founding of the College are fully detailed. Eight pages of notes and corrections,
from other documents seen later, follow the text, as does an appendix including
Alleyn's father's will, the part of Orlando, two legal documents, and the agreement
for the building of the College. See Index, under Alleyn, for additional references.
See 1843.1.

1842.1   CUNNINGHAM, PETER, ed. *Extracts from the Accounts of the Revels at Court in the Reigns of Queen Elizabeth and King James I*. London: Shakespeare Society, 228 pp.

      Contains a lengthy introduction by the editor describing the circumstances of his discovery of these documents, of interest for what it tells us about nineteenth-century antiquarians as well as about the subject itself. Cunningham claims to correct several errors of Malone (1790.1). He provides an index of plays mentioned, although a more complete index would be helpful. These documents were later the subject of a continuing controversy over their genuineness. See Index under Revels Accounts.

1843

1843.1   COLLIER, JOHN PAYNE. *The Alleyn Papers: A Collection of Original Documents Illustrative of the Life and Times of Edward Alleyn.* London: Shakespeare Society, 110 pp.

      Additions to the earlier biography of Alleyn (1841.1), based on additional documents held by Halliwell-Phillipps. The introduction contains Collier's discussion of the documents, which form the bulk of the volume. Collier here concentrates an Alleyn's acquisition of wealth and accumulation of property. He also prints the actor's will. See Index, under Alleyn, for additional references.

1843.2   FAIRHOLT, FREDERICH W[ILLIAM]. *Lord Mayor's Pageants: Being Collections Towards a History of These Annual Celebrations.* Percy Society, no. 10, pt. 1. London: Percy Societv, 178 pp.

      A history of the Lord Mayor's Pageants from 1236 to 1841. Fairholt describes the pageants for each year, based on contemporary records, and prints a selection in a companion volume.

1844

1844.1   BRUCE, JOHN. "Who Was 'Will, My Lord of Leycester's Jesting Player'?" *ShSP* 1: 88-95.

      The phrase alluded to in the title occurs in a letter of Sir Philip Sidney. Bruce narrows the possibilities to three, and concludes that Will Kempe was a likelier candidate than either William Shakespeare or Will Johnson. He then speculates that Leicestar's Men (including Shakespeare) may have accompanied Sidney to the Low Countries in 1585. See also 1958.13; 1959.13.

1844.2   DRAMATICUS [pseud.]. "On the Profits of Old Actors." *ShSP* 1: 21-23.

      A brief note citing corroborative evidence for the profitability of acting around 1600.

1844.3   HALLIWELL[-PHILLIPPS], JAMES ORCHARD. *Tarleton's Jests, and News Out of Purgatory: With Notes, and Some Account of the Life of Tarleton.* London: Shakespeare Society, 182 pp.

    Essentially an edition of the two works. with a brief biography of the famous clown of Shakespeare's company. See Index, under Tarlton, for additional references.

1844.4   HERBERT, J. P. "Additions to *The Alleyn Papers*." *ShSP* 1: 16-20.

    Contains four minor items, including a note signed by dramatist Robert Daborne; an agreement with a tailor signed by William Rowley, Joseph Taylor, and Robert Pallant; verses in the farm of an acrostic by John Day; and a charitable appeal in prose, also by Day. The originals at the time were in the possession of the author, having been collected by his father and grandfather.

1844.5   TOMLINS, THOMAS EDLYNE. "Origins of the Curtain Theatre, and Mistakes Regarding It ." *ShSP* 1: 29-35.

    Repudiates Collier's conjecture (in 1831.1) that the Curtain Playhouse drew its name from the similarly named land on which it stood (which may have been part of the fortifications of London) by publishing the documents Collier cited but did not print.

1845

1845.1   CUNNINGHAM, PETER. "Did General Harrison Kill 'Dick Robinson' the Player?" *ShSP* 2: 11-13.

    Confirms the suggestion (in 1699.1) that actor Richard Robinson was killed by General Harrison at the taking of Basing House by citing a previously unknown tract on the Great Rebellion held in the British Library.

1845.2   _____. "Plays Acted at Court, Anno 1613 (from the Accounts of Lard Harrington, Treasurer of the Chamber to James I)." *ShSP* 2: 123-26.

    The first printing of Joseph Haslewood's notes on the Treasurer's Account, as well as a brief history of the source from which they were derived.

1845.3   FAIRHOLT, FREDERICK WILLIAM. *The Civic Garland: A Collection of Songs from the London Pageants.* Percy Society, no. 12. London: Percy Society, 134 pp.

    The subtitle explains the contents. Fairholt provides a lengthy introduction discussing his sources and a headnote for each of the twenty-eight songs included. Selections range from mid-sixteenth century to 1702.

1845.4   HENSLOWE, PHILIP. *The Diary of Philip Henslowe from 1591 to 1609.* Edited by John Payne Collier. London: Shakespeare Society, 290 pp.

    The first complete printing of the diary, but superseded by the editions of Greg (1904.7; 1907.15; 1908.11), Foakes and Rickert (1961.13), and the facsimile

(1977.8). Collier provides copious annotations and the inventories in an appendix. See also Malone's transcription of part of the diary in 1790.1.

1846

1946.1   COLLIER, JOHN PAYNE. *Memoirs of the Principal Actors in the Plays of Shakespeare.* London: Shakepeare Society, 296 pp.
   Brief biographies of the actors listed as principal players in the First Folio, with the exception of Shakespeare himself. They vary in length and detail, depending, of course, on what Collier knew of the actor. Thus, Richard Burbage is given fifty-six pages while Samuel Crasse rates two. Collier cites relevant documents fully. <u>See</u> Index, under Actors and under names of individuals; and <u>see</u> especially Chambers(1923.2), Nungezer (1929.12), and Bentley 1941.1.

1846.2   RIMBAULT, EDWARD F[RANCIS]. *Who Was "Jack Wilson" the Singer of Shakespeare's Stage?* London: John Russell Smith, 16 pp.
   Attempts to identify the Jack Wilson who played Balthazar in *Much Ado About Nothing* and composed music to several of Shakespeare's songs with Dr. John Wilson, who became Oxford Professor of Music in 1644.

1847

1847.1   REARDON, JAMES PURCELL. "An Unknown Tract by Philip Stubbes, the Enemy of Theatrical Performances in 1583." *ShSP* 3: 15-21.
   A brief antitheatrical tract by the author of *The Anatomy of Abuses*, discovered by Reardon.

1847.2   TOMLINS, THOMAS EDLYNE. "A New Document Regarding the Authority of the Master of the Revels Over Play-Makers, Plays, and Players, in 1581." *ShSP* 3:1-6.
   Discusses details of the lease of the grounds on which Text of the document giving Edmund Tylney extraordinary powers to command the services of any playwright or actor he saw fit and to imprison any who refuse. Tylney was also given the right to require any company to present any of their plays to him at any time.

1847.3   TYSON, WILLIAM. "Heming's Players at Bristol in the Reign of Henry VIII." *ShSP* 3: 13-14.
   A brief note disclosing discovery of a five-shilling payment to"Mr. henings players" in Bristol in 1544. Tyson speculates that this might have been the father of John Heminge,first editor of Shakespeare.

1848.1   CUNNINGHAM, PETER; PLANCHE, J[AMES] R[OBINSON]; and
COLLIER, J[OHN] PAYNE. *Inigo Jones: A Life: Remarks on Some his Sketches
for Masques and Dramas; and Five Court Masques.* London: Shakespeare
Society, 296 pp.
    The earliest biography of Jones to cite records extensively, particularly
with regard to the expenses for the masques of James I. The authors include a
detailed examination of Jones's quarrel with Jonson, as well as a discussion of
their collaboration. The volume places more under emphasis on the architecture
than the theatre work in discussing Jones's career, but the designs for the masques
are discussed in the second essay. Five documents and fifteen costume sketches
are included in an appendix.

1848.2   MACHYN, HENRY. *The Diary of Henry Machyn, Citizen and Merchant-
Taylor of London, from A.D. 1550 to A.D. 1563.* Edited by John Nichols.
Camden Society Publications, No. 42. London: Camden Society, 464 pp.
    Contains first-hand descriptions of the Lord Mayor's Pageants of 1553-57
and 1561-62, and of a variety of interludes and plays. Frequently cited by Collier
in 1879.2.

1849.1   COLLIER, JOHN PAYNE. "Original History of 'The Theatre,' in Shoreditch,
and Connexion of the Burbage Family with It." *ShSP* 5: 63-70.
    Discusses details of the lease of the grounds on which James Burbage built
the Theatre in Shoreditch. Collier assumes that the statement that the Burbages
and others tore down the building and carried the timber away to build another
playhouse cannot be true, since he dates the first Globe to 1594 or 1595 rather
than 1599. See Index, under Burbage, James, and under Theatre Playhouse; see
also Stopes, Charlotte Carmichael, and Wallace, Charles William, for additional
references.

1849.2   _____. "Richard Field (the Printer of Shakespeare's *Venus and Adonis* and
Lucrece), Nathaniel Field, Anthony Munday, and Heenry Chettle." ShSq 4:36-40.
    Discloses details about the apprenticeship bindings of actors Field,
Munday, and Chettle, all of which were broken

1849.3   CUNNINGHAM, PETER. "Sir George Buc and the Office of the Revels."
ShSP 4:143-44.
    A brief note including a letter from Sir George Buc, ca. 1610, dealing with
his loss of a house and his request for help from the Earl of Salisbury.

1849.4   _____. "The Whitefriars Theatre, the Salisbury Court Theatre, and the Duke's Theatre in Dorset Gardens." *ShSP* 4: 89-109.

Consists primarily of five sixteenth-century documents related to theatrical affairs at these three playhouses. Included are the Indenture on 15 July 1629 of the Earl of Dorset; Heton's Instructions for his Patent and Draught of the same; Bird's "Instructions Touching Salisbury Court Playhouse, 14 Septem., 1639," made on behalf of William Beeston; and Tyrrill, Wyndham, and Archer's deposition against Beeston, 1667.

1849.5   DRAMATICUS [pseud.]. "The Players Who Acted in *The Shoemaker's Holiday*, 1600, a Comedy by Thomas Dekker and Robert Wilson." *ShSP* 4: 110-22.

The anonymous author's anonymous friend provided him with a copy of the play with Wilson's name accompanying Dekker's at the end of an epistle to the reader, and the same copy has the names of the actors of the principal roles written in as they enter.

1849.6   FORMAN, SIMON. *The Autobiography and Personal Diary of Dr. Simon Foreman, the Celebrated Astrologer, from A.D. 1552 to A.D. 1602, from the Unpublished Manuscripts in the Ashmolean Museum, Oxford.* Edited by James Orchard Halliwell[-Phillipps]. London: privately printed. 32 pp.

Does not include Forman's eyewitness accounts of four of Shakespeare's plays. See 1876.1.

1849.7   HALLIWELL[-PHILLIPPS], J[AMES] 0[RCHARD]. "Dispute Between the Earl of Worcester's Players and the Corporation of Leicester in 1586: From the Records of that City." *ShSq* 4: 145-46.

Records of an attempt in 1586 by the city fathers of Leicester to bribe Lord Worcester's Players into not performing in their community and the subsequent quarrel that developed.

1849.8   REARDON, JAMES PURCELL. "Two Specimens of the Poetry of Philip Stubbes, Author of *The Anatomy of Abuses*, 1583, and the Enemy of Theatrical Performances, Unknown to Bibliographers." *ShSP* 4: 71-88.

Two brief prose tracts, in the style of the *Anatomy*, and two pieces in rhymed couplets, all opposing the theatre and discovered by Reardon.

1849.9   TOMLINS, T[HOMAS] EDLYNE. "Three New Privy Seals for Players in the Time of Shakespeare." *ShSP* 4: 41-49.

The Privy seals for the Prince's Men, 1607; Queen Anne's Men, 1610; and the Duke of York's Men (later Charles I) are here printed for the first time.

1854.1   L., H. "'Retainers to Seven Shares and a Half.'" *N&Q* 9 (4 March) :199.
        Questions the meaning of the quotation from Crashaw. The editor responds with a brief description of the sharing system, with references to a variety of primary sources and to Collier (1831.1).

1855

1855.1   KELLY, WILLIAM. *Royal Progresses to Leicester*. London: Leicester Mercury, 15 pp.
        Text of a paper read to the Leicester Literary and Philosophical Society on 29 January 1855. Includes accounts of visits by Elizabeth in 1575, 1576, and 1585; and by James I in 1612, 1614, and 1616; as well as by various members of the royal family in 1604, 1608, and 1612. Kelly includes various details of finance and spectacle, taken from historical records.

1857

1857.1   SMITH, WILLIAM HENRY. *Bacon and Shakespeare: An Inquiry Touching Players, Playhouses, and Play-Writers in the Days of Elizabeth*. London: John Russell Smith, pp. 48-78.
        The relevant section examines players and playhouses briefly. Smith covers no new ground, but presents Collier (1831.1) and Malone (1790.1) as the ultimate authorities.

1858

1858.1   HALL, S[AMUEL] C[ARTER], and HALL, Mrs. S[AMUEL] C[ARTER]. "The Book of the Thames, from Its Rise to Its Fall. Part XXI." *ArtJ*, n.s. 4 (September): 277-80.
        In part describes the Paris Garden, or Swan, and the Globe, with illustrations. Of little historical value. Reprinted: 1859.1; 1867.1; 1869.1; 1877.1.

1859

1859.1   HALL, S[AMUEL] C[ARTER], and HALL, Mrs. S[AMUEL] C[ARTER]. The Book of the Thames, from Its Rise to Its Fall. London: A. Hall, Virtue, & Col.
        Includes 1858.1.

1860

1860.1   WRIGHT, GEORGE R. "The English Stage in the Year 1638." *JBArA* 16 (December): 275-76.
        Discusses the list of plays acted "before the King and queene this year of our Lord, 1638." Wright mistakes the Cockpit-in-Court for Beeston's Cockpit (or

Phoenix) Playhouse in Drury Lane. He prints a facsimile of the document. Revised: 1887.13.

1861

1861.1   INGLEBY, CLEMENT MANSFIELD. *A Complete View of the Shakespeare Controversy.* London: Nattali & Bond, 350 pp.

      Examines the question of Collier's alleged forgeries in detail, concluding that he indeed forged portions of at least seven documents used in 1831.1.

1865

1865.1   KELLY, WILLIAM, ed. *Notices Illustrative of the Drama and Other Popular Amusements Chiefly in the Sixteenth and Seventeenth Centuries Incidentally Illustrating Shakespeare and his Contemporaries; Extracted from the Chamberlain's Accounts and Other Manuscripts of the Borough of Leicester.* London: John Russell Smith, 310 pp.

      The first 184 pages consist of a detailed introduction, which serves to focus for the reader the wealth of documentary material contained in the rest of the volume. Prints extracts from documents from 1467 to 1749 illustrating the variety of popular entertainments available in Leicester during those years. Most important for present purposes is the section dealing with visits of the London companies.

1865.2   RYE, WILLIAM BRENCHLEY. *England as Seen by Foreigners in the Days of Elizabeth and James the First: Comprising Translations of the Journals of the Two Dukes of Wartemberg in 1592 and 1610, Both Illustrative of Shakespeare: With Extracts from the Travels of Foreign Princes and Others.* London: J. R. Smith, 300 pp.

      Seventeen translations from five languages, from 1558 to 1617, with three or four scattered theatrical references.

1867

1867.1   HALL, S[AMUEL] C[ARTER], and HALL, Mrs. S[AMUEL] C[ARTER]. *The Book of the Thames, from Its Rise to Its Fall.* London: Alfred W. Bennett.
      Includes 1858.1

1868

1868.1   MANNINGHAM, JOHN. *Diary of John Manningham, of the Middle Temple, and of Bradbourne, Kent, Barrister-at-Law, 1602-1603.* Edited by John Bruce. Westminster: Camden Society. 188 pp.

      An edition of the diary, which contains an eyewitness account of the Middle Temple production of *Twelfth Night* (p. 18) and a bawdy anecdote about Shakespeare and Richard Burbage (p. 39).

1869.1   HALL, S[AMUEL] C[ARTER], and HALL, Mrs. S[AMUEL] C[ARTER]. *The Book of the Thames, from Its Rise to Its Fall.* London and New York: Cassell, Petter, & Galpin.

        Includes 1858.1.

1869.2   HAZLITT, W[ILLIAM] C[AREW], ed. *English Drama and Stage Under the Tudor and Stuart Princes, 1543-1664.* London: Roxburghe Library, 289 pp.

        Compilation of thirty-two documents and thirteen treatises dealing with stage history in the period. Extremely valuable, although largely superseded by subsequent reprintings such as the various Malone Society Collections and the 1972 "Theatrum Redivivum" series of Johnson Reprint corporation.

1870

1870.1   ANON. "The Globe and Blackfriars Theatres." *N&Q* 42 (20 August): 166.

        Announces (erroneously) that it is now certain that Shakespeare was never a proprietor at either playhouse, referring the reader to Halliwell-Phillipps's announcement of the discovery of documents (see 1874.2).

1870.2   BRENDON, HEN[RY] S. "Early London Theatres." *N&Q* 42 (10 December): 515.

        Suggests on the authority of a contemporary letter that the Fortune burnt in December 1621.

1870.3   HALLIWELL-PHILLIPPS, J[AMES] O[RCHARD], ed. *A Collection of Ancient Documents Respecting the Office of Master of the Revels, and Other Papers Relating to the Early English Theatre, from the Original Manuscripts Formerly in the Haslewood Collection.* London: T. Richards, 100 pp.

        Contains documents from the time of Henry VIII to the time of Charles 11, with most drawn from the later period. Included in the collection are several documents tracing the history of the office. This is a valuable source book.

1870.4   RANKIN. GEORGE. "Early London Theatres." *N&Q* 42 (8 October): 306.

        Discusses the legend of the Devil joining in a dance at the Fortune, eventually burning the building down.

1870.5   T., S. W. "Early London Theatres." *N&Q* 42 (10 September): 216.

        Requests information on the supposed seventeen theatres in London 1570-1629. The editor responds with the names of thirteen and refers to various inns as other possibilities.

1872.1   RIMBAULT, EDWARD FRANCIS. *The Old Cheque Book, or Book of Remembrence, of the Chapel*. London: Camden Society, 250 pp.

      An edition of the manuscript documents of the Chapel Royal. While of some importance in the history of music, and while the Children of the Chapel were an important acting company, this work sheds little light on their theatre work.

1872.2   WRIGHT, JAMES. *Historia Histrionica: An Historical Account of the English Stage*. Edited by [Edward] W[illiam] Ashbee. London: Mr. Ashbee's Occasional Fac-Simile Reprints, 32 pp.

      Reprint of 1699.1.

1873

1973.1   KINGSLEY, CHARLES. "Plays and Puritans." In *Plays and Puritans, and Other Historical Essays*. I.ondon: Macmillan, pp. 1-80.

      Essentially an attack on pre-civil war morality as expressed in the plays of the period. Reprinted: 1889. 5.

1874

1874.1   ELLIS, GEORGE. "'The Private House in Drury Lane.'" *N&Q* 49 (27 June): 508.

      Questions the meaning of "private" on title pages. See 1875.1 for a response.

1874.2   HALLIWELL-PHILLIPPS, J[AMES] O[RCHARD]. *Illustrations of the Life of Shakespeare*. Pt. 1. London: Longmans, Green, 128 pp.

      Contains a variety of documents, including the Fortune contract, various licenses to playwrights, and papers related to sharea in the Globe and Blackfriars in an appendix. There is also an intriguing correspondence with the honorary President of the New Shakspere Society concerning unflattering references to some of Halliwell-Phillipps's work.

1874.3   WRIGHT, JAMES. *Historia Histrionica: A Dialogue of Plays and Players*. In *A Select Collection of Old English Plays*. 4th ed. Vol. 3. Edited by W[illiam] C[arew] Hazlitt and Robert Dodsley. London: Reeves & Turner, pp. 399-431.

      Reprint of 1699.1.

1875.1   WYLIE, CHARLES. "'The Private House in Drury Lane. '" *N&Q* 50 (11 July): 35-36.
    Responds to 1874.1, referring Ellis to Collier (1831.1) and Malone (1821.1). Wylie suggests (following Collier) that "private" refers to the possibility of locking the boxes.

1876

1876.1   FORMAN, SIMON. "Dr. Forman's Book of Plays, or Notes in 1611 on Shakspere's *Richard II, Winter's Tale, Cymbeline,* and *Macbeth,* from the Writer's Own Manuscript, Ashmole 208, Article X. With the Lord Treasurer's Payments for the Acting of 6 of Shakspere's Plays in 1613." *TrNShS* 6: 413-20.
    Prints Forman's eyewitness accounts of the four plays and the record of the Lord Treasurer's payments.

1876.2   WRIGHT, JAMES. *Historia Histrionica.* In *A Select Collection of Old English Plays.* 4th ed. Vol. 15. Edited by W[illiam] C[arew] Hazlitt and Robert Dodsley. London: Reeves & Turner, pp. 399-431.
    Reprint of 1699.1.

1877

1877.1   BLANCH, WILLIAM HARNETT. Dulwich College and Edward Alleyn. London: E. Wallen, pp. 55-75.
    The relevant section contains a brief biography of the actor/philanthropist, with little of theatrical interest and no oew information. See 1841.1; 1843.1; see also Index under Alleyn.

1877.2   HALL, S[AMUEL] C[ARTER] and HALL, Mrs. S[AMUEL] C[ARTER]. *The Book of the Thames, from Its Rise to Its Fall.* 2d ed. London: A. Hall, Virtue & Co.
    Includes 1858.1.

1878

1878.1   BAKER, H[ENRY] BARTON. Our Old Actors. Vol. 1. London: R. Bentley & Sons, pp. 3-32.
    The relevant section is the first two chapters, "Burbadge and his Contemporaries" and "The Original Actors of Shakespeare's Plays." Baker discusses Pavy, Tarlton, Burbage, Kempe, Sly, Armin, Lowin, Field, Taylor, and Alleyn, as well as the persecution of the players after the closing of the theatres. The style is rather anecdotal. Reprinted: 1879.1; revised, 1881.1.

1878.2   OVERALL, WILLIAM HENRY, and C., H., eds. *Analytical Index to the Series of Records Known as the Remembrancia: Archives of the City of London, A.D. 1579-1664*. London: E. J. Francis & Co.. DW. 350-57.
        The relevant section deals with "Plays and Players" and lists and abstracts twenty-five documents held in the Town Clerk's Record Room.

1878.3   RENDLE. WILLIAM. "The Bankside. Southwark, and the Globe." In *Rarrison's Description of England in Shakespeare's Youth*, pt. 2. Edited by Frederick J. Furnivall. London: New Shakspere Society. pp. 12-18.
        A brief discussion that puts Harrison's description in perspective for the reader.

1878.4   _____. *Old Southwark and Its People*. London: W. Drewett, 333 pp.
        The only items of theatrical interest concern the residence of various minor players in the area and their disputes.

1879

1879.1   BAKER, HENRY BARTON. *English Actors From Shakespeare to Macready*. Vol. 1. New York: H. Holt & Co., 3-32.
        Reprint of 1878.1.

1879.2   COLLIER, J[OHN] PAYNE. *The History of English Dramatic Poetry to the Time of Shakespeare: And Annals of the Stage to the Restoration*. 2d ed. 3 vols. London: George Bell & Sons. 1540 pp.
        Second edition, much revised and expanded, of 1831.1. The basic structure of the volumes remains unchanged. The most important section is the first, the Annals of the Stage, wherein the documentary evidence is presented. See, however, 1861.1, for indications of Collier forgeries. This work was important in its time, but has since been superseded by (at least) Chambers (1923.2) and Bentley (1941.1; 1956.4; 1968.2). One example of misinformation contained in the preface to the new edition is that Richard Burbage's father is definitely established as Edmond Burbage, a Bedfordshire farmer. See 1886.4.

1880

1880.1   TITTMAN, JULIUS. *Die Schauspiele der englischen Komödianten in Deutschland*. Leipzig: F. A. Brockhaus, 264 pp.
        Essentially an edition of seven plays in German performed by English players in Germany during the sixteenth century, with a lengthy introduction touching on theatrical matters.

1881.1   BAKER, H[ENRY] BARTON. *Our Old Actors*. London: R. Bentley & Sons, pp. 1-12.

Revised and corrected version of 1878.1. Baker eliminates many of the anecdotes of the previous volume. The relevant section is the Prologue, "From the Earliest Times to the Commonwealth." Baker briefly discusses Tarlton, Burbage, Kempe, Field, Taylor, and Alleyn, as well as the persecution of the players during the Interregnum.

1881.2   FLEAY, F[REDERICKI G[ARD]. "On the Actor Lists, 1578-1642." *TrRHS* 9: 44-81.

Examines twelve complete cast lists, three plots of nonextant plays with complete casts, and more than six dozen lists of various companies within the indicated dates. Fleay arranges the actors' names into eight tables for comparison and discussion.

1881.3   HALLIWELL-PHILLIPPS, J[AMES] O[RCHARD]. *Outlines of the Life of Shakespeare*. Brighton: privately printed, 192 pp.

An initial biographical effort of little theatrical value, but later greatly expanded. See the subsequent editions: 1882.3; 1884.2; 1885.5; lm.3; 1887.3; 1889.4; 1890.2; 1891.2; 1898.1; 1907.12.

1881.4   WARNER, GEORGE FREDERIC. *Catalogue of the Manuscripta and Muniments of Alleyn's College of God's Gift at Dulwich*. London: Longman's, Green, & Co. 388 pp.

In two parts, the first describing manuscripts 1-18 and the second the muniments, along with an appendix describing manuscripts 19-36, about which Warner did not initially know. The most important from a theatrical point of view are MS 1, containing Alleyn's theatrical papers; MS 2, containing his papers on the Bear Garden; MS 7, the diary and account book of Philip Henslowe; MS 8, Alleyn's memorandum book; and MS 9, Alleyn's diary and account book. Muniments 1-72 (Section 1) are documents concerned with the Bear Garden. See also the facsimiles, 1977.8.

1882.1   FLEAY, F[REDERICK] G[ARD]. "On the History of the Theatres in London from Their First Opening in 1576 to Their Closing in 1642." *TrRHS* 10: 114-33.

A paper read before the Royal Historical Society, presenting a brief sketch of the changes in the companies and playhouses during the period. Fleay also attempts to assign playwrights to each theatre and company. This, along with 1881.2, was a preliminary work for his more important and complete 1890.1.

1882.2   FURNIVALL, F[REDERICK] J. "The End of Shakspere's Playhouse." *Academy* 22 (28 October): 314-15.

A brief note transcribing manuscript additions to a copy of the 1631 edition of Stow's Survey, with information about the demolition of the Globe, the Blackfriars, the Fortune, the Hope, the Phoenix, and the Salisbury Court.

1882.3   HALLIWELL-PHILLIPPS, J[AMES] O[RCHARD]. *Outlines of the Life of Shakespeare*. 2d ed. London: Longmans, Green & Co., 701 pp.

Second edition of 1881.3, greatly expanded, with information of theatrical interest throughout.

1882.4   NICHOLSON, BRINSLEY. "Kemp and the Play of *Hamlet*--Yorick and Tarlton--a Short Chapter in Dramatic History." *TrRHS* 8: 57-66.

A paper read at a meeting of the Society, 12 March 1880. Nicholson argues that Kempe's quarrel with the company and the lack of a ready replacement for him shaped the play in part.

1883

1883.1   ALBRECHT, ALEXANDER. *Das englische Kindertheater*. Halle: Waisenhauses, 56 pp.

Published version of a doctoral dissertation at Friedrichs-Universitat, Halle-Wittenberg. Albrecht examines the children's theatres of the church and the court as well as the development of the public boys' companies. He clarifies modes of performance and profiles individual actors, concluding with the repertories for the three companies.

1883.2   HALLIWELL-PHILLIPPS, J[AMES] O[RCHARD]. *Outlines of the Life of Shakespeare*. 3d ed. London: Longmans, Green, 736 pp.

Third edition of 1881.3, expanded, with information of theatrical interest throughout.

1884

1884.1   FLEAY, F[REDERICK] G[ARD]. "Shakespeare and Puritnism." *Anglia* 7: 223-31.

Discusses references to Puritanism and Puritans in tile plays rather than Puritan opposition to Shakespeare and his theatre

1884.2   HALLIWELL-PHII.LIPPS, J[AMES] O[RCHARD]. *Outlines of the Life of Shakespeare*. 4th ed. London: Longmans, Green, 480 pp.

Fourth edition of 1881.3, expanded, with information of theatrical interest throughout.

1884.3   HALLIWELL-PHILLIPPS, JAMES ORCHARD. *Old Theatres: Views of the Globe and Bear Garden.* Brighton: privately printed, 3 pp.

      A reprint of a portion of the Visscher view of London, with the two buildings.

1884.4   MIESSNER, JOHANNES. "Die englische Komödianten in Oesterreich." *JDSG* 19: 113-54.

      Chronicles English actors performing in Austria in the sixteenth and seventeenth centuries, based on various city records. <u>See also</u> 1884.5 for a more complete treatment.

1884.5   ___. *Die englischen Komoedianten zur Zeit Shakespeares in Oesterreich.* Beiträge zur deutschen Literatur und des gestigen Lebens in Oesterreich, no. 4. Vienna: Carl Konegen, 188 pp.

      Traces performances by English touring players in Austria in the late sixteenth and early seventeenth centuries, touching on performances in the Netherlands and Germany. Meissner bases his discussion on documentary sources, most frequently the account books of the towns. He also prints an edition of the manuscript play *Der Jud von Venedig.*

<u>1885</u>

1885.1   GREENSTREET, JAMES. "Documents Relating to the Players at the Red Bull, Clerkenwell, and the Cockpit in Drury Lane in the Time of James I." *TrNShS* 10, pt. 3, no. 22: 489-51.2.

      Discusses and prints documents related to various court masques in the early seventeenth century. Queen Anne's Men played at both playhouses for a time, and there was some complicated litigation over the management of the group. <u>See</u> 1885.2-4.

1885.2   _____. "Drury Lane Theatre in the Reign of James I." *Athenaeum,* 21 February, p. 258.

      Prints the bill of complaint and its answer from a Chancery suit of 1623, bearing on the Red Bull and Cockpit companies, the late manager Thomas Greene, and his widow, Susan Browne Greene Baskervile. Continued in 1885.3-4; <u>see</u> 1885.1.

1885.3   _____. "Drury Lane Titeatre in the Reign of James 1." *Athenaeum,* 29 August, p. 282.

      Continuation of 1885.2. Greenstreet prints the will of Thomas Greene, manager of the Red Bull conipany, with particulars of that playhousc, along with the deposition of Henry Herbert, Master of the Revels, in the Baskervile proceedings against the Cockpit company. Continued in 1885.4; 1885.1.

1885.4   GREENSTREET, J[AMES]. "The Red Bull Playhouse in the Reign of James I." *Athenaeum*, 28 November, pp. 709-10,

      Two documents from Woodford v. Holland, a Court of Requests suit, with commentary. The bill of complaint, unfortunately not yet discovered, would probably provide much information about the early history of the Red Bull.. Concludes 1885.2-3; 1885.1.

1885.5   HALLIWELL-PHILLIPPS, J[AMES] O[RCHARD]. *Outlines of The Life of Shakespeare*. 5th ed. London: Longmans, Green, 640 pp.

      Fifth edition of 1881.3, expanded, with information of theatrical interest throughout.

1885.6   ORDISH, T. FAIRMAN. "London Theatres, No. I: The Theatre and Curtain." *Antiquary* 11 (March): 89-97.

      Reviews the state of scholarship in Malone, Collier, Halliwell-Phillipps, and Fleay, supplemented with documentary evidence. See 1885.7-11; 1886.4-8; 1887.5-7.

1885.7   _____. "London Theatres, No. II: The Globe and Lesser Bankside Playhouses, Part I." *Antiquary* 11 (May): 212-18.

      As a prologue to his discussion of the Globe, Ordish sketches the history of Henslowe's Rose, with reference to the diary. See also 1885.6, 8-11; 1886.4-8; 1887.5-7.

1885.8   _____. "London Theatres, No. II: The Globe and Lesser Bankside Playhouses, Part II." *Antiquary* 11 (June): 243-49.

      Continues 1885.7 with a discussion of the Hope, also known as the Bear Garden. See also 1885.9-11; 1886.4-8; 1887.5-7.

1885.9   _____. "London Theatres, No. II: The Globe and Lesser Bankside Playhouses, Part III." *Antiquary* 12 (August):41-49.

      Continues 1885.6-8 with a discussion of the Globe. Ordish accepts Rendle's site south of Maid Lane and relies on the Fortune contract for information as to its construction. Here, as elsewhere, he essentially repeats the conclusions of Malone, Collier, Halliwell-Phillipps, Fleay and others. See also 1885.10-11; 1886.4-8; 1887.5-7.

1885.10   _____. "London Theatres, No. II: The Globe and Lesser Bankside Playhouses, Part IV." *Antiquary* 12 (November): 192-98.

      Discusses the "internal economy, arrangements, and aspect of the playhouse," including time of performance, composition and behavior of audience, and staging and acting conventions. See also 1885.6-9, 11; 1886.4-8; 1887.5-7.

1885.11 _____. "London Theatres: The Globe and Lesser Bankside Playhouses (Concluded)." *Antiquary* 12 (December): 245-48.

Discusses what is known about the Swan (three years before the discovery of the DeWitt/VanBuchell sketch). Ordish concentrates on the competition between the Swan and Blackfriars property, with commentary. Continued in 1888.5.

1885.12 RENDLE, W[ILLIAM]. "The Globe Playhouse." *Walford's Antiquarian Magazine and Bibliographer* 8 (November): 209-16.

The fourth and final in a series; see also 1885.13-15. Rendle cites the "epigrammatic sayings of contemporaries" to write his "brief but real picture of the Globe." In other words, he presents the contemporary reputation of the playhouse.

1885.13 _____. "The Playhouses at Bankside in the Time of Shakespeare, Part I." *[Walford's] Antiquarian Magazine and Bibliographer* 7 (May): 207-12.

The first of a series on the public playhouses south of the Thames. See also 1885.12, 14, 15. Rendle here, as elsewhere, is rather anecdotal, taking the reader on an imaginary tour of the area. He stops first at the Swan, reciting some twenty references to that playhouse from 1594 to 1630.

1885.14 _____. "The Playhouses at Bankside in the Time of Shakespeare, Part II." *[Walford's] Antiquarian Magazine and Bibliographer* 7 (June): 274-79.

Sequel to 1885.13; see also 1885.15, 12. Here Rendle discusses the conditions of the area surrounding the Swan. He concentrates on Holland's Leaguer, a bawdy house.

1885.15 _____. "The Playhouses at Bankside in the Time of Shakespeare, Part III." *[Walford's] Antiquarian Magazine and Bibliographer* 8 (August): 55-62.

The third of a series; see also 1885.12-14. Here Rendle discusses the old Bear Garden; the Hope, or new Bear Garden; and the Rose.

1886

1886.1 COHN, ALBERT. "Englische Komödianten in Köln (1592-1656)." *JDSG* 21: 245-76.

Chronicles the performances of English touring companies in Cologne.

1886.2 GREENSTREET, JAMES. "The Blackfriars Pl.ayhouse: Its Antecedents." *Athenaeum*, 7 January, p. 25.

A document from a Chancery suit of Queen Mary's time, related to the Master of the Revels and his use of the Blackfriars property, with commentary. Continued in 1888.5.

1886.3   HALLIWEL-PHIILIPPS, J[AMES] O[RCHARD]. *Outlines of the Life of Shakespeare*. 6th ed. 2 vols. London: Longmans, Green, 784 pp.
        Sixth edition of 1881.3, expanded, with information of theatrical interest throughout.

1886.4   ORDISH, T. FAIRMAN. "London Theatres, No. III: The Blackfriars Playhouse." *Antiquary* 14 (July): 22-27/
        Discusses Burbage's second Blackfriars, the first being unknown at the time. Here Ordish is primarily concerned with the use of the playhouse by the boy companies before 1608, and with the errors of Collier in 1831.1 and 1879.2. Continued in 1886.7; see also the rest of the series: 1885.6-11; 1886.7-8; 1887.5-7.

1886.5   _____. "London Theatres, No. III: The Blackfriars Playhouse (Continued)." *Antiquary* 14 (August): 55-58.
        Continuation of 1886.4. Ordish here discusses the opposition to the King's Men at this playhouse. Continued in 1886.6; see also the rest of the series: 1885.6-11; 1886.7-8; 1887.5-7.

1886.6   _____. "London Theatres, No. III: The Blackfriars Playhouse (Continued)." Antiquary 14 (September): 108-13.
        Continuation of 1886.4, 5. Discusses the shares and finance of the King's Men at the Blackfriars, as well as the music which accompanied performances. See also the rest of the series: 1885.6-11; 1886.7-8; 1887.5-7.

1886.7   _____. "London Theatres, IV: The Fortune Playhouse." *Antiquary* 14 (November): 205-11.
        Concentrates on Alleyn's career and finances, especially as connected with the Fortune. See also the rest of the series: 1885.6-11; 1886.4-6, 8; 1887.5-7.

1886.8   _____. "London Theatres, No. V: The Red Bull." *Antiquary* 3 (Decernber): 236-41.
        Discusses what is known of the Red Bull, primarily from the work of Greenstreet (1885.1-4) and Collier (1879.2). See the rest of the series: 1885.6-11; 1886.4-7; and see also Ordish's book (1894.4) on the subject, for which these served as the basis.

1886.9   TRAUTMANN, KARL. "Englische Komoedianten in Nürnberg bis zum Schlusse des Dreissigjäher Krieges (1593-1648)." *ArchivL* 14 (Spring) : 113-36.
        Chronicles the performances of English actors in Nuremberg during the years indicated, based on documentary sources held in that city.

1886.10   VATKE, TH[EODOR]. "Das Theater und das London Publikum in Shakespeares Zeit." *JDSG* 21: 226-44.
        Examines the relationship between the audience and the theatre in Shakespeare's time. Vatke traces audience behavior and dress through references

in plays, prologues, inductions, and pamphlets, as well as the growing opposition among the Puritans.

1887

1887.1   ANON. "A Middlesex Sessions Record Touching James Burbage's 'Theater.'" *Athenaeum*, 12 February, pp. 233-34.

> A brief note citing a court record which illuminates the relationship between Burbage and Braynes.

1887.2   CRÜGER, JOHANNES. "Englische Komoedianten in Strassburg im Elsass." *Archiv* (Spring): 113-25.

> Chronicles the visits of English players to Strassburg, 1596-1657, based on official city records of payment.

1887.3   HALLIWELL-PHILLIPS, J[AMES] O[RCHARD]. *Outlines of the Life of Shakespeare.* 7th ed. 2 vols. London: Longmans, Green, 848 pp.

> Seventh edition of 1881.3, expanded, with information of theatrical interest throughout.

1887.4   _____. *The Visits of Shakespeare's Company of Actors to the Provincial Cities and Towns of England. Illustrated by Extracts Gathered from Corporate Records.* Brighton: privately printed, 48 pp.

> A variety of provincial notices of the Chamberlain's/King's Men, arranged alphabetically by town from Barnstaple to Worcester. Fifteen entries in all are included, with the greatest amount of information in the last. This, the earliest work on its subject, has been superseded by various Malone Society Collections and Records of Early English Drama. See Index under Provincial Tours.

1887.5   ORDISH, T. FAIRMAN. "London Theatres, VI: Cockpit, Drury Lane." *Antiquary* 15 (March): 93-97.

> Discusses the destruction of the playhouse by the London apprentices in 1617, the renaming of the theatre as the Phoenix, and several changes of company between 1617 and 1642. See the rest of the series: 1885.6-11; 1886.4-8; 1887.6.

1887.6   _____. "London Theatres, VII: Whitefriars: Salisbury Court." *Antiquary* 15 (June): 262-65.

> Examines the evidence for the existence of an early Whitefriars playhouse, which Ordish dismisses as "a crude stage," in preparation for a more detailed discussion (in 1887.7) of the Salisbury Court. See also the rest of the series: 1885.6-11; 1886.4-8; 1887.5.

1887.7 _____. "London Theatres, VII: Whitefriars: Salisbury Court." *Antiquary* 16 (December):244-47.

In the last article in his series, composed of 1885.6-11, 1886.4-8, and 1887.5-7, Ordish discusses what is known of the last playhouse of the period, the Salisbury Court. He takes his information primarily from Collier (1831.1; 1879.2) and Fleay (1882.1). See also his book (1894.4) based on this series.

1887.8 RENDLE, WILLIAM. "Paris Garden and Christ Church, Blackfriars." *N&Q* 75 (26 March): 241-43.

In essence a review of an 1881 private publication, *The Manor of Old Paris Garden* by Joseph Meymott, Rendle concludes that the dates are often inaccurate in the Elizabethan/Jacobean section of the book, but there is much of value. Despite the title and Rendle's other work in theatre history, there is nothing here of theatrical interest. Continued in 1887.9-10.

1887.9 _____. "Paris Garden and Christ Church, Blackfriars." *N&Q* 75 (30 April): 343.

Continues 1887.8; concluded in 1887.10.

1887.10 _____. "Paris Garden and Christ Church, Blackfriars." *N&Q* 75 (4 June): 442-44.

Concludes 1887.8-9.

1887.11 TRAUTMANN, KARL. "Englische Komoedianten in Stuttgart (1600, 1609, 1613-14) und Tubingen (1597) ." *ArchivL* 15 (Spring): 711-16.

Discusses the visits of English actors to the two cities in the years indicated, based on city records of payment.

1887.12 _____. "Englische Komoedianten in Ulm (1602)." *ArchivL* 15 (Spring): 216-17.

A brief note of a visit of Robert Browne's company.

1887.13 WRIGHT, GEORGE R. "On a Manuscript List of Plays of the Year 1638." In *Archaeologic and Historic Fragments*. London: Whiting & Co., pp. 1-24.

Revision of 1860.1, with the same basic confusion of the Cockpit (Phoenix) in Drury Lane for the Cockpit-in-Court.

1888

1888.1 ARCHER, WILLIAM. "A Sixteenth century Playhouse." *UR* 1 (June): 281-88.

Discusses Gaedertz's discovery of the Swan drawing (see 1888.4), prints it, and speculates on what it tells us. Archer follows Gaedertz in believing that curtains could be drawn between the pillars to form a large inner stage. He concludes with a comparison of the Swan drawing with the *Wits* frontispiece.

1888.2   BOLTE, JOHANNES. "Englische Komoedianten in Dänemark und
          Schweden." *JDSG* 23:99-108.
               Chronicles the performances of touring English players in Denmark and
          Sweden in the sixteenth and seventeenth centuries, based on government
          documents recording payments.

1888.3   FIRTH, C[HARLES] H[ARDING]. "The Suppression of the Drama During the
          Protectorate and Commonwealth." *N&Q* 78 (18 August): 122-23.
               Cites four newspapers of the 16508 to show that private performances
          were frequently given during the Interregnum.

1888.4   GAEDERTZ, KARL THEODOR. *Zur Kenntis der altenglischen Bühne, nebst
          andern Beitrigen zur Shakespeare-Litteratur*. Bremen: C. E. Miller, pp. 1-18.
               Includes DeWitt's description of the Swan and VanBuchell's copy of his
          sketch, discovered by Gaedertz in the Utrecht University Library. He believed,
          however, that curtains were hung up between the posts to divide the platform into
          outer and inner stages. This is certainly among the most important discoveries in
          the field.

1888.5   GREENSTREET, JAMES. "The Blackfriars Playhouse: Its Antecedents."
          Athenaeum, 7 January, pp. 25-26.
               Continuation of 1886.2. Greenstreet prints a Privy Seal Signet Bill from
          1561 authorizing tennis-playing in the neighborhood of Blackfriars, along with
          the actual license, with commentary. He attempts to show something of the
          history of the area's connection with entertainment enterprises. Continued in
          1888.6-7; 1889.3.

1888.6   _____. "The Blackfriars Theatre in the Time of Shakespeare, I." *Athenaeum*, 7
          April, pp. 445-46.
               Abstracts of five documents related to the 1612 Chancery case, Kirkham
          v. Painton. Continued in 1888.7; 1889.3.

1888.7   _____. "The Blackfriars Theatre in the Time of Shakespeare, II." *Athenaeum*,
          21 April, p. 509.
               Continuation of 1888.6. Abstracts of two additional documents from the
          same case. Concluded in 1889.3.

1888.8   _____. "The Whitefriars Theatre in the Time of Shakespeare." *TrNShS* 13, pt.
          3: 269-84.
               Text of a paper read before the Society, 9 November 1888. Greenstreet
          discusses the Chancery suit of 1609 concerning the management of Whitefriars,
          and he prints the documents of the case.

1888.9   LOWE, ROBERT W. *A Bibliographical Account of English Theatrical Literature from the Earliest Times to the Present Day*. London: John C. Nims, 384 pp.

The earliest attempt at a bibliography of theatrical literature. The alphabetical subject listing of books dealing with the theatre as opposed to the drama contains items relevant to this period throughout. See 1970.1, and Index under Bibliographies.

1888.10   RENDLE, WILLIAM. "The Swan Playhouse, Bankside, circa 1596." *N&Q* 78 (22 September): 221-22.

Discusses Gaedertz's discovery and publication of the Swan drawing (1888.4).

1888.11   _____, and NEWMAN, PHILIP P. *The Inns of Old Southwark and Their Associations*. London: Longmans, Green, 437 pp.

Includes references to the Boar's Head, the Rose, the Globe, the Newington Butts, and various inns associated with the playhouses. These are brief mentions, however, in a sort of "walking tour of the area" format. Not of major importance.

1888.12   WHEATLEY, HENRY B. "On a Contemporary Drawing of the Interior of the Swan Theatre, 1596." *TrNShS* 12, pt. 2: 213-25.

A paper read before the Society, 9 November 1888. Wheatley reports on Gaedertz's discovery and printing of the Swan drawing (see 1888.4), questioning the capacity (given by DeWitt as 3000) and commenting on the composition of the building and its arrangements.

1889

1889.1   BAKER, H[ENRY] BARTON. *The London Stage: Its History and Traditions from 1576 to 1888*. Vol. 1. London: W. H. Allen & Co., pp. 1-31.

The relevant section is the first chapter, "The Elizabethan Stage." Baker briefly discusses the Theatre, the Curtain, the Swan, the Hope, the Globe, the Newington Butts, the Blackfriars, the Fortune, the Red Bull, the Cockpit (or Phoenix), the Whitefriars, and the Salisbury Court playhouses; actors, including Burbage and Alleyn; audiences; music: finance; and government regulation. This is a popular work, based on secondary sources. See 1904.2 for a revision.

1889.2   CREIZENACH, W[ILHELM MICHAEL ANTON]. *Die Schauspiele der enslischen Komödianten*. Deutsche National-Literatur, no. 23. Berlin and Stuttgart: W. Spemann, 352 pp.

An essentially literary study of the drama of the English actors in Germany, but with information of theatrical interest throughout.

1889.3   GREENSTREET, JAMES. "Blackfriars Theatre in the Time of Shakespeare." *Athenaeum*, 10 August, pp. 203-4.

   Concludes 1888.5-7. Extracts from the Star Chamber suit alluded to in the Chancery suit abstracted earlier.

1889.4   HALLIWELL-PHILLIPPS, J[AMES] O[RCHARD]. *Outlines of the Life of Shakespeare*. 8th ed. 2 vols. London: Longmans, Green, 896 pp.

   Eighth edition of 1881.3, expanded, with information of theatrical interest throughout.

1889.5   KINGSLEY, CHARLES. "Plays and Puritans." In *Plays and Puritans and Other Historical Essays*. 2d. ed. London: Macmillan, pp. 1-83.

   Second edition of 1873.1.

1889.6   SIMPSON, WILLIAM SPARROW. *Gleanings from Old S. Paul's*. London: Elliot Stock, pp. 101-18.

   The relevant section is Chapter Six, "Plays Acted by the Children of Paul's." Simpson lists thirty-five plays performed by the children, mostly based on title-page claims or the work of Halliwell-Phillipps. He does not examine acting or physical staging. Not of major theatrical importance.

1889.7   YOUNG, WILLIAM. *The History of Dulwich College; With a Life of Edward Alleyn*. Vol. 2. Edinburgh: Morrison & Gibb, pp. 1-265.

   The first three chapters of volume two concern the life of Alleyn, his diary, and the Fortune Playhouse. Young is more careful in his use of records than was Collier in 1841.1, and is able to correct the biography in many details. The diary is printed complete, with a facsimile of three pages. The brief chapter on the Fortune is primarily a compilation of all the material in the Dulwich manuscripts and muniments that deal with that playhouse. See also the facsimile of the Henslowe papers (1977.8) and the catalogue of the papers (1881.4).

1890

1890.1   FLEAY, FREDERICK GARD. *A Chronicle History of the London Stage,1558-1642*. London: Reeves & Turner, 424 pp.

   Divides the period into seven parts, breaking at 1586, 1603, 1613, 1636. and 1642. One chapter is devoted to each section, examining court performances, companies, playhauses, playwrights, and general stage history for the years in question. Fleay presents information chronologically, with sources listed, and he uses many tables to organize the data. A dozen subject indexes round out the volume. This is the most important work between Collier on the one hand (1879.2) and Adams (1917.3) and Chambers (1923.2) on the other.

1890.2   HALLIWELL-PHILLIPPS, J[AMES] O[RCHARD]. *Outlines of the Life of Shakespeare*. 9th ed. 2 vols. London and New York: Longmans, Green, 1084 pp.
  Ninth edition of 1881.3, expanded, with information of theatrical interest throughout.

1890.3   RENDLE, WILLIAM. "Philip Henslowe." *Genealogist,* n.s. 4, no. 3: 149-59.
  A brief biography of the financier and theatre manager, concentrating on the Henslowe v. Henslowe suit in Chancery, the documents of which are held in the Public Record Office.

1891

1891.1   CARGILL, ALEXANDER. "Shakespeare as an Actor." *Scribner's* 9 (May), 613-35.
  A brief biography, concentrating on theatrical matters. Reprinted: 1916.4.

1891.2   PAGET, A[LFRED] H[ENRY]. *The Elizabethan Playhouses*. London: G. Gibbons, 14 pp.
  Reprint of 1891.3.

1891.3   _____. "The Elizabethan Play-Houses." *TrLeLPS* (January): 237-50.
  A paper read before the Leicester Literary and Philosophical Society in 1890. Paget briefly reviews the state of knowledge of the Elizabethan theatre (drawn primarily from Halliwell-Phillipps and Collier) and goes on to examine the discovery space. He postulates a recessed alcove under the required balcony, closed by curtains and used for discoveries. Remarkably moderate for its time. Reprinted: 1891.2.

1892

1892.1   HIPIWELL, DANIEL. "Prices of Admission to Theatres, Temp. Elizabeth." *N&Q* 85 (21 May): 412.
  Records two references to "two penny rooms." See 1892.3 for a response.

1892.2   JUNIUS, PHILIP. "Diary of the Journey of Philip Junius Duke of Stettin-Pomerania Through England in the Year 1602." Edited by Gottfried van Bülow and Wilfred Powell. *TrRHS* 6: 1-67.
  A facing-page translation of the diary, including accounts of performances the Duke attended.

1892.3   NICHOLSON, BR[INSLEY]. "Prices of Admission to Theatres, Temp. Elizabeth." *N&Q* 85 (18 June): 499.
  Responds to 1892.1, pointing out the commonness of the term and its parallel to the gallery.

1892.4   STOPES, CHARLOTTE CARMICHAEL. "William Hunnis." *JUSG* 27: 200-17.

>   A brief biography and list of publications of the playwright and Master of the Queen's Chapel. See also 1900.3 and especially 1910.19.

1893

1893.1   ARCHER, THOMAS. *The Highway of Letters and Its Echoes of Famous Footsteps*. London: Cassell; New York: Randolph, pp. 189-220.

>   The relevant section examines "Dramatists, Plays and Players." While the Elizabethan period is touched on, this is not of great theatrical importance.

1893.2   BOLTE, JOHANNES. *Die Singspiele der englischcn Komödianten und ihrer Nachfolger* in Deutschland, Holland und Skandinavien. Theatergeschichte Forschungen, no. 7. Hamburg and Leipzig: Leopold Voss. 194 pp.

>   Discusses the origins and characteristics of the English plays with music performed on the continent during the sixteenth and seventeenth centuries. The Angel-like Roland (1596) is the most important, and Bolte prints both text and music.

1894

1894.1   CALMOUR, ALFRED CECIL. *Fact and Fiction about Shakespeare, with Some Account of the Playhouses, Players, and Playwrights of His Period*. Stratford-upon-Avon: George Boyden, 112 pp.

>   A slight volume intended for the general reader and riddled with errors of fact and interpretation. Of little interest to the theatre historian.

1894.2   ORDISH, T. FAIRMAN. *Early London Theatres--In the Fields*. London: Elliot Stock, 298 pp.

>   Histories of the Theatre, the Curtain, the amphitheatres, Newington Butts, the Rose, the Bear Garden, the Hope, the Paris Garden, and the Swan. The Globe is excluded since Ordish proposes to examine it in a separate volume; the same is true of the city theatres. Neither projected volume ever appeared. Staging is not considered. This is the most comprehensive survey of its time, roughly equivalent to Fleay (1890.1), but was superseded by Adams (1917.3). Ordish based his book on his earlier series of articles: 1885.6-11; 1886.4-8; and 1887.5-7. Reprinted: 1899.2; 1971.13.

1895

1895.1   BOLTE, JOHANNES. *Das Danziger Theater im 16. und 17. Jahrhundert*. Hamburg and Leipzig: Leopold Voss, 296 pp.

>   Essentially a chronicle history, citing documentary evidence on a year-by-year basis. Of interest because of the English actors who performed in Danzig

before the Restoration. Bolte includes in an appendix a German version of a Marston play performed by one such group. <u>See also</u> 1979.19.

1895.2   PENNIMAN, JOSIAH HARMAR. "The War of the Theatres." Ph.D. dissertation, University of Pennsylvania, 168 pp.
>   Published: 1897.2.

<u>1897</u>

1897.1   LOGEMAN, 11. "Johannes de Witt's Visit to the Swan Theatre." *Anglia* 19: 117-34.
>   Suggests that the play depicted in the Swan drawing is *Twelfth Night*, and tries to show that the date of the play and the date of DeWitt's visit may have coincided. <u>See also</u> 1951.7.

1897.2   PENNIMAN, JOSIAH H[ARMAR]. *The War of the Theatres*. Publications of the University of Pennsylvania Series in Philology, Literature, and Archaelogy, vol. 4, no. 3. Boston: Ginn & Co., 168 pp.
>   Published version of 1895.2. Penniman examines the quarrels of Marston and Dakker with Jonson, which found expression in fifteen satirical plays. Despite the title this study is almost completely literary in approach and consequently of only passing theatrical interest.

<u>1898</u>

1898.1   HALLIWELL-PHILLIPPS, J[AMES] O[RCHARD]. *Outlines of the Life of Shakespeare*. 10th ed. 2 vols. London: Longmans, Green. 848 pp.
>   Tenth addition of 1881.3, expanded, with information of theatrical interest throughout.

<u>1899</u>

1899.1   BINZ, GUSTAV. "Londoner Theater und Schauspiele im Jahre 1599." *Anglia* 22: 456-64.
>   Discusses Thomas Platter's observations. See also 1929.13; 1937.9; 1956.29.

1899.2   ORDISH, THOMAS FAIRMAN. *Early London Theatres in the Fields*. London: E. Stock, 298 pp.
>   Reprint of 1894.2.

1900.1   BOLTE, JOHANNES. "Englische Komödianten in Munster und Ule." *JDSG* 36: 273-75.

  Using municipal records, Bolte chronicles five performances, from 1601 to 1647, of English touring players in the two cities.

1900.2   GREG, W[ALTER] W[ILSON]. "Webster's *White Devil*." *MLQ* 3 (December): 112-40.

  Though primarily a literary study, of interest because of Greg's discussion of the alternation theory, called here "dramatic enjambement," in the second part of the essay. Reprinted: 1966.7.

1900.3   STOPES, CHARLOTTE CARMICHAEL. "William Hunnis, the Dramatist." *Athenaeum* 31 March, pp. 410-12.

  A brief recitation of the achievements of the Master of the Chapel Royal, focusing on the plays performed for the Queen. See 1910.8 for a more detailed treatment.

<u>1901</u>

1901.1   DOBELL, BERTRAM. "Newly Discovered Documents of the Elizabethan and Jacobean Periods, II: Letters of George Chapman and Ben Jonson." *Athenaeum*, 30 March, pp. 403-4.

  Three letters of Chapman and excerpts from seven of Jonson, relating to their quarrel over *Eastward Ho*, part of the War of the Theatres. See also 1897.2; 1923.7.

1901.2   MAAS, HERMAN. *Die Kindertruppen: Ein Kapitel aus der Geschichte der englischen Theatergesellschaften in dem Zeitraume von 1559 bis 1642*. Breman: Grube & Dathe, 35 pp.

  Published version of a Gottingen Ph.D. dissertation. This is one chapter of a projected longer work. Maas outlines the activities and repertories of the children's companies during the reigns of Elizabeth, James, and Charles. Most sources are secondary. See also his more comprehensive treatment, 1907.16, as well as Index under Children's Companies.

1901.3   MALONE, EDMOND. "An Historical Account of the English Stage." In *Complete Works of Shakespeare*. New York: P. F. Collier & Son, 522 pp.

  Reprints 1790.1, with additions from 1813.1 and 1821.1.

1901.4   MANZIUS, KARL. *Skuespilkunstens Historie*. Vol. 3. *Engelske Theaterforhold i Shakesparetiden*. Copenhagen: P. Hegel & Son, 236 pp.

  The English Renaissance volume of Manzius's comprehensive history of theatre. See 1904.9 for an English translation. Reprinted: 1937.6.

1902.1   ANON. "A London Theatre Temp. Queen Elizabeth." *Builder* 82 (10 May): 468-69.

Describes an exhibition held in the Hall of Clifford's Inn of maps, views, and models of sixteenth- and seventeenth-century London and models of playhouses of Shakespeare's time. The author describes the model of the Globe, based on the Swan drawing and the Fortune contract, in detail.

1902.2   BROTANEK, RUDOLPH. *Die englischen Maskenspiele*. Wiener Beitrage zur englischen Philologie, no. 15. Vienna and Leipzig: W. Braumüler, 371 pp.

By the sixteenth century, disguises as a dramatic form were enjoyed by courtly audiences and peasants alike. In the seventeenth century, disguises on stage were seldom a performance in themselves but rather enhancements to a speech, song, instrumental music, or dance. France exerted a strong influence on the development of the English masque. Brotanek concludes with a chronological register and bibliography of masques.

1902.3   DURAND, W[ALTER] Y[ALE]. "Notes on Richard Edwards." *JEGP* 4 (July): 348-69.

Argues that *Damon and Pythias* was performed at Whitehall on Christmas, 1564; and that the lost *Palaemon and Arcyte* was not Shakespeare's source for *Two Noble Kinsmen*.

1902.4   GRABAU, CARL. "Zur enelischen Bühne um 1600." *JDSG* 38: 230-36.

Examines stage directions in *The Cuck-Queanes* and *Cuckolds Errant* and *The Faery Pastorall or Forrest of Elues*, two manuscript plays not printed until the nineteenth century. Grabau finds evidence for three doors, each representing a different location throughout, indicated by signs. Further, there is an indication that the playhouse at St. Paul's may not have had a trap.

1902.5   LAWRENCE, W[ILLIAM] J[OHN]. "History of a Peculiar Stage Curtain." *GMg* 293 (July): 53-59.

Traces the history of the front curtain, noting its use in Jonson's *Masque of Blackness* (1605) and in Charles I's royal entry into Edinburgh in 1633. Reprinted: 1912.15.

1902.6   MEYER, C. F. "Englische Komödianten am Hofe des Herzog Philip Julius [*sic*] von Pommern-Wolgast." *JDSG* 38: 196-211.

Examines the visits of touring English players to the court of Archduke Philip Junius in the first quarter of the seventeenth century. See also 1892.2.

1902.7   SCHELLING, FELIX E. "The Elizabethan Theatre." *Lippincott's* 69 (March): 309-23.

        A general discussion for a popular audience, with illustrations. Schelling first establishes the political and geographical backgrounds and then examines the public playhouses, most notably the Globe.

1903

1903.1   CREIZENACH, WILHELM MICHAEL ANTON. *Geschichte des neueren Dramas.* Vols. 2 and 3. Halle: S. M. Niemaeyer.

        See English translation, 1916.5. Second edition, 1923.4.

1903.2   HALE, EDWARD EVERETT, Jr. "The Influence of Theatrical Conditions on Shakespeare." *MP* 1 (June):171-92.

        Attempts to examine the conditions under which Shakespeare wrote as an aid to understanding the plays. Hale stresses the "rhetorical" nature of performances, the absence of a front curtain, the use of the upper stage for separate scenes, the use of costumes and properties, the habit of improvisation on the part of the clowns, and the need for imagination on the part of the audience.

1903.3   HERZ, EMIL. *Englische Schauspieler und englisches Schauspiel zur Zeit Shakespeares in Deutschland.* Theatergeschichtliche Forschungen, no. 18. Hamburg and Leipzig: L. Voss, 143 pp.

        Published version of a Bonn Ph.D. dissertation. Each of the first ten chapters treats an English company touring in Germany. The second section then discusses the repertory of these companies in detail, concentrating on Shakespeare's plays as presented in Germany.

1903.4   LAWRENCE, WILL1AM J[OHN]. "A Forgotten Stage Conventionality." *Anglia* 26 (June): 447-60.

        Argues that the English proscenium doors with balconies above, in use during the Restoration and eighteenth century, were derived from the stage doors of the Elizabethan period and used for the same purposes. Reprinted: 1912.15.

1903.5   LAWRENCE, W[ILLIAM] J[OHN]. "The Mounting of the Stuart Masques." *English Illustrated Magazine*, n.s. 30 (November): 174-81.

        Examines recently discovered designs for masques by Inigo Jones and the texts of *The Triumph of Peace* and *Temple of Love*. Reprinted: 1912.15.

1903.6   _____. "Some Characteristics of the Elizabethan-Stuart Stage." *EStudien* 32: 36-51.

        Discusses the absence of the front curtain and its implications, and the use of the traverse. Lawrence also argues against accepting the Swan drawing because it is "hearsay evidence," undated, self-contradictory, and shows no upper and lower traverses.

1903.7   SYMMES, HAROLD S. *Les débuts de la critique dramatique en Angleterre jusqu'à la mort de Shakespeare.* Peris: Ernest Leroux, 218 pp.

        Published version of a University of Paris Ph.D. dissertation. Symmes discusses three stages in the early development of dramatic criticism in England: the early Puritan attacks, the beginning of the development of classical ideals, and the more sophisticated use of classical ideals in the Restoration. When compared with France and Italy, according to Symmes, England's critics lagged far behind, holding to medieval values until well into the seventeenth century.

1903. 8   THOMPSON, ELBERT NEVIUS SEBRING. "The Controversy between the Puritans and the Stage." Ph.D. dissertation, Yale University, 275 pp.

        Published: 1903.9.

1903.9   THOMPSON, ELBERT N[EVIUS] S[EBRINGI. *The Controversy between the Puritans and the Stage.* Yale Studies in English, no. 20. New York: H. Holt & Co., 275 pp.

        Published version of 1903.8. Thompson divides his work into two parts, the Puritan attack on the stage (17 chapters) and the dramatists' reply to the Puritans (3 chapters). The detailed accounts of various treatises are especially clear. Of most interest to the theatre historian are Chapter Four on the Gosson-Lodge debate, Chapter Ten on legislation covering the stage, and all of Part Two.

1903.10   WOOLF, ARTHUR H. *Shakespeare and the Old Southwark Playhouses.* London: privately printed, 19 pp.

        Text of a lecture delivered at the Southwark town hall on 23 April 1903. Woolf simply presents the main facts concerning Shakespeare's connection with the area and its playhouses. He discusses the Rose (placing Shakespeare there for the initial performance of *Henry VI* and *Titus*) and the Globe (stating that it was built from the timbers of the demolished Curtain, rather than the Theatre) in some detail. Similar minor errors of fact are scattered throughout.

1904

1904.1   ADAMS, JOHN CHESTER. "The Predecessors of the XVII Century Court Masque in England." Ph.D. dissertation, Yale University, pp. 106-66.

        The relevant section discusses masking during Elizabeth's reign. Adams distinguishes between "masking entertainments" and true masques with speeches and scenery, concentrating on the latter. The masques performed outside the Elizabethan court are the true predecessors of the seventeenth-century court masques, with the *Masque of Proteus* as the most significant.

1904.2   BAKER, H(ENRY] BARTON. History of the London Stage and Its Famous Players (1576-1903). London: G. Routledge & Sons; New York: E. P. Dutton & Co., pp. 3-29.

        Revision of 1889.1. The relevant section is Chapter One of Part One, covering the period 1576-1642. Since Baker attempts to discuss all the playhouses in twenty-seven pages, the work is necessarily general, and it is riddled with such common misstatements as "the Globe was a hexagonal building."

1904.3   BANG[-KAUP], W[ILLY]. "Zur Biihne Shakespeares." *JDSG* 40: 223-27
Responds to Brodmeier (1904.5), suggesting a slightly different arrangement for the curtains to the rear stage.

1904.4   BRANDL, A[LOIS]. "Englische Komödianten in Frankfurt a. M." *JDSG* 40: 229-30.
A brief note citing Moryson's description of a play he saw in Frankfurt.

1904.5   BRODMEIER, CECIL. *Die Shakespeare-Bühne nach den alten Büchenweisungen*. Weimar: A. Haschke, 121 pp.
Published version of a Jena Ph.D. dissertation. Brodmeier reconstructs a typical Elizabethan public playhouse from stage directions in a wide variety of plays. He locates the curtains between the pillars, and places a trap, two doorways, and a spacious upper stage in this "hinterbühne." He also discusses the use of properties and music. This is one of the clearest statements of the alternation theory. See 1904.3; 1904.8.

1904.6   FURNIVALL, F[REDERICK] J. "The Fortune Theatre in 1649." *N&Q* 109 (30 January): 85.
Cites a 1649 Chancery suit showing that the Fortune was held by Edward Alleyn's College of God's Gift in Dulwich, and leased one to Lisle. Lisle wanted to convert the playhouse to some other use, but the College refused.

1904.7   HENSLOWE, PHILIP. *Henslowe's Diary*. P. 1,Text. Edited by Walter Wilson Greg. London: A. H. Bullen, 240 pp.
For many years the standard edition of the most important extant document from the Elizabethan playhouses. In the Introduction Greg describes the manuscript and its contents, discusses Collier's forgeries (see 1845.3), and gives his general plan for the projected three volumes. This one contains only the diary and notes; see 1908.11 Greg's commentary and 1907.15 for other Henslowe papers. See also 1961.13 for another edition and 1977.8 for the facsimile of the diary and papers.

1904.8   KELLER, WOLFGANG. "Nochmals zur Bühne Shakespeares." *JDSG* 40: 225-27.
Responds to Brodmeier (1904.5) and Bang (1904.3), suggesting an alternative arrangement of curtains, with one set dividing the front stage from the rear stage and second set at the back of the rear stage between the two doors.

1904.9   MANZIUS, KARL. *A History of Theatrical Art in Ancient and Modern Times.* Vol. 3. *The Shakespearean Period in England.* Translated by Louise von Cassel. London: Duckworth & Co., 250 pp.

Translation of 1901.4. The three major sections of this popular treatise examine the theatres, general theatrical conditions, and acting. Mantzius discusses the Theatre, the Globe, the Fortune, the Curtain, the Blackfriars, the Rose, Newington Butts, the Red Bull, the Swan, the Phoenix, and the Salisbury Court playhouses, as well as such miscellaneous topics as hours of performance, expenses, and playbills. The section on acting treats Tarlton, Kempe, Burbage, Alleyn, and Field. Reprinted: 1937.6.

1904.10   SCHELLING, FELIX E. "'An Aery of Children, Little Eyases.'" In *The Queen's Progress and Other Elizabethan Sketches.* London: T. W. Laurie, pp. 103-28.

Examines the boy actors, concentrating on court and legal records concerning them and the plays which they presented.

1904.11   _____. "Plays in the Making." In In *The Queen's Progress and Other Elizabethan Sketches.* London: T. W. Laurie, pp. 149-70.

Examines Henslowe's management practices as revealed in the diary, concentrating on the "thraldom" of the playwrights (notably Dekker) who worked for him.

1905

1905.1   DURAND, W[ALTER] Y[ALE]. "*Palaemon and Arcyte, Progne, Marcus Geminus,* and the Theatre in Which They Were Acted as Described by John Bereblock (1566). *PMLA* 20 (September): 502-28.

Essentially a translation of relevant sections of Bereblock's Latin account, with commentary. Durand describes the preparations made for production as paralleling the preparations made at an innyard. Particularly interesting is his argument that "every main feature of the early playhouse can be traced to the conditions either of the hall or the innyard."

1905.2   LAWRENCE, W[ILLIAM] J[OHN]. "A Forgotten Restoration Playhouse." *EStudien* 35 (Spring): 279-89.

Using records of a French actor who visited London in 1661 and Pepys's diary, Lawrence suggests that the Phoenix in Drury Lane was rebuilt, fitted with scenes, and operated during the Restoration.

1905.3   MONKEMEYER, PAUL. *Prolegomena zu einer Darstellung der englischen Volksbühne zur Elisabeth- und Stuart-Zeit nach den alten Büchen-Anweisungen.* Hanover and Leipzig: Hanische Buchhandlung, 94 pp.

Published version of a Gottingen Ph.D. dissertation. The three chapters of this "Prologue to an Examination of the Elizabethan and Stuart Public Theatre Through the Old Stage Directions" examine staging before 1576, the choice of materials for the study, and the stage directions in selected plays. Since this is but a prologue, Monkemeyer reaches no conclusions.

1905.4 MURRAY, JOHN TUCKER. "English Dramatic Companies in the Towns Outside of London, 1550-1600." *MP* (April):539-59.

Attempts an account of the customs of the touring companies--their methods of performance, relations to town authorities, amounts paid, and so on. Murray identifies three types of company (London, Nobleman's, Town) and follows them through typical activities. See also 1910.15; 1920.30.

1905.5 REYNOLDS, GEORGE FULLMER. "Some Principles of Elizabethan Staging." Ph.D. dissertation, University of Chicago, 63 pp.

Published in two parts: 1905.6-7; see also 1905.8.

1905.6 REYNOLDS, GEORGE F[ULLMER]. "Some Principles of Elizabethan Staging, Part I." *MP* 2 (April): 581-614.

First part of published version of 1905.5; continued in 1905.7. Also published in monograph form: 1905.8.

1905.7 _____. "Some Principles of Elizabethan Staging, Part II." *MP* 3 (June): 69-97.

Continuation of 1905.6; published version of 1905.5. Also published in monograph form: 1905.8.

1905.8 _____. *Some Principles of Elizabethan Staging*. Chicago: University of Chicago Press, 63 pp.

Published version of 1905.5; also published as 1905.6-7. Reynolds examines the alternation theory and finds it wanting, then develops a theory of simultaneity similar to medieval practice. The theory is based on the passages in plays of the period that render alternation unlikely or impossible. Other items touched on are the scene boards indicating location, the existence of three stage doors at least in some theatres, and the availability of a curtained alcove for discoveries. For later contributions to the field, see Index under Reynolds.

1905.9 STOPES, CHARLOTTE CARMICHAEL. "Mary's Chapel Royal and Her Coronation Play." *Athenaeum,* 9 September, pp. 346-47.

Examines the membership of Queen Mary's Chapel Royal and the events of her coronation, including the play presented, and speculates on its content and authorship.

1906

1906.1 CHAMBERS, E[DMUND] K. "Court Performances before Queen Elizabeth." *MLN* 2 (0ctober): 1-13.

Lists previously unknown court performances, from the Declared Accounts of the Treasurer of the Chamber, in effect abstracts of the Original Accounts, which unfortunately have several missing years. For each entry

Chambers shows the date, the company, and the payees, which leads to a number of deductions concerning companies and actors.

1906.2 _____. *Notes on the History of the Revels Office Under the Tudors.* London: A. H. Bullen. 80 pp.

Brief history based on available documentary evidence. Chambers begins with the late fifteenth century, with most of the material belonging to Elizabeth's reign.

1906.3 CORBIN, JOHN. "Shakespeare and the Plastic Stage." *Atlantic* 97, no. 3 (March): 369-83.

A discussion of Elizabethan staging methods for the general reader, attempting to correct the "bare stage and a blanket" impression. Corbin focuses on the use of properties (citing Henslowe's diary for corroboration) and the holdover of medieval conventions.

1906.4 GRABO, CARL H. "The Stage for Which Shakespeare Wrote, I: The Mystery Plays." *Chautauquan* 44 (September): 98-106.

Despite the main title, this deals exclusively with medieval drama as background for the rest of the series. See also 1906.5-7; 1907.10-11.

1906.5 _____. "The Stage for Which Shakespeare Wrote, II: The Ancestry of the English Theater." *Chautauquan* 44 (October): 711-19.

Discusses the Cornish rounds and the Tudor inns, as additional background for the series. See 1905.6-7; 1907.10-11.

1906.6 _____. "The Stage for Which Shakespeare Wrote, III: Theatres of Elizabeth's London." *Chautauquan* 44 (November): 354-66.

Continuation of 1905.4-5. Discusses the various playhouses, placing considerable importance on the Fortune contract and the Swan drawing. Grabo stresses the lack of a curtain in the modern sense and the rapid flow of action. Continued in 1906.7; 1907.10-11.

1906.7 _____. "The Stage for Which Shakespeare Wrote, IV: The Stage Properties and Costumes." *Chaurauquan* 45 (December): 79-89.

Continuation of 1906.4-6. Grabo discusses the use of props and costumes, beginning with an examination of the stage doors and location signs (citing Reynolds, 1905.8) and continuing with the prop lists and costume notes from Henslowe's diary. He concludes that "stage properties and costumes were . . . as elaborate and accurate as circumstances would permit." Continued in 1907.10-11.

1906.8 PLOMER, HENRY R. "Fortune Playhouse." *N&Q* 114 (11 August): 107.

Cites an advertisement in a London newspaper from 1660/61, which offers the Fortune Playhouse and its adjoining ground for the building of tenements and a street.

1906.9   RAVN, V[ILHELM] C[ARL]. "English Instrumentalists at the Danish Court in the Time of Shakespeare." *SIMG* 7: 550-63.

Examines a small group of English "instrumentalists" who also, apparently, presented dances and interludes in Denmark during 1579-1586. Ravn also discusses Leicester's Men, including Will Kempe.

1906.10   WALLACE, CHARLES WILLIAM. "Old Blackfriars Theatre: Fresh Discovery of Documents." *Times* (London), 12 September, p. 6.

Letter to the editor announcing discovery of four lawsuits bearing on the Blackfriars and offering some conclusions drawn from them. Wallace's arguments are developed more fully in 1908.18, the published version of his dissertation (1906.11).

1906.11   _____. "The Children of the Chapel at Blackfriars, 1597-1603." Ph.D. dissertation, Freiburg University, 207 pp.

Published: 1908.18.

1907

*1907.1   ARCHER, WILLIAM. "The Fortune Theatre, 1600." *Tribune* (London) 12 October.

Cited in 1, col. 1385. Abstract of 1908.2.

1907.2   BOAS, FREDERICK S. " A 'Defence of Oxford Plays and Players.'" *FortR* 88 (August): 309-19.

Discusses a previously unknown defense of the academic stage by playwright William Gager, from 1592, directed to John Rainolds. Gager answers Rainolds's attack point for point. See also 1916.17-18; 1974.3.

1907.3   CHAMBERS, E[DMUND] K. "The Elizabethan Lords Chamberlain." MSC 1, pt. 1: 31-42.

Traces the succession of Lords Chamberlain from 1558 to 1603. Chambers includes brief biographies of William Howard, Thomas Ratliffe, Henry Carey, and William Brooke, as well as brief notes on the various companies connected with the Chamberlain's office.

1907.4   _____. "The Stage of the Globe." In *The Works of Shakespeare*. Vol. 10. Edited by A. H. Bullen. Stratford: Shakespeare Head Press, pp. 351-62.

After a lengthy preamble setting forth the problems of reconstruction, Chambers describes the Globe on the model of the Fortune contract, "eighty feet square without and fifty-five feet square within." The description of the stage follows Brodmeier (1904.5), with three divisions of the stage (inner, outer, upper) and scenes alternating among them. Chambers believes, however, that there were no stage posts at the Globe. His inner stage is smaller than Brodmeier's, and more in line with Reynolds's "alcove" (1905.8).

1907.5   _____, and GREG, W[ALTER] W[ILSON], eds. "Dramatic Records from the City of London: The Remembrancia." *MSC* 1, pt. 1: 43-100.

   A selection of letters and other documents from the Rememhrancia preserved in the Office of the Town Clerk in the City of London. See also 1878.2: 1956.35.

1907.6   CLARK, ANDREW. "Maldon Records and the Drama." *N&Q* 115 (9 March): 181-83.

   Examines the archives of the borough of Maldon, Essex, for information on dramatic production from 1447 to 1635; lists all recorded payments for theatrical purposes. See also 1909.10. Continued in 1907.7-9.

1907.7   _____. "Maldon Records and the Drama." *N&Q* 115 (4 May): 342- 43.
   Continues 1907.6; continued in 1907.8-9.

1907.8   _____. "Maldon Records and the Drama." *N&Q* 115 (1 June): 422- 23.
   Continues 1907.6-7; concluded in 1907.9.

1907.9   _____. "Maldon Records and the Drama." *N&Q* 116 (20 July): 43-44.
   Concludes 1907.6-8; see also 1909.10.

1907.10   GRABO, CARL H. "The Stage for Which Shakespeare Wrote, V: The Staging of *Macbeth* and *Romeo and Juliet*." *Chautauquan* 45 (January): 206-18.

   Continuation of 1906.4-7. Grabo here discusses the two plays in terms of stage directions for each scene. Concluded in 1907.11.

1907.11   _____. "The Stage for Which Shakespeare Wrote, VI: Some Effects of Elizabethan Stage Conditions upon Shakespeare's Method." *Chautauquan* 45 (February): 331-43.

   Concludes the series consisting of 1906.4-7 and 1907.10. The time of performances, the nature of the acting, and the modification or shaping of dramatic structure are Grabo's topics. In all, this series is balanced in its approach and deserving of a wider reputation than it has in the field.

1907.12   HALLIWELL-PHILLIPPS, J[AMES] OIRCHARD]. *Outlines of the Life of Shakespeare*. 11th ed. 2 vols. London: Longmans, Green, 946 pp.

   Eleventh edition of 1881.3, expanded, with information of theatrical interest throughout.

1907.13   HARRIS, CHARLES. "English Actors in Germany in the Sixteenth and Seventeenth Centuries." *WRUB*, n.s. 10, no. 6 (November): 136-63.

   A general discussion, summarizing the state of research in the field. See Index under Actors--English on Continent.

1907.14 _____. "The English Comedians in Germany before the Thirty Years War: The Financial Side." *PMLA* 22, no. 3:446-64.

   Analyzes playgoing expenses recorded in *Moryson's Itinerary* in order to estimate the income of a touring English company around 1600. Harris puts the average income at around $55, a quite substantial sum at the time.

1907.15 HENSLOW, PHILIP. *Henslowe Papers: Being Documents Supplementary to Henslowe's Diary*. Edited by Walter W[ilson] Greg. London: A. H. Bullen, 187 pp.

   Contains abstracts of selected documents relating to the theatres and the Bear Garden, to the drama and stage, and to bearbaiting; Edward Alleyn's memorandum book; and miscellaneous notes and papers. Three appendixes contain a list of documents not at Dulwich, dramatic plots, and Alleyn's part in *Orlando Furioso*. 1977.8.

1907.16 HAAS, HERMAN. *Aussere Geschicte der englischen Theatertuppen in dem Zeitraum von 1559 bis 1647*. Materialienzur Kunde des Blieren englischen Dramas, no. 19. Ediied by Willy Bang[-Kaup.] Louvain: A. Uystpruyst, 283 pp.

   A comprehensive examination of the acting companies of the period. Seven chapters treat the adult groups and five the children's, with chronological coverage. This is primarily a compilation of documentary sources rather than an interpretive history. At the time of publication this work stood as the most important in its field, but it has since been superseded by Murray (1910.15), Chambers (1923.2), and Bentley (1941.1).

1907.17 PERCY, EUSTACE. *The Privy Council under the Tudors*. Oxford: B. Blackwell, 74 pp.

   The Stanhope Essay, 1907. While this is an excellent historical analysis of a most important political body, there is nothing here of theatrical interest. Included because of listing in NCBEL 1, col. 1383.

1907.18 REYNOLDS, GEORGE F[ULLMER]. "'Trees' on the Stage of Shakespeare." *MP* 5 (October): 153-68.

   Examines the use of forest and tree settings to illustrate Elizabethan staging methods. Reynolds argues here that such settings existed, included real trees, and were used to suggest solitude and desolation. He bases his conclusions on textual references and Simon Forman's descriptions of four plays he saw. Essentially this is an argument for simultaneous staging in the public theatres.

1907.19 STOPES, CHARLOTTE CARMICHAEL. "Elizabethan Stage Scenery." *FortR* 87 (June): 1107-17.

   Attempts first to account for differences in staging styles by comparing what she calls "the national spirit" of the Elizabethan period and her own time, then to counter the modern notion of scenery with the Elizabethan usage of properties and hangings.

1907.20   WEGENER, RICHARD. *Die Bücheneinrichtung des Shakespeareschein Theaters nach den zeitgenössischen Dramen.* Haile: Max Niemeyer, 164 pp.

An attempt at a comprehensive reconstruction of staging practices based on stage directions and textual allusions in published plays and surviving manuscripts. The Swan drawing is taken as the basis for the public theatres, the Globe in particular. Wegener also examines the second Blackfriars. Probable uses of stage structures for scenes set in homes, battlefields, and other locations are discussed, with the focus on the flexible use of stage doors, the traverse, end the upper stage. One of the most moderate of the German studies of its time. 1909.24.

1908

1908.1   ALBRIGHT, VICTOR EMANUEL. *A Typical Shakespearian Stage: The Outer-Inner Stage.* New York: Knickerbocker Press, 42 pp.

The third chapter of 1909.1 and 2. Albright seeks to dismiss the Swan drawing while accepting the *Messalina* title page as valid visual evidence. He argues backwards from the Restoration stage, specifically the Duke's Theatre of 1671, and advocates the alternation theory.

1908.2   ARCHER, WILLIAM. "The Fortune Theatre, 1600." *JDSG* 44: 159-66.

Discusses the Fortune contract and attempts a reconstruction of the playhouse based on it. Abstracted in 1907.1.

*1908.3   _____. "The Swan Drawing." *Tribune* (London), 11 January.

Cited in *NCBEL*, col. 1385.

1908.4   CHAMBERS, E[DMUND] K., and GREG, WALTER W[ILSON], eds.; "Dramatic Records from the Lansdowne Manuscripts." *MSC* 1, pt. 2: 143-215.

Documents drawn from the Burghley Papers, accumulated by Sir William Cecil. A total of twenty-two entries are included, from 1562 to after 1595. Excluded are all but one of the documents published by Feuillerat in 1908.6.

1908.5   DURAND, WALTER YALE. "Some Errors Concerning Richard Edwards." *MLN* 23 (May): 129-31.

Points out minor errors regarding the life and works of Edwards in John Farmer's edition of *Damon and Pithias.*

1908.6   FEUILLERAT, ALBERT, ed. *Documents Relating Co the Office of the Revels in the Time of Queen Elizabeth.* Materalen zur Kunde des älteren englischen Dramas, no. 21, edited by Willy Bang[-Kaup.] Louvain: A. Uystpruyst, 513 pp.

Part I contains the documents related to the Office and Officers of the Revels, while Part I1 contains extracts from the account books from 1558 to 1601. Feuillerat appends a chronological list of plays and masques mentioned in the documents, fifty pages of explanatory notes, and three indexes.

1908.7   G., G. M. *The Stage Censor, an Historical Sketch: 1544-1907*. London: S. Low, Marston & Co., pp. 5-64.

      The relevant section is the first two chapters, dealing with the stage censor under the Tudors and Stuarts. This is a simple survey, with little depth and less objectivity. The writer's purpose seems to be to show how the stage censor has from the beginning abrogated the rights of every Englishman.

1908.8   GILDERSLEEVE, VIRGINIA CROCHERON. "Government Regulation of the Elizabethan Drama." Ph.D. dissertation, Columbia University, 259 pp.
      Published: 1908.9.

1908.9   _____. *Government Regulation of the Elizabethan Drama*. Columbia University Studies in English, series 11, no. 4. New York: Columbia University Press, 259 pp.

      Published version of 1908.8. An account of the laws and regulations, local and national, which affected the drama and theatre during the period. The work is based on the official documents of the time as they appear in government collections. Gildersleeve first examines the national regulations and the office of the Master of the Revels, and then moves into the local regulations in London from 1543 to 1592 and from 1592 to 1642. She concludes with an analysis of the Puritan victory over the stage in 1642.

1908.10   GODFREY, WALTER H. "An Elizabethan Playhouse." *ArchR* (Spring): 239-44.

      A conjectural reconstruction of the Fortune, complete with perspective rendering, floor plans, and section drawings. Godfrey reprints the relevant section of the contract and bases his work on that. His Fortune is complete with inner stage, obliquely set doors, curtained upper stage, and balcony boxes above the doors. The stage pillars are set far to the sides, and there is a railing around the stage. Godfrey suggests that the Swan drawing is inaccurate, since "the rear wall as there represented is merely a temporary stage property with its imitation of heavy barred doors, required for the one play, concealing in this exceptional case the more usual inner stage." He presents little evidence for his reconstruction aside from the contract. Reprinted: 1913.5; <u>see also</u> 1911.2-3; 1912.8; 1916.1.

1908.11   HENSLOWE, PHILIP. *Henslowe's Diary. Pt. 2, Commentary*. Edited by Walter Wilson Greg. London: A. H. Bullen, 400 pp.

      The four main chapters treat Henslowe's family and private affairs, Henslowe and the stage, and plays and persons mentioned in the diary. A final chapter provides twelve tables of reference. Greg examines the Rose, the Fortune, and the Hope in detail; he also discusses several acting companies associated with Henslowe at one time or another. The chapter on plays lists 280, performed by 12 companies at various playhouses, and the chapter on persons mentioned includes detailed references. <u>See also</u> 1904.7; 1907.15; and other editions of the diary, 1845.3; 1961.13.

1908.12   JARVIS, ROYAL PRESTON. "Investigations on Jigging." Ph.D. dissertation, Columbia University, 71 pp.
> Published: 1908.13.

1908.l3   ___. *Investigations on Jigging.* Transactions of the American Institute of Mining Engineers. New York: AIME, 71 PP.
> Published version of 1908.12. This has nothing to do with the theatrical jig of the Elizabethan period. Instead, the jig discussed is a device used in mining for separating minerals of different specific gravities. Included because of mistaken listing in *ADDT,* p. 49.

1908.14   LAWRENCE, W[ILLIAM] J[OHN]. "Music in the Elizabethan Theatre." *JDSG* 44: 36-50.
> Examines the use of inter-act music, the use of music to set a mood, and the location of the musicians in the private theatres. Reprinted: 1912.15.

1908.l5   _____. "The Situation of the Lord's Room." *EStudien* 39, no. 3 (Summer): 402-12.
> Argues that the boxes for the nobility "were originally situate aloft in the tyring house, and that before 1609 the position had been abandoned." Reprinted: 1912.15.

1908.16   SCHELLING, FELIX E. *Elizabethan Drama 1558-1642: A History of the Drama in England from the Accession of Queen Elizabeth to the Closing of the Theaters, to Which Is Prefixed a Résumé of the Earlier Drama from Its Beginnings.* Vol. 1. Boston and New York: Houghton, Mifflin & Co., pp. 141-93.
> The relevant section is Chapter Four, "The London Playhouse." Schelling bases his discussion of the companies on Fleay (1890.1) and his discussion of the theatres on Ordish (1894.2). His examination of the structure of the stage is drawn from Reynolds (1905.8), but here he includes more documentation. Schelling also examines costuming and management practices in his broad survey. Reprinted: 1911.24; 1935.14.

1908.17   SMITH, WINIFRED. "Italian and Elizabethan Comedy." *MP* 5 (April): 555-56.
> Examines Italian commedia actors and their drama in the sixteenth century for their influence on England. Smith here discusses character types and improvisation. <u>See also</u> 1912.21.

1908.18   WALLACE, CHARLES WILLIAM. *The Children of the Chapel at Blackfriars 1597-1608: Introductory to the Children of the Revels, Their Origins, Courses, and Influences. A History Based upon Original Records, Documents, and Plays, Being a Contribution to Knowledge of the Stage and Drama of Shakespeare's Time.* UNS, no. 8. Lincoln: University of Nebraska, 207 pp.
> Published version of 1906.11. Particularly valuable in its day for the new documentary evidence provided, it remains an important contribution. Wallace

deals with the Blackfriars building, the organization and maintenance of the Children of the Chapel under Queen Elizabeth, the custom of sitting on the stage and its origin, the relationship of the Children at Blackfriars with other companies and playhouses, and s variety of other issues. The notes are, as Wallace indicates, the most important part of the book, since he lays out his evidence in some detail. Certain parts of the volume, however, such as the discussion of the stage at Blackfriars and its furnishings, are "reserved for the complete work" (a standard phrsse in German dissertations of the time), projected for three volumes. That work never appeared, but see also 1909.30-34; 1910.21-25; 1911.29; 1912.24; 1913.18; 1914.25-26. Wallace was an indefatigable searcher of documents, and while perhaps not overly modest he made many extremely important contributions to the field. See 1911.4.

1908.19   WILSON, J[OHN] DOVER. "The Missing Title of Thomas Lodge's Reply to Gosson's *School of Abuse*." *MLR* 3 (January): l66-68.
Claims that the work in question is the Honest Excuses mentioned by Gosson in his *Apologie for the School of Abuse*.

<u>1909</u>

1909.1   ALBRIGHT, VICTOR E. "The Shakespearian Stage." Ph.D. dissertation, Columbia University, 194 pp.
Published: 1909.2.

1909.2   _____. *The Shakespearian Stage*. Columbia University Studies in English, series 11, no. 6. New York: Columbia University Press, 194 pp.
Published version of 1909.1. The third chapter reprints 1908.1. The additional information is contained in Chapters Four and Five, "The Shakespearian Method of Stage Presentation." Basically Albright argues backwards from the Restoration mode of staging. He is a strong exponent of the inner stage and the alternation theory.

1909.3   ANON. "The Globe Theatre, Southwark, and Its Site." *Builder* 97 (25 September): 333-34.
Briefly describes the monument to be unveiled at the supposed site of the Globe. The writer includes a brief history of the playhouse, including its relationship to the Fortune contract and the Swan drawing. Rendle is the authority used to set the site.

1909.4   ANON. "Site of the Globe Theatre, Southwark." *Builder* 97 (13 November): 516.
Briefly reviews Hubbard's (1909.13) and Martin's (190919-21) arguments about the site, favoring Martin.

1909.5   ANON. "Where Did the 'Wooden O.,' the Globe Theatre, Stand?" *Illustrated London News* 135 (9 October): 500-01.
Several pictures illustrating the dispute over the location of the Globe (north or south of Maid Lane?), of interest at the time because of Wallace's charges (in 1909.32) that the memorial tablet was set up in the wrong location.

1909.6   [ARKWRIGHT, GODFREY EDWARD PELLEW.] "Early Elizabethan Stage Music." *MusAnt* 1 (October): 30-40.
Discusses the music for five songs extracted from plays of the boy companies and six others that may have been so extracted. Arkwright prints "Pandolpho," one of the songs.

1909.7   BOAS, F[REDERICK] S., and GREG, W[ALTER] W[ILSON], eds. "James I at Oxford in 1605: Property Lists from the University Archives." *MSC* 1, pt. 3: 247-59.
Extracts from documents in the Oxford University Archives related to plays performed during the visit of King James from 27 to 31 August 1605, with commentary. The documents are concerned with the London hire of apparel and furniture for the occasion.

1909.8   CHAMBERS, E[DMUND] K. "Court Performances under James I." *MLR* 4 (January): 153-66.
Chambers uses previously neglected records to add to our list of plays performed at Court, 1603-1616. The play, the date, and the members of the royal family in attendance are noted where possible. The new information clarifies the status of companies and actors in some cases.

1909.9   _____, and GREG, W[ALTER] W[ILSON], eds. "Dramatic Records from the Patent Rolls: Company Licenses." *MSC* 1, Pt. 3: 260-84.
Fourteen theatrical licenses from the Patent Rolls, plus two from the Signet Office, with commentary.

1909.10   CLARK, ANDREW. "Players or Companies on Tour, 1548-1630." *N&Q* 20 (17 July): 41-42.
Examines the records of the borough of Saffron Walden, Essex, for information about theatrical activities from 1547 to 1631, listing all recorded payments to companies and actors. See also 1907.6-9.

1909.11   FLECKNOE, RICHARD. "A Short Discourse of the English Stage." In *Critical Essays of the Seventeenth Century*. Vol. 2. Edited by Joel Elias Spingarn. Oxford: Clarendon Press, pp. 91-96.
Reprint of 1664.1.

1909.12 HELMHOLTZ-PHELAN, ANNA AUGUSTA. "The Staging of the Court Drama to 1595." *PMLA* 24 (June): 185-206.

    Examines staging at court in the sixteenth century and earlier. The relevant section (discussing the reign of Elizabeth) is based on the Revels Accounts. Helmholtz-Phelan discusses Lyly's *Woman in the Moon* in detail. She speculates on the use of a front curtain and perspective scenery.

1909.13 HUBBARD, G[EORGE]. "The Site of the Globe Theatre of Shakespeare on Bankside as Shown by Maps of the Period." *JRIBA*, 3d series, 17:26-28

    Argues for a site north of Maid Lane based on the visual evidence of early maps and views of London. Hubbard is one of the strongest supporters of the north site.

1909.14 JACKSON, RICHARD C. "The Site of Shakespeare's Globe Playhouse." *Athenaeum* (30 October): 525-26.

    Responds to Wallace in 1909.32, 33, questioning the validity of both his documents and his diagram, and presenting evidence for a site south of New Park Street, earlier known as Maid Lane.

1909.15 LAW, ERNEST. "Shakespeare in London." *Times* (London) (11 October): 10.

    A letter to the editor, seconding Lee's appeal in 1909.18 for a thorough search of the Public Records, and speculating on Shakespeare's post-1611 connection with the King's Men.

1909.16 LAWRENCE W[ILLIAM] J[OHN]. "Early French Players in England." *Anglia* 32: 60-89.

    Chronicles French actors in England from the time of Henry VII through the Restoration. Reprinted: 1912.15.

1909.17 _____. "Title and Locality Boards on the Pre-Restoration Stage." *JDSG* 45: 146-70.

    Examines the evidence for the use of title and location boards on the Tudor and Stuart stage. Lawrence concludes that title boards were frequently used, but that there is insufficient evidence concerning the general use of location boards, although we know they were used at Paul's, ca. 1600. See 1910.6. Reprinted: 1912.15.

1909.18 LEE, SIDNEY. "Shakespeare in London." *Times* (London), (5 October): 8.

    A letter to the editor commenting on Wallace's pieces in the previous two issues (1909.32-33). Lee challenges Wallace's assertion of the value of his discoveries, awaiting the full argument, and urges more systematic study of the lawsuits and other documents held in the Public Record Office.

1909.19   MARTIN, WILLIAM. "Shakespeare in London." *Times* (London), (7 October): 8.

        A letter to the editor clarifying Tree's letter of the previous day (1909.28). Martin interprets Wallace's evidence for situating the Globe north of Maid Lane (in 1909.32-33) as actually referring to a position south of that street. See also 1909.21.

1909.20   _____. "Shakespeare in London." *Times* (London), (8 October): 10.

        A letter to the editor summarizing the contents of six documents that trace the property of the Globe from 1626 to 1787, at which time it can be located exactly. Martin again places the site to the south of Maid Lane. See 1909.21.

1909.21   _____. "The Site of Shakespeare's Globe Playhouse." *Times* (London), (9 October): 425.

        Responds to Wallace in 1909.32-33, arguing for the south side of Maid Lane, based on maps and views of London, conveyances of property, tradition, and an alternate reading of Wallace's evidence. Martin presents much the same arguments as in 1909.19 and 20.

1909.22   McDONNELL, MICHAEL, F.J. *A History of St. Paul's School*. London: Chapman & Hall, pp. 143-55.

        The earliest complete history of Paul's. The relevant section of Chapter Nine deals with the headmastership of Mulcaster (1596-1608), but there is little mention of theatrical matters. For more information on Mulcaster's theatrical connection, see 1943.3; 1970.5; 1972.6; 1974.10.

1909.23   REYHER, PAUL. *Les masques anglais: Etude sur les ballets et la vie de court en Angleterre (1512-1640)*. Paris: Hachet, 563 pp.

        Published version of his Ph.D. dissertation, University of Paris. Reyher differentiates masques from other forms of court entertainment, and discusses the literary and theatrical elements, including scenery, costume, music, and dance.

1909.24   SKEMP, ARTHUR R. "Some Characteristics of the English Stage before the Restoration." *JDSG* 45: 101-25.

        Examines the Messalina print and what is shows of the shape of the stage, the character of the upper stage, and the traverse. Skemp also discusses the heavens, the mistaken tradition of the front curtain, and later modifications of the public stage. In his section on the private theatre he stresses the size end shape of the Blackfriars stage. Primarily a refutation of Wegener (1907.20).

1909.25   STOPES, CHARLOTTE CARMICHAEL. "The Burbages and the Transportation of 'The Theatre.'" Athenaeum, 16 October, pp. 470-72.

        Discusses the problems involved in moving the playhouse to its new site south of the river, based on information found in various court cases. See also 1913.19. Reprinted 1913.15; 1914.24.

1909.26   STOPES, C[HARLOTTE] C[ARMICHAEL]. "Burbage's 'Theatre.'" *FortR* 31 (1 July): 49-59.

> A discussion of the life and achievements of James Burbage, father of James and Cuthbert and builder of the first public playhouse. Stopes draws much of her information from previously unknown lawsuits in various courts, held in the Public Record Office. Reprinted: 1913.15; 1914.24; see also 1914.22.

1909.27   _____. "Giles and Christopher Alleyn of Holywell." *N&Q* 120 (30 October): 341-43.

> Biographical notes on the men who leased James Burbage the land on which he built the Theatre. Much of the information is draw from various court records.

1909.28   TREE, HERRERT BEERBOHM. "Shakespeare in London." *Times* (London), (6 October): 10.

> A letter to the editor disagreeing with Wallace's assertion that the Globe was located north of Maid Lane (see 1909.32). While himself not a historian, Tree bases his objection on Martin's discovery of a reference to the Globe in a Sacrament Token book from Southwark Cathedral. See also Martin's letter of the next day, 1909.19.

1909.29   UNWIN, GEORGE. *The Gilds and Companies of London*. London: Methuen; New York: Charles Scribner's Sons, pp. 267-92.

> The relevant section is Chapter 16, dealing with the Lord Mayor's Shows. While the entire history of the Shows is traced, Unwin pays special attention to the Jacobean period, described as "the Golden Age of the Lord Show." He examines the relationship of the Show to court masque and discusses the contributions of Middleton, Munday, Webster, Dekker, and other major playwrights. Reprinted: 1925.18; 1938.10; 1963.19.

1909.30   WALLACE, CHARLES WILLIAM. *Advance Sheets from Shakespeare, the Globe, and Blackfriars*. Stratford: Shakespeare Head Press, 16 pp.

> A portion of a plea at the Common Law in a case set for trial in February 1616. The plaintiff's bill reveals "the origin and history of shares in the Globe and Blackfriars in outline up to the date of the trial, gives the number of shares owned in each by Shakespeare and his associates at various dates, estimates the value of a share in 1615-16, and places an indefinite but clearly excessive estimate upon the profits." Wallace here reprints the Latin text "for private circulation only."

1909.31   _____. *Globe Theatre Apparel*. London: privately printed, 11 pp.

> The documents of the Taylor v. Hemynges case, concerning costumes of the King's Men, from 1612. Wallace prints the Bill of Complaint and two Answers.

1909.32 _____. "Shakespeare in London: Fresh Documents on the Poet and His Theatres, the Globe and the Blackfriars." *Times* (London), (2 October): 9.

Discusses Shakespeare's financial holdings in the Globe and Blackfriars, based on the discovery of the records of a lawsuit (see 1909.30). Wallace also attempts to locate the Globe, contributing to the controversy that raged for the next fifteen years by placing the building to the north of Maid Lane. Continued in 1909.33. See 1909.14, 18, 21.

1909.33 _____. "Shakespeare in London: Fresh Documents an the Poet and His Theatres, the Globe and Blackfriars." *Times* (London), (4 October): 9.

Continuation of 1909.32, giving the translated text of the documents. See also 1909.14, 18, 21, 30.

1909.34 _____. "Three London Theatres of Shakespeare's Time." University Studies (Nebraska) 9 (October) :287-342.

Information about the Red Bull, the Fortune, and the Bear Garden, drawn from suits in the Court of Requests, preserved in the Public Record Office. Wallace prints the documents, as well as his deductions from them. He includes the Woodford v.Holland case, bearing on the Red Bull; the Smith v. Beeston suit, dealing with Queen Anne's Men; and the Alleyn v.Henslowe proceedings, about the Fortune and the Red Bull.

1910

1910.1 ANON. "Shakespeare Discoveries." *Outlook* 94 (26 March): 655-56.

Announces Wallace's discovery of documents described in 1910.22.

1910.2 ANON. "The Site of the Globe Theatre, Bankside." *Builder* 108 (26 March): 353.

Cites the testimony of Mrs. Thrale in 1781 that she saw the foundations of the Globe, "hexagonal in form without . . . round within." Whatever she saw, it was south of Maid Lane.

1910.3 ARONSTEIN, PHILIP. "Die Organisation des englischen Shauspiels im Zeitalter Shakeapeares, I." *GRM* 2: 165-75.

Discusses government regulation and royal patronage of the drama. Continued in 1910.4.

1910.4 _____. "Die Organisation des englischen Schauspiels im Zeitalter Shakespeares, II." *GRM* 2: 216-31.

Continuation of 1910.3. Aronstein here discusses the system of sharers, housekeepers, hired men, and boys used i the Elizabethan playhouses.

1910.5   CHILD, HAROLD H. "The Elizabethan Theatre." In *Cambridge History of English Literature*. Vol. 6, *The Drama to 1642*, Pt. 2. Edited by A. W. Ward and A. R. Waller. Cambridge: University Press, pp. 241-78.

Surveys the field: includes discussions of the companies, the playhouses, methods of staging, costumes, the audience, and the financial arrangements Reprinted: 1919.3; 1932.3; 1939.1; 1949.4; 1950.6.

1910.6   CONRAD, HEWN. "Bemerkungen zu W. J. Lawrence Aufsatz 'Title and Locality Boards.'" *JDSG* 46: 106-13.

Responds to Lawrence in 1909.17, claiming that "title" is a general term and does not necessarily refer to a board bearing the title of the play posted in the theatre.

1910.7   FEUILLERAT, ALBERT. *Le Bureau des Menus-Plaisirs (Office of the Revels) et la mise en scène a la cour d'Elizabeth*. Louvain: A. Uystpruyst, 88 pp.

Published version of his Pi1.D. dissertation, University of Paris. Intended as an introduction to and discussion of the documents in 1908.6. The two major chapters give a brief history of the Office of the Revels and discuss the function and administration of the Office.

1910.8   _____. "Quelques documents nouveaux sur le Théâtre de Blackfriars." In *Mélanges littéraires publiés par la Faculté des Lettres de Clermont-Ferrand*. Clemont-Ferrand: Universite Faculté des Lettres et Sciences Humaines, pp. 267-76.

Announces the discovery of three documents that establish the existence of the first Blackfriars as a separate theatre in 1576. Feuillerat briefly discloses the transactions between Farrant and Hunnis connected with the playhouse and its early history. See also 1911.13; 1912.6, 17, 23; 1913.3.

1910.9   FORESTIER, A[MEDEE]. "Origins of the English Stage, No. VI: A Shakespeare Play at the Old Globe in Shakespeare's Day." *Illustrated London News* 136 (19 March): 423.

A conjectural illustration of 1 Henry IV, showing the theatre, stage, actors, and audience, with five lines of commentary.

1910.10   LAW, ERNEST. "Shakespeare at Whitehall: on All Hallow's Day, 1604." *Times* (London), (31 October): 10.

Discusses in general terms the performance in the Whitehall banqueting house. Law also touches on the performance of *Merry Wives of Windsor* in the Great Hall that same year. Continued in 1910.11.

1910.11   _____. "Shakespeare's Christmas, St. Stephen's Day, 1604: The First Night Performance of *Measure for Measure*." *Times* (London), (26 December): 10.

Continuation of 1910.10. Law discusses the December twenty-six court performance in the Great Hall, arguing that the "gross dialogues" were cut for the occasion.

1910.12   MANLY, J[OHN] M[ATTHEWS]. "The Children of the Chapel Royal and Their Masters." In *Cambridge History of English Literature*. Vol. 6, *The Drama to 1642*, pt. 2. Edited by A. W. Ward and A. R. Waller. Cambridge: University Press, pp. 279-92.

    Discusses the series of seventeenth-century masters of the Children of the Chapel and their possible and known dramatic contributions as well as the professional troupe which presented public performances at Blackfriars. Reprinted: 1919.12; 1932.10; 1934.10; 1949.10; 1950.13.

1910.13   MARTIN, WII.LIAM. "The Site of the Globe Playhouse of Shakespeare." *Surrey Archaeological Collections* 23: 149-202.

    Reviews the evidence that determined the position of the plaque commemorating the site of the Globe on the south side of Park Street, formerly Maid Lane. Martin considers three classes of evidence: legal, semi-legal, and business documents; printed and oral accounts of the site; and contemporary maps, views, and plans. He follows Rendle (1878.3) in the interpretation of most documents. The many illustrations help the reader to follow the argument. This is Martin's major contribution to the controversy over the site of the Globe and is frequently drawn on by others. See Index under Globe Playhouse--Site of.

1910.14   MÜLLER, C. "Zue Geschichte der Hirtenspiele in dem Entertainments der Königin Elisabeth und König Jakobs I." *GRM* 10: 456-83.

    Examines the songs in the entertainments of Elizabeth and James during progresses, with a chronicle of such entertainments.

1910.15   MURRAY, JOHN TUCKER. *English Dramatic Companies, 1558-1642*. Vol. 1, *London Companies*; Vol. 2, *Provincial Companies*. London: Constable & Co.; Boston: Houghton-Mifflin, 804 pp.

    An attempt at a comprehensive history of all dramatic companies in London and the provinces during the reigns of Elizabeth, James, and Charles. While there is little new in the first volume, the second presents the results of the first systematic search of records of a dozen provincial cities. The appendixes include many newly discovered documents. See 1920.30. Superseded by Chambers (1923.2) and Bentley (1941.1).

1910.16   NEUENDORFF, BERNHARD. *Die englische Volksbühne im Zeitalter Shakespeares nach den Bühnenweisungen*. Berlin: E. Felber, 770 pp.

    Examines the typical Elizabethan stage, based on a study of the stage directions in printed texts. Neuendorff supports the inner-outer stage hypothesis and advocates the alternation theory.

*1910.17   STOPES, CHARLOTTE CARMICHAEL. "The Rose and the Swan, 1597." *Stage* (London), (6 January).

    Cited in 1917.3.

1910.18   STOPES, CHARLOTTE C[ARMICHAEL]. "Shakespeare's Fellows and Followers." *JDSG* 46: 92-105.

>   Information drawn from the Lord Chamberlain's papers, concerning various actors, managers, and playwrights. <u>See also</u> 1931.2.

1910.19   _____. "The Theatre." *Archiv* 124 (January): 129-31.

>   A brief review of her research since 1889 on Burbage's playhouse and Shakespeare's connection to it. <u>See also</u> 1913.15, 19.

1910.20   STOPES, C[HARLOTTE] C[ARMICHAEL]. *William Hunnis and the Revels of the Chapel Royal: A Study of the Influences Which Affected Shakespeare.* Materialien zur Kunde des älteren englischen Dramas, no. 29. Ed. Willy Bang[-Kaup]. Louvain: A. Uystpruyst, 362 pp.

>   An attempt at a biography of the Master of the Children of the Chapel Royal, 1566-1597, with documentary notes.

1910.21   WALLACE, C[HARLES] W[ILLIAM] . "Gervase Markham, Dramatist ." *JDSG* 46: 345-50.

>   Records from the Court of Requests of a suit (1623) between Markham and various actors.

1910.22   WALLACE, CHARLES WILLIAM. "New Shakespeare Discoveries: Shakespeare as a Men among Men." *Harper's* 120 (March):489- 510.

>   Discusses the discovery of documents in the Court of Requests, preserved in the Public Record Office, bearing on Shakespeare's life in London. There is little of theatrical interest.

1910.23   WALLACE, CHARLES W[ILLIAM]. "Shakespeare and His London Associates as Revealed in Recently Discovered Documents." *University Studies* (Nebraska) 10, no. 4 (October): 261-360.

>   Transcripts of fifty-six documents of the period bearing on theatrical affairs, with commentary. Thirty-nine of the documents are from the Belott-Mountjoy case, earlier reported in 1910.22. Eight are from the Witter-Heminges case, earlier reported in 1910.24. The final nine are from the Keysar-Burbage case, earlier reported in 1906.10.

1910.24   WALLACE, CHARLES WILLIAM. "Shakspere and the Blackfriars." *Century* 80 (September): 742-52.

>   Discusses Shakespeare's association with the Blackfriars, based upon a variety of records of court eases discovered by Wallace. The most important case centers on a charge of conspiracy against the Blackfriars shareholders.

1910.25   _____. "Shakespere's Money Interest in the Globe Theater." *Century* 80 (August): 500-12.

>   Discusses the business affairs of Shakespeare in the organizing, building, rebuilding, and management of the Globe, drawn from a variety of records of

court cases discovered by Wallace. He concludes, for example, that Shakespeare in fact owned an interest in the Globe after he retired to Stratford, and that his income from his share was less than previously supposed.

1910.26   WILSON, J[OHN] D[OVER]. "The Puritan Attack on the Stage." In *Cambridge History of English Literature*. Vol. 6, *Drama to 1642*. Pt. 2. Edited by A. W. Ward and A. R. Waller. Cambridge: University Press, pp. 373-409.
    Discusses the puritan background and the major publications (including those of Gosson, Lodge, Stubbes, Rankins, Rainolds, and Prynne) of the attack. Reprinted: 1919.20; 1932.12; 1934.20; 1949.17; 1950.21.

1911

1911.1   ADAMS, JOSEPH QUINCY, Jr. "The Four Pictorial Representations of the Elizabethan Stage." *JGGP* 10 (April): 329-33.
    Examines Albright's treatment of the Swan, Red Bull, *Messalina*, and *Roxana* drawings in 1909.2 and finds it wanting. The *Messalina* and *Roxana* illustrations "offer practically no proof of Mr. Albright's typical stage," while Albright's rejection of the Swan drawing "will not do." Adams rejects Albright's theories.

1911.2   ANON. "At the Sign of St. Paul's." *Illustrated London News* 140 (9 September): 402.
    Four photographs of James P. Maginnis's model of the Fortune, from designs by Godfrey in 1908.10.

1911.3   ANON. "The Elizabethan Playhouse." *Architect and Builder's Journal*, (16 August): 167-71.
    Summarizes 1908.10 and reprints the sections and floor-plans from that reconstruction.

1911.4   BASKERVILL, C[HARLES] R[EED]. "The Custom of Sitting on the Elizabethan Stage." *MP* 8 (April): 581-90.
    Takes issue with Wallace's conclusion in 1908.18 that the custom of sitting on the stage began at the Blackfriars in 1597, citing a variety of sources showing a broader application.

1911.5   CHAMBERS, E[DMUND] K. "Commissions for the Chapel." *MSC* 1, pts. 4 & 5: 357-63.
    Commissions issued to Nathaniel Giles in 1604 and 1606, bearing on the use of boys far dramatic purposes.

1911.6   _____. "A Jotting by John Aubrey." *MSC* 1, pts. 4 & 5: 341-47.
    A facsimile of a page of Aubrey's notes, concerning Fletcher, Jonson, Shakespeare, and John Ogilby the dancing master, with commentary. William Beestan apparently served as the source of the information.

1911.7   _____. "Plays of the King's Men in 1641." *MSC* 1, pts. 4 & 5: 364-69.
          A warrant and schedule from the Lord Chamberlain's Warrant Books in
the Public Record Office, with commentary. The lists contains sixty plays,
apparently all of the repertory of the King's Men not yet in print and thus
reserved for that company.

1911.8   _____. "Two Early Player Lists." *MSC* 1, pts. 4 & 5: 348-56.
          A letter listing the Earl of Wocester's Men in 1572 and a certificate listing
Queen Elizabeth's Men in 1588, with commentary.

1911.9   _____, and GREG, W[ALTER] W[ILSON], eds. "Dramatic Records from the
Privy Council Register, 1603-42." *MSC* 1, pts. 4 & 5: 370-95.
          Transcripts of all entries bearing on dramatic history from the Privy
Council Register during the reigns of James and Charles. Chambers and Greg list
twenty-four entries in all. See also 1912.21.

1911.10   COLLINS, CHURTON. "Shakespearian Theatres." *ContempR* 99 (January):
96-108.
          A popular general survey of playhouses, acting, and theatrical conditions
of Shakespeare's tine. Collins is rather anecdotal, taking the reader on an
imaginary tour and to an imaginary performance. There are many minor errors of
fact.

1911.11   CORBIN, JOHN. "Shakespere His Own Stage-Manager." *Century* 83
(December): 260-70.
          A popular treatment, arguing for the presentation of the plays as
Shakespeare intended them. Corbin includes drawings of a reconstruction with
inner stages above and below, and octagonal shape. He also describes productions
he participated in at the New Theatre.

1911.12   CUNLIFFE, J[OHN] W[ILLIAM], ed. "The Queenes Majesties Entertainment
at Woodstocke." *PMLA* 926 (March): 92-141.
          An edition of the entertainment, based on the 1585 quarto, with critical
commentary including information of theatrical interest.

1911.13   FEUILLERAT, A[LBERT]. "Shakespeare's Blackfriars: Discovery of
Important Documents." *Daily Chronicle* (London), no. 15,552 (22 December): 4.
          Announces the discovery of nine documents among the Loseley
manuscripts concerning the history of the first Blackfriars. A rough history of the
theatre is sketched in less than two newspaper columns. A more complete
history with full documentation is left for another time. See also 1912.6, 17, 23;
1913.3.

1911.14   FORESTIER, A[MEDEE]. "Where Money Came from for Dulwich College; Chief Rival to Shakespeare's Theatre, the Globe: The Fortune." *Illustrated London News* 140 (12 August): 776-77.

        Two drawings, a section and a perspective rendering, of Forestier's reconstruction, with notes. This version of the Fortune has obliquely set doors with balconies above them, and large inner stages above and below. It is very similar to Godfrey's reconstruction (1908.10).

1911.15   LAW, ERNEST. "Cunningham's Extracts from the Revels Books, 1842, I." *Athenaeum,* (9 September): 297-99.

        Responds to Stopes in 1911.26, 27, arguing for the genuineness of the Revels extracts. Law answers her objections point by point, with reference to many contemporary documents. Here he deals with the genuineness of the ink, the punctuation, and the spelling of the 1604-5 entry. Continued in 1911.16-17; 1912.13-14. For response <u>see</u> 1911.29. <u>See also</u> 1911.18; 1912.20; 1913.8; 1920.12-13, 26; 1922.8; 1925.20; 1928.16; 1930.9.

1911.16   _____. "Cunningham's Extracts from the Revels Books, 1842, II." *Athenaeum,* (16 September): 324.

        Continuation of 1911.15, in response to 1911.26-27. Here Law examines word usage in the 1604-5 document. For a response <u>see</u> 1911.29. Continued in 1911.17. <u>See also</u> 1911.18; 1912.20; 1913.8; 1920.12-13, 26; 1922.8; 1925.20; 1928.16; 1930.9.

1911.17   _____. "Cunningham's Extracts from the Revels Books, 1842, III. *Athenaeum,* (30 September): 388.

        Continuation of 1911.15, 16. Here Law answers Stopes's objections to the incompleteness of the 1604-5 document. Continued in 1912.13-14; for a response <u>see</u> 1911.29. <u>See also</u> 1911.18; 1912.20; 1913.8; 1920.12-13, 26; 1922.8; 1925.20; 1928.16; 1930.9.

1911.18   LAW, ERNEST PHILIP ALFHONSE. *Some Supposed Shakespeare Forgeries.* London: G. Bell & Sons, 80 pp.

        Records the history of the controversy over the supposedly forged Revels Accounts of 1604 and 1611, ultimately arguing for their genuineness. Based on 1911.15-17 and 1912.13-14. <u>See also</u> 1911.27-29; 1912.20; 1913.8; 1920.12-13, 26; 1922.8; 1925.20; 1928.16; 1930.9.

1911.19   LAWRENCE, W[ILLIM] J[OHN]. "The Evolution and Influence of the. Elizabethan Playhouse." *JDSG* 47: 18-41.

        Chronicles the changes in the playhouses and the manner of presentation from the Theatre until the closing of the playhouses in 1642. Reprinted: 1912.15.

1911.20 _____. 'The Seventeenth Century Theatre: Systems of Admission." *Anglia* 35: 526-38.

Discusses the gathering of admissions at the various points in the Elizabethan playhouse and the survival of the custom in the Restoration and eighteenth century. Reprinted: 1913.9.

1911.21 PILCH, LEO. "Shakespeare als Regisseur." *ZFEU* 10, no. 4 (Fall): 385-406.

Examines Shakespeare's function as director, citing lines from *Midsunmer Night's Dream*, *1 Henry IV*, and *Henry V* that provide stage directions for action.

1911.22 REESE, GEORG HERMANN. *Studien und Beiträge zur Geschicte der englischen Schauspielkunst in Zeitalter Shakespeares*, Jena: G. Neuerhahn. 36 pp.

Published version of his Jena Ph.D. dissertation, Reese examines costume practices during the period based on textual allusions and stage directions in the published plays. The two sections deal with costumes for Jewish characters and historical costumes.

1911.23 REYNOLDS, G[EORGE] F[ULLMER]. "What We Know of the Elizabethan Stage." *MP* 9 (July): 47-82.

A review of the literature, divided into three parts: treatment of sources, construction of the stage, and principles of stage management. The point of departure is Reynolds's own argument, presented in 1905.8, for an essentially medieval method of staging. He emphasizes the need to consider each playhouse individually and to use evidence from published plays with great care. In an appendix Reynolds considers several miscellaneous issues. This is among the most important of the pre-World War I articles, indispensible for tracing the history of the field.

1911.24 SCHELLING, FELIX E. *Elizabethan Drama 1558-1642: A History of the Drama in England from the Ascension of Queen Elizabeth to the Closing of the Theatres, to Which is Prefixed a Resume of the Earlier Drama from Its Beginnings.* Vol. 1. Boston and New York: Houghton, Mifflin & Co., pp. 141-93.

Reprint of 1908.16.

1911.25 SPENCER, M. LYLE. Corpus Christi Pageants in England. New Yark: Baker & Taylor, 276 pp.

While the final chapter, dealing with the passing of the pageants, covers the sixteenth and seventeenth centuries, there is little here of importance to the Elizabethan stage. Included because of listing in previous bibliographies.

1911.26 [STOPES, CHARLOTTE CARMICHAEL.] "Cunningham's Extracts from the Revels Books, 1842, I." *Athenaeum*, (22 July): 101-2.

Writing as "Audi Alterem Partem" ["Let the Other Side be Heard"], Stopes questions the genuineness of the extracts, based on the use of the paper, the handwriting, and the spelling. Continued in 1911.27; Law responds in

1911.15-17, and Scopes responds to the response in 1911.28. See also their books on the subject: Law, 1911.18, 1913.8; Stopes, 1922.8. Other treatments, with arguments pro and con, may be found in 1920.12-13, 26; 1925.20; 1928.16; and 1930.9.

1911.27 _____."Cunningham's Extracts from the Revels Books, 1842, II." *Athenaeum*, (29 July): 130-31.

        Continuation of 1911.26, written as "Audi Alterem Partem." Here Stopes questions the 1604-5 documents on the basis of the use of words compared to the usage found in other Revels Accounts, as well as their incompleteness. She also challenges the 1636 account on the basis of the place of performance. See Law's response, 1911.15-17; Stopes's rebuttal, 1911.28; and the rest of the controversy, 1911.18; 1912.13-14. 20: 1913.8; 1920.12-13, 26; 1922.8; 1925.20; 1928.16; and 1930.9.

1911.28 _____. "Cunningham's Extracts from the Revels Books." *Athenaeum*, (7 October): 421-22.

        Writing as "Audi Alterem Partem," Stopes responds to Law in 1911.15-17, attempting to refute his argument about the genuineness of the 1604-5 document. Law responds in 1912.13-14; Stopes offers her rebuttal in 1912.20. See their books: Law, 1911.18, 1913.8; Stopes, 1922.8; as well as other contributions to the controversy in 1920.12-13, 26; 1925.20; 1928.16; 1930.9.

1911.29 WALLACE, CHARLES WILLIAM. "The Swan Theatre and the Earl of Pembroke's Servants." *EStudien* 43, no. 3 (July): 340-95.

        A set of documents from the Court of Requests, held in the Public Record Office, bearing on the Swan, with sixteen conclusions about the playhouse and its company that Wallace draws from the evidence presented.

<u>1912</u>

1912.1 ADAMS, JOSEPH QUINCY, Jr. "Lordinge (alias 'Lodowick') Barry." *MP* 9 (April): 567-70.

        Discusses the common error of calling Lordinge Barry, playwright and manager of the King's Revels company at Whitefriars, by the wrong name, Lodowick. See also 1917.8.

1912.2 BELL, WALTER GEORGE. "The Whitefriars Playhouses." In *Fleet Street in Seven Centuries*. London: Isaac Pitman & Sons, pp. 305-37.

        Discusses the possible playhouse in 1580, the Whitefriars of the Queen's Revels of 1610-13, and the Salisbury Court of 1629-64. Most of the information is drawn from Collier (1879.21), Fleay (1890.1). and Murray (1910.15). Bell also discusses the Dorset Garden Playhouse of the Restoration.

1912.3   BRERETON, J[OHN] LE GAY. "Stage Arrangement in Peele's *David and Bethsabe*, I.i." *MLR* (July): 373-74.

Draws attention to a 1537 German illustration, in relation to a stage direction in Peele's text that indicates Bethsabe is discovered bathing, with "David above viewing &." The implication is that he sits above an obliquely set door in order to see into the discovery space. Reprinted: 1948.5.

1912.4   CLAPHAM, ALFRED W. "On the Topography of the Dominican Priory of London." *Archaeologia* 63: 57-84.

A paper read 18 January 1912. Clapham reconstructs the Blackfriars precinct, including the site of the playhouse.

1912.5   CULLEN, CHARLES. "Puritanism and the Stage." *PRPSG* 43: 153-81.

Text of a paper read before the Historical and Philological section of the Society, 20 March 1912. Cullen sketches the intellectual and cultural backgrounds, briefly describes the theatrical situation, and broadly traces the arguments of the Puritans, especially Stubbes and Prynne.

1912.6   FEUILLERAT, ALBERT. "The Origins of Shakespeare's Theatre: Recent Discovery of Documents." *JDSC* 48: 81-103.

Discusses the documents found among the Loseley Manuscripts that verify the existence of the first Blackfriars Playhouse, built by Richard Farrant in 1576-77. Feuillerat also prints six letters and Farrant's lease for the first time. Abridged in 1911.13.

1912.7   FLOOD. W. H. GRATTAN. "Master Sebastian of Paul's." *MusAnt* 3 (January): 149-57.

A brief biography of Sebastian Wstcott, early Master of the Children of Paul's, touching on theatrical matters,

1912.8   GODFREY. WALTER H. "A Scale Model of the Fortune Theatre." *ArchR* 31 (January): 53-55.

Photographs of a scale model built to Godfrey's plans in 1908.10. See also 1911.3.

1912.9   GRAVES, THORNTON SHIRLEY. "The Court and London Theatres during the Reign of Elizabeth." Ph.D. dissertation, University of Chicago, 93 pp.

Published as 1913.6.

1912.10   GRAVES,T[HORNTON] S[HIRLEY]. "A Note on the Swan Theatre." *MP* 9 (January): 431-34.

Discusses a letter of 1602 that demonstrates that the Swan was fitted with "hangings and curtains" (which Graves takes to be different) for at least one performance.

1912.11   GRAVES, T[HORNTON] S[HIRLEY]. "Some Allusions to Religious and Political Plays." *MP* 9 (April): 545-54.

Discusses references to anti-Catholic plays in 1559 and plays about a possible marriage for Elizabeth (and other political matters) in 1565.

1912.12   HUBBARD, GEORGE. "On the Exact Site of the Globe Playhouse of Shakespeare." *TrLMArchS*, n.s. 2, pt. 3: 334-57.

Text of a paper read to the Society, 26 February 1912. Hubbard argues for a site north of Maid Lane, based on the existence of a property known as "the Park" different from the Bishop of Winchester's Park to the south. He also cites the discovery of the possible foundations of the playhouse in 1907. See Index under Globe Playhouse--Site of.

1912.13   LAW, ERNEST. "Cunnigham's Extracts from the Revels Books, 1842, IV." *Athenaeum,* (6 April): 390.

Responds to 1911.28, continuing 1911. Here Law argues for the genuineness of the 1611-12 play list contained in 1912.13: Stopes replies in 1912.20. 1911.18; 1913.8; 1920.12-13, 26; 1922.8; 1925.20; 1928.19; 1930.9

1912.14   ____. "Cunningham's Extracts from the Revels Books, 1842, V." *Athenaeum,* (27 April): 470-71.

Conclusion of 1911.15-17; 1912.13. Here Law examines the record of 1636-37, which he finds genuine. Stopes based her objection on the place of performance listed, which she found to be false on the basis of payments made to the players. Law reads the same evidence differently, finding the listed place of performance to be genuine. See 1911.18; 1912.20; 1913.8; 1920.12-13, 26; 1922.8; 1925.20; 1928.16, 1930.9.

1912.15   LAWRENCE, W[ILLIAM] J[OHN]. *The Elizabethan Playhouse and Other Studies*. Stratford: Shakespeare Head Press, 265 pp.

A collection composed of one new essay (1912.17) and revisions of eight others (1902.9; 1903.4-5; 1908.14-15; 1909.16-17; 1911.19). Lawrence includes a preface, a bibliography, and an index. See also 1913.9.

1912.16   ____. "Light and Darkness in the Elizabethan Theatre." *EStudien* 45 (September): 181-200.

Discusses the bringing in of lights as "emblematic of the lateness of the hour," rather than for purposes of illumination. Lawrence argues that stages were never darkened for realistic effect. Reprinted: 1913.9. See also 1913.7; 1915.15. -

1912.17   ____. "New Facts about the Blackfriars: Monsieur Feuillerat's Discoveries." In *The Elizabethan Playhouse and Other Studies*. Stratford: Shakespeare Head Press, pp. 225-44.

Briefly traces the history of the first Blackfriars, as set out by Feuillerat (only 1911.13 had yet been published; 1912.6 was still to come) and then attempts to place that theatre into the general mold of "Elizabethan private theatre."

1912.18 _____. "Windows on the Pre-Restoration Stage." *Anglia* 36 (November): 450-78.

        Examines the issue of the upper stage generally, and the windows belonging to the area particularly. Lawrence discusses casements, bay windows, windows with curtains, gated windows, conjunctive windows, upper back windows, and lower-stage windows, citing a variety of plays from many theatres. Reprinted: 1913.9.

1912.19 SMITH, WINIFRED. *The Commedia dell'Arte: A Study in Italian Popular Comedy.* Columbia University Studies in English and Comparative Literature, no. 2. New York: Columbia University Press, pp. 170-99.

        The relevant section is Chapter Six, "The Commedia dell'Arte in Elizabethan and Jacobean England." Smith traces Italian entertainers in England and commedia influences on the drama. Based on 1908.17.

1912.20 [STOPES, CHARLOTTE CARMICHAEL.] "Cunningham's Extracts from the Revels Books." *Athenaeum,* (27 April): 469-70.

        Writing as "Audi Alterem Partem," Stopes responds to Law(1912.13). She reiterates her reasons for considering the 1611-12 list a forgery, primarily that only thirteen of the thirty-two performances are listed and that the list contains errors. See Law's final response, 1912.14. See also 1911.18; 1913.8; 1920.12-13, 26; 1922.8; 1925.20; 1928.16; 1930.9.

1912.21 STOPES, C[HARLOTTE] C[ARMICHAEL]. "Dramatic Records from the Privy Council Register, James I and Charles I." *JDSG* 48: 103-15.

        Extracts from the Registers, 1613-1639, bearing on theatrical affairs, with commentary. See also 1911.9.

1912.22 SULLIVAN, MARY. "Court Masques of James I: Their Influence on Shakespeare and Public Theatres." Ph.D. dissertation, University of Nebraska, 259 pp.

        Published as 1913.16.

1912.23 WALLACE, CHARLES WILLIAM. *The Evolution of the English Drama up to Shakespeare, with a History of the First Blackfriars Theatre: A Survey Based upon Original Records Now for the First Time Collected and Published.* Schriften der deutschen Shakespeare-Gesselschaft, no. 4. Berlin: Georg Reimer, 246 pp.

        Attempts to trace the early history of theatre and drama in Renaissance England, based on documents rediscovered by Wallace and his wife over many years. The most important section from a theatrical perspective is Chapters 14 through 19, dealing with the first Blackfriars. Wallace prints excerpts from many documents to support his case. The final chapters contain a table of plays and masques performed before Elizabeth 1558-1585 and a list of payments for plays at Court during the same period. This is among the most important of Wallace's many contributions to scholarship in the field.

1913.1   ALBRIGHT, VICTOR E. "Two of Percy's Plays as Proof of the Elizabethan Stage." *MP* 11 (October): 237-46.
Challenges the use of *Cuckqueens and Cuckolds Errant* and *Faery Pastoral*, both manuscript plays by Percy, as evidence of Elizabethan staging practices, since it is unlikely that the manuscripts reflect actual productions. See also 1914.21.

1913.2   COWLING, GEORGE HERBERT. *Music on the Shakespearian Stage.* Cambridge: University Press, 116 pp.
Examines the role of music, both instrumental and vocal, on the stage of Shakespeare and his contemporaries. The seven chapters treat pre-Shakespearan music; a general view of the Elizabethan stage and its music; the instruments of the period and their uses; the use of incidental music; the musicians, the singers, and the songs in the plays; the share in the drama that the music had; and literary allusions to music in Elizabethan plays. Cowling concludes that music was an important part of Elizabethan performances and could be used simply as entertainment, to reveal character, or to increase dramatic intensity. See Index under Music.

1913.3   FEUILLERAT, ALBERT. "Blackfriars Records." *MSC* 2, pt. 1: 1-136.
A selection of documents which locate Shakespeare's Blackfriars and show its relationsllip to Farrant's. Feuillerat divides the text into four sections, dealing with a general survey of the conventual buildings, Farrant's playhouse, Burbage's playhouse, and the sale of the property adjoining the latter.

1913.4   POWELL, FRANK, and PALMER, FRANK. Censorship in England. London: Frank Palmer, pp. 1-93.
The relevant section is the first four chapters, dealing with the origin of censorship, Sir Henry Herbert and his fees, the work of the early censors, and the work of the censors during the Interregnum. Chapter Three, "The Early Censors at Work," gives numerous examples of the Master of the Revel's comments and modifications.

1913.5   GODFREY, WALTER M. "The Fortune Theatre, London (1600)." In *Some Famous Buildings and Their Story.* By Alfred W. Clapham and Walter H. Godfrey. Westminster: Technical Journals, pp. 13-28.
Reprint of 1908.10.

1913.6   GRAVES, THORNTON SHIRLEY. *The Court and London Theatres during the Reign of Queen Elizabeth.* Menasha, Wisc.: Collegiate Press, 93 pp.
Published version if 1912.9. Graves approaches the London playhouses before 1603 from the perspective of the court stage, and points out the probability of influence. He divides his discussion into four parts: the structural elements of the Elizabethan theatres; the inn-yard and its relation to the London theatres; and

the influence of the court on methods of production. The major development here is the theory of the "canopy" stage, a permanent curtained booth used for discoveries instead of an "inner stage."

1913.7   GRAVES, T[HORNTON] S[HIRLEY]. "Night Scenes in the Elizabethan Theatres." *EStudien* 47 (August): 63-71.
>Responds to Lawrence (1912.16), suggesting that black hangings could also be used to suggest night. Graves also argues that there were night performances in the public theatres. <u>See also</u> Lawrence's reply, 1915.15.

1913.8   LAW, ERNEST PHILIP ALPHONSE. *More about Shakespeare "Forgeries."* London: D. Bell & Sons, 70 pp.
>Reprint of 1911.15-17; 1912.13-14.

1913.9   LAWRENCE, W[ILLIAM] J[OHN]. *The Elizabethan Playhouse and Other Studies.* Second Series. Stratford: Shakespeare Head Press, 261 pp.
>Contains revisions of three previously published essays (1911.20; 1912.16, 18) and three new essays (1913.10-12) decline with the theatre of the period, as well as a preface, bibliography, and index.

1913.10   _____. "The Origin of the English Picture-Stage." In *Elizabethan Playhouse and Other Studies.* Second Series. Stratford: Shakespeare Head Press, pp. 119-48.
>Examines possible uses of scenery in the private theatres before 1642 and D'Avenant's productions during the Interregnum as preparation for a discussion of the use of scenery after 1660.

1913.11   _____. "The Origin of the Theatre Programe." In *The Elizabethan Playhouse and Other Studies.* Second Series. Stratford: Shakespeare Head Press, pp. 55-92.
>Examines the advertising, playbills, and posters used to attract audiences during this period as preparation for tracing the later history of the program.

1913.l2   _____. "The Persistence of Elizabethan Conventions." In *The Elizabethan Playhouse and Other Studies.* Second Series. Stratford: Shakespeare Head Press, pp. 149-88.
>Examines possible influences on later periods of Elizabethan uses of music, masques, the visualization of dreams, spectators sitting on the stage, passing over the stage, the bearing of bodies from the stage, the terminal dance, and the custom of announcing the next performance.

1913.13   MARTIN, WILLIAM. "An Elizabethan Theatre Program." *SMNN* 24, no. 277 (January): 16-20.
>Discusses and prints the Swan "Plat" of England's Joy, which Martin assumes was printed for the audience like a modern program.

1913.14   POEL, WILLIAM. *Shakespeare in the Theatre*. London and Toronto: Sidgwick & Jackson, pp. 3-28.

> The relevant section contains part of "The Elizabethan Playhouse," a paper read before the Elizabethan Literary Society on 1 November 1893. Instead of stage structures, Poel discusses general principles of performance that can be adapted in the modern theatre.

1913.15   STOPES, C[HARLOTTE] C[ARMICHAEL]. *Burbage and Shakespeare's London*. London: Alexander Moring, The De la More Press, 272 pp.

> Contains reprints of 1909.25-26. The three chapters examine the lives of James Burbage, builder of the Theatre; his sons, Richard and Cuthbert; and their descendents. The last half of the volume consists of twenty-eight documentary from which Stopes draws her material. The Preface sheds some light on her competition with the Wallaces. Stopes includes considerable information about the building of the Theatre, but she concentrates on biography. See also Wallace, 1913.19.

1913.16   SULLIVAN, MARY. *Court Masques of James I: Their Influence on Shakespeare and the Public Theatres*. New York and London: G. P. Putnam's Sons, Knickerbocker Press, 259 pp.

> Published version of 1912.22. The first four chapters treat the periods 1603-1608, 1608-1614, 1614-1616, and The final two chapters examine the cost of dramatic productions at Court and the influence of diplomatic conditions upon literature. A valuable appendix prints eighty-seven excerpts from letters, dispatches, and other documents related to court masques of James I. Sullivan's central thesis is that the occasion of the masque is the most important determinant of content.

1913.17   THORNDIKE, ASHLEY HORACE. "From Outdoors to Indoors on the Elizabethan Stage." In *Anniversary Papers by Colleagues and Pupils of George Lyman Kittredge*. Boston: Ginn, pp. 273-79.

> Discusses the use of curtains and the inner stage for the representation of location whenever desired by use of the principle of alternation, specifically when characters move from an outdoor location to an indoor location. Thorndike uses *A Yorkshire Tragedy* as his main example. For more details on Thorndike's approach to the Elizabethan stage, see 1916.16.

1913.18   WALIACE, CHARLES WILLIAM. "A London Pageant of Shakespeare's Time: New Information from Old Records." *Times* (London), (28 March): 6.

> Discusses the pageant on the Thames in 1610 in honor of the creation of Prince Henry as Prince of Wales. Anthony Mundav was employed as poet, and Richard Burbage and John Rice were the two orators on behalf of the city.

1913.19 _____. *The First London Theatre: Materials for a History*. *UNS* 13, nos. 1-3, 297 pp.

       Presents the documents Wallace found concerning the Burbage-Brayne controversy and the Burbage-Allen litigation as well as an essay (pp. 1-35) interpreting the evidence they present. The 99 documents are printed chronologically. <u>See</u> 1913.15; 1979.2.

1913.20 WITHINGTON, ROBERT. "English Pageantry, an Historical Outline." Ph.D. dissertation, Harvard University.

       Published as 1918.4 and 1920.32.

<u>1914</u>

1914.1 ANON. "More Light on Shakespeare." *Outlook* 107 (11 July): 587-89.

       Announces additional Wallace discoveries, described in a variety of scholarly and popular publications.

1914.2 ARKWRIGHT, G[ODFREY] E[DWARD] P[ELLEW]. "Elizabethan Choirboy Plays and Their Music." *PMusA* 40: 117-38.

       A paper read before the association 21 April 1914. Arkwright traces the history of the Children of the Chapel and the Children of Paul's, including their dramatic performances. He then examines the lyrics contained in the plays.

1914.3 A[RKWRIGHT], G[ODFREY] E[DWARD] P[ELLEW]. "Proposals for Building an Amphitheatre in London, 1620." *N&Q* 130 (19 December): 481-82.

       Three documents related to the proposed Amphitheatre, held in the Bodleian Library, with brief commentary. Arkwright prints the proposal, the King's approval, and the King's ultimate disapproval. Continued in 1914.4.

1914.4 _____. "Proposals for Building an Amphitheatre in London, 1620." *N&Q* 130 (26 December): 502-03.

       Completes 1914.3.

1914.5 BOAS, FREDERICK S. *University Drama in the Tudor Age*. Oxford: Clarendon Press, 414 pp.

       Primarily a literary study, but Boas does consider "the general relations between the academic and the professional stage." He also includes scattered information concerning stage arrangements, actors, and properties, as well as a discussion of the controversy over the propriety of acting in a University.

1914.6 GRAVES, T[HORTON] S[HIRLEY]. "The Origin of the Custom of Sitting on the Stage." *JEGP* 13 (January): 104-09.

       Examines the possibility that the custom of sitting on the stage originated at the first Blackfriars and demonstrates that it predates even that theatre. Graves cites Bereblock's description of the performance of *Palemon and Arcyte* (<u>see</u> 1905.1) to show that Elizabeth sat upon the stage in 1566 and concludes that "the gentlemen who occupied the stage were paying for the privilege of sitting where they had seen their superiors sit at private performances."

1914.7 _____. "The Political Use of the Stage during the Reign of James I." *Anglia* 38: 137-56.
    Argues that plays were mare often used for political purposes than has been supposed, with numerous examples drawn from plays and records of the period.

1914.8 _____. "The Shape of the First London Theatre." *SAQ* 13 (July): 280-82.
    Argues briefly that the Theatre was round, based on documents printed by Wallace in 1913.19.

1914.9 HILLEBRAND, HAROLD NEWCOMB. "The Child Actors of the Sixteenth and Seventeenth Centuries." Ph.D. dissertation, Harvard University, 355 pp. Published as 1926.6.

1914.10 JENKINSON, WILBERFORCE. "The Early Play-Houses and the Drama as Referred to in Tudor and Stuart Literature." *ContempR* 105 (June): 847-56.
    Traces allusions to plays and playhouses from 1547 to 1643.

1914.11 JONAS, MAURICE. "The Red Bull Theatre." *N&Q* 129 (21 February): 150.
    Requests information for the beginning of playing at this theatre, since Lawrence estimates 1600 while everyone else estimates 1609. See 1914.12, 20.

1914.12 JONES, TOM. "The Red Bull Theatre." *N&Q* 129 (11 April): 298.
    Responds to 1914.11, referring Jonas and the reader to 1885.2-4.

1914.13 K. L. L. "Site of the Globe Theatre." *N&Q* 130 (12 September): 209-10.
    Initiates a series of queries, replies, and counters on this subject in *N&Q* by requesting more information on the dispute between Stopes and Wallace on the location of the Globe. This is probably the major controversy of the century in the field. See Index under Globe Playhouse--Site of. The definitive work is Braines (1923.11). Continued in 1914.15. See 1914.18.

1914.14 _____. "Site of the Globe Theatre." *N&Q* 130 (10 October): 290-91.
    Responds to Martin (1909.21) and Jackson (1909.14), suggesting the north side of Maid Lane, as did Wallace. See Index under Globe Playhouse--Site of. Continued in 1914.15.

1914.15 _____. "Site of the Globe Theatre." *N&Q* 130 (24 October): 335.
    Concludes 1914.13-14. See Index under Globe Playhouse--Site of.

1914.16   KEITH, WILLIAM GRANT. "The Designs for the First Movable Scenery on the English Public Stage." *BMg* 25 (April): 29-33.

Primarily concerned with the 1656 production of Siege of Rhodes, but includes a brief discussion of the pre-Commonwealth designs of Inigo Jones. Continued in 1914.17.

1914.17   _____. "The Designs for the First Movable Scenery on the English Public Stage. *BMg* 25 (May): 85-98.

Continues 1914.16.

1914.18   MARTIN, WILLIAM. "Site of the Globe Theatre." *N&Q* 130 (24 October): 335.

Responds to L. L. K. (1914.13-14), referring to his earlier paper on the subject (1910.13), in which he set out his reasons for supposing the Globe to have been situated on the south side of Maid Lane. He also refers L. L. K. to the new documents discovered by Wallace (1914.25-26). See Index under Globe Playhouse--Site of.

1914.19   NAIRN, J. ARBUTHNOTT. "Boy Actors under the Tudors and Stewarts." *TrRSL,* 2d series 32: 61-78.

A paper read before the Society, 26 February 1913. Nairn divides the boy companies into two types, the choir boys and the school boys, and discusses each in turn. He also provides a few biographical facts about Nathaniel Field and Salathiel Pavy, from the Children of the Chapel, as examples.

1914.20   NORMAN, WILLIAM. "The Red Bull Theatre." *N&Q* 129 (14 March): 212.

Responds to 1914.11, citing three plays produced at the Red Bull in 1612, 1620, and 1622.

1914.21   REYNOLDS, GEORGE F[ULLMER]. "William Percy and his Plays, with a Summary of the Customs of Elizabethan Staging." *MP* 12 (October) : 241-60.

Answers Albright's objections (in 1913.1) to the use of Percy's manuscript plays as evidence of Elizabethan staging practices, pointing out that they contradict Albright's alternation theory. The second section of the paper summarizes Reynolds's findings from a study of the plays presented at the Rose, the first Globe, and the first Fortune. He again emphasizes the medieval as opposed to modern nature of the staging. Reynolds concludes with a brief resume of Percy's life. See also his study of the Red Bull plays, 1940.10.

1914.22   STOPES, CHARLOTTE CARMICHAEL. "The Burbages, Founders of the Modern Stage." *TrRSL,* 2d series 32: 107-45.

A paper delivered 23 October 1912. Stopes includes a discussion of the theatrical world of early Elizabethan England, as well as a history of the family's involvement with the Theatre, the second Blackfriars, and the Globe. She concludes with an evaluation of Richard as a performer.

1914.23 _____. "'The Queen's Players' in 1636 [*sic*]." *Athenaeum*, (24 January): 143.
Despite the title (which was probably an editorial error), this transcribes a reference to Queen Jane's players in a suit in Chancery in 1536. Reprinted: 1914.24.

1914.24 _____. *Shakespeare's Environment*. London: G. Bell, 369 pp.
A collection of thirty previously-published essays, including 1909.75-26 and 1914.23.

1914.25 WALLACE, CHARLES WILLIAM. "Further New Documents." *Times* (London), (1 May): 4.
Continuation of 1914.26. Wallace here examines the history of the Globe property through the eighteenth century, as contained in seven documents he discovered in 1909. They deal with the family of Thomas Brend, and are used to argue once again for a site of the Globe north of Maid Lane. See Index under Globe Playhouse--Site of.

1914.26 _____. "Shakespeare and the Globe: New Documents Examined." *Times* (London), (30 April): 9-10.
Reiterates his arguments, set out in 1909.32, that the Globe was located north of Maid Lane, in response to the heated debate about its location then going on. He here brings to bear the Sewer Commission documents, not seen by him until 1911. Continued in 1914.25; see also Index under Globe Playhouse--Site of.

1915

1915.1 BAYLEY, A[RTHUR] R[UTTER]. "Shakespeare and the Blackfriars Theatre." *N&Q* 132 (7 August):108.
Responds to 1915.13, stating that while it is possible that Shakespeare acted at Blackfriars there is no evidence either way.

1915.2 [BRAINES, WILLIAM WESTMORELAND.] *Holywell Priory and the Site of the Theatre*, Shoreditch. Indications of Houses of Historical Interest in London, no. 43. London: London County Council, 32 pp.
Through the device of tracing the property through transfers, bequests, conveyances, and wills down to a time when it is described in terms of boundaries identifiable through modern maps, Braines is able to fix the site of the Theatre to within a few feet. He cites freely and fully from various documents. See also 1917.5 and his definitive siting of the Globe, 1921.1 and 1923.11.

1915.3 GRAVES, THORNTON SHIRLEY. "The 'Act-Time' in Elizabethan Theatres." *SP* 12 (July): 103-34.
An attempt to show the weakness of the arguments for continuous performance on the Elizabethan stage, by establishing "beyond all reasonable doubt that the 'five act form' with regular act intermissions was the rule in

London." <u>See also</u> Lawrence, 1912.15.

1915.4   GRAVES, T[HORNTON] S[HIRLEY]. "Tricks of Elizabethan Showmen."
SAQ 14 (April): 138-48.
Discusses questionable advertising methods of Elizabethan players.
Graves argues that they often claimed patronage that was not theirs, that they
knew the value of catchy and suggestive titles, and that they were not above a
quick exit with the cash box. He concludes, as Lawrence did in 1913.11, that
"showmanship did not begin with Barnum."

1915.5   HILLEBRAND, HAROLD NEWCOMB. "Sebastian Westcott, Dramatist and
Master of the Children of Paul's." *JEGP* 14 (October): 568-84.
An attempt at a brief biography of the dramatist, including linkage of his
name for the first time with *The Contention between Liberality and Prodigality*,
published in 1602 but probably written many years earlier for the Children of
Paul's. Hillebrand suggests in passing that the theatre at Paul's might have
preceded both the first Blackfriars and Burbage's Theatre.

1915.6   HUBBARD, GEORGE. "The Site of the Globe." *N&Q* 132 (3 July): 11-13.
Responds to Stopes (1915.23), suggesting that the Globe Alley that
presents evidence for the south site was a later, second alley bearing that name,
the original being to the north of Maid Lane. He also asserts that the Globe was
built on the site of the old Bear Ring, and that two warehouses were built upon the
site. Their construction revealed the foundations of the Globe. Continued in
1915.7-12. <u>See also</u> Index under Globe Playhouse--Site of, and 1915.14, 16-19.

1915.7   _____. "The Site of the Globe." *N&Q* 132 (17 July): 50-51.
Continues 1915.6. Here Hubbard interprets the "Sewer Presentments"
evidence for a north site. Continued in 1915.8-12. <u>See also</u> Index under Globe
Playhouse--Site of, and 1915.14, 16-19.

1915.8   _____. "The Site of the Globe." *N&Q* 132 (24 July): 70-71.
Continues 1915.6-7. Hubbard argues for the north site on the basis of
visual evidence of maps and views of London. Continued in 1915.9-12; <u>See also</u>
Index under Globe Playhouse--Site of, and 1915.14, 16-19.

1915.9   _____. "The Site of the Globe." *N&Q* 132 (11 September): 201-2.
Replies to Martin (1915.16-19), again arguing for the site north of Maid
Lane, on the earlier evidence. <u>See</u> 1915.6-8; <u>See also</u> Index, under Globe
Playhouse--Site of, and 1915.14, 16-19.

1915.10   _____. "The Site of the Globe." *N&Q* 132 (18 September): 224-25.
Continues 1915.9. <u>See</u> Index, under Globe Playhouse--Site of, and
1915.14, 16-19.

1915.11   _____. "The Site of the Globe." *N&Q* 132 (2 October): 264-66.
           Continues 1915.9-10. <u>See</u> Index, under Globe Playhouse--Site of, and
1915.14, 16-19.

1915.12   _____. "The Site of the Globe." *N&Q* 132 (30 October): 347-48.
           Responds to L. L. K. (1915.14), reasserting his previous arguments in
favor of a site north of Maid Lane. <u>See</u> 1915.6-11, 16-19. <u>See also</u> Index, under
Globe Playhouse--Site of.

1915.13   JONAS, MAURICE. "Shakespeare and the Blackfriars Theatre." *N&Q* 132
           (17 July): 47.
           Asks for information on Shakespeare acting at this playhouse. <u>See</u> 1915.1.

1915.14   K., L. L. "The Site of the Globe." *N&Q* 132 (9 October): 289.
           Responds to Hubbard (1915.6-8) briefly, pointing out that Wallace differs
with Hubbard on the position of a crucial parcel of land. <u>See</u> Hubbard's response,
1915.12; <u>see also</u> Index under Globe Playhouse--Site of.

1915.15   LAWRENCE, W[ILLIAM] J[OHN]. "Night Performances in the Elizabethan
           Theatres: A Reply to Dr. T. S. Graves." *EStudien* 48 (January): 213-30.
           Replies to 1913.7, arguing that night Performances in the public theatres
were exceptional and that black hangings were not used to signify night.

1915.16   MARTIN, WILLIAM. "The Site of the Globe." *N&Q* 132 (3 July): 10-11.
           Responds to Stopes (191523), reviewing the argument and suggesting
again that the evidence for placing the Globe north of Maid Lane derives from a
clerical accident with an upside down map. <u>See</u> Index under Globe Playhouse--
Site of.

1915.17   _____. "The Site of the Globe." *N&Q* 132 (14 August): 121-23.
           Responds to Hubbard (1915.6-0), arguing for a site to the south of Maid
Lane. Here Martin takes issue with the assumption of an earlier Globe Alley.
Continued in 1915.18-19.

1915.18   _____. "The Site of the Globe." *N&Q* 132 (21 August): 143-44.
           Continuation of 1915.17, in response to Hubbard (1915.6-8). Here Martin
questions the assumption of a second "Park," separate from the Bishop's Park, as
well as Hubbard's interpretation of the Sewer Commission records. Continued in
1915.19.

1915.19   _____. "The Site of the Globe." *N&Q* 132 (28 August): 161-63.
           Continuation of 1915.17-18, in response to Hubbard (1915.6-8). Here
Martin questions Hubbard's treatment of contemporary maps and views and his
assertion that the foundations of the Globe were discovered without citing
corroborative evidence. <u>See</u> Hubbard's reply (1915.9), and the definitive work of
Braines (1923.11). <u>See also</u> Index under Globe Playhouse--Site of.

1915.20   POLLOCK, ARTHUR. "The Evolution of the Actor, II: The Rise of the Modern Actor." *Drama* 20 (November): 651-63.

Includes a brief sketch of Elizabethan actors and acting conditions. Continued in 1916.12.

1915.21   PORTER, CHARLOTTE. "Playing *Hamlet* as Shakespeare Staged It in 1601." *Drama* 19 (August): 511-26.

An anecdotal reconstruction of a performance of at the Globe. Continued in 1915.22.

1915.22   ___. "Playing *Hamlet* as Shakespeare Staged It, II." *Drama* 20 (November): 675-89.

Continuation of 1915.21, including a plan of the Globe.

1915.23   STOPES, C[HARLOTTE] C[ARMICHAEL]. "The Site of the Globe." *N&Q* 131 (12 June): 447-49.

Argues for the site south of Maid Lane, as did Martin (1909.19-21; 1910.13). Based on a court suit, the Sewer Commission order, various leases, and the archaeological discoveries of her husband, Henry Stopes, between 1880 and 1890. See particularly Martin's response, 1915.16: see also Index under Globe Playhouse--Site of.

1916

1916.1   ARCHER, WILLIAM, and LAWRENCE, W[ILLIAM] J[OHN]. "The Playhouse." In *Shakespeare's England: An Account of the Life and Manners of his Age*. Vol. 2. Edited by Sidney Lee, Charles Talbut Onions, and Walter A. Raleigh. Oxford: Clarendon Press, pp. 283-310.

Surveys the London playhouses chronologically, from the Theatre to the Salisbury Court. Archer and Lawrence also discuss the structure of the playhouse in generalized terms, including a recessed inner stage. On this point the Swan drawing is held to be inaccurate. The stage doors and upper stage, as well as the audience and its management, are topics for discussion. While intended for the general reader, this study is fully documented. Archer and Lawrence also reprint Godfrey's illustration of the Fortune as an example (see 1908.10). Reprinted: 1950.1.

1916.2   BRERETON, J[OHN] LE GAY. "DeWitt at the Swan." In *A Book of Homage to Shakespeare*. Edited by Israel Gollancz. London: Oxford University Press, pp. 204-06.

Attempts to reconstruct what DeWitt actually saw on his visit to the Swan by determining the copying errors of Van Buchell. Brereton places DeWitt in the second gallery to the right of center, and makes allowances for this position. In effect, he is trying to provide reasons for the drawing not conforming to his idea of what it should be.

1916.3   CARGILL, ALEXANDER. "The 'Globe' Theatre on the Bankside." In *Shakespeare the Player and Other Papers Illustrative of Shakespeare's Individuality*. London: Constable & Co., pp. 136-39.

Appendix B to the volume, with a general discussion and illustration from the Holler engraving.

1916.4   _____. "Shakespeare the Player." In *Shakespeare the Player and Other Papers Illustrative of Shakespeare's Individuality*. London: Constable & Co., pp. 1-34.
Reprint of 1891.1.

1916.5   CREIZENACH, WILHELM [MICHAEL ANTON]. *The English Drama in the Age of Shakespeare*. Translated by Cecile Hugon. London: Sidwick & Jackson, pp. 1-57, 353-430.

Translation of *Geschichte des neueren Dramas*, vol. 4 (1903.1). Book I, "The English Theatre from 1570 to 1587," and Book VIII, "Staging and Histrionic Art," are the relevant sections. The former is a general survey of little interest. The latter is more specifically theatrical, discussing stage doors, discoveries, the upper stage, and so on, but the discussion is of generalized "Elizabethan stage," using evidence from a wide variety of times and places. Creizenach also discusses acting and actors, particularly Burbage and Alleyn. See second edition, 1923.4.

1916.6   DICKINSON, THOMAS H. "Some Principles of Shakespeare Staging." In *Shakespeare Studies by Members of the Department of English of the University of Wisconsin*. Madison: University of Wisconsin. pp. 125-47.

Discusses in general terms the flexibility of Elizabethan staging and the difference between foreground and background. Much of the essay is then devoted to suggestions for modern staging.

1916.7   GRAVES, T[HORNTON] S[HIRLEY]. "The Ass as Actor." *SAQ* 15 (April): 175-82.

Briefly traces the ass as character from the medieval period through the eighteenth century, including the Elizabethan period. While the scholarship is genuine, the tone is tongue-in-cheek.

*1916.8   LAWRENCE, W[ILLIAM] J[OHN]. "Acting in Shakespeare's Day: Early Histrionic Conditions." *Stage* (London), 27 April.
Cited in *TN* 11 (April 1957): 71.

1916.9   _____. "A Forgotten Playhouse Custom of Shakespeare's Day." In *A Book of Homage to Shakespeare*. Edited by Israel Gollancz. London: Oxford University Press, pp. 707-11

Examines the practice of free admission after the fourth act. Lawrence draws his evidence from the extant plots and from a legal document of 1612. The custom apparently survived until well into the Restoration, when it was suppressed.

1916.10 ____. "New Light on the Elizabethan Theatre." *PortR* 105 (May): 820-29.
Discusses the difference between the public and private playhouses, and argues that changes in the public theatres came about because of competition with the private houses. The most important change was the roofing of the public playhouses, beginning with the Fortune in 1623 and followed shortly by the Red Bull.

1916.11 POEL, WILLIAM. *Some Notes on Shakespeare's Stage and Plays.* Manchester: University Press, 17 pp.
A general discussion by the founder and director of the Elizabethan Stage Society. Poel briefly discusses the Globe, the Fortune contract, the costumes, and the acting companies. His main point is that modern productions of Shakespeare should be based on Elizabethan theatrical conditions.

1916.12 POLLOCK, ARTHUR. "The Actor in England." *Drama* 24 (November): 550-59.
Continues 1915.20, beginning with Elizabethan actors and acting conditions.

1916.13 PORTER, CHARLOTTE. "How Shakespeare Set and Struck the Scene for *Julius Caesar* in 1599." *MLN* 31 (May): 281-87.
Discusses the staging of *Julius Caesar* based on original stage directions and dialogue references. Porter assumes upper and lower inner stages, and the visual appearance of all properties mentioned in the dialogue.

1916.14 SIMPSON, PERCY. "Actors and Acting." In *Shakespeare's England: An Account of the Life and Manners of his Age.* Vol. 2. Edited by Sidney Lee, Charles Talbut Onions, and Walter A. Raleigh. Oxford: Clarendon Press, pp. 240-82.
Examines Puritan attacks on actors and their defense, boy companies, Shakespeare's descriptions of acting, the clowns, and rehearsal and performance procedures. Aimed at the general reader, but well documented. Reprinted: 1950.16.

1916.15 ____."The Masque." In *Shakespeare's England: An Account of the Life and Manners of his Age.* Edited by Sidney Lee, Charles Talbut Onions, and Walter A. Raleigh. Oxford: Clarendon Press, pp. 311-33.
Discusses mumming and disguises in the sixteenth century as predecessors of the masque, as well as the form and performance of the masque itself. Other sections examine the Office of the Revels and the art of Inigo Jones. Intended for the general reader but well documented. Reprinted: 1950.17.

1916.16 THORNDIKE, ASHLEY H. *Shakespeare's Theater.* New York: Macmillan, 472 pp.
An attempt at a comprehensive survey of all that was known of the Elizabethen stage. Thorndike includes chapters on playhouses, the physical stage,

stage presentation, court theatres, companies, government regulation, actors and acting, and the audience. He subscribes to most commonplace ideas of his day, such as the inner stage and the alternation theory.

1916.17   YOUNG, KARL. "An Elizabethan Defence of the Stage." In *Shakespeare Studies by Members of the Department of English of the University of Wisconsin*. Madison: University of Wisconsin. pp. 101-71.

      Two letters, from Rainolds to Thornton and from Gager to Rainolds, from 1592 and 1593, concerning Rainolds's attack on the stage. See also 1916.18; 1974.3.

1916.18   _____. "William Gager's Defence of the Academic Stage." *TrWASAL* 18, pt. 2: 593-638.

      Traces the controversy between Gager end John Rainolds, including the text of one substantial letter from Gager in defense of the stage. See also 1916.17; 1974.3.

1917

1917.1   ADAMS, JOSEPH QUINCY. "The Conventual Buildings of Blackfriars, London, and the Playhouses Constructed Therein." *SP* 14 (April): 64-87.

      An attempt to reconstruct the ancient Dominican Priory of Blackfriars, and to point out the location, size, shape, and other details of the two playhouses constructed there. Because of the discovery of important documents among the Loseley Manuscripts (E 1913.3), Adams is able to correct Clapham's earlier attempt (see 1912.4) in many details. Adams places the first Blackfriars Playhouse in the Buttery section, a room 46 feet long and 25 feet wide, with a platform stage at one end equipped with multiple settings after the court fashion. There were no galleries, just benches for spectators. The second playhouse was built in the Halland Parlor, the combined length of which was 66 feet, with a width of 46 feet. Adams thinks there were two galleries, possible because of the width and height of the rooms.

1917.2   ADAMS, JOSEPH QUINCY, ed. *The Dramatic Records of Sir Henry Herbert, Master of the Revels, 1623-1673*. New Haven: Yale University Press, 155 pp.

      Composed of the important Office Book, containing entries from 1622 to 1642, and two sets of miscellaneous documents dated 1622-1642 and 1660-1670. While the Office Book itself had, unfortunately, vanished by 1917, Adams attempted to reconstruct it as best he could by piecing together the quotations from it scattered through the works of Malone and Chalmers (see, for example, 1821.1). In a brief Introduction Adams traces the history of the office up to Herbert and what is known about the Office Book and its disposal. He divides the Office Book itself into sections dealing with a veriety of areas, the most important being "Censorship of Plays," "Licenses of Plays," "Licenses of Playhouses and Companies," and "Plays and Masques at Court." The Index appears complete and analytical. This work is certainly among the most important to a study of the Elizabethan theatre. See also Lawrence (1923.15) for additions.

1917.3   ADAMS, JOSEPH QUINCY. *Shakespearean Playhouses: A History of English Theatres from the Beginnings to the Restoration.* Boston: Houghton Mifflin, 473 pp.
  Includes histories of seventeen permanent playhouses and five temporary or projected buildings, as well as a chapter on the early inn-yard theatres. Adams cites documentary sources at length and is generally quite careful in his interpretations. He does not attempt to reconstruct staging practices or make conjectural drawings of the theatre interiors, but rather contents himself with the histories of the buildings themselves. He quietly corrects the errors of Malone, Halliwell-Phillipps, Collier, Fleay, Ordish, and so on, and modestly hopes to be so corrected himself when further evidence is discovered or his interpretations are proven wrong. This book stood among the most important published in the field for years, and still ranks as indispensable more than sixty years later. The 316-item bibliography, with the more important items specially marked, is among the best guides to early scholarship in the field.

1917.4   BAYLEY, A[RTHUR] R[UTTER]. "Second Fortune Theatre." *N&Q* 134 (30 December): 537.
  Responds to 1917.7, suggesting that this playhouse was dismantled rather than burned in 1649, citing Lawrence.

1917.5   BRAINES, WILLIAM WESTMORELAND. "The Site of the Theatre, Shoreditch." *London Topographical Record* 11 :1-27.
  Contains the same information as in 1915.2.

1917.6   GRAVES, THORNTON SHIRLEY. "'Playing in the Dark' During the Elizabethan Period." *SP* 3 (January): 93-108.
  Discusses performances in the late afternoon during winter, and evening performances, and speculates about the on the rear stage and artificial lighting that would have been necessary. A continuation of the running feud between Graves and Lawrence on the subject; see also 1912.16; 1913.7; 1915.15.

1917.7   JONAS, MAURICE. "Second Fortune Theatre." *N&Q* 134 (18 November): 408.
  Requests corroboration of the burning of this playhouse. See1917.4, 10 for replies.

1917.8   LAWRENCE, W[ILLIAM] J[OHN]. "The Mystery of Lodowick Barry." *SP* 14 (April): 52-63.
  Lawrence shows that the Lording Barry who bought a controlling interest in the Whitefriars Playhouse in 1608 was also the author of *Ram Alley*. Further, "Lording" is not a Christian name (see 1912.1) but a polite title for the son of a

Lord. Lawrence concludes that the Lo. Barry listed as the author was actually David Oge Barry, son of general Lord Barry, who died in 1610 at the age of 24.

1917.9   LÜDEKE, HENRY. "Ludwig Tiecks Shakespeare-Studien: Zwei Kapitel zum Thema: Ludwig Tieck und das englische Theater." Ph.D. dissertation, University of Frankfurt, 62 pp.

    The two chapters alluded to in the title deal with Tieck's study of the old English theatres throughout his life, and the romantic period in Tieck's Shakespeare criticism. According to the foreword, these are Chapters Two and Four of a longer work. Tieck created a conjectural reconstruction of an Elizabethan playhouse in an 1836 short story.

1917.10   STEWART, ALAN. "Second Fortune Theatre." *N&Q* 134 (30 December 7): 577.

    Responds to 1917.7, suggesting that, according to Prynne, this playhouse burned in 1649. <u>See also</u> 1917.4.

1917.11   STRUNK, W[ILLIAM], Jr. "The Elizabethan Showman's Ape." *MLN* 32 (April): 215-21.

    Discusses the exhibition of trained apes in the period and several references to the practice in Shakespeare and elsewhere. <u>See</u> 1920.3.

1918

1918.1   LAWRENCE, W[ILLIAM] J[AMES]. "The Elizabethan Stage Throne. *TR* 3 (January): 93-108.

    Argues that the stage throne, when required, was placed on the rear stage and discovered or thrust out, and was not permanently in place. Lawrence uses stage directions and allusions from a variety of plays to support his case.

*1918.2   THALER, ALWIN. "Finance and Business Management of the Elizabethan Theatre." Ph.D. dissertation, Harvard University.

    Cited in *ADDT*, p. 92.

1918.3   THALER, ALWIN. "Shakespeare's Income." *SP* 15 (April): 82-96.

    Reexamines Shakespeare's income from all sources--as actor/sharer, housekeeper, playwright, and investor--placing his annual income at about £350. This figure would place him among the well off but not the fabulously wealthy. Based on research from 1918.2.

1918.4   WITHINGTON, ROBERT. *English Pageantry: An Historical Outline*. Vol. 1. Cambridge: Harvard University Press, pp. 198-238.

    Published version of 1913.20. The relevant section deals with Elizabethan pageantry, 1558-1602, and the royal entry in the seventeenth century. Nichols (1823.1) is the main source for the Elizabethan section. Both chapters present chronological listings of pageants and royal entries for the years indicated. <u>See also</u> vol. 2 (1920.32).

1919

1919.1   ADAMS, JOSEPH QUINCY. "An 'Hitherto Unknown' Actor of Shakespeare's Troupe?" *MLN* 34 (January): 46-48.
       A brief analysis of the letter from William Wilson to Edward Alleyn, concluding that Wilson was not, in fact, an actor but rather a gatherer or perhaps a stagekeeper.

1919.2   _____. "The Housekeepers of the Globe." *MP* 17 (May): l-8.
       Discusses the disposition of the housekeeper's shares in the Globe from 1598 to 1644.

1919.3   CHILD, HAROLD H. "The Elizabethan Theatre." In *Cambridge History of English Literature*. Vol. 6, *The Drama to 1642*. Pt. 2. Edited by A. W. Ward and A. R. Waller. Cambridge: University Press, pp. 241-78.
       Reprint of 1910.5.

1919.4   GRAY, HENRY DAVID. "The Dumb Show in *Hamlet*." *MP* 17 (May): 51-54. Rejects the supposition that the dumb show was presented above while Claudius was on the throne in the inner stage as an explanation of his non-reaction to the recreation of his crime.

1919.5   GREG, W[ALTER] W[ILSON]. "'The Seven Deadly Sins.'" *TLS* (2 October): 532.
       A letter to the editor in response to Spens (1919.18), disagreeing with the assertion that this plot was rejected by one company and sold to another.

1919.6   _____. "The 'Stolne and Surreptitious' Shakespearian Texts." *TLS* (28 August): 461.
       A letter to the editor, in response to Lawrence (1919.10), pointing out two fallacies in Lawrence's case.

1919.7   LAWRENCE, W[ILLIAM] J[OHN]. "'He's for a Jig or --.'" *TLS* (3 July): 363-64.
       Examines the history and practice of the jig, which was "in essence a primitive ballad-opera." It was a rhymed farce, completely sung, generally arranged for four or five characters, and served strictly as an afterpiece. After 1612, in order to get around an order forbidding the jig after the play, it was presented in the middle. <u>See also</u> Baskervill (1929.1).

1919.8   _____. "Horses on the Elizabethan Stage." *TLS* (5 June): 312.
          A refutation of the idea (adopted by many, based on Simon Forman's diary) that horses were used on the Elizabethan stage. Lawrence compares Forman's commentary with the play, concluding that Forman presents "a coloured narrative of the story unfolded."

1919.9   _____. "The King's Revels Players of 1619-1623." *MLR* 14 (October): 416-18.
          Argues that with the death of Queen Anne in 1619, the company in her service became the Company of the King's Revels. Lawrence cites title pages of several plays and the records of the Master of the Revels to substantiate his case.

1919.10   _____. "The 'Stolne and Surreptitious' Shakespearian Texts." *TLS* (21 August): 449.
          A letter to the editor, in response to Wilson and Pollard's theories of the "bad" quartos as cut copies for touring (see 1919.14-16, 21, 22). Lawrence argues that there was no need for touring cut versions of plays, given adequate doubling. See the responses of Greg (1919.6), Pollard (1919.13), and Wilson (1920.31).

1919.11   _____. "Wilkinson's View of the Supposed Fortune Theatre, and What it Really Represents." *ArchR* 46 (September): 70-71.
          Asserts that the picture of the Fortune printed by Wilkinson in 1825.1 was actually a picture of the post-Restoration "Nursery" in Barbican. Lawrence presents no evidence to support his assertion, but claims he has it.

1919.12   MANLY, J[OHN] M[ATTHEWS]. "The Children of the Chapel Royal and their Masters." In *Cambridge History of English Literature*. Vol. 6, *The Drama to 1642*. Pt. 2. Edited by A. W. Ward and A. R. Waller. Cambridge: University Press, pp. 279-92.
          Reprint of 1910.12.

1919.13   POLLARD, ALFRED W. "The 'Stolne and Surreptitious' Shakespearian Texts." *TLS* (28 August): 461.
          A letter to the editor, in response to Lawrence (1919.10). Pollard defends his view that the "bad" quartos represent cut touring versions of the plays.

1919.14   POLLARD, A[LFRED] W., and WILSON, J[OHN] DOVER. "The 'Stolne and Surreptitious' Shakespearian Texts, I: Why Some of Shakespeare's Plays Were Pirated." *TLS* (9 January): 18.
          Proposes that the "bad" quartos were cut versions of the plays, used for the 1593 provincial tour of the Chamberlain's Men. They were thus less valuable in London, and more easily printed. Continued in 1919.15-16, 21-22.

1919.15 _____. "The 'Stolne and Surreptitious' Shakespearian Texts: *Henry V* (1600)."
TLS (13 March): 134.
Continuation of 1919.14, 21. Uses the theories earlier advanced to show
that the "bad" quarto of was derived from a cut touring version augmented by an
actor's memory. Continued in 1919.16, 22.

1919.16 _____. "The 'Stolne and Surreptitious' Shakespearian Texts: *Merry Wives of
Windsor*." *TLS* (7 August):420.
Continuation of 1919.14-15, 21, applying the theories to the *Merry Wives
of Windsor* "bad" quarto. For responses see 1919.6, 10, 18. Continued in 1919.22.

1919.17 REYNOLDS, GEORGE FULLMER. "Two Conventions of the Elizabethan
Stage." *MP* 17 (May): 35-43.
Discusses the use of the stage doors to change locations and the
conventional suppression of other doors when only one was needed for the action
on stage. See 1920.1.

1919.18 SPENS, J. "The 'Stolne and Surreptitious' Shakespearian Texts." *TLS* (18
September): 500.
A letter to the editor, in response to Pollard (1919.13). Spens suggests that
the companies might furnish early outlines, plots, rejected drafts, and cut versions
to other dramatists for a fee.

1919.19 THALER, ALWIN. "Playwrights' Benefits and 'Interior Gathering' in the
Elizabethan Theatre." *SP* 16 (April): 187-96.
Examines the beginning of the tradition of playwrights' benefits,
concluding that they did not begin before 1603, and the collection of entrance
fees. Thaler differs with Lawrence on both issues (see 1913.9). Based on Thaler's
dissertation (1918.2).

1919.20 WILSON, J[OHN] D[OVER]. "The Puritan Attack upon the Stage." In
Cambridge History of English Literature. Vol. 6, *Drama to 1642,* Pt. 2. Edited by
A. W. Ward and A. R. Waller. Cambridge: University Press, pp. 373-409.
Reprint of 1910.26.

1919.21 WILSON, J[OHN] DOVER, and POLLARD, A[LFRED] W. "The 'Stolne
and Surreptitious' Shakespearian Texts, II: How Some of Shakespeare's Plays
Were Pirated." *TLS* (16 January): 30.
Continuation of 1919.14. Suggests that the pirate was a minor actor of the
company, adding to abridged touring copies from memory. Continued in 1919.15-
16, 22.

1919.22 _____. "The 'Stolne and Surreptitious' Shakespearian Texts: *Romeo and
Juliet*, 1597." *TLS* (14 August): 434.
Continuation of 1919.1471, 15-16, applying the theory to *Romeo and
Juliet*. There is some evidence that the pirate played the role of Capulet.

1920.1   BRERETON, JOHN LE GAY. "One-Door Interiors on the Elizabethan Stage." *MLN* 35 (February):119-20.

A brief note in response to Reynolds (1919.17), arguing that the Swan drawing is incorrect, since it shows only two doors instead of the three that Brereton thinks were actually there.

1920.2   GRAVES, THORNTON S[HIRLEY]. "The Devil in the Playhouse." *SAQ* 19 (April): 131-40.

A humorous chronicle of claims of the devil's actual appearance in various playhouses throughout history. Graves repeats the story about the Fortune's destruction (see 1870.4).

1920.3   _____. "The Elizabethan Trained Ape." *MLN* 35 (April): 248-49.

A brief note adding a few references to those cited by Strunk (1917.11).

1920.4   _____. "Notes on the Elizabethan Theatres." *SP* 17 (April): 170-82.

Minor additions to studies of the audience and the playbill.

1920.5   _____. "Organized Applause." *SAQ* 19 (July): 236-48.

Discusses the use of the claque before the nineteenth century, including during the Elizabethan period.

1920.6   _____. "Richard Rawlidge on London Playhouses." *MP* 18 (May): 41-48.

Cites Rawlidge himself, rather than Prynne's misquotation, to show that he was far from vehemently opposed to the London playhouses of his time. Rawlidge's references to the putting down of "playhouses" in 1580 probably means "gaming-houses."

1920.7   GRAY, HENRY DAVID. "The Sources of *The Tempest*." *MLN* 35 (June): 321-30.

Argues that Shakespeare based his play on the scenarios of several comedia dell'arte performances he had seen. The scenarios survive in a 1622 manuscript and contain most of the dramatic elements Shakespeare employed. See also 1920.22.

1920.8   GREG, W[ALTER] WILSON. "Doubled Parts on the Elizabethan Stage." *TLS* (12 February): 105.

A letter to the editor, in response to Lawrence (1919.10), pointing out the frequency of sharers doubling parts. See also Lawrence's reply (1920.15).

1920.9   GREG, W[ALTER] W[ILSON]. "Doubled Parts on the Elizabethan Stage." *TLS* (4 March): 155.

A letter to the editor, in response to Lawrence's response to 1920.8. Greg argues for doubling by sharers on the basis of the playhouse documents.

1920.10 _____. "Was *Sir Thomas More* Ever Acted?" *TLS* (8 July): 440.
Questions Lawrence's disputation of Greg's opinion, expressed in his edition of the play, that *Sir Thomas More* was never acted. See also 1920.23.

1920.11 HILLEBRAND, HAROLD N. "The Early History of the Chapel Royal." *MP* 18 (September) : 233-68.
Attempts to trace the history of the Chapel Royal from the time of Henry I, adding the most information to our knowledge of the Chapel in the sixteenth century. Hillebrand prints a Bodleian manuscript that adds information to Rimbault's Cheque Book (1872.1). There is little of specifically theatrical interest.

1920.12 LAW, ERNEST. "Shakespeare's Plays in the Revels Accounts." *TLS* (23 December): 876.
A letter to the editor in response to Stopes (1920.26), again arguing for the genuineness of the Revels Accounts, on the same evidence. See Index under Revels Accounts for the entire controversy. Continued in 1920.13.

1920.13 _____. "Shakespeare's Plays in the Revels Accounts." *TLS* (30 December): 891.
Continuation of 1920.12. See Index under Revels Accounts for the complete controversy.

1920.14 LAWRENCE, W[ILLIAM] J[OHN]. "Dekker on 'Steering the Passage of Scaenes.'" *MLR* 15 (April): 166-68.
Points out that the passage from *The Guls Horn-booke* is not a literal indication of scenery on the stage, as some have assumed. but rather s poetic allusion, as is made clear by the prologue Dekker wrote for *All's Lost by Lust* and *A Wonder of a Kingdome*.

1920.15 _____. "Doubled Parts on the Elizabethan Stage." *TLS* (26 February): 140.
A letter to the editor, in response to Greg (1920.8). Lawrence points out that the eleven cast lists from the period indicate no doubling by sharers. See Greg's reply (1920.9).

1920.16 _____. "Early Touring Companies." *TLS* (5 February): 86-87.
A letter to the editor, in response to Wilson (1920.31). Lawrence differs with him over the splitting of Shakespeare's company for touring the provinces.

1920.17 _____. "The King's Players at Court in 1610." *MLR* (January): 89-90.
A brief note discussing the court performance of *Mucedorus* and the prologue's mention of an earlier "unwilling errour" of the company.

1920.18 _____. "The Masque in *The Tempest.*" *FortR* 113 (June): 940-46.
Argues that the betrothal masque in *The Tempest* was not originally part of the play, but rather was written "in anticipation of the coming nuptials of the Elector Palatine and the Princess Elizabeth." Lawrence bases his theory on stage directions from the First Folio and several textual allusions.

1920.19 _____. "Music in the Elizabethan Theatre." *MusAnt* 6 (April): 192-205.

Discusses the use of music in public and private playhouses. Lawrence examines preliminary, entre-act, and incidental music, as well as the instruments used.

1920.20 _____. "The Mystery of *Macbeth*: A Solution." *FortR* 114 (November): 777-83.

Argues that the witch scenes in the play as we have it were added by another hand after Shakespeare's retirement, and that Middleton's The Witch was the source. See also Flatter and Cutts: 1957.6; 1958.6; 1959.5; 1960.5-7. Reprinted: 1928.9.

*1920.21 _____. "On the Underrated Genius of Dick Tarleton." *London Mercury* (2 May).

Cited in *TN* 11 (April 1957): 72.

1920.22 _____. "Shakespeare and the Italian Comedians." *TLS* (11 November): 736.

Responds to Gray's suggestion (in 1920.7) that *The Tempest* was based on five cornmedia dell'arte scenarios that survive. Lawrence shows that a company that might have presented the performances was in London in 1610, the year before *The Tempest* was presented at Court. But see 1921.3 for a correction by Chambers.

1920.23 _____. "Was *Sir Thomas More* Ever Acted?" *TLS* (1 July): 421.

Disputes the validity of Greg's contention in his Malone Society edition of the play that it was never acted. See Greg's reply, 1920.10.

*1920.24 _____, and GODFREY, WALTER H. "The Bear Garden Contract of 1606 and What It Implies." *ArchR* 47 (June).

Cited in *TN* 11 (April 1957): 72.

1920.25 LIEBSCHER, FRIEDA MARGOT. "Wie ersetzt Shakespeare seinem Publikum Theaterzettel, Bühnendekorationen und künstliche Beleuchtung? Nachgewiesen am *Hamlet*, zugleich ein Beitrag sum Kenntnis des altenglischen Theaters." Ph.D. dissertation, Leipzig, 89 pp.

Examines, among other matters, Shakespeare's setting of scene with language and implicit stage directions in dialogue. Handwritten.

1920.26 STOPES, CHARLOTTE CARMICHAEL. "The Seventeenth Century Revels Books." *TLS* (2 December): 798.

A lengthy letter to the editor, arguing that the three seventeenth-century accounts published by Cunningham in 1842 were forgeries. See also Law's reply (1920.12-13) and Index under Revels Accounts for the entire controversy

1920.27   THALER, ALWIN. "The Elizabethan Dramatic Companies." *PMLA* 35 (March): 123-59.

Discusses the role of the actor/sharer and the business manager of the company, as well as the value and distribution of shares. Based in large part an his Ph.D. dissertation (1918.2).

1920.28   _____. "The 'Free-list' and Theatre Tickets in Shakespeare's Time and After." *MLR* 15 (April): 124-36.

Discusses the development of these two elements of theatrical management from Shakespeare to Sheridan. Based in large part on his Ph.D. dissertation (1918.2).

1920.29   _____. "The Players at Court, 1564-1642." *JEGP* 19 (January): 19-48.

Examines "the financial relations between the court and the professional players and playwrights from the beginning of the Shakespearian era to the closing of the theatres in 1642." Thaler includes tables of payments made to companies for court performances during the reigns of Elizabeth, James, and Charles. Based on his Ph.D. dissertation (1918.2).

1920.30   _____. "The Travelling Players in Shakespare's England." *MP* 17 (January): 489-514.

Additions to Murray's information (see 1905.4; 1910.15) based on research in connection with 1918.2. Thaler focuses on the financial end of the touring companies, both London-based and provincial. Reprinted: 1941.13.

1920.31   WILSON, J[OHN] DOVER. "Early Touring Companies." *TLS* (29 January): 68.

A letter to the editor, in response to Lawrence (1919.10). Wilson reiterates his argument that the four Shakespeare "bad" quartos were cut-down versions for touring.

1920.32   WITHINGTON, ROBERT. *English Pageantry: An Historical Outline*. Vol. 2. Cambridge: Harvard University Press, pp. 3-42.

Second volume of the published version of 1913.20. The relevant section deals with the Lord Mayor's Show, 1209-1635. No records exist 1636-1642. See also 1970.3; 1918.4 (vol. 1); and Index under Lord Mayor's Show.

<u>1921</u>

1921.1   BRAINES, WILLIAM WESTMORELAND. *The Site of the Globe Playhouse, Southwark*. London: London County Council, 43 pp.

An attempt to settle the issue of the Globe's location north or south of Maid Lane, based on documentary evidence only. The case for the north side is made and refuted, and the case for the south side prevails. Further, the actual site of the property leased for the purpose of building the Globe is pinpointed, through bequests, bills of sale, and other court documents. G. Topham

Forrest adds an appendix on the architecture of the playhouse. See also second edition (1924.3); and Index under Globe Playhouse--Site of.

1921.2   CAMPBELL, LILY BESS. "Scenes and Machines on the English Stage during the Renaissance: A Classical Revival." Ph.D. dissertation, University of Chicago, 302 pp.
          Published as 1923.1.

1921.3   CHAMBERS, E[DMUND] K. "Italian Players in England." *TLS* (12 May): 307.
          Corrects Lawrence's assertion (in 1920.22) that an Italian company performed in London in 1607-8 by demonstrating that "Princes" in a municipal accounts book was misread as "Venice."

1921.4   FLOOD, W[ILLIAM] H[ENRY] GRATTAN. "The King's Players at Dunwich in 1607." *TLS* (28 April): 276.
          Based on the Corporate Records of Dunwich, Flood lists several visits of players to that city, including one by the King's Men in 1607.

1921.5   FORREST, G. TOPHAM. "Blackfriars Theatre: Conjectural Reconstruction." *Times* (London), (21 November): 5.
          While published by Forrest, the actual reconstruction was prepared by J. H. Farrar and R. L. Martin, architects of the London County Council. The drawing shows the interior of the playhouse, complete with a curtained inner stage, two obliquely set doors, and no boxes on the platform level; a curtained space above in the center of the gallery; benches in the pit; two audience galleries; and candles serving as footlights. For other reconstructions of the second Blackfriars, see 1954.17; 1964.14; 1970.13; 1975.15.

1921.6   GRAVES, THORNTON S[HIRLEY]. "Notes on Puritanism and the Stage." *SP* 18 (April) :141-69.
          A few apparently overlooked instances of attack or defense of the stage, and a consideration of the defense from 1642 to 1660.

1921.7   _____. "The Stage Sword and Dagger." *SAQ* 20 (July): 201-12.
          Anecdotal discussion of fencing in the theatre, including the Elizabethan period.

1921.8   GREG, WALTER W[ILSON]. "'Bengemenes Johnsones Share.'" *MLR* 16 (October): 323.
          Responds to Thayer's explanation of the entry in Henslowe's diary (see1921.16) by pointing out that it was not possible for Jonson to have held a share in the Admiral's Men at the time. Greg suggests that Henslowe had arranged to receive certain money out of what was due Jonson as a sharer in Pembroke's Men.

1921.9   LAWRENCE, W[ILLIAM] J[OHN]. "The Earliest Private-Theatre Play." *TLS* (11 August): 514.

    Argues that *The Warres of Cyprus* was written by Farrant and first presented ca. 1578, making it the earliest extant play performed in a private playhouse.

1921.10   _____. "Early Substantive Theatre Masques." *TLS* (8 December): 814.

    Discusses details of the initial productions of *The World Tost at Tennis*, *The Sun's Darling*, and *Microcosmus*, the earliest masques produced in the playhouses.

1921.11   _____. "The Phallus on the Early English Stage." *Psyche and Eros* 2, no. 3 (May-June): 161-65.

    Discusses the use of the phallus on the English stage, based on the illustration published with *The World Tost at Tennis* showing a devil with erect phallus. The editor of the journal (S.A.T.) appends a note indicating that Lawrence also detects the use of the phallus in *Two Noble Kinsmen*.

1921.12   RHODES, R. CROMPTON. "Shakespeare's Prompt Books, I: Stage Directions." *TLS* (21 July): 467.

    Examines the stage directions of Shakespeare and sorts the plays into three groups, depending upon the adequacy of their directions for Elizabethan production. *Titus Andronicys, Henry VI, Tempest, Henry VIII, Coriolanus,* and *Timon of Athens* are particularly rich in stage directions, while *Two Gentlemen of Verona, Merry Wives of Windsor, Measure for Measure,* and *Winter's Tale* are particularly scanty. Continued in 1921.13.

1921.13   _____. "Shakespeare's Prompt Books, 11: The Curtains." *TLS* (28 July): 482.

    Continuation of 1921.11. Rhodes examines possible uses of curtains for revealina the "inner stage" at the Globe, despite the fact that there are no stage-directions in the plays requiring them.

1921.14   ROLLINS, HYDER E. "A Contribution to the History of the English Commonwealth Drama." *SP* 18 (July): 267-333.

    While technically concerned only with events after 1642, Rollins includes several references to happenings before that date and to the playhouses involved during the Interregnum, most notably the Phoenix and the Red Bull. Most comments towards this history of Commonwealth drama are based upon the Thomason collection in the British Museum.

1921.15   SISSON, CHARLES J[ASPER]. *Le goût public et le théàtre élisabéthain jusqu'à la mort de Shakespeare*. Dijon: University of Dijon, 197 pp.

    Examines the public taste in relation to English theatre to 1616. The two major sections deal with public taste in general and the public's response to theatrical entertainment. The second section contains chapters on the scenic embellishment, comedy, tragedy, historical drama, and romance. Sisson concludes that changing public tastes were reflected in the changing repertories of the public and private playhouses.

1921.16   THALER, ALVIN. "'Bengemenes Johnsones Share. '" *MLR* 16 (January): 61-65.
　　　　　　Explains an entry in Henslowe's diary by suggesting that Jonson was an actor-sharer in 1597 and was repaying a loan he had taken from Henslowe. <u>See also</u> 1921.8. Reprinted: 1941.10.

1921.17   ____. "Was Richard Brome an Actor?" *MLN* 36 (February): 88-91.
　　　　　　A brief note arguing for Brome's having acted, after serving an apprenticeship with Ben Jonson. Reprinted: 1941.10.

<u>1922</u>

1922.1   GRAVES, THORNTON S[HIRLEY] . "Some Aspects of Extemporal Acting." *SP* 19 (October): 429-56.
　　　　　　Examines the approval of extemporal wit, commedia dell' arte, and censorship influences on Elizabethan and later acting.

1922.2   _____. "Some References to Elizabethan Theatres." *SP* (July): 3I7-27.
　　　　　　A compilation of mare than twenty contemporary references to a variety of Elizabethan playhouses. All are of minor importance, and none reveals anything new.

1922.3   HILLEBRAND, HAROLD NEWCOMB."The Children of the King's Revels at Whitefriars." *JEGP* 21 (April): 318-34.
　　　　　　Discusses the conduct of business and the plays produced by this ill-founded and short-lived group. Hillebrand shows that the founder of the company was Thomas Woodford, not Michael Drayton as had been supposed, and that the company was in operation in August of 1607. He dates the beginning of the enterprise as late 1606, with Lording Barry, the playwright, taking over from Woodford in 1607. Hillebrand cites liberally from various court cases to support his assertions. In the final five pages he discusses seven extant plays performed at Whitefriars, although he does not attempt to reconstruct staging practices.

1922.4   HIND, ARTHUR MAYGAR. *Wenceslaus Hollar and His Views of London and Windsor in the Seventeenth Century*. London: John Lane, 92 pp.
　　　　　　The first twenty-five pages consists of a sketch of Hollar's life and works, valuable background for the theatre historian concerned with the period. The heart of the volume, however, is the set of sixty-four plates and the descriptions of the 132 etchings.

1922.5   LAWRENCE, W[ILLIAM] J[OHN]. "Notes on a Collection of Masque Music." *M&L* 3 (January): 49-58.

> Discusses the contents of a manuscript held in the British Library, containing music for several masque dances. Lawrence lists the contents and comments on each item, attempting to assign each to its source entertainment. See also 1954.5.

1922.6   _____. "A Plummet for Bottom's Dream." *FortR* 117 (May): 833-44.

> Argues that *Midsummer Night's Dream* was a public play adapted for private performance, not vice-versa, and that the quarto text reflects both versions. Reprinted: 1928.9.

1922.7   RHODES, R. CROMPTON. *The Stagery of Shakespeare*. Birmingham: Cornish Brothers, 102 pp.

> "An attempt to ascertain the nature of Shakespeare's Stagery from an intensive study of the Stage-directions in the original texts in Quarto, authorised and unauthorised, and in Folio." Rhodes develops the old alternation theory into a theory of "the triple stage--placing far more importance on the upper stage. Rhodes rejects the Swan drawing "because in so many particulars it is obviously inexact." Includes reprints of 1921.12-13.

1922.8   STOPES, CHARLOTTE CARMICHAEL. *The Seventeenth-Century Accounts of the Master of the Revels*. London: Shakespeare Association, 36 pp.

> Examines the three supposed seventeenth-century account books that survive, finding them all to be nineteenth-century forgeries, probably by Cunningham. For her exchanges with Law over the genuineness of the documents, and others' opinions, see Index under Revels Accounts.

1922.9   THALER, ALWIN. "Minor Actors and Employees in the Elizabethan Theater." *MP* 20 (August): 49-60.

> Brief notes on the hired men, the boy actors, the gatherers, tiremen, prompters, stagehands, and musicians. Reprinted: 1941.10.

1922.10   _____. *Shakespere to Sheridan: A Book about the Theatre of Yesterday and Today*. Cambridge: Harvard University Press, 339 pp.

> An attempt to show the continuity of theatrical tradition from Shakespeare through the eighteenth century. The chapters on playwrights, players, managers, and playhouses all touch on the Elizabethan period. Thaler includes three appendices on rates of admission and capacity that deal only with the earlier period.

1922.11   _____. "Strolling Players and Provincial Drama After Shakespere." *PMLS* 37 (June): 243-80.

> Primarily concerned with the Restoration and eighteenth century, although the general remarks about the types of companies and their management are relevant to the earlier period.

1923.1   CAMPBELL, LILY B[ESS]. *Scenes and Machines on the English Stage during the Renaissance: A Classical Revival.* Cambridge: University Press, 302 pp.

Published version of 1921.2. The four parts deal with the classical revival of stage decoration in Italy and stage decoration in England in three successive periods: sixteenth century, pre-Restoration seventeenth century, and post-Restoration seventeenth century. Campbell includes fifteen figures and eight plates. She concludes that "the history of stage spectacle during the sixteenth and seventeenth centuries appears as fundamentally a history of the Renaissance conceptions of the ancient classical stage as these conceptions were modified by the conditions of the age into which they were projected." This work is especially important for its treatment of the masques and the machinery used in the public theatres.

1923.2   CHAMBERS, EDMUND R. *The Elizabethan Stage.* 4 vols. Oxford: Clarendon Press, 1930 pp.

Synthesis of literally all material on English theatre from 1558 to 1616 available at the time. composed of twenty-four chapters and thirteen appendixes contained in four volumes. The volumes are further subdivided into five major books. Book I and Book II, in volume 1, deal with the court and the control of the stage respectively. Book III examines the companies, with separate chapters on the boy companies, adult companies, and international companies; it includes a biographical sketch of all known actors of the period. Book IV looks at the playhouses and staging, with chapters on the public theatres, the private theatres, the structure and conduct of the theatres, staging at court, staging in the playhouses in the sixteeenth century, and staging in the playhouses in the seventeenth century. Book III and most of Book IV compose volume 2. Book V, composing the remainder of volume 3 and part of volume 4, deals with plays and playwrights. The three chapters of this Book examine the printing of plays, the individual playwrights and their work, and anonymous works. The appendixes, dealing with miscellaneous information, form the remainder of volume 4. The method of the work is partly documentary and partly interpretive. That is, Chambers presents all available documentary evidence on each subject to enable the reader to make his or her own judgments, but he also presents his own interpretation of the evidence from time to time. While in need of revision in the light of later scholarship, this work remains one of the two or three most important contributions to the field. See 1925.4-5.

1923.3   CHAMBERS, E[DMUND] K., ed. "Four Letters on Theatrical Affairs." *MSC* 2, pt. 2: 145-49.

Letters from 1569, 1576-7 (in Italian), 1599-1601, and 1608.

1923.4   CREIZENACH, WILHELM MICHAEL ANTON. *Geschichte des neuren Dramas.* 2d ed. Vols. 2 and 3. Halle: S. M. Niemaeyer.

Second edition of 1903.1: see translation of that edition, 1916.5.

1923.5   EVANS, M. BLAKEMORE. "Traditions of the Elizabethan Stage in Germany." *PQ* 2 (October): 310-14.

    Uses German drama based on English sources to show the comic aspect of madness in Elizabethan tragedy and the tradition of Pyramus falling on his scabbard rather than his sword in *Midsummer Night's Dream*.

1923.6   GREG, WALTER W[ILSON]. *Two Elizabethan Stage Abridgements: The Battle of Alcazar & Orlando Furioso: An Essay in Critical Bibliography*. Oxford: Clarendon Press, 366 pp.

    Contains facsimiles and detailed discussion of the plot of *The Battle of Alcazar* and the actor's part of *Orlando*, especially in relation to the "bad" quartas of both plays. Greg includes historical information about the Lord Admiral's company 1589-1594 and 1597-1602.

1923.7   HARRISON, G[EORGE] B[AGSHAWE]. *Shakespeare's Fellows: Being a Brief Chronicle of the Shakespearean Age*. London: Bodley Head, 207 pp.

    Intended as "a brief introduction to the study of the personal side of Elizabethan drama." The relevant chapters are the first, discussing "Stage and University," the third, examining "The Chamberlain's and the Admiral's," and the fourth, "Poetomachia," dealing with the war of the theatres. Partially incorporated into 1956.14.

1923.8   HERFORD, C[HARLES] H[AROLD]. *Sketch of Recent Shakespearian Investigations, 1853-1923*. London: Blackie & Son, pp. 8-15.

    Not meant to be a comprehsive bibliography but rather "a conspectus of prevailing tendencies." The relevant section deals with publications on the Elizabethan stage, all of which have been incorporated into the present bibliography.

1923.9   HOLZKNECHT, KARL J. "Theatrical Billposting in the Age of Elizabeth." *PQ* 2 (October): 267-81.

    Investigates "the origin of the custom of theatrical billposting and . . . the character and extent of the practice in the theatre of the Elizabethan time." Holzknecht concludes that billposting was common, that posts were frequently used for the purpose, that the type of play would be on the bill but not the dramatis personae, that the bills were posted the morning of the performance by minor members of the company, and that the printing of bills became the subject of a monopoly.

1923.10   HOTSON, JOHN LESLIE. "Sir William Davenant and the Commonwealth Stage." Ph.D. dissertation, Harvard University.

    Published, in expanded version: 1928.7.

1923.11   HUBBARD, GEORGE. *On the Site of the Globe Playhouse of Shakespeare.* Cambridge: University Press, 47 pp.

>   Perhaps the most important of the arguments for placing the site of the Globe to the north of Maid Lane, in direct response to Braines (1921.1). Braines responded once more, in 1924.3, to settle the issue. This exchange is the culmination of the controversy over the site of Shakespeare's playhouse that dominated the early years of the century. <u>See</u> Index under Globe Playhouse--Site of.

1923.12   KINGSLAND, GERTRUDE SOUTHWICK. "The First Quarto of *Hamlet* in the Light of the Stage." Ph.D. dissertation, Columbia University.

>   Excerpts published as 1923.13.

1923.13   _____. *The First Quarto of "Hamlet" in the Light of the Stage.* Oshkosh: Castle-Pierce Press, 63 pp.

>   Published version of 1923.12. Attempts to support the theory that the first quarto of is an actor's version excised from the complete text by comparing it to acting versions of the play from the time of Betterton to 1920. The five parts of the Introduction are abstracts of the five chapters of the complete dissertation. The concluding chapter is printed in full.

1923.14   LAMBORN, EDMUND ARNOLD GREENING, and HARRISON, G[EORGE] B[AGSWAWE]. *Shakespeare: The Man and His Stage.* London: Oxford University Press, pp. 76-104.

>   The relevant section discusses the theatres and actors in general terms.

1923.15   LAWRENCE, W[ILLIAM] J[OHN]. "New Facts from Sir Henry Herbert's Office Book." *TLS* (29 November): 820.

>   Seven additions to 1917.2, discovered by Lawrence in the Malone collection at the Bodleian Library. Reprinted: 1937.5.

1923.16   _____. "A New Shakespeare Test." *Criterion* 2, no. 5 (October): 77-94.

>   Discusses the instrument called for in stage directions for incidental music, focusing on the cornet and trumpet. Since trumpets were used on the public stage and cornets on the private stage before 1609, any stage directions that call for both must be from after that date. Reprinted: 1928.9.

1923.17   _____. "Shakespeare's Workshop." *FortR* 119 (April): 589-99.

>   Discusses the influence of the audience, the playhouse, and the classical leanings of the University Wits on Shakespeare and the drama. Reprinted: 1928.9.

1923.18   LOUNSBURY, THOMAS R. "A Puritan Censor of the Stage." *YR* 12 (July): 790-810.

>   Examines Prynne's life and works, particularly *Histriomastix*. The tone throughout is derogatory.

1923.19   ROLLINS, HYDER E. "The Commonwealth Drama: Miscellaneous Notes."
SP 20 (January): 52-69.
A variety of notes, some of which pertain to actors of the earlier period.
Rollins also includes notices of provincial entertainments after the closing of the
theatres.

1923.20   SMITH, G. C. MOORE, ed. "The Academic Drama at Cambridge: Extracts
from College Records." *MSC* 2, pt. 2: 150-230.
Records of plays produced by members of the various colleges.

1924

1924.1   ADAIR, E[DWARD] R[OBERT]. *The Sources of the History of the Council in
the Sixteenth & Early Seventeenth Centuries*. Helps for Students of History, no.
51. London: Society for Promoting Christian Knowledge, 96 pp.
An annotated bibliography with an extended introductory essay. The effect
of the Privy Council on English theatrical affairs during this period was far from
negligible, but this volume is of only peripheral interest. Included in *NCBEL* 1,
col. 1384.

1924.2   ARCHER, WILLIAM. "Elizabethan Stage and Restoration Drama." *QR* 24
(April): 399-418.
Essentially a lengthy review article, focusing on Chambers (1923.2).
Archer attacks the Swan drawing, since it contains no rear stage, which "was from
a very early date, in constant demand," and since the two doors entering onto the
stage are not obliquely set. He also, however, argues for the primacy of the
platform, with inner and upper stages serving as auxiliary acting spaces.

1924.3   BRAINES, WILLIAM WESTMORELAND. *The Site of the Globe Playhouse,
Southwark*. 2d ed. London: London County Council, 47 pp.
Revised and enlarged edition of 1921.1. The new information includes a
discussion of the pictorial evidence of the early maps and views of London; a
consideration (and refutation) of Hubbard (1923.11); and an appendix discussing the sites of the Southwark Bear Gardens. This work stands today as the
definitive study of the site of Shakespeare's public playhouse. For the entire
controversy, <u>see</u> Index under Globe Playhouse--Site of.

1924.4   GREG, W[ALTER] W[ILSON]. "The Masque of the Twelve Months." *TLS* (30
October): 686.
A letter to the editor, in response to Lawrence (1924.6) Greg admits the
reasonableness (but not the inevitability) of Lawrence's identification of one of
Jones's designs.

1924.5   LAWRENCE, W[ILLIAM] J[OHN]. "Bells on the Elizabethan Stage." *FortR* 122 (July): 59-70.
        Discusses the various uses of bells in the theatre for dramatic effect. Reprinted: 1935.7.

1924.6   _____. "Inigo Jones: An Identification." *TLS* (23 October): 667 .
        A letter to the editor, assigning one of Jones's designs to *The Masque of the Twelve Months*. <u>See</u> Greg's response, 1924.4.

1924.7   _____. "John Kirke, the Caroline Actor-Dramatist." *SP* 21 (October): 586-93.
        Discusses the acting and playwriting career of the author of *The Seven Champions of Christendome*. Kirke was originally a strolling provincial player who became a Groom of the Chamber in 1635.

1924.8   _____. "The Rose Theatre of Shakespeare's Day." *TLS* (21 February): 112.
        A letter to the editor concerning the supposed end of the Rose. Lawrence suggests that Collier did not in fact forge the poem about the burning of the Rose; the reference was actually to the fire at the King's Theatre in 1671-72.

1924.9   _____. "Was Peter Cunningham a Forger?" *MLR* 29 (January): 25-34.
        Argues for the genuineness of the Revels Accounts, in direct answer to Stopes's final attack in 1922.8. Lawrence deals with the three Revels Accounts published by Cunningham in 1842 and finds no reason to doubt their authenticity. <u>See also</u> Index under Revels Accounts for the entire contraversy.

1924.10   SIMPSON, PERCY, and BELL, C[HARLES] F[RANCIS]. *Designs by Inigo Jones for Masques and Plays at Court*. Oxford: Malone and Walpole Societies, 158 pp.
        "A descriptive catalogue of drawings for scenery and costumes mainly in the collection of his Grace the Duke of Devonshire." Simpson and Bell divide their work into two sections, drawings for known masques and plays, and doubtful and unidentified drawings. The detailed introduction traces Jones's artistic achievement. <u>See also</u> 1924.6; 1973.10, 21; and Index under Jones, Inigo.

1924.11   STEELE, MARY SUSAN. "Plays and Masques at Court, 1558-1642." Ph.D. dissertation, Cornell University, 367 pp.
        Published as 1926.10-51.

1924.12   WHANSLAW, HARRY WILLIAM. *The Bankside Stage-Book*. Redhill, Surrey: Wells Gardner, Darton & Co., 256 pp.
        A guide for children to building a practical model of a Tudor playhouse, based on the Fortune contract and a large dose of speculation. Whanslaw includes a general history of theatre from the Greeks through the early twentieth century. His model includes an inner below and inner above.

1925.1   ARONSTEIN, P[HILIP] . "Das englische Renaissancetheater." *NS* 33 (July-August): 265-80.

Essentially a lengthy review of Chambers (1923.2), with an outline of previous scholarship in the field, from Malone to Stopes, Greg, Feuillerat, and Wallace.

1925.2   BOAS, F[REDERICK] S. "Crosfield's Diary and the Caroline Stage." *FortR* 123 (April): 514-24.

Excerpts from the diary of Thomas Crosfield from 1626 to 1640. Crosfield was elected a Fellow of queen's College, Oxford, in 1627, and he noted many dramatic performances in his diary. Boas includes Crosfield's notes from an interview with Richard Kendall, an actor at Salisbury Court, concerning the London companies in 1634.

1925.3   BRADNER, LEICESTER. "Stages and Stage Scenery in Court Drama before 1558." *RES* 1 (October): 447-48.

Demonstrates that a raised stage and Serlian "houses" were used in the Universities before 1550, and speculates that the same would have been used at Court.

1925.4   CHAMBERS, EIDMUND] K. "Elizabethan Stage Gleanings." *RES* 1 (January): 75-78.

Four notes adding to the information presented in 1923.2. Continued in 1925.5.

1925.5   _____. "Some Elizabethan Stage Gleanings." *RES* 1 (April): 182-86.

Continuation of 1925.4, with six additional bits of information.

1925.6   GAW, ALLISON. "Actors' Names in Basic Shakespearean Texts, with Special Reference to *Romeo and Juliet* and *Much Ado*." *PMLA* 40 (September): 530-50.

Argues that the use of actors' names for minor parts not taken from Shakespeare's sources reflects the work of the playwright, not the prompter.

1925.7   _____. "John Sincklo as One of Shakespeare's Actors." *Anglia* 49: 289-303.

Discusses Romeo's description of the Apothecary in the second quarto of Romeo and Juliet, and applies the description to John Sincklo, previously one of Strange's Men and Pembroke's Men.

1925.8   GRANVILLE-BARKER, HARLEY. "A Note Upon Chapters XX. and XXI. of *The Elizabethan Stage*." *MR* 1 (January): 60-71.

Dissents from Chambers's view that the inn-yard theatres were less important than the court theatres during the sixteenth century, asserting that it was in the inn-yards that "emotional" acting developed. Granville-Barker brings no concrete evidence to bear on the issue; instead, he draws upon his extensive production experience.

1925.9   GRAVES, THORNTON SHIRLEY. "Women on the Pre-Restoration Stage." *SP* 22 (April): 184-97.
Reexamines the evidence for female actors before 1642, finding that while women were never regularly employed, "the sporadic appearance of women on special occasions may have been more frequent than has been generally recognized."

1925.10   GREG, W[ALTER] W[ILSON]. "The Elizabethan Stage." *RES* 1 (January): 97-111.
An extended review of Chambers (1923.2).

1925.11   _____. "The Evidence of Theatrical Plots for the History of the Elizabethan Stage." *RES* (July): 257-74.
Considers the casts revealed by the seven complete and three fragmentary plots in light of the companies and vice-versa. Greg is able to clarify the relationship between the Admiral's and Strange's company as well as tentatively set the date of *The Battle of Alcazar* as winter, 1598-99.

1925.12   _____. "Prompt Copies, Private Transcripts, and the Playhouse Scrivener." *Library*, 4th ser. 6 (September): 148-56.
Discusses bibliographical problems of several manuscript plays of the period. It seems possible that the playhouses kept the author's foul papers as well as a fair copy of the play.

1925.13   HAINES, C. M. "The 'Law of Re-Entry' in Shakespeare." *RGS* 1 (October): 449-51.
Examines a variety of exits at the end of one scene with immediate reentrance to start another in Shakespeare, concluding that normally this is not the case.

1925.14   KEITH, WILLIAM GRANT. "John Webb and the Court Theatre of Charles II." *ArchR* 57 (February): 49-55.
Traces Webb's career and analyzes several of his scene designs. While dealing primarily with the Restoration, Keith also touches on Webb's earlier work under Jones. He makes the mistake, however, of assigning the construction of the Cockpit-in-Court to the later period.

1925.15   MARCHAM, FRANK, and GILSON, J[ULIUS] P[ARNELL], eds. *The King's Office of the Revels, 1610-22: Fragments of Documents in the Department of Manuscripts, British Museum*. London: Frank Marcham, 48 pp.
Photographs and transcriptions of eighteen fragments from the Cotton Manuscript Tiberius E. X.

1925.16   NICOLL, ALLARDYCE. "The Rights of Beeston and D'avenant in
            Elizabethan Plays." *RES* 1 (June): 84-91.
                While primarily concerned with the Restoration stage here, Nicoll does
            summarize some of the activities of William Beeston, Davenant, and Killigrew
            before 1642.

1925.17   T.-D., G. "Whitehall in 1642." *RES* 1 (October): 462.
                Brief excerpts from a 1642 quarto describing masque production.

1925.18   UNWIN, GEORGE. *The Gilds and Companies of London*. 2d ed. London:
            Methuen, pp. 267-92.
                Reprint of 1909.29.

1925.19   WOOD, D. T. B. "The Revels Books: The Writer of the Malone Scrap." *RES*
1   (January): 72-74.
                Identifies Sir William Musgrave as the probable copier of this important
            document. See also 1925.20.

1925.20   ____. "The Suspected Revels Books." *RES* 1 (April): 166-72.
                Examines the external appearance of the Revels Books for 1604-5, 1611-
            12, and 1636, suspected of being forgeries. Wood concludes that the documents
            are probably genuine, but if they are not then Sir William Musgrave must have
            had a hand in the forgery. See also 1925.19 and Index under Revels Accounts.

1925.21   YATES, FRANCES A. "English Actors in Paris during the Lifetime of
            Shakespeare." *RES* 1 (October):392-403.
                Primarily a summary of what is known of the two English companies that
            performed in Paris before 1616, including a suggestion that *Richard III* might
            have been one of the plays performed. Yates does print two letters, discovered
            in the Public Record Office, that bear on the matter, one of which confirms a
            previously unknown performance in 1603.

                                        1926

1926.1   BALDWIN, T[HOMAS] W[HITFIELD]. "Nathaniel Field and Robert
            Wilson." *MLN* 41 (January): 32-34.
                Brief notes concerning Nathaniel Field, arguing that the actor and the
            printer were in fact the same man, and Robert Wilson, arguing that the Queen's
            Company member in 1583 had died by 1588, and that later records belong to
            others of that name.

1926.2   BORCHERDT, HANS HEINRICH. *Der Renaissancetil des Theaters; ein
            prinzipieller Versuch*. Halle: Max Niemeyer, 44 pp.
                Examines the development of the Renaissance playhouse on the continent,
            with comparisons to English practice.

1926.3   DENKINGER, EMMA MARSHALL. "Actors' Names in the Register of St. Botolph Aldgate." *PMLA* 41 (March): 91-109.

A collection of entries in the parish register concerning fifteen actors from 1592 to 1622. The list is alphabetical, with previously known biographical information summarized.

*1926.4 ENGELEN, J[OHANNES]. *Die schauspieler-Ökonomie in Shakespeares Dramen*. Münster.

Unlocatable. Cited in *NCBEL* 1, col. 1395.

1926.5   GRANVILLE-BAKER, HARLEY. "The Stagecraft of Shakespeare." *FortR* 126 (July): 1-17.

A lecture delivered at the Sorbonne, 26 January 1926. Granville-Baker here concentrates on the differences between Shakespearean stage conditions and our own, mentioning four: language change; a different sense of the past; women's parts played by boys; and primary appeal to the ear rather than to the eye. He concludes that to appreciate Shakespeare, "we must go back and meet him on his own ground."

1926.6   HILLEBRAND, HAROLD NEWCOMB. *The Child Actors: A Chapter in Elizabethan Stage History*. *ISLL,* vol. 11, nos. 1 and 2. Urbana: University of Illinois, 355 pp.

Published version of 1914.9. Based primarily on previously discovered documents, but a fuller treatment than available earlier. Hillebrand begins with a general survey of children on the stage since the twelfth century, and gives detailed histories of the major bays' troupes during the reigns of Henry VIII and Elizabeth. He discusses the Children of the Chapel Royal, the Children of Paul's, the King's Revels, and the Queen's Revels in turn. In an important final chapter Hillebrand deals with the influence of the child actors on the plays. Three appendixes contain some of the more obscure documents used. See Index under Children's Companies for other references.

1926.7   HUNTER, MARK. "Act- and Scene-Division in the Plays of Shakespeare." *RES* 2 (July): 295-310.

Argues that Elizabethan plays (including Shakespeare's) were written in the five-act structure. See 1927.19; 1928.7, 17-18 for replies.

1926.8   MARCHAM, FRANK. "The King's Office of the Revels." *RES* 2 (January): 95-96.

A brief note in response to a review of 1925.15 by Chambers.

1926.9   RANNIE, DAVID WATSON. "Scenery in Shakespeare's Plays." In *Scenery in Shakespeare's Plays and Other Studies*. Oxford: Basil Blackwell, pp. 125-76.

Refers not to stage scenery, but to poetic scenery: "references, in the speeches of his characters, to exterior and interior backgrounds and surroundings, and secondly, similes, metaphors or other figures of speech, taken from phenomena of landscape or atmosphere."

1926.10   STEELE, MARY SUSAN. *Plays and Masques at Court during the Reigns of Elizabeth, James, and Charles. Cornell Studies in English.* Ithaca: Cornell University Press, 300 pp.

        Published version of 1924.11. A chronicle listing of all plays and masques presented at Court 1558-1642. Steele includes presentations before the sovereign on progress. The main sources are the official records from the Revels Office books and contemporary allusions from diaries, letters, and so on. The three chapters give the details of the reigns of Elizabeth, James, and Charles by season. The two indexes treat authors and titles. Same as 1926.11.

1926.11   _____. *Plays and Masques at Court, 1558-1642.* New Haven: Yale University Press, 300 pp.

        Same as 1926.10.

1926.12   WILSON, F[RANK] P[ERCY]. "Ralph Crane, Scrivener to the King's Players." *Library*, 4th ser. 7 (September): 194-215.

        Examines manuscripts from the King's Men, shown by Greg to be by the same hand (see 1925.12), and claims that Ralph Crane was the transcriber. Wilson also ties Crane to three other extant manuscripts and shows that he was transcribing for the company before 1621. Reprinted: 1968.3.

1926.13   WRIGHT, LOUIS B. "Will Kempe and the Commedia delllArte." *MLN* 41 (December): 516-20.

        A brief note arguing for the commedia influence on Kempe, and assigning him the parts of Costard and Launce as well as Peter and Dogberry.

1927

1927.1   BALDWIN, THOMAS WHITFIELD. *The Organization and Personnel of the Shakespearean Company.* Princeton: Princeton University Press. 464 pp.

        Comprehensive examination of the Chamberlain's/King's Men from 1558 to 1642. The major chapters treat government regulation and theatrical custom, membership, housekeepers, hired men and the bookkeeper, finance, the division of labor, the Beaumont and Fletcher actor lists, and the actors of Shakespeare's plays. The appendixes include discussions of the Admiral's Men before 1595, the apprentices and their roles, and Jonson's plays for the company. Baldwin establishes lines of parts and assigns actors to them. His many charts yield valuable comparisons. While somewhat devalued by more recent research, this work remains an important contribution to the field.

1927.2   BALDWIN, T[HOMAS] W[HITFIELD]. "Posting Henslowe's Accounts."
         JEGP 26 (January): 42-90.
              Uses one of the principles developed in 1927.1 to examine the accounts of
         the Admiral's Men as revealed in Henslowe's diary. Baldwin clarifies the amounts
         of loans Henslowe furnished the company, their schedule of repayment, and the
         actors' income from the galleries. He finally traces the membership of the
         company.

1927.3   BRETTLE, R[OBERT] E[DWARD]. "Samuel Daniel and the Children of the
         Queen's Revels, 1604-5." *RES* 3 (April): 162-68.
              Two documents discovered in the declared accounts of the Treasurer of
         the Chamber that clarify Daniel's standing with the company. Both were
         previously published by Hillebrand in 1926.2.

1927.4   BYRNE, M[URIEL] St. CLARE. "Shakespeare's Audience." In *A Series of
         Papers on Shakespeare and the Theatre together with Papers on Edward Alleyn
         and Early Records Illustrating the Personal Life of Shakespeare.* London: Oxford
         University Press for the Shakespeare Association, pp. 186-216.
              A reevaluation of the evidence from contemporary accounts and from the
         plays. Byrne sets out the different classes that attended the theatre and attempts to
         analyze audience taste as reflected in the plays presented. Rather than a superior
         imaginative capacity, Byrne would credit the Elizabethan audience with "an
         immense capacity for . . . the childish faculty of over-looking without effort
         discrepancies which shatter the illusion of reality!' She concludes that the first
         demand of the audience was for a good story, and that Shakespeare and the other
         dramatists did their best to oblige.

1927.5   COWLING, G[EORGE] H[ERRERT]. "Shakespeare and the Elizabethan
         Style." In *A Series of Papers on Shakespeare and the Theatre together with
         Papers on Edward Alleyn and Early Records Illustrating the Personal Life of
         Shakespeare.* London: Oxford University Press for the Shakespeare Association,
         pp. 157-85.
              Summarizes what was known or thought about the Elizabethan stage in
         1927. Cowling describes the public theatres as having two or three doors, a
         gallery above, and an arras covering the center door and possible a "recess"--
         the inner stage. The private theatres, according to Cowling, had "a great curtain
         which concealed the whole of the rear wall beneath the gallery or balcony." The
         effect of a proscenium arch was thought to be made by the heavens and the pillars
         in the public theatres. In the second section Cowling surveys Shakespeare's use of
         these elements, and in the third he shows how the stage influenced Shakespeare's
         dramaturgy.

1927.6   GRAY, AUSTIN K. "Robert Armine, the Foole." *PMLA* 42 (September): 673-85.

> Discusses the change in Shakespeare's fools when Armin replaced Kempe in the company in about 1600. Armin played Touchstone, Feste, Lear's fool, and the drunken porter, as well as a variety of other roles. Gray also examines Armin's contributions to literature.

1927.7   GREG, W[ALTER] W[ILSON]. "Edward Alleyn." In *A Series of Papers on Shakespeare and the Theatre, Together with Papers on Edward Alleyn and Early Records Illustrating the Personal Life of Shakespeare*. London: Oxford University Press for the Shakespeare Association, pp. 1-34.

> A brief but comprehensive examination of the Alleyn life records. Especially important are the inferences Greg draws from various contemporary records. He traces the travelling of the Lord Admiral's Men from London during times of plague and briefly summarizes Alleyn's relationship with Henslowe and the founding of Dulwich College. <u>See also</u> Index under Alleyn for other references.

1927.8   HAINES, C. M. "The Development of Shakespeare's Stagecraft." In *A Series of Papers on Shakespeare and the Theatre, Together with Papers on Edward Alleyn and Early Records Illustrating the Personal Life of Shakespeare*. London: Oxford University Press for the Shakespeare Association, pp. 35-61.

> Attempts to trace the development of Shakespeare's use of the elements of Elizabethan staging through his plays. Haines assumes, as did most writers on the subject at the time, an inner stage and a balcony flanked by windows and containing an upper inner stage. He goes through the plays by chronological and thematic groups and discusses Shakespeare's use of the physical features of the stage and his growing adeptness at localizing action. *Antony and Cleopatra* and *Coriolanus* are called "his greatest achievements in this field."

1927.9   HARRISON, G[EORGE] B[AGSHAW]. "Shakespeare's Actors." In *A Series of Papers on Shakespeare and the Theatre together with Papers on Edward Alleyn and Early Records Illustrating the Personal Life of Shakespeare*. London: Oxford University Press for the Shakespeare Association, pp. 62-87.

> Proposes not to add to our information, but to reexamine it to see if there are any additional inferences possible. Harrison concentrates on the years 1597-1605, and he examines the plays for the impact of the actors on them, coming to the standard conclusion that Shakespeare wrote the plays with the actors who would play the parts in mind. Known biographical facts, then, have an impact on our understanding of characters and plays, and Harrison discusses what we know of Burbage and Kempe.

1927.10   ISAACS, J[ACOB]. "Shakespeare as Man of the Theatre." In *A Series of Papers on Shakespeare and the Theatre together with Papers on Edward Alleyn and Early Records Illustrating the Personal Life of Shakespeare*. London: Oxford University Press for the Shakespeare Association, pp. 88-119.

       Examines Shakespeare's sense of the stage and applies the modern notion of the director to Shakespeare's art. Isaacs first establishes a theatrical tradition throughout Europe before Shakespeare, then fits Shakespeare into that tradition.

1927.11   _____. "Shakespeare's 'Abridgement' in the Light of Theatrical History." *RES* 3 (July): 339-40.

       Relates the French use of outlines (similar to Elizabethan "Plots") to Shakespeare's use of the term in *Hamlet* and *Midsummer Night's Dream*.

1927.12   LAWRENCE, W[ILLIAM] J[OHN]. "John Honeyman, the Caroline Actor-Dramatist." *RES* (April): 220-22.

       A brief note tracing the career of this member of the King's Men.

1927.13   _____. *The Physical Conditions of the Elizabethan Public Playhouse*. Cambridge: Harvard University Press, 129 pp.

       Based on a series of lectures given at Harvard and Radcliffe in 1925-26. While modifying some of his earlier judgments, Lawrence is still four-square for the inner stage. His treatment of textual evidence is doubtful, as he cites stage directions from nineteenth-century editions in support of several of his contentions, and those directions are not found in the original texts. This is the only one of Lawrence's many publications where he attempts a lengthy discussion of his views on the subject; all his other books are collections of articles, most of which were previously published.

1927.14   _____. *Pre-Restoration Stage Studies*. Cambridge: Harvard University Press, 435 pp.

       Essays selected from the Harvard-Radcliffe lectures of 1925-26, tied together only by their applicability to the stagecraft of the period. Topics examined include the innyard plays and playing spaces, the practice of doubling, the stage jig, Shakespeare's staging of *Hamlet*, stage traps, illusions of sound, stage realism, stage spectacle, the use of properties, and the evaluation of early prompt books.

1927.15   NOBLE, RICHARD. "Shakespeare's Songs and Stage." In *A Series of Papers on Shakespeare and the Theatre together with Papers on Edward Alleyn and Early Records Illustrating the Personal Life of Shakespeare*. London: Oxford University Press for the Shakespeare Association, pp. 120-33.

       Examines the development of Shakespeare's use of song to delineate character, move the plot forward, and help set the scene. Noble believes the songs were sung to existing popular tunes, known to the audience.

1927.16   NUNGEZER, EDWIN. "A Dictionary of Actors and of Other Persons Associated with the Public Representation of Plays in England before 1642." Ph.D. Dissertation, Cornell University, 665 pp.
    Published as 1929.12.

1927.17   SHAKESPEARE ASSOCIATION. *A Series of Papers on Shakespeare and the Theatre together with Papers on Edward Alleyn and Early Records Illustrating the Personal Life of Shakespeare.* London: Oxford University Press for the Shakespeare Association, 239 pp.
    Contains 1927.4-5; 7-10; 15.

1927.18   SISSON, C[HARLES] J[ASPER]. Introduction to *Believe as You List*, by Philip Massinger. Malone Society Reprints, London: Oxford University Press, v-xxxiv.
    A detailed introduction to an edition of the manuscript play, including valuable information about the prompter's notations and the cast. Reprinted: 1968.3.

1927.19   WILSON, J[OHN] DOVER. "Act- and Scene-Divisions in the Plays of Shakespeare: A Reply to Sir Mark Hunter." *RES* 3 (October): 385-97.
    In response to 1926.7, Wilson points out the lack of act-division in many manuscript plays of the period 1590-1610, when Shakespeare was actively writing. The pause between acts was not usual until the King's Men began playing at Blackfriars.

1927.20   WRIGHT, LOUIS B. "Animal Actors on the English Stage before 1642." *PMLA* 42 (September): 656-69.
    Discusses the use of animal actors, especially when it approached an "animal act" or extraneous show, as in Two Gentlemen of Verona. Wright concludes that "in the variety-entertainment that helped to attract Elizabethan theatrical audiences animal acts held a recognized place."

1927.21   _____. "Elizabethan Sea Drama and Its Staging." *Anglia* 51: 104-18.
    Examines the staging of sea drama. Wright concludes that "sea atmosphere was induced in Elizabethan theatres not only by vivid descriptions, sea songs, etc., but also through simulation of actual ship scenes by the arrangement and skillful use of the stages, by the use of simple properties, and by appropriate costuming." He cites many plays of the period.

1927.22   _____. "Juggling Tricks and Conjuring on the English Stage before 1642." *MP* 24 (February): 269-84.
    Points out instances of the use of legerdemain, tricks of sleight, and elaborate spectacles of conjuring in English Renaissance drama. Most such instances were gratuitous, included purely for entertainment values. Wright cites contemporary sources for methods of feigning executions and other stage tricks.

1927.23   _____. "Stage Dueling in the Elizabethan Theatre." *MLR* 22 (July): 265-75.
Points out the use of stage combats to furnish dueling spectacles in the course of play performances on the Elizabethan stage. Players were skilled fencers, and the audience enjoyed the spectacle of a good match, as in *Hamlet*. Reprinted: 1968.3.

1927.24   _____. "Variety Entertainment by the Elizabethan Strolling Players." *JEGP* 26 (April): 294-303.
Examines the evidence for variety entertainment (acrobatics, music, juggling, magic, dance, and so on) by the touring actors, in the provinces and on the continent.

1928

1928.1   BENTLEY, G[ERALD] E[ADES]. "*The Dumb Band of Venice*." TLS (6 December): 966.
Reveals the discovery of a warrant for payment to the King's Men for presentation of this previously unknown play at Court in 1628. But see 1929.4.

1928.2   _____. "Shakespeare's Fellows." *TLS* (15 November): 856.
Examines the records of the Church of St. Saviour, Southwark, and prints those relating to actors and other theatrical personalities who lived in the parish.

1928.3   FREDÉN,GUSTAF. "A propos du théâltre anglais en Allemagne: L'auteur inconnu des *Comedies et tragedies anglaises* de 1620." *RLC*, no. 3 (July-September): 420-32.
Discusses the possible authorship of a seventeenth-century German collection of English plays. See also 1939.3.

1928.4   GREG. W[ALTER] W[ILSON]. "Act Divisions in Shakespeare." *RES* 4 (April): 152-58.
Examines all plays printed 1591-1610 for evidence of act division. Only about 45 percent of the plays are divided. After excluding plays not intended for the regular stage, only about 40 percent are divided. And if plays meant for the children's companies are excluded, only about 20 percent of the plays are divided.

1928.5   HAINES, C. M. "Shakespeare's 'Curtains.'" *TLS* (10 May): 358.
Responds to Noble (1928.11) suggesting that even if the final scene in began with a discovery (which Haines considers unlikely), it certainly did not end with the drawing of a curtain. The trunk scene in Cymbeline is the only Shakespearean scene to both begin and end with the curtain. Haines tentatively suggests some sort of mechanical device might have allowed the pulling of the curtain from backstage.

1928.6   HOTSON, [JOHN] LESLIE. *The Commonwealth and Restoration Stage.*
Cambridge: Harvard University Press, 424 pp.
        Expanded, published version of 1923.10. While on the surface dealing
with the period after 1642, this book is of great importance to the study of the pre-
Commonwealth stage. Because of Hotson's careful search of public records, and
his publication of excerpts from many of the more than one hundred documents
he discovered, we learn a great deal about the playhouses and personalities of the
Caroline period. The section dealing with the private playhouses that survived
until the Restoration (the Phoenix and the Salisbury Court) is especially
important.

1928.7   LAWRENCE, W[ILLIAM] J[OHN]. "Act-Intervals in Early Shakespearian
Performances." *RES* 4 (January): 78-79.
        A brief note, in response to Hunter (1926.17) and Wilson (1927.19),
pointing out that a parody of the lovers sleeping through the act in *Midsummer
Night's Dream* occurs in *Histriomastix*, which must have been written before
1608. Thus, if it is based on *Midsummer Night's Dream*, there must have been an
act-time for the lovers to sleep through at the Globe, since the King's Men did not
start playing at Blackfriars until that date. <u>See</u> Wilson (1928.18) for a response.

1928.8   _____. *Shakespeare's Workshop.* Oxford: B. Blackwell; Boston and New York:
Houghton-Mifflin, 161 pp.
        Reprints essays from a variety of publications, including four of theatrical
interest: 1920.20, 1922.6; 1923.16, 17.

1928.9   _____. "Turrets in Early Elizabethan Theatres." *RES* 4 (April): 208-09.
        A brief note suggesting that the Theatre and the Curtain possessed towers
or turrets, based on a passage in Stubbes's *Anatomy of Abuses*.

1928.10   MARSCHALL, WILHELM. "Das 'Sir Thomas Moore'-Manuskript und die
englische 'Commedia dell'arte.'" *Anglia* 52:193-241.
        Examines the influence of comedia dell'arte practices on the *Sir Thomas
More* manuscript and speculates on Shakespears's part in its writing.

1928.11   NOBLE, RICHARD. "Shakespeare's 'Curtains.'" *TLS* (3 May): 334.
        Argues that the final scene of was "discovered by means of drawing aside
the curtain of the inner stage." *See* Haines's response, 1928.5.

1928.12   SACK, MARIA. *Darstellerzahl und Rollenverteilung bei Shakespeare.*
Beitrage zur englische Philologie, no. 8. Leipzig: Bernard Tauchnitz, 76 pp.
        Examines the doubling of roles and the actors required for Shakespeare's
plays. Sack includes detailed discussions of *King Lear, Macbeth, Midsummer
Night's Dream, Merchant of Venice, Taming of the Shrew, Richard III,* and
Romeo and Juliet. Eleven adults and three boys, most of whom were versatile
enough to play several roles, as well as a few walk-ons, were apparently always
available.

1928.13   SHARPE, ROBERT BOIES. "The Real War of the Theatres: The Rivalry of the Admiral's Men and the Chamberlain's Men during the Last Decade of Queen Elizabeth's Reign, 1594-1603." Ph.D. dissertation, Yale University, 259 pp.
>   Published as 1935.16.

1928.14   SYMONDS, E. M. "The Diary of John Greene (1635-57)." *EHR* 43 (July): 385-94.
>   Contains notices of Greene's attendance at the Blackfriars and the Phoenix.

1928.15   TANNENBAUM, SAMUEL A. *Shakespeare Forgeries in the Revels Accounts*. New York: Columbia University Press, 109 pp.
>   Examines the supposed Revels Accounts of 1604-5 and 1611-12, published by Cunningham in 1842, concluding that they are in fact forgeries by Collier. Tannenbaum prints many transcripts and facsimiles of the documents to support his case. For the rest of the controversy, see Index under Revels Accounts.

1928.16   TURNER, CELESTE. *Anthony Mundy, an Elizabethan Man of Letters*. University of California Publications in English, vol. 2, no. 1. Berkeley: University of California Press, 234 pp.
>   Essentially a biographical study of the playwright, with some account of the composition of his plays and pageants. Of little theatrical interest. Included because of listing in *NCBEL* 1, col. 1402.

1928.17   WILLOUGHBY, EDWIN ELLIOT. "The Heading, Actus Primus, Scaena Prima, in the First Folio." *RES* 4 (July): 323-26.
>   In response to Hunter (1926.17), Willoughby points out that the act divisions of the First Folio are of typographical rather than theatrical origin.

1928.18   WILSON, J[OHN] DOVER. "'They Sleepe All the Act.'" *RES* 4 (April): 191-93.
>   A brief response to Lawrence (1928.7) regarding sleeping through the act time in *Midsummer Night's Dream*, suggesting that there was probably no act time in *Histriomastix* and that Lawrence's conjecture does not hold up.

1928.19   WINNINGHOF, ELISABETH. *Das Theaterkostüm bei Shakespeare*. Munich: H. Buschmann, 85 pp.
>   Published version of a University of Munich Ph.D. dissertation. Examines general costuming practices of the Elizabethan period. Brilliant color and fine detail were expected by the audience and presented by the players. Costuming was used to delineate characters and identify social standing, occupation, and history. Royal costumes for men and women were the most elaborate, followed by noblemen, clergy, academicians, craftsmen, and servants. The fool wore an individual costume, and foreigners were immediately recognizable. Special costumes were used for fairies, gods, witches, animals, and so on. Winninghof

concludes that costumes were an important part of the theatre of the time. This was the first comprehensive treatment of the subject. For other costume references, <u>see</u> Index under Costumes.

1928.20   WRIGHT, LOUIS B. "Variety-Show Clownery on the Pre-Restoration Stage." *Anglia* 52: 51-68.
Examines extraneous clownery inserted into Elizabethan plays to add to audience enjoyment. Wright finds little change from the beginning of the period until the closing of the theatres.

1928.21   _____. "Vaudeville Dancing and Acrobatics in Elizabethan Plays." *EStudien* 63 (September): 59-76.
Discusses the place of incidental dancing and acrobatics in the regular drama. Wright provides numerous examples of the use of both, and concludes that they were often used to enhance entertainment values in a play.

<u>1929</u>

1929.1   BALDWIN, T[HOMAS] W[HITFIELD]. "The Revels Books of 1604-5 and 1611-12." *Library*, 4th ser. 10 (December): 327-38.
Examines the Revels Accounts for the two years that have been suspected of being forged, arguing for their genuineness. For the complete controversy, <u>see</u> Index under Revels Accounts.

1929.2   BASKERVILL, CHARLES READ. *The Elizabethan Jig and Related Song Drama*. Chicago: University of Chicago Press, 642 pp.
A comprehensive examination of the Elizabethan jig, in two parts: history and texts. Part I deals with the rise of the jig, major types and practitioners, and the decline of the form, while Part I1 contains the texts of thirty-six extant English and continental jigs. The many notes serve as a guide to previous scholarship in the area.

1929.3   BECKWITH, ADA. "A Typical Elizabethan Playhouse." *ShAB* 4 (January): [inside back cover].
A drawing, after a design by Tannenbaum. Both inner and upper stages extend the full width of the back wall, fully curtained, with door and windows inside each. The stage doors, flanked by smaller windows, are obliquely set.

1929.4   BENTLEY, G[ERALD] E[ADES]. "The Dumbe Band of Venice." *TLS* 2 (21 February): 142.
Replies to 1928.1, following Greg's suggestion that this play is probably Henry Shirley's *Dumb Baud*.

1929.5 _____. "New Actors of the Elizabethan Period." *MLN* 44 (June): 368-72.

Lists information about fourteen previously unknown actors found primarily in the registers of London churches. Part of the research for his Ph.D. dissertation (1929.7), which eventually became 1941.1.

1929.6 _____. "Records of Players in the Parish of St. Giles, Cripplegate." *MLN* 44 (September): 789-826.

A collection of 288 entries concerning 80 actors and dramatists, mostly connected with the Fortune Playhouse. Bentley's list is alphabetical, with a brief recital of what is known of each individual along with the information drawn from the parish register. Part of the research for his Ph.D. dissertation (1929.7), which became 1941.1.

1929.7 BENTLEY, GERALD EADES. "Studies in the Theatrical Companies and Actors of 'Elizabethan' Times with Special Reference to the Period 1616-1642." 2 vols. Ph.D. dissertation, University of London, 695 pp.

Perhaps the most important dissertation ever produced in the field, these two volumes served as the basis for much of Bentley's later Jacobean and Caroline Stage (1941.1). The first volume corrects and supplements the then out-of-date histories of the companies by Collier (1879.2), Fleay (1890.1), and Murray (1910.15); the second volume, dealing with the actors of the later part of the period, is wholly original. Almost all information on actors and companies comes from primary sources: Bentley breaks a good deal of new ground; particularly in the parish registers of the London churches (see 1929.5-6). Bentley deals with the London companies only in London; there is no discussion here of the companies in the provinces.

1929.8 BOSWELL, ELEANORE. "'Young Mr. Cartwright.'" *MLR* 24 (April): 125-42.

A biographical sketch of William Cartwright, one of the few Restoration actors who began a career before 1642. His father was an actor with Henslowe, and the younger man was at the Salisbury Court Playhouse in the 1630s. After 1642 he became a bookseller, and then joined Killigrew's King's company in 1660.

1929.9 LAWRENCE, W[II,LIAM] J[I]OHN]. "The English Jig." *TLS* (23 May): 419-20.

A letter to the editor commenting on a review of Baskervill (1929.2). Lawrence suggests that "no jig was ever acted by living human beings at the Bear Garden until it was reconstructed as the Hope Theatre in 1613."

1929.10 MOORE, JOHN ROBERT. "The Songs of the Public Theatres in the Time of Shakespeare." *JEGP* 28 (April): 166-202.

Discusses "the growing sense of dramatic fitness in the dramatic songs of Elizabeth's last decade." Moore contends that the singer of what he calls the Romantic plays "had ceased to be the mere clown of the Moralities and Inter-ludes," and had not yet become the "mere singer" of the later drama.

1929.11   MOTTER, THOMAS HUBBARD VAIL. *The School Drama in England.* Oxford, London: Longmans, Green & Co., 325 pp.

After an initial chapter tracing the development of the boy actor, Motter outlines theatrical activities at a 1930-variety of schools, including Eton, St. Peter's College in Westminster, the Merchant Taylors', St. Paul's, Harrow's,

1929.12   NUNZEGER, EDWIN. *A Dictionary of Actors and Other Persons Associated with the Public Representation of Plays in England before 1642.* Cornell Studies in English, no. 13. New Haven: Yale University Press, 438 pp.

Published version of 1927.16. An attempt to "assemble all the available information regarding actors, theatrical proprietors, stage attendants, and other persons known to have been associated with the representation of plays in England before the year 1642," primarily from secondary sources. Alleyn is allotted eight pages; Richard Burbage, eleven and a half; most receive a scant paragraph. The thirty-three page bibliography is perhaps the most useful feature.

1929.13   PLATTER, THOMAS. *Thomas Platters des Jüngeren Englandfahrt im Jahre 1599.* Edited by H. Hecht. Halle: M. Niemayer, 180 pp.

The standard scholarly edition of Platter's diary, containing a brief description of a performance at an Elizabethan playhouse. See 1937.9 for a translation.

1929.14   SISSON, CHARLES [JASPER]. "Henslowe's Will Again." *RES* 5 (July): 308-11.

A brief note based on discoveries among the Star Chamber proceedings in the Public Record Office.

1929.15   SMITH, WINIFRED. "Italian Actors in Elizabethan England." *MLN* 44 (June): 375-77.

Notes on Drusiano Martinelli and "Scoto of Mantua" (Dianisio), two commedia actors found in London in the early seventeenth century, drawn from manuscript sources held in Italy.

1929.16   WARD, B[ERNARD] M[ORDAUNT]. "John Lyly and the Office of the Revels." *RES* 5 (January): 57-59.

A transcript of a document from the Exchequer Account Books, revealing that Blagrave was promoted from Clerk of the Revels to Surveyor of the Works in 1586, and that he drew salary from both positions until he died in 1590. Further, it is possible that John Lyly, on loan from Lord Oxford, was involved as Clerk of the Revels from 1590 to 1603.

1930.1   BENTLY, GERALD EADES. "Players in the Parish of St. Giles in the Fields."
RES 6 (April): 149-66,
Information gleaned from the parish registers and from a nineteenth-century history of the parish whose author apparently had access to other records. Bentley briefly summarizes the known facts about each actor listed and prints the new information. Based on his dissertation (1929.7) and included in 1941.1.

1930.2   DICKSON. M. J. "William Trevell and the Whitefriars Theatre." *RES* 6 (July): 309-12.
A brief history of Trevell's associations with Whitefriars, based on a Court of Requests bill Dickson discovered. See also 1930.3

1930.3   DOWLING, MARGARET. "Further Notes on William Trevell." *RES* 6 (October): 443-46.
More information on Trevell, based on the same Court of Requests bill. See 1930.2.

1930.4   GRAY, HENRY DAVID. "The Roles of William Kemp." *MLR* 25 (July): 261-73.
Speculates on the casting of Shakespeare's early clown. Gray sees Kempe as a comic character actor, and casts him as Polonius/First Gravedigger, Dogberry, Christopher Sly, and Falstaff. See also 1927.1; 1931.1, 8.

1930.5   LAWRENCE, W[ILLIAM] J[OHN]. "The Elizabethan Private Playhouse."
Criterion 9, no. 36 (April): 420-29.
Discusses the difference between the terms "private house" and "private playhouse." Lawrence argues that the former was used as a device to get around the law prohibiting London performances: the plays were to be "rehearsed" in the "private house" of the company menager. The revival of the boy companies at the second Blackfriars signaled the change in nomenclature. Reprinted: 1935.7.

1930.6   _____. "The Nut-Cracking Elizabethans." *Nation & Athenauem* (13 September): 729-30.
Discusses the audience habits of eating and talking through a performance, alluded to in a variety of contemporary documents. Lawrence concludes with a slap at those who hold that scenery was in use before 1642, based on lines from a 1671 play. Reprinted: 1935.7.

1930.7   _____. "The Stage Directions in *King Henry VIII.*" *TLS* (18 December): 1085.
Argues that the stage directions for the coronation procession were derived from an outside, and authoritative, source.

1930.8   REYNOLDS, GEORGE F[ULLMER]. "'Lines' of Parts in Shakespeare's Plays." *ShAB* 5 (July): 102-103.

        Compares Baldwin's casting in 1927.1 of the Chamberlain's Men in Shakespeare's plays with the 1930 casting of the Stratford-upon-Avon company, concluding that "it is practically impossible on the evidence we have to make even a tentative casting of Shakespeare's or an arrangement of the parts into many significant 'lines.'"

1930.9   STAMPS, ALFRED EDWARD. *The Disputed Revels Accounts*. London: Oxford University Press for the Shakespeare Association, 42 pp.

        A revised version of a paper read before the Association in 1929, with copies of the complete Accounts for 1604-5 and 1611-12. Stamps argues for the authenticity of the documents, based on analysis of the paper and ink, the handwriting habits of Buc, and other evidence. For the complete controversy, <u>see</u> Index under Revels Accounts.

1930.10   TAYLOR, GEORGE C. "Another Renaissance Attack on the Stage." *PQ* 9 (January): 78-81.

        An excerpt from a 1586 treatise that includes an attack on the stage couched in usual terms. Taylor speculates that there might have been some common source, some yet to be discovered "reference books on commonplace themes," since so many of the attacks sound so much alike.

1931

1931.1   BALDWIN, T[HOMAS] W[HITFIELD]. "Will Kemp Not Falstaff." *MLR* 26 (April): 170-72.

        Differs with Gray (1930.4) over the assignment of the role of Falstaff to William Kempe, since the same actor who played Falstaff apparently also played Sir Toby Belch in 1601, by which time Kempe had left the company. <u>See also</u> 1927.1 and Gray's reply, 1931.8.

1931.2   BOSWELL, ELEANOR, and CHAMBERS, E[DMUND] K., eds. "Dramatic Records: The Lord Chamberlain's Office. *MSC* 2, pt. 3: 321-416.

        Sixteen selections from the records of the Lord Chamberlain of the Household, preserved in the Public Record Office. Entries range from 1603 to 1637.

1931.3   CHAMBERS, E[DMUND] K. "Players at Ipswich." *MSC* 2, pt. 3: 258-84.

        Extracts from the municipal archives at Ipswich from 1554 to 1624-25, primarily recording payments to players.

1931.4   COLLINS, FLETCHER, Jr. "The Relation of Tudor Halls to Elizabethan Public Theatres." *PQ* 10 (July): 313-16.

        Argues that the Tudor Hall combined with the innyard to influence the Elizabethan public theatre. The Swan drawing is an accurate reflection of this influence. Collins anticipates Hosley's work by more then thirty years; <u>see</u> 1963.15, 1964.17, 1970.13, 1973.12.

1931.5   COOPER, CHARLES WILLIAM. "John Lacy, the Comedian: A Study in the Early Restoration Theatrical Tradition." Ph.D. dissertation, University of California at Berkeley, 244 pp.

Examines the career of comic actor and playwright John Lacy. Part Three, "John Lacy in the Theatrical Tradition," is especially important, since Cooper traces Lacy's role in the transmission of theatrical customs and traditions from the pre-Commonwealth stage to the Restoration theatre, a largely neglected area. As the principal dancing-master of the Theatre Royal in the early Restoration, as one of the foremost men of business at the same playhouse, and as a leading low comedian, as well as a playwright, Lacy exerted a strong influence on Restoration theatre practice, an influence that Cooper claims was strongly rooted in his earlier experience.

1931.6   EBISCH, WALTHER, and SCHÜCKING, LEVIN L. *A Shakespeare Bibliography*. Oxford: Clarendon Press, pp. 119-34, 138.

The relevant section lists works dealing with Shakespeare's stage and the production of his plays. Ebisch and Schücking provide minimal annotations but they list major reviews. The terminal date is 1930. Supplemented: 1937.3. All relevant items have been incorporated into the present bibliography.

1931.7   FITZGIBBON, H. MACAULAY. "Instruments and Their Music in the Elizabethan Drama." *MusQ* 17 (July): 319-29.

Surveys the use of music and catalogues mentions of specific instruments in stage directions and texts.

1931.8   GRAY, HENRY DAVID. "Shakespeare and Will Kemp: A Rejoinder." *MLR* 26 (April): 172-74.

Answers Baldwin's objections to his casting of Kempe as Falstaff. <u>See</u> 1927.1; 1930.4; 1931.1.

1931.9   GREG, W[ALTER] W[ILSON]. *Dramatic Documents From the Elizabethan Playhouse: Stage Plots; Actor's Parts; Prompt Books*. 2 vols. Oxford: Clarendon Press, 432 pp.

Facsimiles and transcripts for eight plots, the part of Orlando, and selected pages from nine prompt books from the Elizabethan period, along with commentary on each. This is without question one of the more important works in the field, since it presents the actual material used in the playhouses. Greg includes a section on the extant actor lists, including as much relevant information as possible on each actor mentioned. He concludes with a complete descriptive list of manuscript plays. Reprinted: 1969.5.

1931.10   LAWRENCE, W[ILLIAM] J[OHN]. "Old-Time Rehearsal." *Times* (London), (5 November): 20.

> Argues that the playwrights rehearsed their own plays, based on Flecknoe's comment to that effect (in 1664.1) and Johannes Rhenanus's preface to an adaptation of an old English play asserting the same thing. Lawrence also discusses rehearsal practices in the Restoration and eighteenth century. Reprinted: 1935.4.

1931.11   LEA, KATHLEEN M. "English Players at the Swedish Court." *MLR* 26 (January): 78-80.

> Four previously unknown English actors and musicians can be placed at the Swedish court between 1592 and 1608 because of the discovery of their names in correspondence among uncalendared Swedish State Papers.

1931.12   McKERROW, RONALD B. "The Elizabethan Printer and Dramatic Manuscripts." *Library*, 4th ser. 12 (December): 253-75.

> A paper read before the Bibliographical Society on 19 October 1931. McKerrow establishes four classes of evidence in a printed text that mark it as having been set in print from prompt copy. Reprinted: 1974.21.

1931.13   MILL, ANNA JEAN, and CHAMBERS, E[DMUND] K., eds. "Dramatic Records from the Cify of London: The Repertories, Journals and Letter Books." *MSC* 2, pt. 3: 285-320.

> Sixty extracts from various records of the City of London, supplementing those published earlier. Entries range from 1522 to 1615.

1931.14   PARADISE, N. BURTON. *Thomas Lodge: The History of an Elizabethan.* New Haven: Yale University Press, 254 pp.

> A study of the life and works of one of the earliest defenders of the stage against the Puritans. Chapter Five specifically examines his work as a playwright, but from a literary rather than a theatrical perspective. Included because of listing in *NCBEL,* col. 1402.

1931.15   SMITH, MILTON. "Shakespeare in the Schools." *ShAB* 6 (April): 39-47.

> Discusses teaching Shakespearean scholarship, including the theatrical. Of little scholarly value.

1931.16   THALER, ALWIN. "*Faire Em* (and Shakspere's Company?) in Lancashire." *PMLA* 46 (September): 647-58.

> Discusses *Faire Em* (presented by Lord Strange's Men, 1593) as a country play complimenting Sir Edmond Trafford. Reprinted: 1941.11,

1931.17   WRIGHT, LOUIS B. "Madmen as Vaudeville Performers on the Elizabethan
           Stage." *JEGP* 30 (January): 48-54.
                   Points out "certain examples of the employment of insanity as extrneous
           vaudeville entertainment in regular play performances." Wright includes *The
           Duchess of Malfi* and *The Changeling* among his examples. The introduction of
           madmen and madwomen served to enhance the comic spectacle demanded of
           even serious plays

1932

1932.1   ADAMS, JOSEPH QUINCY. "Elizabethan Playhouse Manuscripts and Their
          Significance for the Text of Shakespeare." *Hopkins Alumni Magazine* 21
          (October): 21-52.
                  Text of a lecture before the Tudor and Stuart Club, Johns Hopkins
          University, 23 February 1932. Adams clarifies the preparation of dramatic
          manuscripts for sale to the actors and traces them to the printers. The playwright
          first prepares an outline of the plot, gains the approval of the company, then
          composes the speeches of the characters in "foul sheets." A "fair copy" is
          prepared, with stage directions in the right margin and speaker designations in
          the left. The finished play is read to the company, submitted for license, and used
          as a prompt book. Abbreviated prompt books were frequently prepared for
          touring. Printed plays were sat in type from both kinds of prompt books,
          often with editing of stage directions. This is probably the clearest discussion of
          manuscripts and printed plays available. See also Bentley (1971.2).

1932.2   BRADBROOK, MURIEL CLARA. *Elizabethan Stage Conditions: A Study of
          Their Place in the Interpretation of Shakespeare*. Cambridge: University Press;
          New York: Macmillan, 149 pp.
                  The Harness Prize Essay, 1931. After reviewing Shakespearean criticism
          in the eighteenth, nineteenth, and twentieth centuries, Bradbrook discusses the
          effect of Shakespeare's stage on his dramatic structure and poetry, among other
          matters. Reprinted: 1968.9.

1932.3   CHILD, HAROLD H. "The Elizabethan Theatre." In *Cambridge History of
          English Literature*. Vol. 6, *The Drama to 1642*. Pt. 2. Edited by A. W. Ward and
          A. R. Waller. Cambridge: University Press, pp. 241-78.
                  Reprint of 1910.5.

1932.4   GREG, W[ALTER] W[ILSON]. "Elizabethan Dramatic Documents." *RES* 8
          (October): 457-58.
                  Greg replies in a letter to Lawrence's review of 1931.9, clarifying his
          position on two minor points.

1932.5   HART, ALFRED. "The Length of Elizabethan and Jacobean Plays." *RES* 8 (April): 139-54.

        Based on line-counts of 233 plays (all but two of the extant plays written for the public stage, 1590-1616), Hart comes up with an average length of 2500 lines. He examines the repertories of the main companies separately, and finds that they each conform to this length as well, indicating no substantial difference between lengths of plays at different companies. Continued in 1932.6 and 1934.2. Reprinted: 1934.3; 1970.11.

1932.6   _____. "The Time Allotted for Representation of Elizabethan and Jacobean Plays." *RES* 8 (October): 395-413.

        Based on his line-count in 1932.5 and contemporary references, Hart concludes that slightly cut versions of the plays were performed in two hours, plus the time needed for music and the concluding dance. Continued in 1934.2. Reprinted: 1934.3; 1970.11.

1932.7   LAWRENCE, W[ILLIAM] J[OHN]. "A 'Piece of Perspective.'" *TLS* (21 July): 532.

        A letter to the editor regarding Jonson's *Cynthia's Revels*. Lawrence argues that the quotation cannot refer to stage scenery since perspective scenery was unknown in England before 1600.

*1932.8   _____. "Shakespeare's Use of Animals." *Dublin Magazine* (January-March).

        Cited in *TN* 12 (April 1958): 79. Reprinted: 1935.7.

*1932.9   _____. "Stage Dummies." *New Statesman* (14 May).

        Cited in *TN* 12 (April 1958): 80. Reprinted: 1937.5.

1932.10   MANLY, J[OHN] M[ATTHEWS]. "The Children of the Chapel Royal and Their Masters." *Cambridge History of English Literature*. Vol. 6, *The Drama to 1642*. Pt. 2. Edited by A. W. Ward and A. R. Waller. Cambridge: University Press, pp. 279-92.

        Reprint of 1910.12

1932.11   THALER, ALWIN. "The Original Malvolio?" *ShAB* 7 (April): 57-71.

        Suggests that William Ffarington, steward to Lord Strange, patron of Shakespeare's company, served as the model for the character. Reprinted: 1941.12.

1932.12   WILSON, J[OHN] D[OVER]. "The Puritan Attack upon the Stage." In *Cambridge History of English Literature*. Vol. 6, *Drama to 1642*. Pt. 2. Edited by A. W. Ward and A. W. Waller. Cambridge: University Press, pp. 373-409.

        Reprint of 1910.26.

1933.1   BATY, GASTON. "La scène élizabéthaine." In *Le théâtre élizabétaine: Études et traductions*. Edited by Georgette Camille. Les Cahiers du Sud. 10. Paris: Les Cahiers du Sud, pp. 98-102.

A general discussion of stages and staging, based on Adams (1917.3). Albright (1909.2), Chambers (1923.2), Campbell (1923.1), and Mönkmeyer (1905.3).

1933.2   BOAS, F[REDERICK] S. "Tewkesbury Abbey's Theatrical Gear." TLS (16 March): 184.

Lists a variety of entries in the Tewkesbury Churchwardens Accounts from 1563 to 1703 dealing with theatrical costumes and other "gear."

1933.3   ECCLES, MARK. "Sir George Buc, Master of the Revels." In *Thomas Lodge and Other Elizabethans*. Edited by C[harles] J[asper] Sisson. Cambridge: Harvard University Press, pp. 409-506.

A biographical study, encompassing Buc's work as Master of the Revels, but containing little of specifically theatrical interest.

1933.4   ISAACS, JACOB. *Production and Stage Management at the Blackfriars*. London: Oxford University Press for the Shakespeare Associetion, 28 pp.

Originally a lecture delivered to the Shakespeare Association on 25 November 1932, with added references and corroborative material. Isaacs draws his evidence from prologues and stage directions in prompt copies and published plays. He examines 100 texts, "of which some seventy were unquestionably performed at the Blackfriars." There is no distinction between practices at Blackfriars and elsewhere, however. Isaacs examines the production staff, lighting, music, prompt books, plots, grouping, upper and lower stages (with two sets of curtains), and scenery (which was "definitely used" in the 1630s).

1933.5   LAWRENCE, W[ILLIAM] J[OHN]. "A Quaint Old Playhouse Trick." *Stage* (London), (28 September): 8.

Discusses the practice of a character in a play referring to the actor who played the character, much to the delight of the audience. Thomas Green is Lawrence's prime example, but he also cites Nathan Field, William Ostler, and Richard Robinson. Reprinted: 1937.5.

1933.6   REYNOLDS, GEORGE F[ULLMER]. "Elizabethan Stage Railings." *TLS* (16 February): 108.

Draws attention to a reference to the stage railing in The Hector of Germany, a Red Bull play printed in 1615.

1933.7   SISSON, CHARLES J[ASPER]. "Thomas Lodge and His Family." In *Thomas Lodge and Other Elizabethans*. Edited by C[harles] J[asper] Sisson. Cambridge: Harvard University Press, pp. 1-63.
        A general discussion of the life of the playwright and his works, of only peripheral theatrical interest. Included because of listing in *NCBEL* 1, col. 1402.

1933.8   TILLOTSON, GEOFFREY. "*Othello* and *The Alchemist* at Oxford in 1610." *TLS* (20 July): 494.
        Production of these plays at Oxford In 1610 is verified by William Fulman's transcription of a letter from Henry Jackson.

1933.9   WALKER, ALICE. "The Life of Thomas Lodge." *RES* 9 (October): 410-32.
        Supplements biographical information provided by Paradise (1931.14) and Sisson (1933.7). Continued in 1934.18.

1933.10   WARD, B[ERNARD] M[ORDAUNT]. "The Chamberlain's Men in 1597." *RES* 9 (January): 55-58.
        Extracts from the account books at Faversham, Rye, and Dover, bearing on the Lord Chamberlain's company's tour in the summer and autumn of 1597.

1933.11   WILLIAMS, IOLO A. "Hollar: A Discovery." *Connoisseur* 92 (November): 318-21.
        Announces discovery of the Hollar sketch of Southwark containing the second Globe, later engraved as the "I.ong Bird's Eye View of London."

1934

1934.1   CHILD, HAROLD H. "The Elizabethan Theatre." In *Cambridge History of English Literature*. Vol. 6, *The Drama to 1642*. Pt. 2. Edited by A. W. Ward and A. R. Waller. Cambridge: University Press, pp. 241-78.
        Reprint of 1910.5.

1934.2   HART, ALFRED. "Acting Versions of Elizabethan Plays." *RES* 10 (January): 1-28.
        Based on his earlier work (1932.5, 6). Hart concludes that plays were routinely cut for Elizabethan presentation. Evidence to support that conclusion is drawn from extant manuscripts containing lines marked for omission and comparison of so-called "bad" quartos based on acting copies with "good" quartos. Reprinted: 1934.3; 1970.11.

1934.3   _____. "Play Abridgement: The Length of Elizabethan and Jacobean Plays, Time Allotted for the Presentation of Elizabethan and Jacobean Plays, Acting Versions of Elizabethan and Jacobean Plays." In *Shakespeare and the Homilies, and Other Pieces of Research into the Elizabethan Drama*. Melbourne: Melbourne University Press, pp. 77-153.
        Reprints of 1932.6; 1932.7; 1934.2. *See also* 1970.11.

1934.4   HARTLEB, HANS. "Landgraf Moritz der Gelehrte von Hessen-Kassel als Fürderer der englische Komödianten und Erbauer des ersten deutschen Theaters." Ph.D. dissertation, Ludwig- Maximilians University, Munich, 162 pp.
        Published as 1936.12.

1934.5   LAWRENCE, W[ILLIAM] J [OHN]. "The Italian Comedian of 1610." *TLS* (7 June): 408.
        A letter to the editor, referring to a Calendar of State Papers entry concerning payments to an "Italian Comedian." Lawrence suggests it was an individual, rather than a company, referred to also in Jonson's 115th epigram.

1934.6   _____. "The Sharing Table." *Stage* (London), (6 December): 16.
        Discusses the process of sharing the day's receipts after the hired men had been paid. Lawrence finds similarities with the French system of the seventeenth century. Reprinted: 1935.4.

1934.7   _____. "Speeding up Shakespeare." *Criterion* 14, no. 54 (October): 78-85.
        Argues that "by virtue of Shakespeare's own testimony we are compelled to conclude that Shakespeare's plays were written in the conventional five acts, and acted in his own day with four intervals." Reprinted: 1937.5.

1934.8   LEA, KATHLEEN MARGARITE. *Italian Popular Comedy: A Study in the Commedia dell'Arte, 1500-1620, with Special Reference to the English Stage. Vol. 2. Oxford: Clarendon Press, pp. 339-455.*
        The relevant section forms the bulk of the second volume, wherein Lea discusses the contacts and comparisons with the English drama and theatre. She shows the contact to be "considerable" but the influence, "sporadic and superficial."

1934.9   LEECH, CLIFFORD E. J. "Sir Henry Lee's Entertainment of Elizabeth in 1592." *MLR* 30 (January): 52-55.
        Examines a manuscript of Sir Henry Lee's Devices, held in the British Library, which confirms the history of the 1592 entertainment at Woodstock and clarifies the proceedings of 20 and 21 September.

1934.10   MANLY, J[OHN] M[ATTHEWS]. "The Children of the Chapel Royal and Their Masters." In *Cambridge History of English Literature*. Vol. 6, *The Drama to 1642*. Pt. 2. Edited by A. W. Ward and A. R. Waller. Cambridge: University Press, pp. 279-92.
        Reprint of 1910.12.

1934.11   MEPHAM, W[ILLIAM] A. "A XVI Century Village Play at Heybridge, Essex." *N&Q* 166 (4 August): 75-79.
        Enumerates early sixteenth-century performances in Heybridge, based on contemporary accounts preserved in a scrap book. See also 1934.12; 1937.6.

1934.l2 _____. "Village Plays at Dunmow, Essex, in the Sixteenth Century." *N&Q* 166 (19 May): 345-48.

    Lists the early sixteenth-century performances, based on the city account book records of payments to actors. See also 1934.11, 1937.6; continued in 1934.13.

1934.13 _____ "Village Plays at Dunmow, Essex, in the Sixteenth Century." *N&Q* 166 (26 May): 362-66.

    Continuation of 1934.12. See 1934.11; 1937.6.

1934.14 SISSON, C[HARLES] J[ASPER]. "The Theatres and the Companies." In *A Companion to Shakespeare Studies*. Edited by Harley Granvllle-Barker and G[eorge] B[agshawe] Harrison. Cambridge: University Press; New York: Macmillan, pp. 9-43

    A brief general history, divided into sections covering the conditions of Shakespeare's art; the actors, companies, and playhouses; Elizabethan staging; the masques; the repertories; the performances; the actors; the audience; opposition to the stage; and a typical structure of the public theatre, including Godfrey's reconstruction of the Fortune (1908.10). Reprinted: 1960.19.

1934.15 WALKER, ALICE. "The Life of Thomas Lodge, II." *RES* 10 (January): 46-54.

    Continuation of 1933.9.

1934.16 WHITE, BEATRICE. *An Index to "The Elizabethan Stage" and "William Shakespeare," by Sir Edmund Chambers*. London: Oxford University Press, 161 pp.

    Comprehensive index to 1923.2.

1934.17 WILSON, J[OHN] D[OVER]. "The Puritan Attack on the Stage." In *Cambridge History of English Literature*. Vol. 6, *Drama to 1642*. Pt. 2. Edited by A. W. Ward and A. R. Waller. Cambridge: University Press, pp. 373-409.

    Reprint of 1910.26.

<u>1935</u>

1935.1 ADAMS, JOHN CRANFORD. "The Structure of the Globe Playhouse Stage." Ph.D. dissertation, Cornell University, 335 pp.

    Expanded version published: 1942.1.

1935.2 BAESECKE, ANNA. *Das Schauspiel der englischen Komödiandten in Deutschschland: Seine dramatische Form und seine Entwicklung*. Studien zur englischen Philologie, no. 8. Halle: Martin-Sändig, 154 pp.

    Published version of a 1934 Halle Ph.D. dissertation. Baesecke examines the form and development of the song- drama of the English actors in Germany during the sixteenth and scventeenth centuries. She divides the time considered into four periods (1560-1600, 1600-1620, 1620-1648, and 1648-1700) and traces the development of the form during each.

1935.3   HUNT, THEODORE B. "The Scenes as Shakespeare Saw Them." In *The Parrott Presentation Volume*. Edited by Herding Craig. Princeton: Princeton University Press, pp. 205-12.

     An argument for the reconstruction of Shakespeare's imagined settings for scenes based on information included in the text. The "lobby" in Hamlet, for example, is shown to be "a sunny, elevated portico opening on the ramparts, not far from the entrance to the palace." while Polonius's "house" is an apartment in the palace.

1935.4   LAWRENCE, W[ILLIAMI J[OHN]. *Old Theatre Days and Ways*. London: George Harrap & Co., 256 pp.

     A collection of previously published essays, some extensively revised, including 1931.10 and 1935.5. Pertinent studies examine the use of trumpet and drum to announce the players, the role of the prompter, the complex systems of admission used, rehearsal procedures, Elizabethan acrobats, and the sharing system. Almost all range freely through time, discussing foreign as well as English production methods.

1935.5   _____. "The Original Staging of *Romeo and Juliet*, Act 111, Scene V." *TLS* (19 September): 580.

     Argues for the playing of the second balcony scene entirely on the upper stage. See also Sampson (1935.13; 1936.21): Adams (1936.1): and Granville-Barker (1936.10).

1935.6   _____. "The Site of the Whitefriars Theatre." *RES* 11 (April): 6-11.

     Lawrence sides with Chambers (1923.2) against J. C. Adams (1917.3) on the site of the Whitefriars, based upon the authority of an eighteenth-century history of the precinct.

1935.7   _____. *Those Nut-Cracking Elizabethans: Studies of the Early Theatre and Drama*. London: Argonaut Press, 217 pp.

     A collection of previously published essays, some extensively revised, including 1930.5, 6 and 1932.8. The title essay examines the eating habits of the audience; others treat Shakespeare's use of animals, the use of bells, the stage furniture and its removers, and the development of the private playhouse.

1935.8   LEECH, CLIFFORD [E. J.] "The Plays of Edward Sharpham: Alterations Accomplished and Projected." *RES* 11 (January): 69-74.

     Examines the hasty adaptation of *Cupid's Whirligig* and "The Fleire" to the production needs of the moment. The latter play exists in manuscript in the British Library and is clearly marked by the adaptor.

1935.9   LEECH, CLIFFORD E. J. "Private Performances and Amateur Theatricals (Excluding the Academic Stage) from 1580 to 1660, with an Edition of *Ranguaillo D'Oceano*, 1640." Ph.D. dissertation, London University, 475 pp.

      Examines "those types of dramatic performances in the period 1580-1660 which were not conditioned by the exigencies of a regular theatre and a paying audience." The eight major chapters treat the end of the mysteries, May games, private entertainments, private masques, amateur and household plays, private professional performances, and irregular country performances, with the second, sixth, and eighth chapters containing the most new information.

1935.10   McKERROW, R[ONALD] B. "A Suggestion Regarding Shakespeare's Manuscripts." *RES* 11 (October): 459-65.

      Suggests that printed plays where character naming in stage directions and speech headings is inconsistent might have been printed from the author's foul papers, while consistency in naming signals printing from a fair copy, perhaps made by a playhouse scribe.

1935.11   NICOLL, ALLARDYCE. "Royal Divertisements ." *ThArts* 19 (February): 139-48.

      Describes the contents of a collection at Turin, bearing on the production of masques and ballets at the Savoy palace. Of some interest because of the parallels to the masques of Jonson and Jones.

1935.12   REWICK, W[ILLIAM] L[INDSAY]. "Alfonso Ferrabosca." *RES* 11 (April): 184-85.

      A document in the Vatican Archives explains why the Exchequer held up Ferrabosco's annuity after 1583: this contributor to Elizabeth's masques left for Italy in that year.

1935.13   SAMPSON, GEORGE. "The Staging of *Romeo and Juliet*." *TLS* (9 November): 722.

      Responds to Lawrence (1935.5). agreeing with the placement of the second balcony scene and arguing for continuity rather than act division in modern editions.

1935.14   SCHELLING, FELIX E. *Elizabethan Drama 1558-1642: A History of the Drama in England from the Accession of Queen Elizabeth to the Closing of the Theaters, to Which Is Prefixed a Resumé of the Earlier Drama from Its Beginnings*. Vol. 1. Boston and New York: Houghton, Mifflin & Co., pp. 141-93.

      Reprint of 1908.16.

1935.15   SEE, L. H. "Shakespeares erste Verleger." *Weltkunst* 9 (8 December): 3.

      A brief note on Heminge and Condell on the "Bibliophile" page.

1935.16   SHARPE, ROBERT BOIES. *The Real War of the Theatres: Shakspeare's Fellows in Rivalry with the Admiral's Men, 1594-1603. Repertories, Devices, and Types.* Modern Language Association Monograph Series, no. 5. Boston: D. C. Heath & Co., 260 pp.

Expanded, published version of 1928.14. A chronological survey of the theatrical "vents of the last decade of Elizabeth's rule, focusing on the rivalry between the Lord Chamberlain's Men and the Lord Admiral's Men. Sharpe sees political overtones in the rivalry, which culminated in the history plays that each side presented.

1935.17   SMALL, GEORGE WILLIAM. "Shakespeare's Stage." *ShAB* 10 (January): 31-35.

Argues for a rectangular rather than a tapered stage, as suggested by the Swan drawing and the Fortune contract.

1935.18   SPRAGUE, ARTHUR COLBY. *Shakespeare and the Audience.* Cambridge: Harvard University Press, 327 pp.

Not actually a study of the audience, but criticism of the plays attempting to establish Shakespeare's intended effect on the audience.

1936

1936.1   ADAMS, JOHN C[RANFORD]. "*Romeo and Juliet* as Played on Shakespeare's Stage." *ThArts* 20 (November): 869-904.

Discusses Shakespeare's use of what Adams thought were the seven stages available to him--the platform, the curtained inner stage, the "tarras," the "chamber," the two window stages, and the third-level music room. Illustrated with diagrams and photographs of a model of Adam's reconstruction of the Globe. Based partially on 1935.1; see also 1936.2; 1942.1.

1936.2   _____. "Shakespeare's Stage: New Facts and Figures." *ThArts* 20 (October): 812-18.

Describes, without providing evidence, his reconstruction of the Globe, complete with seven stages. Based on 1935.1; *see also* 1936.1; 1942.1.

1936.3   _____. "The Staging of *Romeo and Juliet*." *TLS* (15 February): 139.

In response to Lawrence (1935.5) and Sampson (1935.13), Adams explains how the second balcony scene would be staged in his reconstruction of the Globe. The entire scene would be played on the three upper stages. See also Granville-Barker (1936.10) and Lawrence (1936.15) and Adams's response, 1936.4.

1936.4   _____. "The Staging of *Romeo and Juliet*." *TLS* (23 May): 440.

Replies to Granville-Barker (1936.10) and Lawrence (1936.15), reasserting his previous argument (see 1936.3).

1936.5 BRANDL, ALOIS. "Shakespeare-Müglichkeiten." In *Forschungen und Charakteristiken*. Berlin and Leipzig: Walter de Gruyter & Co., pp. 177-82.

Discusses the extant illustrations of the Elizabethan stage and how the upper stage would have been used.

1936.6 BROWN, IVOR. "The Boy-Player." *ThArts* 20 (May): 385-91.

Examines the ways in which Shakespeare's use of boys for women's roles shaped the plays. Brown follows Granville-Barker in finding that young women in Shakespeare are essentially lacking in "sex appeal." See also 1937.1.

1936.7 CRUNDELL, H. W. "Visits of Dramatic Companies to Bristol, 1584-1600." *N&Q* (11 July): 24.

Corrects some misreadings in Murray (1910.15), from the Audit Books of the Bristol City Chamberlain.

1936.8 ELLIS-FERMOR, UNA M. "The Jacobean Stage." In *The Jacobean Drama: An Interpretation*. London: Methuen, pp. 273-83.

A general survey of the stage and audience, intended to supply background for her literary study in the previous chapters. Reprinted: 1947.3; 1953.5; 1958.8; 1961.9; 1964.10; 1965.8; 1969.4.

1936.9 GAW, ALLISON. "The Impromptu Mask in Shakspere (With Especial Reference to the Stagery of *Romeo and Juliet*, I, iv-v)." *ShAB* 11 (July): 149-60.

Argues that the mask Shakespeare used for getting Romeo into the Capulets' house led to an awkward bit of staging involving a march around the stage to signify a change of locale. With the entry of the Capulet servants, the scene becomes the Capulet house, despite the fact that Romeo and his group have never left the stage. Further, Gaw claims, the scene made heavy demands on the company, and keeping the masked characters on stage helped create the illusion of a large number of characters.

1936.10 GRANVILLE-BARKER, HARLEY. "The Staging of *Romeo and Juliet*." *TLS* (22 February): 163.

In answer to Lawrence (1935.5) and Adams (1936.31), Granville-Barker argues that the second balcony scene would be more effective if staged on the platform rather than on the upper stage.

1936.11 HARBAGE, ALFRED. *Cavalier Drama: An Historical and Critical Supplement to the Study of the Elizabethan and Restoration Stage*. New York: Modern Language Association, pp. 191-214, passim.

Examines the writing and presentation of plays "by fashionable gentry active in the Caroline court and on the Royal side in the Civil Wars--by the 'Cavaliers.'" While not of primary theatrical interest, there are references throughout to playhouses and actors. The most important section for present purposes is Part Two, Chapter V, "Caroline and Commonwealth Private Theatricals."

1936.12 HARTLEB, HANS. *Deutschlands erster Theaterbau. Eine Geschichte des Theaterlebens und der englischen Komödianten unter Landaraf Moritz dem Gelehrten von Hessen-Kassel.* Berlin and Leipzig: Walter de Gruyter, 162 pp.
Published version of 1934.4. Hartleb discusses the English actors in Kassel and their repertory in the seventeenth century, and Landgraf Moritz's building of the first German theatre.

1936.13 JOUVET, LOUIS. "The Elizabethan Theatre: Reconstruction after the Manner of Cuvier." *ThArts* 20 (March): 222-23.
Not a reconstruction but a rather poetic wish for one.

1936.14 LAWRENCE, W[ILLIAM] J[OHN]. "Something New about Shakespeare." *London Mercury* 34 (July): 224-28.
Argues that the absence of Shakespeare's heroes in the fourth act is purposeful, and has to do with the gradual slowing down of the plot.

1936.15 _____. "The Staging of *Romeo and Juliet*." *TLS* (29 February): 184.
Takes issue with Adams's placement of the second balcony scene in a side window area and his placement of IV.v. on the upper stage. See also 1936.3.

1936.16 LEWES, GEORGE HENRY. "Shakespeare: Actor and Critic." *ThW* 21 (October): 41-50.
Discusses Shakespeare's probable shortcomings as an actor, based primarily on Hamlet's advice to the players. Lewes uses this as a springboard to discuss the general problem of the actor: to play emotions without getting lost in them.

1936.17 LINTHICUM, MARIE CHANNING. "Costume in the Drama of Shakespeare and His Contemporaries." Ph.D. dissertation, University of Iowa, 307 pp.
Published as 1936.18.

1936.18 LINTHICUM, M[ARIE] CHANNING. *Costume in the Drama of Shakespeare and His Contemporaries.* London: Oxford University Press, 307 pp.
Published version of 1936.17. A comprehensive treatment of color, fabric, garment style, and accessories from the sixteenth and seventeenth centuries, including selected references from the plays of Shakespeare and his contemporaries. Linthicum draws upon many earlier works (including manuscripts) for her historical discussion. While not dealing precisely with theatre practice, this volume is helpful in gaining a full understanding of that practice. Linthicum includes two appendixes, but this volume is somewhat marred by the lack of an introduction or conclusion.

1936.19 NICOLL, ALLARDYCE. "Scenery between Shakespeare and Dryden." *TLS* (15 August): 658.
Discusses two drawings used for staging *Candy Restored* by amateurs in 1640-41.

1936.20   SAMPSON, GEORGE. "The Staging of *Romeo and Juliet*." *TLS* (22 February): 163.

      Responds to Adams's reply (1936.3) to his previous letter (1935.13), reasserting his interest in continuity in modern (not Elizabethan) stage directions.

1936.21   SISSON, C[HARLES] J[ASPER]. "Mr. and Mrs. Browne of the Boar's Head." *L&LT* 15, no. 6 (Winter): 99-107.

      Discusses the theatre at the Boar's Head, the manager, and his wife, based on records of court cases held in the Public Record Office. The treatment here is rather anecdotal and without notes. <u>See also</u> 1972.29.

1937

1937.1   BOAS, GUY. "The Influence of the Boy-Actor on Shakespeare's Plays." *ContempR* 52 (July): 69-77.

      Argues that the range and emotional resources of the boy actors were limited, and that the roles they were required to play were also limited in order to fit their abilities.

1937.2   CRUNDELL, H. W. "*The Taming of the Shrew* on the XVII. Century Stage." *N&Q* 173 (18 September): 207.

      Argues that the Epilogue (not printed in the First Folio but preserved in the text of *The Taming of a Shrew*) was Shakespeare's.

1937.3   EBISCH, WALTHER, and SCHÜCKING, LEVIN L. *A Shakespeare Bibliography: Supplement for the Years 1930-1935*. Oxford: Clarendon Press, pp. 41-44.

      Continuation of 1931.6 until April 1936. All relevant items have been incorporated into this bibliography.

1937.4   KERNODLE, GEORGE RILEY. "Perspective in the Renaissance Theatre: The Pictorial Sources and the Development of Scenic Forms." Ph.D. dissertation, Yale University, 325 pp.

      Expanded version published: 1944.7.

1937.5   LAWRENCE, W[ILLIAM] J[OHN]. *Speeding Up Shakespeare: Studies of the Bygone Theatre and Drama*. London: Argonaut Press, 220 pp.

      Collection of previously published essays, some with substantial revision, including 1923.15: 1932.9; 1933.5: 1934.7. Included are discussions of the speed of performance; the habit of actors referring to themselves while in character; an evaluation of Richard Tarleton; the use of dummies on stage; the origin of the custom of the Gravediggers in wearing several waistcoats; and additions to Adams's edition of Henry Herbert's office book.

1937.6   MEPHAM, W[ILLIAM] A. "The History of the Drama in Essex from the Fifteenth Century to the Present Time." Ph.D. dissertation, London University, pp. 1-284.

        The relevant chapters are two through nine, covering the fifteenth through seventeenth centuries. In the sixteenth century, London professional companies regularly visited Maldon and Saffron Walden, and religious plays were still produced by prominent men of the districts. The visits of the professional companies ceased by 1639, as Essex was predominantly Puritan. Mepham bases most of his conclusions on information gathered from a variety of Churchwardens' Accounts and municipal archives in Essex. The more modern information is largely gleaned from contemporary newspapers. See also 1934.11-12.

1937.7   MITCHELL, LEE. "The Advent of Scene Design in England." *QJS* 23 (April): 189-97.

        Examines Inigo Jones's designs for the court masques, with frequent references to Italian practices.

1937.8   NICOLL, ALLARDYCE. *The Stuart Masque and the Renaissance Stage.* London: G. Harrap, 224 pp.

        A study of the staging of the Stuart masques produced at Whitehall during the reigns of James I and Charles I. After a brief review of the form of the masque, Nicoll examines in detail the Whitehall banqueting house and the extant designs for performances there, with frequent reference to Italian practices. The almost 200 illustrations add significantly to the work.

1937.9   PLATTER, THOMAS. *Thomas Platter's Travels in England, 1599.* Translated by Clare Williams. London: Jonathan Cape, 245 pp.

        A translation of and commentary on the contemporary diary containing a brief description of a play that Platter saw. Based on 1929.13.

1938

1938.1   ADAMS, JOHN C[RANFORD]. "The Staging of *The Tempest*, 111, iii." *RES* 14 (October): 404-19.

        Examines the three important stage directions in the scene, concluding that the banquet disappeared into a false table-top; that Ariel descended and ascended with the flying machinery, in a prone or inclined position; and that Prospero appeared on a third level rather than on the usual second level (or upper stage) in order to cue the musicians.

1938.2   ANON. "English Humor 1500 to 1800." *TLS* (21 May): 360.

        Includes a brief discussion of Richard Tarlton.

1938.3   BENTLEY, GERALD EADES. "The Diary of a Caroline Theatregoer." *MP* 35 (August): 61-72.

        Extracts from the manuscript diary of Sir Humphrey Mildmay, held in the British Library, with commentary. Mildmay attended plays regularly, and his diary records his attendance from 1633 until the theatres closed in 1642. He also records his expenses. Mildmay frequented the Blackfriars, but he also visited the Globe and the Phoenix.

1938.4   DAVIES, W. ROBERTSON. *Shakespeare's Boy Actors*. London: J. M. Dent & Sons, 207 pp.

        Investigates the influence which the convention of the boy actor for female parts may have exercised over the Elizabethan dramatist, and the interpretation of the parts given by the bay actors in general. Davies includes conjectural accounts of the training given the boys and a consideration of the devices used by the playwrights to bring the part within the scope of the young male actor.

1938.5   GREG, W[ALTER] W[ILSON]. "A Fragment from Henslowe's Diary." *Library*, 4th ser. 19 (September): 180-84.

        A detailed account and facsimile of an acquitance by Dekker for payment, apparently cut from the diary. <u>See also</u> 1940.1.

1938.6   KELLY, F[RANCIS] M[ICHAEL]. *Shakespearian Costume for Stage and Screen*. London: Adam & Charles Black, pp. 9-58.

        Contains little of historical interest, except the section containing an analysis of actual clothing worn during the period 1560-1620.

1938.7   MOODY, DOROTHY BELLE. "Shakespeare's Stage Directions: An Examination for Bibliographical and Literary Evidence." Ph.D. dissertation, Yale University, 434 pp.

        Attempts to show what Shakespeare's stage directions "reveal as to the history of his text, and to set forth such literary information as they yield . . . . Since the matter of staging has been fully discussed elsewhere, for the most part I ignore it."

1938.8   R. "Actors in Shakespeare's Plays." *N&Q* 174 (28 May): 387.

        A brief paragraph noting the printing of actors' names in the First Folio *Much Ado about Nothing*.

1938.9   SKOPNIK, GUNTER. "Niederländische Bühnenformen des 16. Jahrhunderts." *DuV* 39 (November): 411-26.

        Discusses methods of production in the Netherlands in the sixteenth century, including those of touring English companies.

1938.10   UNWIN, GEORGE. *The Gilds and Companies of London.* 3d ed. London: G. Allen & Unwin, 397 pp.
Reprint of 1909.29.

1939

1939.1   ETCH, LOUIS M. "Ned Alleyn versus Dick Burbage." *SpMon* 6:110-26.
A comparison of the two great Elizabethan actors, based on contemporary references. Alleyn played the stage "heavies," such as Barabas, Faustus, Tamburlaine, and Hieronimo, and apparently displayed a tendency to "strut and bellow." Burbage, on the other hand, was apparently more restrained, playing Biron, Romeo, Prince Hal, Brutus, and the heroes of the four great tragedies. Eich concludes that Burbage was the better actor.

1939.2   ELIOT, SAMUEL A., Jr. "The Lord Chamberlain's Company as Portrayed in *Every Man Out of His Humour.*" *SCSML* 21 (October): 64-80.
Discusses the casting of Jonson's play, based on a published cast list and the types of the characters.

1939.3   FREDÉN, GUSTAF. *Friedrich Menius und das Repertorie der englischen Komödianten in Deutschland.* Stockholm: P. A. Palmers. 527 pp.
Examines the life and work of Menius, an early seventeenth-century German theatrical personality, in relation to the touring English players. Fredén pays special attention to the plays presented, bath straight adaptations of English originals (such as *Titus Andronicus*, which was very popular) and hybrid Germen works featuring Pickelherring. He concludes that Menius edited the 1620 collection of plays by the English comedians. See also 1941.7.

1939.4   GRAY, M[ARGARET] M[URIEL]. "Queen Elizabeth's Players." *TLS* (14 January): 25-26.
A letter to the editor, citing and commenting on a 1589 letter that demonstrates that the Queen's Men were in Scotland in that year.

1939.5   GRIFFIN, WILLIAM JAMES. "Tudor Control of Press and Stage." Ph.D. dissertation, University of Iowa, 198 pp.
A systematic collection of data, arranged historically and comparatively, concerning the action and attitude of Tudor government toward the press and stage. The most useful section is the second chapter, which sets forth a calendar of evidence used in the narrative first chapter. The study includes data from 1485 to 1603. Griffin has used Archer's Transcript of the Registers of the Company of Stationers of London, 1554-1640 extensively.

1939.6   HARBAGE, ALFRED. "Elizabethan Acting." *PMLA* 54 (September): 685-708.
An attempt to define both "formal" and "natural" acting styles and to defend the former while attacking the latter. Harbage considers Betterton to be the first "natural" actor in England, with Burbage, Alleyn, and the rest belonging

to the "formal" school. He cites the preface to a manuscript play, "The Cyprian Conqueror," and subsequent acting manuals, for their formal approach.

1939.7   SOUTHERN, RICHARD. "He, Also, Was a Scene Painter (Wm. Lyzarde 1572)." 23 *L&LT* (November): 294-300.
       An anecdotal look st William Lyzarde, scene painter to Elizabeth, based primarily on his accounts from 1572. Southern concentrates on Lyzarde's pigment order.

1939.8   STUNZ, ARTHUR NESBITT. "The Contemporary Setting of *Macbeth*." Ph.D. dissertation, University of Iowa, 81 pp.
       Attempts to date *Macbeth* accurately (he proposes May/June 1606), and to investigate the possible effect of contemporary political attitudes. Of little theatrical interest.

1940

1940.1   ADAMS, JOSEPH QUINCY. "Another Fragment from Henslowe's Diary." *Library*, 4th ser. 20 (September): 154-58.
       Discussion of paper containing the signatures of Dekker and two others, held in the Folger Shakespeare Library and apparently removed from the diary. See also Greg (1938.5).

1940.2   BATESON, F[REDERICK] W[ILSE], ed. *The Cambridge Bibliography of English Literature*. Vol. 1, *600-1660*, Cambridge: University Press. pp. 497-513.
       The relevant section is Parts I1 and I11 of the Renaissance Drama listings, dealing with "Theatres and Actors" and "The Puritan Attack Upon the Stage." There are also a variety of subsections in each category. Relevant items have been included in this bibliography. See also the Supplement (1957.16) and (1974.25).

1940.3   CASTLE, EDUARD. "Zu dem Problem: Shakespeare und seine Truppe." *JDSG* 76: 57-111.
       Examines Shakespeare's plays and company, and attempts to establish lines of business and assign actors to them. Castle includes many pages of tables to help support his contentions. *See also* Baldwin (1927.1).

1940.4   CHAMBERS, E[DMUND] K. "William Shakespeare: An Epilogue." *RES* 16 (October): 385-401.
       Considers, among many other matters, the acting style of the period, the length of representation of plays, and allusions to the stage and acting in Shakespeare. Reprinted: 1944.6.

1940.5   GORELIK, MODECHAI. *New Theatres for Old*. New York: S. French, pp 100-105.
       The relevant section is titled "Shakespeare, Liberator," where, as part of a larger argument about the coming of naturalism, Gorelik discusses how Shakespeare used his resources in a masterful way. Reprinted: 1947.4.

1940.6   GREG, W[ALTER] W[ILSON]. "The Staging of *King Lear*." *RES* 16 (July): 300-303.

    Discusses the simplicity of the stage directions for *King Lear*, concluding that no "rear stage," and probably no balcony, was available for its initial production.

1940.7   HARBAGE, ALFRED. *Annals of English Drama, 975-1700*. Philadelphia: University of Pennsylvania Press, 264 pp.

    A comprehensive listing, unannotated and undocumented, arranged chronologically, with company and date of performance. The "Index of Dramatic Companies" and "List of Theatres" are relevant, although outdated. Revised: 1964.13.

1940.8   LEWIS, JOHN COLBY. "A Correlation of the Theatre with the Graphic Arts, According to the Dominant Artistic Theories of Several Times, from the Middle Ages to the Present Day." Ph.D. dissertation, Cornell University, pp. 60-105.

    The relevant section deals with the Renaissance, primarily in Italy, although English practice (chiefly in the masques) is touched on.

1940.9   PASCAL, R[OY]. "The Stage of the 'Englische Komödianten'--Three Problems." *MLR* 35 (July): 367-76.

    Examines the entrances, the balcony, and the curtain used by the English actors in Germany during the seventeenth century. Apparently there were usually two or three doorways opening on to a booth stage set up in a rectangular building open in the center. A balcony was used at times, and the open stage was hung with arras. Parallels with the Elizabethan stage are clear.

1940.10   REYNOLDS, GEORGE FULLMER. *The Staging of Elizabethan Plays at the Red Bull Theatre, 1605-25*. New York: Modern Language Association, 203 pp.

    Widely recognized as a model of scholarship and perhaps the most influential staging study ever published. Reynolds found, in surveying the state of historical scholarship in the thirties, that "many of our present conclusions rest on unsound foundations which demand re-examination." In this book he proposes to offer "such a re-examination with stricter methods of procedure and severer checks on conclusions." Reynolds examines all the evidence presented by a group of plays selected objectively. Each scene of each play is looked at in detail on each point; the plays as a whole are examined; and then all plays are considered in relation to each other. Reynolds is the first to divide the plays of the repertory he establishes for the Red Bull into groups depending upon the reliability of the evidence they provide, and he draws his primary evidence only from those plays that provide the best evidence--the evidence most clearly linked to playhouse practices. Briefly, he concludes that "the Red Bull plays, in spite of their use of spectacle, could be given on a stage structurally like that of the Swan drawing, with the single important addition of a third stage door." Reynolds then speculates that a portable curtained booth might have been used for discoveries.

1940.11   SISSON, C[HARLES] J[ASPER]. "The Mouse-Trap Again." *RES* 16 (April): 129-36.

Examines the staging of the play-within-a-play scene of *Hamlet*, focusing on the preliminary dumb show. Sisson places it on the "inner stage" and freezes the action (except for Hamlet and Ophelia) on the "outer stage."

<u>1941</u>

1941.1   BENTLEY, GERALD EADES. *The Jacobean and Caroline Stage*. Vols. 1-2. Oxford: Clarendon Press, 748 pp.

The first two volumes of Bentley's seven-volume reference work (<u>see also</u> 1956.4; 1968.2), based on his Ph.D. dissertation (1929.7) but greatly expanded. The major purpose is to carry on the survey begun by Chambers (1923.2) from 1616 to 1642, beginning in these volumes with a survey of the companies (vol. 1) and the actors (vol. 2). Bentley treats the companies in roughly the order of their importance, beginning with the King's Men and continuing through Beeston's Boys. First, he summarizes the history of each company to 1616 (from Chambers), and then he traces it until it disbands or the theatres are closed in 1642. In this latter narrative, all relevant documentary evidence is presented in detail. Each chapter concludes with a series of lists and tables presenting the evidence of the actor lists, provincial notices, plays at court, and so on, and a listing of the company's repertory. Volume two contains the information on the actors, with a minimum of comments by Bentley. Instead he cites "every scrap of biographical evidence" in chronological order. The appendix to volume 2 prints many important documents and discusses plague closings.

1941.2   CAMPBELL, LILY B[ESS]. "Richard Tarlton and the Earthquake of 1580." *HLQ* 4 (January): 293-96.

Establishes the clown Tarlton as the author of a poem on the earthquake.

1941.3   CRUNDELL, H. W. "Actors' Parts and Elizabethan Texts." *N&Q* 180 (17 May): 350-51.

Argues that Pope first made the suggestion that same plays of the First Folio (*Merry Wives of Windsor* in particular) were assembled from actors' parts.

1941.4   LEECH, CLIFFORD [E. J.] "The Caroline Audience." *MLR* 36 (July): 304-19.

An examination of tone in Caroline plays through a study of the audience for which they were intended. Leech sees two reasons for a change in Caroline drama from the Jacobean: the refinement of the Court and the new group of young writers. Most evidence for the character of the audience comes from the prologues and epilogues of the plays. The most important audience requirement was for variety and a retreat from the actual. Reprinted: 1950.11.

1941.5   McNEIR, WALDO F. "Gayton on Elizabethan Acting." *PMLA* 56 (June): 579-83.

> Responds to Harbage (1939.6) with previously uncited evidence from a 1654 book by Edmund Gayton, arguing for a fomal acting style.

1941.6   MITCHELL, LEE. "Elizabethan Scenes of Violence and the Problem of Their Staging." Ph.D. dissertation, Northwestern University, 121 pp.

> The three chapters enumerate Elizabethan scenes of violence by type and discuss the Elizabethan and modern staging of such scenes. Stabbing is most often used for sudden and unexpected murders, poisoning for reversal, shooting for the climax of a struggle, battles and executions for spectacular terminal catastrophes, and the melee for surprising terminal action. The use of stage properties, visible blood, and effigies of bodies, heads, and limbs was common. The expert use of optical illusion or misdirection of attention was also employed.

1941.7   [PASCAL, ROY.] "Elizabethan Plays in Germany." *TLS* 2 (26 April): 208.

> Discusses the career of Fredriech Menius, apparent editor of an important 1620 collection of English plays presented in Germany. See Fredén (1939.3).

1941.8   REYNOLDS, GEORGE F[ULLMER]. "Some Problems of Elizabethan Staging." *CUS*, general series (A), 26, no. 4 (November): 3-19.

> The sixth annual Kesearch Lecture of the University of Colorado, delivered 5 May 1941, based on 1940.10. Reynolds includes some interesting personal information as well as his concerns with circumspect treatment of the evidence for staging practices. Contains nothing new.

1941.9   SCHUCKING. LEVIN L. "Die Kindertruppenstelle in *Hamlet*." *Archiv* 179, no. 1: 8-14.

> Examines the allusions in Hamlet to the boy companies, and places them in historical context.

1941.10   THALER, ALWIN. "Ben Jonson, Richard Brome, and Minor Actors." In *Shakespeare and Democracy*. Knoxville: University of Tennessee Press, pp. 266-86.

> Reprint of 1921.16-17; 1922.9.

1941.11   _____. "*Faire Em* (and Shakespeare's Company?) in Lancashire." In *Shakespeare and Democracy*. Knoxville: University of Tennessee Press. pp. 141-56.

> Reprint of 1931.16.

1941.12   _____. "The Original Malvolio?" In *Shakespeare and Democracy*. Knoxville: University of Tennessee Press, pp. 119-37.

> Reprint of 1932.11.

1941.13 _____. "Travelling Players in Shakespeare's England." In *Shakespeare and Democracy*. Knoxville: University of Tennessee Press, pp. 157-84.
Reprint of 1920.30.

1942

1942.1 ADAMS, JOHN CRANFORD. *The Globe Playhouse: Its Design and Equipment*. Cambridge: Harvard University Press, 420 pp.
Expanded, published version of 1935.1. Perhaps the single most influential work in the field, and one of the most misleading. In this, the first comprehensive attempt to reconstruct the Globe, Adams includes chapters on the property and shape of the building; the playhouse frame; the auditorium; the platform stage; the exterior of the tiring house; the first, second, and third levels and stairs of the tiring house; and the superstructure It was Adams who popularized the ideas of the "study," the "tarras," the "chamber," and the "music gallery." The major problem is Adams's use of evidence from too wide a variety of sources. While almost completely discredited in scholarly circles, this reconstruction of the Globe is the most widely known and accepted, perhaps because of the ubiquitous models that appeared in high schools throughout the country. See also the second edition, 1961.1.

1942.2 BENTLEY, GERALD E[ADES]. "A Good Name Lost: Ben Jonson's Lament for S. P." *TLS* (30 May): 276.
Argues that the first name of the well-known boy actor was not Salathiel, as had been supposed, but rather Salmon (Pavy). Bentley cites ten seventeenth-century appearances of the name, one of which was previously unknown, and traces the substitution of the Christian name to Gifford's 1816 edition of Jonson.

1942.3 BRAWNER, JAMES PAUL. *"The Wars of Cyrus": An Early Classical Narrative of the Child Actors*. ISLL, vol. 28, nos. 3-4. Urbana: University of Illinois, 163 pp.
A critical edition, with notes and commentary, of the earliest private theatre play. Section V of the Introduction deals with "Staging of the Play," but Brawner provides nothing new. He believes that multiple staging would have been employed.

1942.4 MILES, THEODORE. "Place Realism in a Group of Caroline Plays." *RES* 18 (October): 428-40.
Examines six private theatre plays from 1631 to 1635 that have London place-names as titles. It has been elsewhere assumed that specific representational scenery might have been used in staging those plays. See 1972.12.

1942.5 RINGLER, WILLIAM [A.]. "The First Phase of the Elizabethan Attack on the Stage, 1558-79." *HLQ* 5 (July): 391-418.
A different view of the attack on the stage, suggesting that: 1) it began suddenly in 1577; 2) the causes were internal, resulting from changes within the

theatres themselves; and 3) the attack was led by laymen, not clergy, and that it was not initially theological.

1942.6   RINGLER, WILLIM A. *Stephen Gosson: A Biographical and Critical Study.* Princeton Studies in English, no. 35. Princeton: Princeton University Press, 151 pp.

    The most important section from a theatrical perspective is the fourth chapter, detailing the Puritan attach on the stage and the role in it of Gosson's *Schoole of Abuse.*

1942.7   SISSON, C[HARLES] J[ASPER]. "Notes on Early Stuart Stage History." *MLR* 37 (January): 25-36.

    The first part consists of a wealth of notes on theatrical personalities of the early seventeenth century, derived from the close study of various legal documents. The second part (pp. 30-34) discusses the shares in the Red Bull company. The final section (pp. 34-36) discusses the wages of the hired men. Sisson is particularly noted for his skill at dealing with documentary evidence.

1942.8   SISSON, CHARLES J[ASPER]. "Shakespeare's Quartos as Prompt-Copies, with Some Account of Cholmeley's Players and a New Shakespeare Allusion." *RES* 18 (April): 129-43.

    Argues that the usage of published quartos as prompt copies by both provincial and London companies was general. Information about Cholmeley's Players (also known as the Simpson's Company), a provincial but professional group in Yorkshire, is derived from Star Chamber documents.

<u>1943</u>

1943.1   ABEGGLEN, HOMER N. "A Dissertation in Five Parts. 1. The Methods of Staging in London Theatres in the Last Half of the Nineteenth Century. 2. Theatrical Satire on the American Business Man, 1900-1940. 3. The Staging of Medieval and Elizabethan Plays. 4. A Comparison Between Plautine Farce and Romantic Comedy. 5. The Premiere of Wycherly's *The Plain Dealer.*" Ph.D. dissertation, Western Reserve University, pp. 36-70.

    The relevant part is the third, a highly personalized and anecdotal essay examining different types of scenes and approaches to their staging. Abegglen simply reports on what various scholars have written (he cites fewer than ten sources), concluding that "no one method was adhered to by all the producers of the seven different theatres."

1943.2   BALD, R[OBERT] C[ECIL]. "Leicester's Men in the Low Countries." *RES* 19 (October): 195-97.

    Selections from Halliwell-Phillipps's scrapbooks, containing excerpts from Leicester's household account book, bearing on the company's tour of 1585-86.

1943.3   BRAWNER, JAMES PAUL. "Early Classical Narrative Plays by Sebastian Westcott and Richard Mulcaster." *MLQ* 4 (December): 455-64.

    Claims Westcott and Mulcaster wrote several of the plays presented by their children's companies in the sixteenth century. See also 1951.4.

1943.4   DAVIS, JOE LEE. "The Case for Comedy in Caroline Theatrical Apologetics." *PMLA* 58 (June) : 353-71.

    Discusses Prynne's attacks on Caroline comedy in *Histriomastix* and its defense In Randolph's *The Muse's Looking Glass* and Baker's *Theatrum Redivivum.*

1943.5   GRIFFIN, WILLIAM J. "Notes on Early Tudor Control of the Stage." *MLN* 58 (January): 50-54.

    Corrects Gildersleeve (1908.9) on two minor points and adds two minor instances of control of the stage in the 1540s.

1943.6   PARROTT, THOMAS MARC, and BALL, ROBERT HAMILTON. *A Short View of Elizabethan Drama, Together with Some Account of Its Principal Playwrights and the Conditions under Which It Was Produced.* New York: Charles Scribner's Sons, pp. 45-62.

    Primarily concerned with major plays and "the personality of the dramatist." but also considers theatrical conditions briefly. The relevant section is Chapter Three, "Actors and Theatres," which includes in its general discussion a drawing and description of J. C. Adams's reconstruction of the Globe (see 942.1). Reprinted: 1958.15.

1943.7   SISSON, C[HARLES] J[ASPER]. "A Note on Sebastian Westcott." *RES* 19 (April): 204-5.

    A brief note on the Master of the Children of Paul's, derived from a Chancery suit involving his brother.

1943.8   STEVENSON, ALLEN H. "Shirley's Years in Ireland." *RES* 20 (January):19-28.

    While Shirley's years as resident dramatist at the Werbaugh Theatre, Dublin, are the concern of this essay, the dates of his departure and his return to London are clarified.

<u>1944</u>

1944.1   B[ARRELL], C[HARLES] W[ISNER]. "Documentary Notes on the Swan Theatre." *ShFQ* 5 (January): 8-9.

    Discusses the Swan drawing (with a translation of DeWitt's description) and the suit against Langley and Shakespeare. Barrell thinks that the scene illustrated in the drawing is from *Twelfth Night* and that the Earl of Oxford wrote it.

1944.2   BARRELL, CHARLES WISNER. "Lord Oxford as Supervising Patron of Shakespeare's Theatrical Company." *ShFQ* 5 (July): 33-40.

Argues that Edward de Vere, seventeenth Earl of Oxford, was the "Lord Chamberlain" who lent his name to Shakespeare's company.

1944.3   BENNETT, H[ENRY] S[TANLEY]. "Shakespeare's Audience." *PBA* 30: 3-16.

The annual Shakespeare Lecture of the British Academy, delivered 26 April 1944, examining the audience of the Theatre, the Curtain, and the Globe, 1595-1609. Bennett discusses the varied composition of the audience and the methods the playwright used to appeal to each class. The end of the essay, however, consists of a plea to avoid criticism that removes the play from the realm of the theatre.

1944.4   BETHEL, S[AMUEL] L[ESLIE]. *Shakespeare and the Popular Dramatic Tradition.* Westminster: P. S. King and Staples, pp. 31-41,

The relevant section is chapter two, "Planes of Reality," in which Bethel stresses those elements of the playhouse that Shakespeare used to reinforce his themes. Reprinted: 1948.2.

1944.5   CHAMBERS, E[DMUND] K. "The Stage of the Globe." In *Shakespearean Gleanings.* London: Oxford University Press, pp. 98-110.

Reprint of 1907.4.

1944.6   _____. "William Shakespeare: An Epilogue." In *Shakespearean Gleanings.* London: Oxford University Press, pp. 35-51.

Reprint of 1940.3.

1944.7   KERNODLE, GEORGE R. *From Art to Theatre: Form and Convention in the Renaissance.* Chicago: University of Chicago Press, pp. 130-53.

Published version of 1937.4. The relevant section examines the Elizabethan stage in the context of the architectural symbol, along with the Flemish and Spanish popular theatres. Kernodle claims the public stage was similar in many ways to the Flemish Rederyker stage facade, since they were both derived from the same traditions of art and pageantry.

1945

1945.1   JENKIN, BERNARD. "*Antony and Cleopatra*: Some Suggestions on the Monument Scenes." *RES* 21 (January): 1-14.

An imaginative reconstruction of the staging of the monument scenes as Shakespeare saw them. Jenkin concludes that: 1) the First Folio contains two confused versions of the beginning of the scene; 2) the hauling of Antony aloft was required by Shakespeare's source and accepted by him; and 3) the inner stage and upper stage were used in combination in these scenes. See 1964.21.

1945.2   McDOWELL, JOHN H. "Tudor Court Staging: A Study in Perspective." *JEGP* 44 (April): 194-207,
> Considers the causes for the lack of interest in perspective in the Tudor period. McDowell begins with a survey of the Tudor attitudes toward science, then turns to a survey of sixteenth-century court staging practices, which he sees as "multiple staging." He concludes with a discussion of Serlian methods, ultimately disagreeing with Campbell (1923.1) on the use of perspective.

1945.3   SPRAGUE, ARTHUR COLBY. "Off-Stage Sounds." *UTQ* 915 (October): 70-75.
> Discusses how sound effects can enhance mood in the performance of Shakespeare and other dramatists.

1946

1946.1   ADAMS, JOSEPH QUINCY. "The Author-Plot of an Early Seventeenth-Century Play." *Library*, 4th ser. 26 (June): 17-27.
> Discusses and edits the author plot for a tragi-comedy from about 1630, tentatively titled *Philander, King of Thrace*, held in the Folger Shakespeare Library

1946.2   BARBETTI, EMILIO. "Note storiche sul teatro inglese: 'la claque.'" *Anglica* 1 (April-June): 96-99.
> "The existence and organization of the *claque* in the London theatres is traced from Elizabethan times to the present century" (from the English abstract).

1946.3   CHAMBRUN, [CLARA] LONGWORTH. "La compagnie de Shakespeare." *RTh*, no. 2 (August-September):176-86.
> Discusses the evolution of Shakespeare's company, from Lord Strange's Men through the Lord Chamberlain's Men to the King's Men. Chambrun examines the major actors of the company, focusing on Burbage and Kempe, but including an evaluation of Shakespeare as an actor. She includes contemporary portraits of Burbage, Sly, and Lowin.

1946.4   McCALMON, GEORGE. "A Study of the Renaissance and Baroque Factors in the Theatre Style of Inigo Jones." Ph.D.dissertation, Case Western Reserve University, 852 pp.
> Examines the designs for scenery and costumes, tracing Italian and other influences on Jones's work.

1946.5   ORSINI, NAPOLEONE. "La scene italiana in Inghilterra: Il trattato del Serlio." *Anglica* 1 (April-June): 100-02.
> "A mistake in the Jacobean translation of Serlio's treatise on the stage suggests a darker picture of *Cinque-cento* morality than is warranted by the text" (from the English abstract).

1946.6   WATKINS, RONALD. *Moonlight at the Globe*. London: M. Joseph, 135 pp.
          An imaginative reconstruction of an Elizabethan production of
Midsummer Night's Dream, based on J. C. Adams's reconstruction of the Globe
(1942.1). Watkins discusses the stage and its settings, the music, and the
costumes. Of little historical value. Reprinted: 1947.10.

1947

1947.1   BURRELL, JOHN. "Réflexions sur la mise en scène des tragedies de
          Shakespeare." *RTh* 5 (April): 169-70.
          A brief note citing Shakespeare's original staging as justification for
methods employed at the Old Vic in the 1947 season.

1947.2   DAWSON, GILES E. "Copyright of Plays in the Early Seventeenth Century."
          EIE. New York: Columbia University Press, 169-92.
          Discusses the practices of the Stationers' Company and, after 1607, the
Master of the Revels. Dawson discusses both the establishment and the transfer of
copyright, although that particular word is not used until 1734. The copyright
history of *Devil of Edmonton* is traced as an example.

1947.3   ELLIS-FERMOR, UNA M. "The Jacobean Stage." In *The Jacobean Drama:
          An Interpretation*. 2d ed. London: Methuen, pp. 273-83.
          Reprint of 1936.8.

1947.4   GORELIK, MORDECHAI. *New Theatres for Old*. London: Dennis Dobson,
          pp. 100-105.
          Reprint of 1940.5.

1947.5   HODGES, C[YRIL] WALTER. "The Globe Playhouse: Some Notes on a New
          Reconstruction." *TN* 1 (July): 108-11.
          Hodges sets out his differences from Adams (1942.1) on a few small
points. His later reconstructions are more complete and more original. <u>See also</u>
1953.9; 1968.16.

1947.6   MITCHELL, LEE. "Shakespeare's Sound Effects." *SpMon* 14: 127-38.
          Examines the instruments named in Shakespeare's stage directions and the
function of each, and the nonmusical sounds called for and the dramatic purpose
of each. Mitchell lists information on fifteen sound effects and ten instruments,
concluding that there was progressively greater use of sound effects and an
increasing variety of instruments available from the early plays to the late.

1947.7   SABOL, ANDREW JOSEPH. "Music for the English Drama from the
          Beginnings to 1642." Ph.D. dissertation, Brown University, 275 pp.
          Chapters two and three treat secular music in the English drama and music
for the English masque. Sabol not only discusses the music but also provides

many examples culled from contemporary sources. Especially valuable is the music from the boy companies and the music for the masques.

1947.8   SOUTHERN, RICHARD. "Observations on Lansdowne MS. No. 1171." *TN* 2 (October): 6-19.
      Discusses the evidence of the manuscript for the staging of the masques and prints fifteen plates from it. Southern deduces a theory of the pre-Restoration groove from one of the sketches.

1947.9   STURMAN, BERTA. "Renaissance Prompt Copies: *A Looking Glasse for London and England.*" Ph.D. dissertation, University of Chicago, 95 pp.
      Examines an undated copy of the play held at the University of Chicago, which contains manuscript notes in a seventeenth-century hand and was apparently used as a prompt book during the first half of the century. Sturman examines the notes in seven classes: entrances, exits, corrections, properties, sound effects, spectacle, and stage business. All appear to be the work of a single prompter preparing the text for performance and making corrections, perhaps in rehearsal. Other prompt scripts are also considered, and Sturman assigns this revival to Queen Anne's Men in 1606. The third appendix contains a checklist of printed prompt texts.

1947.10   WATKINS, RONALD. *Moonlight at the Globe.* London: M. Joseph, 135 pp.
      Reprint of 1946.6.

1947.11   WILSON, J[OHN] D[OVER], and HUNT, R[ICHARD] W[ILLIAM]. "The Authenticity of Simon Forman's Booke of Plaies." *RES* 23 (July): 193-200.
      Rejects the notion, put forward by Tannenbaum and others, that this document is a Collier forgery. The evidence presented is linguistic and paleographic, Wilson providing the former and Hunt the latter. See also 1849.6; 1876.1; 1907.8; 1919.8: 1959.1.

<u>1948</u>

1948.1   BENTLEY, GERALD EADES. "Shakespeare and the Blackfriars Theatre." *ShS* 1: 38-50.
      Originally a lecture for the Shakespeare Conference, Stratford-upon-Avon August 1947. Bentley places Shakespeare in the context of the London commercial theatre and the organized professional acting troupe, and discusses his relationship with the King's Men's private playhouse. Jonson, Beaumont and Fletcher, and Shakespeare were the playwrights for the new theatre, and Bentley contends that all of Shakespeare's post-1608 plays (*Cymbeline, Winter's Tale, Tempest, Two Noble Kinsmen*) were written with the Blackfriars in mind.

1948.2   BETHEL, S[AMUEL] L[ESLIE]. *Shakespeare and the Popular Dramatic Tradition.* Westminster: P. S. King & Staples, pp. 31-41.
      Reprint of 1944.4.

1948.3   BOWERS, ROBERT H. "Gesticulation in Elizabethan Acting." *SFQ* 12 (Spring): 267-77.

        Generally supports Harbage's theory of "formal" acting in the Elizabethan period (see 1939.4), presenting information from the plays on posture end gesture. See also Index under Acting--Style.

1948.4   BRERETON, J[OHN] LE GAY. "The Elizabethan Playhouse." In *Writings on Elizabethan Drama*. Edited by Robert Guy Howarth. Carlton, Victoria: Melbourne University Press, pp. 81-88.

        A general discussion of the public theatres based on the Swan drawing and of the private theatres based on the *Roxana* and *Messalina* vignettes. See also 1916.2.

1948.5   _____. "Stage-Arrangement in Peele's *David and Bethsabe*, I.i." In *Writings on Elizabethan Drama*. Edited by Robert Guy Howarth. Carlton, Victoria: Melbourne University Press, pp. 93-96.

        Reprint of 1912.3.

1948.6   HODGES, C[YRIL] WALTER. *Shakespeare and the Players*. London: E. Benn, 100 pp.

        A popular treatment for a juvenile audience of Shakespeare's career, including an early Hodges attempt at a conjectural reconstruction of the Globe, complete with inner stages above and below. A detailed discussion of the staging of *Richard III* forms one of the key chapters. Reprinted: 1949.6; second edition: 1970.12. See also Index, under Hodges, for his more serious work on the Globe.

1948.7   McDOWELL, JOIIN H. "Conventions of Medieval Art in Shakespearian Staging." *JEGP* 47 (July): 215-29.

        Discusses the influence of medieval srt on theatres and staging practices of the Elizabethan period. McDowell assumes an inner stage used to localize interiors and relates it to the convention of the "house" structure in art. He similarly relates the curtains used for discoveries, and the iconographic value of stage properties.

1948.8   MITCHELL, LEE. "Shakespeare's Lighting Effects." *SpMon* 15, no. 1: 72-84.

        A reexamination of Shakespearean lighting in terms of the playwright's intentions. Those lights required by the stage action or mentioned in the dialogue are subjected to three questions: 1) what are they; 2) why are they there; and 3) how are they used? Only three different kinds of lights are required: torches, lanterns, and tapers. Mitchell describes four purposes for the use of those lights: chronographic, symbolic, ceremonial, and metaphoric. In answer to the final question, Mitchell finds lights used for important stage business, for spectacle, and for providing imagined stage darkness.

1948.9   [NICOLL, ALLARDYCE.] "A Note on the Swan Theatre Drawing." *ShS* 1: 23-24.

> A brief note transcribing the text accompanies the reproduction.

1948.10   NICOLL, ALLARDYCE. "Studies in the Elizabethan Stage since 1900." *ShS* 1:   1-16.

> Reviews scholarship in the field from 1900 to 1947 with the emphasis on the years following Chambers (1923.2). Nicoll concludes with a section considering "The Needs of the Future."

1948.11   SHAPIRO, I. A. "The Bankside Theatres: Early Engravings." *ShS* 1: 25-38.

> An attempt to survey the pictorial evidence for the sixteenth-century Bankside theatres and collate it with the documentary data. After rejecting several early views as inaccurate, or printed much later, Shapiro uses Norden's *Civitas Londini* to settle the question of the site of the Globe while at the same time rejecting its evidence for polygonal structure. Holler's "Long View," as Braines suggested (see 1924.31, provides reliable evidence of the Bear Garden and the Globe, with the names interchanged.

1948.12   SMITH, WARREN D. "Shakespeare's Stagecraft as Denoted by the Dialogue in the Original Printing of His Plays." Ph.D. dissertation, University of Pennsylvania, 256 pp.

> Revised version published: 1975.29.

1948.13   STRATMAN, CARL J. "Dramatic Performances at Oxford and Cambridge, 1603-1642." Ph.D. dissertation, University of llinois, 416 pp.

> A chronological discussion of professional and amateur theatricals at the two major Universities, based on records of payment and chronologies of events held in Oxford and Cambridge archives.

1948.14   WILSON, J[OHN] DOVER. *"Titus Andronicus* on the Stage in 1595." ShS 1: 17-22.

> Discusses the Peachum illustration and its accompanying text.

1949

1949.1   BACHRACH, A[LFRED] G[USTAV] H[ERBERT]. "The Great Chain of Acting." *Neophil* 33 (Spring): 160-72.

> A review of research on Elizabethan acting, focusing on Bertram Joseph's 1948 lecture series at Oxford on the subject (see1950.10: 1951.18). Bachrach ties acting to the methods of Renaisssnce education and the ideas of Elizabethan psychology. On the whole he describes a formal style. See also Index under Acting--Style.

1949.2   BAKER, RENNIE. "The Structure of the First Globe Theatre." *ShAB* 24
         (April): 106-11.
                 Argues for an octagonal structure for the Globe, on the authority of the
         Fortune contract and pictorial evidence.

1949.3   BENNET, H[ENRY] S[TANI.EYl. "Shakespeare's Stage and Audience."
         Neophil 33 (Winter): 40-51.
                 General discussion of the arrangement and structure of the Elizabethan
         stage and of the nature of the audience. While he cites no sources he is apparently
         indebted to Adams (1942.1) in his description of the inner stage and "tarras." In
         the second section Bennet considers the use made of the stage to change time and
         place at will, and in the third the composition, nature, and expectations of the
         audience.

1949.4   CHILD, HAROLD H. "The Elizabethan Theatre." In *Cambridge History of
         English Literature*. Vol. 6, *The Drama to 1642*, Pt. 2. Edited by A. W. Ward and
         A. R. Weller. Cambridge: University Press, pp. 241-78.
                 Reprint of 1910.5.

1949.5   DARLINGTON, WILLIAM AUBREY. *The Actor and His Audience*. London:
         Phoenix House, pp. 31-35.
                 The relevant section is the first half of Chapter Three, "Burbage and
         Betterton." Darlington bases his evaluation of Burbage's acting on the description
         in Flecknoe (1664.1) and Hamlet's advice to the players, delivered by Burbage
         and presumably describing him.

1949.6   HODGES, C[YRIL] WALTER. *Shakespeare and the Players*. New York:
         Coward-McCann, 101 pp.
                 Reprint of 1948.6.

1949.7   HOPPE, HARRY R. "English Actors at Ghent in the Seventeenth Century."
         REH 25 (October): 305-21.
                 Based on research in the Municipal Archives of Ghent and the Grand
         Archives at Brussels. Records of payments from the city treasury for preview
         performances exist from 1598 on. Several previously unknown English actors on
         the continent performed in Ghent, and several new names are added to the rolls of
         continental performers.

1949.8   HOTSON, [JOHN] LESLIE. "The Projected Amphitheatre." *ShS* 2: 24-35.
                 Discusses the three letters on the subject revealed by Collier and the
         documents printed in 1914.3-4, as well as a new document from the Privy Seal
         office granting a license to build the Amphitheatre. In addition to combats
         and animal acts, the buiding was also to house plays presented by a regular acting
         troupe, perhaps the King's Men. The building was to seat 12,000, at a cost of
         £12,000. The license, however, was stayed in 1626; another attempt to build the
         Amphitheatre was made in 1634, and another at a later time. Hotson presents new

documentary evidence for these last three. The building was, of course, never constructed.

1949.9   KIRSCHBAUM, LEO. "Shakespeare's Stage Blood and Its Critical Significance." *PMLA* 61 (June): 517-29.
Considers the implications of the particularly bloody scenes in *Julius Caesar* and *Coriolanus*, concluding that Shakespeare intended the blood to be displayed on the stage for the purpose of amplifying the theatricality of the moment.

1949.10   MANLY, J[OHN] M[ATTHEWS]. "The Children of the Chapel Royal and Their Masters." In *Cambridge History of English Literature*. Vol. 6, *The Drama to 1642*. Pt. 2. Edited by A. W. Ward and A. R. Waller. Cambridge: University Press, pp. 279-92.
Reprint of 1910.12.

1949.11   McDOWELL, JOHN H. "Medieval Influences in Shakespearian Staging." *Players* 26 (December): 52-53.
Identifies the "inner stage" with the medieval mansion, advocating the alternation theory.

1949.12   MITCHELL, LEE. "Shakespeare's Legerdemain." *SpMon* 16 (August): 144-61.
An examination of Shakespeare's use of magic. Mitchell finds that ventriloquism, levitation, and the illusion of vanishing, among other techniques, were used to mystify--and hence to entertain--the audience. The cauldron scene in Macbeth and the banquet scene in are examples of important uses of illusion. Magic was always well integrated into the scene and never in Shakespeare was used for its own sake.

1949.13   REYNOLDS, GEORGE F[ULLMER]. "Staging Elizabethan Plays." *Listener* 42 (11 August): 223-24.
A radio broadcast on the BBC Third Programme. Reynolds discusses the division of plays into a large number of short scenes and the unchanging background for the action that could accommodate any and all locations. Reprinted: 1949.14.

1949.14   ____. "Staging Elizabethan Plays." *ShAB* 24 (October): 258-63.
Reprint of 1949.13.

1949.15   SHAPIRO, I. A. "An Original Drawing of the Globe Theatre." *ShS* 2: 21-23.
Reprints and discusses Hollar's drawing of the Globe that served as the basis for his "Long View." See also 1933.11.

1949.16   WILSON, EDWARD M., and TURNER, OLGA. "The Spanish Protest against *A Game at Chesse*." *MLR* 44 (October): 476-82.
        Prints "two reports sent to Madrid by the Spanish Ambassador in London" pertaining to the scandal caused by this play, with translations.

1949.17   WILSON, J[OHN] D[OVER]. "The Puritan Attack on the Stage." In *Cambridge History of English Literature*. Vol. 6, *The Drama to 1642*. Pt. 2. Edited by A. W. Ward and A. R. Waller. Cambridge: University Press, pp. 373-409.
        Reprint of 1910.26.

1950

1950.1   ARCHER, WILLIAM, and LAWRENCE, W[ILLIAMl J[OHN]. "The Playhouse." In *Shakespeare's England: An Account of the Life and Manners of His Age*. Vol. 2. Edited by Sidney Lee, Charles Talbut Onions, and Walter A. Raleigh. Oxford: Clarendon Press, pp. 283-310.
        Reprint of 1916.1.

1950.2   BETHEL, S[AMUEL] L[ESLIE]. "Shakespeare's Actors." *RES*, n.s. 1 (July): 193-205.
        Based on a paper read at the Shakespeare Association Conference at Stratford-upon-Avon in the summer of 1948. Bethel reexamines the known facts and theories about the casting of Shakespeare's plays and the style of Elizabethan acting. He doubts the existence of "lines" for actors (see Baldwin, 1927.1) and sides with the proponents of the "formal" school of acting.

1950.3   BROCK, JAMES WILSON. "A Study of the Use of Sound Effects in Elizabethan Drama." Ph.D. dissertation, Northwestern University, 156 pp.
        Analyzes musical and nonmusical sound effects in Elizabethan drama "in terms of their dramatic purpose, function, and use." Brock eliminates orchestral interludes, songs, and dance as stage music instead of sound effects. The five major parts examine the dramatic purpose of sound effects; the functions as specified in stage directions; conjectural effects, based an references in the texts; the production of sound effects; and their employment in the plays. Brock concludes that the Elizabethan audience readily accepted a wider range of conventional sound effects than does the contemporary audience, that effects were less important in comedy, and that the function of sound effects in the Elizabethan theatre is paralleled by their function in radio drama and film.

1950.4   BROMBERG, MURRAY. "The Reputation of Philip Henslowe." *SQ* 1 (Autumn): 135-39.
        Examines Henslowe's contemporary reputation, attempting to show that he was not being satirized in Day's *Parliament of Bees*, as Fleay and Chambers thought.

1950.5   BROOK, DONALD. *A Pageant of English Actors*. London: Rockliffe, pp. 9-35.

   The relevant section is the first four chapters, biographies of Richard Burbage, Richard Tarlton, William Kenpe, and Edward Alleyn. Brook uses only secondary sources in this work for a popular audience.

1950.6   CHILD, HAROLD H. "The Elizabethan Theatre." In *Cambridge History of English Literature*. Vol. 6, *The Drama to 1642*. Pt. 2. Edited by A. W. Ward and A. R. Waller. Cambridge: University Press, pp. 241-78.
   Reprint of 1910.5.

1950.7   FELDMAN, ABRAHAM. "Hans Ewouts, Artist of the Tudor Court Theatre." *N&Q* 195 (10 June): 257-58.

   A biographical sketch of the Dutch painter who influenced the Elizabethan theatre. Ewouts was in the service of the court theatre in 1572-74. Feldman conjectures that the anonymous *Wisdom of Doctor Dodypoll* has a Dutch character based on the painter.

*1950.8   FRONIUS, HANS. *Zeichungen um Shakespeare*. Vienna-Linz: Gurlit Verlag.
   Cited in 1963.14. Eight lithographs of Shakespeare and the Globe playhouse.

1950.9   HODGES, C[YRIL] WALTER. "Unworthy Scaffolds: A Theory for the Reconstruction of Elizabethan Playhouses." *ShS* 3: 83-94.

   Examines the evidence for the platform itself, rather than the tiring house facade. Hodges suggests the booth stage as the prototype for the Platform. The Swan drawing, and the Fortune contract support this view. He suggests that large props and horses may have been brought into the yard.

1950.10   JOSEPH, BERTRAM R. "How the Elizabethans Acted Shakespeare." *Listener* 43 (5 January): 17-18.

   A radio broadcast on the BBC Third Programme. Joseph argues for a formal acting style based on John Bulwer's *Chirologia* and *Chironamia*. See also 1951.18 and Index under Acting--Style.

1950.11   LEECH, CLIFFORD [E. J.] "The Caroline Audience." In *Shakespeare's Tragedies and Other Studies in Seventeenth-Century Drama*. London: Chatto & Windus, pp.   159-81.
   Reprint of 1941.5.

1950.12   LÜDEKE, H[ENRY]. "Shakespeares Globus-Theater: Nach den neuesten Ergebuissen der Forschung." *JDSG* 84-86: 131-39.

   Discusses the needs of a reconstruction of the Globe, along with photographs of a model built to Adams's specifications (see 1942.1).

1950.13   MANLY, J[OHN] M[ATTHEWS]. "The Children of the Chapel and Their Masters." In *Cambridge History of English Literature*. Vol. 6, *The Drama to 1642*. Pt. 2. Edited by A. W. Ward and A. R. Waller. Cambridge: University Press, pp. 279-92.
          Reprint of 1910.12.

1950.14   PURDOM, C. B. *Producing Shakespeare*. London: Sir Isaac Pitman & Sons, 220 pp.
          Intended primarily as a guide to the modern director, containing historical backgroud culled from secondary sources only.

1950.15   ROBERTS, J. R. H., and GODFREY, W[ILLIAM] H., eds. *London County Council Survey of London*, no. 22. London: London County Council, pp. 66-77.
          Chapter Eight, "The Bankside Playhouses and Bear Gardens," contains a brief review of Braines and Chambers on the Rose, the Swan, and the Globe, with one or two new pieces of information added. The building of the Rose Playhouse is set at 1588 rather than 1592, on the basis of a Sewer Commission order, and Shakespeare's supposed residence in Southwark (proposed by Malone and Collier), while not here disproved, cannot be verified, because of documents either forged or no longer extant.

1950.16   SIMPSON, PERCY. "Actors and Acting." In *Shakespeare's England: An Account of the Life and Manners of his Age*. Vol. 2. Edited by Sidney Lee, Charles Talbut Onions, and Walter A. Raleigh. Oxford: Clarendon Press, pp. 240-82.
          Reprint of 1916.14.

1950.17   _____. "The Masque." In *Shakespeare's England: An Account of the Life and Manners of his Age*. Vol. 2. Edited by Sidney Lee, Charles Talbut Onions, and Walter A. Raleigh. Oxford: Clarendon Press, pp. 311-33.
          Reprint of 1916.15.

1950.18   TRIEBEL, L. A. "Sixteenth-Century Stagecraft in European Drama: A Survey." *MLQ* 11 (March): 7-16.
          A general treatment, primarily of continental medieval staging, but venturing into Elizabethan staging via the Swan drawing. Triebel, however, subscribes to the "inner below" and alternation theories, without citing evidence.

1950.19   WATKINS, RONAI.D. *On Producing Shakespeare*. London: Michael Joseph; New York: Norton, 335 pp.
          Discusses elements of Shakespearean stagecraft, concentrating on methods of staging and acting. Watkins summarizes Adams (1942.1) as his discussion of the playhouse, but is more original (if anecdotal) in other areas. As he did earlier with *Midsummer Night's Dream* (1946.6). Watkins gives a complete description of the staging of *Macbeth*.

1950.20   WENTERSDORF, KARL. "Shakespeares erste Truppe: Ein Beitrag zur
            Aufklärung des Problems der sog. 'verlorenen Jahre.'" *JDSG* 84-86: 114-30.
                In an attempt to fill in the "lost years" in Shakespeare's biography,
            Wentersdorf examines the possibility that he was a member of Penbroke's Men.

1950.21   WILSON, [JOHN] D[OVER]. "The Puritan Attack on the Stage." In
            Cambridge History of English Literature. Vol. 6, *The Drama to 1642*. Pt. 2.
            Edited by A. W. Ward and A. R. Waller. Cambridge: University Press. 373-409.
            Reprint of 1910.26.

1951

1951.1   ADAMS, JOHN CRANFORD. "'That Virtuous Fabric.'" *SQ* 32 (Winter): 3-11.
                Adapted from a lecture at the Folger Shakespeare Library on 23 April
            1950, presenting Adams's reconstruction. See also 1942.1.

1951.2   ALDUS, PAUL JOHN. "The Use of Physical Comic Means in English Drama
            from 1420 to 1603." Ph.D. dissertation, University of Chicago, 207 pp.
                Discusses three types of physical comedy: simple episodic routines,
            complex episodic routines, and connate routines (by which he means "relevant to
            the mainstream of the play"), as well as the use of properties for comic effect,
            physical scenes of improbability and reversal, and the evolution of physical to
            verbal means. Part of his conclusions concern the vast increase in the use of
            physical comedy in plays after 1590.

1951.3   BROMBERG, MURRAY. "Theatrical Wagers: A Sidelight on the Elizabethan
            Drama." *N&Q* 196 (8 December): 533-35.
                Examines various types of theatrical wagers, including those between
            actors and playwrights, from a variety of contemporary sources.

1951.4   BROWN, ARTHUR. "A Note on Sebastian Westcott and the Plays Presented
            by the Children of Paul's." *MLQ* 12 (March): 134-36.
                A refutation of Brawner's contention (in 1943.3) that Sebastian Westcott
            was the author of several plays performed by Paul's Boys while they were under
            his direction.

1951.5   BUDDE, FRITZ. "Shakespeare und die Prage der Raumbühne." In
            Studien: Festschrift für Heinrich Mutschmann. Edited by Walther Fischer and
            Karl Wentersdorf. Marburg: N. G. Elwert, pp. 21-47.
                The question-of stage space referred to in the title is the question of
            scenery. Budde compares the modern illusionistic theatre with Shakespeare's
            staging, finding the latter much more flexible.

1951.6   CAPOCCI, VALENTINA. "Poeti e attori nel drams elisabettiano." *Il Ponte* 7 (December): 1593-1600.
   Examines the roles of the playwright and the improvisations of the actor in Elizabethan drama, with examples drawn from Shakespeare, Marlowe, Jonson, and Brome.

1951.7   CHAPMAN, RAYMOND. "*Twelfth Night* and the Swan Theatre." *N&Q* 196 (27 October): 468-70.
   Examines the possibility of an early version of *Twelfth Night* at the Swan, seen by DeWitt in 1596 and serving as the basis for the Swan drawing. Chapman suggests that this early version was the lost *Love's Labours Won*, with the plot as described by Jonson in *Every Man Out of His Humour*.

1951.8   DOWNER, ALAN S. "The Tudor Actor: A Taste of His Quality." *TN* 5 (April): 76-81.
   Originally a paper read at the MLA convention in 1950, concerning acting in the interludes.

1951.9   EDINBOROUGH, ARNOLD. "The Early Tudor Revels Office." *SQ* 2 (Winter): 19-25.
   Examines the history of the Revels Office from approximately 1540 to 1552. Inventories of the office, the accounts of specific court functions, and the accounts of the building of a banqueting house in 1552 are presented.

1951.10   EMPSON, WILLIAM. "The Staging of *Hamlet*." *TLS* (23 November): 749.
   Suggests that Shakespeare wanted to stage the closet scene in the balcony but the players wouldn't allow such an important scene to be played in an auxiliary playing space.

1951.11   FLATTER, RICHARD. "The Dumb-Show in *Macbeth*." *TLS* (23 March): 181.
   Suggests that the eighth king (who would have been James) held a mirror up for the King to see himself.

1951.12   ____. "Outer, Inner, or Upper Stage?" *ShQ* 2 (Spring): 171.
   Questions some of J. C. Adams's pronouncements in 1951.1 on where particular scenes took place, with a request for some substantiation for such assertions.

1951.13   FREEMAN, SIDNEY LEE. "The Forms of the Non-Proscenium Theatre: Their History and Theories." Ph.D. dissertation, Cornell University, pp. 29-32, passim.
   The relevant section discusses the actor-audience relationship in general terms; throughout the rest of the study there are occasional references to the Elizabethan theatre.

1951.14   GRAY, CECIL G. "Shakespeare's Co-Plaintiffs in the Blackfriars Lawsuit of 1615." *N&Q* 196 (10 November): 490-91.

Identifies the first three complainants as Sir Thomas Bendishe, Edward Newport, and William Thoresbie, who owned land in the neighborhood of Dunmow.

1951.l5   _____. "The Sixteenth-Century Burbages of Stratford on Avon." *N&Q* 196 (10 November): 490.

Using a Court of Requests suit of 1610, shows that the John Burbage, bailiff of Stratford-on-Avon in 1555, was not related to the William Burbage who was a tenant of Shakespeare's father.

*1951.16   HAYWARD, WAYNE CLINTON. "The Globe Theatre, 1599-1608." Ph.D. dissertation, University of Birmingham, 215 pp.

Cited in *DEAL*, p. 476.

1951.17   HODGES, C[YRIL] WALTER. "DeWitt Again." *TN* 5 (January): 32-34.

A brief note evaluating the Swan drawing. Hodges finds that the drawing presents us with "a large area of reliable information," despite some undecipherable or uncertain elements.

1951.18   JOSEPH, B[ERTRAM] R. *Elizabethan Acting*. Oxford English Monographs. London: Oxford University Press, 157 pp.

Examines Elizabethan acting from the point of view of rhetorical training. Joseph finds that there were specified manners of speech and gesture for each role, and that Elizabethan acting was far more formal than what we would accept as natural. See also 1950.10; second edition, 1964.25. For the entire controversy over this subject, see Index under Acting--Style.

1951.19   LELYVELD, TOBY BOOKHOLZ. "Shylock on the Stage: Significant Changes in the Interpretation of Shakespeare's Jew." Ph.D. dissertation, Columbia University, 196 pp.

Traces the significant changes in the manner in which Shylock has been interpreted in *Merchant of Venice* in England and America. While there is a discussion of the place of the Jew in Elizabethan society, there is no actual evidence presented for this period.

1951.20   LINN, JOHN GAYWOOD. "The Court Masque and Elizabethan Dramatic Structure." Ph.D. dissertation, Cornell University, 184 pp.

The four major chapters treat the masque before 1595; the masque 1595-1604; and the relationship between the masque and the drama in both periods. Linn concludes that the sharing of elements is not synonymous with "influence," and that prior to the period of the great Jacobean masques there was far less influence in terms of form than has previously been assumed.

*1951.21   LONG, JOHN H. "Shakespeare's Use of Music: A Study of the Music and Its Performance in the Original Performances of Seven Comedies." Ph.D. dissertation, University of Florida, 184 pp.
        Cited in *ADDT*, p. 58.

1951.22   McMANAWAY, JAMES G. "A New Shakespeare Document." *SQ* 2 (Spring): 119- 22.
        A warrant from the Lord Chamberlain for payment to the King's Men, and the schedule of twenty-one plays presented at the Cockpit-in-Court annexed to it.

1951.23   PRIOR, MOODY E. "The Elizabethan Audience and the Plays of Shakespeare." *MP* 49 (November): 101-23.
        Attacks most studies of the audience for having preconceived ideas and engaging in circular reasoning, and surveys attempts to deal with the audience's effect on the plays. A general failing in this type of criticism, Prior says, is a lack of understanding of the limits of the method. See also Index under Audience.

1951.24   PURDOM, C. B. "The Dumb-Show in *Macbeth*." *TLS* (20 April): 245.
        Responds to Ure (1951.31) and Flatter (1951.11).

1951.25   REYNOLDS, GEORGE F[ULLMER]. "Was There a 'Tarras' in Shakespeare's Globe?" *ShS* 4: 97-100.
        The "tarras"--the front part of the balcony in most reconstructions of the Globe, stretching more than twenty feet from window to window, three or four feet deep (as in Adams, 1942.1)--is examined. Reynolds finds little evidence for such a structure, suggesting that the context of references to the "tarras" is always theatrical, and that one upper acting area would suffice for all uses. He blames the arguments for the tarras on insistence on modern realistic conventions in the Elizabethan period, which is inappropriate.

1951.26   RICHEY, DOROTHY. "The Dance in the Drama of the Elizabethan Public Theatre: A Production Problem." Ph.D. dissertation, Northwestern University, 212 pp.
        Examines those dances that form an integral part of the plots of Elizabethan plays presented at the public playhouses and reconstructs, complete with choreographic charts, the specific dances suggested by stage directions and lines of dialogue. The five chapters deal with the pavane, measures, alman, cordion, galliard, volt, basse-danse, morris, sword, country dances, coranto, brawl, canary, jig, hornpipe, and round. While historical information is included, this study is of more use to the director than the theatre historian.

1951.27   SHIELD, H. A. "Links With Shakespeare, VII." *N&Q* 196 (19 June): 250-52.
        An attempt to identify Agnes Bennet, named in Augustine Phillips's will.

1951.28   SMITH, IRWIN. "Notes of the Construction of the Globe Model." *SQ* 2 (Winter): 13-18.
          Adapted from a speech delivered at the Hofstra College Shakespeare Festival, 24 March 1950, explaining some of the decisions behind details of the Adams model of the Globe. <u>See</u> 1942.1.

1951.29   SMITH, WARREN D. "Evidence of Scaffolding on Shakespeare's Stage." *RES*, n.s. 2 (January): 22-29.
          Presents textual evidence for a raised platform on the Globe stage from *Hamlet, Richard III, Troilus and Cressida, Julius Caesar,* and *Antony and Cleopatra.* Smith envisions a smell portable platform, perhaps with three steps up. The same platform would bear the throne of state when it was required.

1951.30   STAMM, RUDOLF. *Geschichte des englischen Theaters.* Bern: A Francke, pp. 55-115.
          The relevant section discusses the theatre of Shakespeare's time. Stam is more concerned with the drama than the theatre, despite the title, but he does attempt to place the drama in its theatrical context. He includes general discussions of playhouses and acting, depending heavily on Chambers (1923.2), Bentley (1941.1), and Hotson (1928.7), among others.

1951.31   URE, PETER. "The Dumb-Show in *Macbeth.*" *TLS* (6 April): 213.
          Responds to Flatter (1951.11). <u>See</u> 1951.24.

1951.32   VENEZKY, ALICE S. "Pageantry on the Shakespearean Stage." Ph.D. dissertation, Columbia University, 242 pp.
          Published: 1951.33.

1951.33   _____. *Pageantry on the Shakespearean Stage.* New York: Twayne, 242 pp.
          Published version of 1951.32. Analyzes the influence of the most popular forms of public display--the procession, pageant, and progress--on the Elizabethan drama, 1581-1603. The four major chapters cover entries and triumphs; royal receptions; pageants, progresses, and plays; and Shakespeare's use of pageant imagery. Venezky hopes her "comparative examination" will "reveal a fuller significance in many scenes" and "contribute to the appreciation and enjoyment of Shakespeare in the study and upon the stage."

<u>1952</u>

1952.1   BALD, R[OBERT] C[ECIL]. "The Entrance to the Elizabethan Theatre." *SQ* 3 (Winter): 17-20.
          Speculates on the location of the entrances to the Elizabethan public theatres, concluding that there were two, one on each side, located with the external staircases. The speculation is based on the Swan drawing and the Hollar "Long View" engraving.

1952.2　BORDINAT, PHILIP. "A Study of the Salisbury Court Theatre." Ph.D. dissertation, University of Birmingham, 280 pp.

Examines the last of the pre-Commononwealth playhouses. The six major chapters deal with the history of the building, its structure and use, the structure of the stage, production techniques at this playhouse, and the use of the playhouse after the Restoration. Bordinat finds that the staging methods used--two doors, an inner stage, an upper stage, and a trap, properties and costumes utilized for purposes of dramatic illusion, one use of partial scenery--were standard for the period.

1952.3　BROWN, ARTHUR. "Sebastian Westcott at York." *MLR* 47 (January): 49-50.

A brief note announcing discovery of a document in York allowing Westcott, Master of the Children of St. Paul's in the 1550s, to take children into his group from anywhere in the realm.

1952.4　CROUCH, JACK HERBERT. "Some Shakespearean Stage Conventions Developed from a Study of the Architectural Antecedents of the Elizabethan Public-Outdoor Playhouse and a Staging Study of *Romeo and Juliet* and *Antony and Cleopatra*." Ph.D. dissertation, Cornell University, pp. 1-73, 253-83.

The relevant sections discuss the general features of the public playhouses and relate them to "manorial-domestic architecture," especially the great hall and its screen.

1952.5　FELDMAN, ABRAHAM BRONSON. "Dutch Theatrical Architecture in Elizabethan London." *N&Q* 197 (11 October): 444-46.

Discusses Dutch influence on the Elizabethan public stage, including the Rhetoric Theatres and the Dutch heritage of Peter Street, Burbage's carpenter.

1952.6　FURNISS, W[ARREN] TODD. "Ben Jonson's Masques and Entertainments." Ph.D. dissertation, Yale University, 290 pp.

Essentially a literary analysis of Jonson's masques, concluding that the masques fit into the tradition of the literature of monarchy, with its unconventional imagery and typical methods. While the study is interesting in itself, it is of little theatrical value.

1952.7　GREENSLADE, S. L. "The Elizabethan Theatre." *TLS* (25 April): 281.

Two payments to players from the Chapter Vouchers, Durham Cathedral, 1590-91.

1952.8　HARBAGE, ALFRED. *Shakespeare and the Rival Traditions*. New York: Macmillan, 393 pp.

Presents "a new synthesis of the facts about Elizabethan theatres and the content of Elizabethan plays, as a means of defining Shakespeare's materials and intentions." The main point is the duality of Elizabethan drama and theatre: the popular plays of the public stage are contrasted to the "coterie" plays of the private stage, and the companies, repertories, and styles of the rivals are also contrasted.

1952.9   HOSKING, GEORGE LLEWELLYN. *The Life and Times of Edward Alleyn.* London: Jonathan Cape, 285 pp.
      The first thirteen chanters (pp. 17-133) contain the relevant information about Alleyn's theatrical career, based primarily on the records held at Dulwich College. The most complete information concerns Alleyn's partnership with Henslowe. Essentially a popular biography coupled with a history of the College.

1952.10   HOSLEY, RICHARD. "A Stage Direction in *Romeo and Juliet.*" *TLS* (13 June): 391.
      Sets the entrance of the musicians at IV.v.95 rather than IV.v.32, on the authority of the "bad" first quarto.

1952.11   HOTSON, [JOHN] LESLIE. "False Faces on Shakespeare's Stage." *TLS* (16 May): 336.
      Asserts that the curtains for discoveries were drawn by two disguised stage-keepers who were visible to the audience throughout the performance. Further, the visors they wore were often used on stage for purposes of disguise.

1952.12   _____. *Shakespeare's Motley.* London: Hart-Davis; New York: Oxford University Press. 133 pp.
      Examines the fool and his clothing, finding that the "motley coat" was a long coat of mixed color, like tweed. The most important chapter is the last, "Robert Armin, Shakespeare's Fool," which examines the life and works of the actor.

1952.13   MEAD, ROBERT SMITH. "A Study of Factors Influencing the Development of Acting Techniques in England, 1576-1642, with Applications to the Problems of Educational Theatre." Ph.D. dissertation, Northwestern University, 306 pp.
      An attempt at a comprehensive view of all factors affecting the actor's work during the period. The first six chapters introduce the study and examine the changing political and social conditions and the development of acting style and technique. Mead concludes that "Elizabethan acting changed greatly during the period and developed into an art during the last two decades of the sixteenth century."

1952.14   SAUNDERS, F. R. "Capacity of the Second Globe Theatre." *TLS* (14 November): 743.
      Presents contemporary evidence from the Spanish State Archives (first published in 1949.16) that the Globe held 3000 people for each of four performances of *A Game at Chess*, 1624.

1952.15   SCHLESS, HOWARD H. "False Faces on Shakespeare's Stage." *TLS* (6
         June): 377.
                   Responds to Hotson (1952.11).

1952.16   SEMPER, I. J. "Jacobean Playhouses and Catholic Clerics." *Month*, n.s. 8
         (July): 28-39.
                   Examines the controversy over playhouse attendance by secular priests in
         1617 and 1618, based on manuscripts held in the Folger Shakespeare Library.
         William Harrison, on 9 March 1617/18, prohibited their attendance; Thomas
         Lake, on 25 April 1618, wrote a letter of protest; and John Colleton, Harrison's
         assistant, replied. While the grounds of the prohibition are similar to the protests
         of the Puritans, Semper maintains that as a general rule Catholics did not
         disapprove of the drama; the prohibition of attendance had more to do with
         maintaining a low profile in London. See also 1952.17.

1952.17   _____. "The Jacobean Theatre through the Eyes of Catholic Clerics." *SQ* 3
         (Winter): 45-51.
                   Discusses the controversy among Catholic clerics about attending the
         theatre in the early seventeenth century, based on a manuscript held at the Folger
         Shakespeare Library. The prohibition sparked a lively and learned debate, and
         was finally lifted in 1618. See also1952.16.

1952.18   SMITH, IRWIN. "Theatre into Globe." *SQ* 3 (Spring): 113-20.
                   Examines the transformation of the Theatre into the Globe, based on a
         study of Tudor joinery and carpenter's marks. Smith concludes that Peter Street
         supervised the tearing down and transportation of the timbers, and that the basic
         frame of the building was reproduced exactly on the new site.

1952.19   SOUTHERN, RICHARD. *Changeable Scenery: Its Origin and Development
         in the British Theatre.* London: Faber & Faber. 411 pp.
                   Partly based on twelve unpublished volumes by W. J. Lawrence, written
         from 1887 to 1912, and presented to Southern by Lawence in 1939. The relevant
         section in this comprehensive history is Part One, "The Rise of Changeable
         Scenery at Court." The six chapters in this section treat an overview of the field;
         the static scene, the house, and the moving cloud; the rise of the shutter and its
         frame; the grooves; the so-called "scenes of relieve;" and the great scenic
         controversy between Jonson and Jones. Part One includes detailed discussions of
         the designs of Inigo Jones.

1952.20   _____, and HODGES, C[YRIL] WALTER. "Colour in the Elizabethan
         Theatre." *TN* 6 (January): 57-59.
                   Southern contributes a note on imitation marbled classical columns in the
         Swan, while Hodges briefly discusses a seventeenth-century ceiling possibly
         related to the decorated "heavens" of the public theatre.

1952.21   WALKER, JOHN ANTHONY. "The Functions of Stage Lighting in the
           Changing Concepts of Stage Design." Ph.D. dissertation, Cornell University, pp.
           112-36.
                    The relevant section is Chapter Three, section B, which examines lighting
           in Renaissance England. The most important discussion is of Inigo Jones and
           lighting in the court masques. See also 1976.10.

1952.22   WHITE, ERIC WALTER. "A Note on the Reconstruction of Farce Jigs." TN
           26 (January): 39-42.
                    Briefly reviews the current state of knowledge of both text and music of
           the Elizabethan jig, suggesting that "there is enough material extant for some of
           these jigs to be edited for stage performance today."

1953

1953.1   BECKERMAN, BERNARD. "The Globe Playhouse at Hofstra College, II:
           Notes on Direction." ETJ 5 (March): 6-11.
                    Discusses mounting productions on the full-sized reproduction of J. C.
           Adams's reconstruction of the Globe. See also 1942.1; 1953.27.

1953.2   BROWN, JOHN RUSSELL. "On the Acting of Shakespeare's Plays." QJS 39
           (December): 477-84.
                    Argues for an essentially "natural" style, "although some vestiges of an old
           formalism remained." Brown believes that there was a development of methods.
           Here he attempts to answer objections to his position, citing a variety of
           contemporary texts in support. See also Index under Acting--Style. Reprinted:
           1968.3.

1953.3   CLINTON-BADDELEY, V. C. "Elizabethan Players in Sherborne." TN 7
           (July): 83.
                    Draws attention to several entries in the account books from the former
           Church House, showing payments to actors from 1571 to 1603. The Long Room,
           in which they played, still exists.

1953.4   DeBANKE, CECILE. Shakespearean Stage Production: Then and Now. New
           York: McGraw-Hill, 342 pp.
                    The four parts examine staging, actors and acting, costume, and music and
           dance, both in Shakespeare's time and in the 1950s. DeBanke depends largely on
           the work of others, especially J. C. Adams (1942.1). The work is intended as an
           aid to modern staging rather than a piece of historical scholarship.

1953.5   ELLIS-FERMOR, UNA M. "The Jacobean Stage." In The Jaeobean Drama:
           An Interpretation. 3d ed. London: Methuen, pp. 273-83.
                    Reprint of 1936.8.

1953.6　FELDMAN, ABRAHAM B. "Playwrights and Pike-Trailers in the Low Countries." *N&Q* 198 (May): 184-87.

Examines possible Low Country war experiences of George Gascoigne, Christopher Marlowe, and Ben Jonson.

1953.7　FLATTER, RICHARD. "Shakespeare, der Schauspieler." *JDSG* 89: 35-50.

Examines the documentary and textual evidence for Shakespeare as an actor. Flatter argues that the texts of the plays show clear signs of Shakespeare's sensitivity to the sound of his words and pause patterns, a sensitivity that would have been enhanced by his acting experience.

1953.8　HARBAGE, ALFRED. "Shakespeare's Inner Stage." *RenN* 6 (Summer): 18-19.

Abstract of Harbage's response to two papers (including 1953.13) presented at the New England Conference on Renaissance Studies, 24 April 1953. He concludes by stating that the idea of the "inner stage" may be overemphasized.

1953.9　HODGES, C[YRIL] WALTER. *The Globe Restored: A Study of the Elizabethan Theatre.* London: Ernest Benn, 199 pp.

A conjectural reconstruction of the first Globe, especially interesting because of the author's awareness of the problems of reconstruction and his gathering of relevant evidence. Hodges devotes his central chapters to the platform and the tiring house, breaking with Adams (1942.1) over the "inner stage" and agreeing with Reynolds (1940.10) that a portable curtained booth might have been used for discoveries and scenes above. See also revised edition, 1968.16.

1953.10　_____. "Some Comments upon Dr. Leslie Hotson's 'Shakespeare Arena.'" *ShStage* 3 (December): 26-29.

A detailed review of Hotson's 1953.11.

1953.11　HOTSON, [JOHN] LESLIE. "Shakespeare's Arena." *SR* 61 (Summer): 347-61.

Presents Hotson's theory on the use of mansions in the medieval manner set forth on the platform stage for interior and above scenes, with the audience on all four sides. This idea is further developed in 1959.9.

1953.12　_____., ed. *Queen Elizabeth's Entrtainment at Mitcham: Poet, Painter and Musician.* New Haven: Yale University Press, 57 pp.

An edition of the manuscript entertainment of 12-13 September 1598, from the British Library. Hotson includes historical and descriptive notes.

1953.13　HOTSON, [JOHN] LESLIE. "Shakespeare's Arena-Stage at Court." *RenN* 6 (Summer): 17-18.

A summary of 1953.11, delivered at the New England Conference on Renaissance Studies, 24 April 1953. See also 1953.8 for Harbage's response.

1953.14   KREMPEL, DANIEL SPARTAKUS. "The Theatre in Relation to Art and to the Social Order from the Middle Ages to the Present." Ph.D. dissertation, University of Illinois, 373 pp.

      The chapter dealing with the Elizabethan theatre treats it primarily as an extension of medieval practice.

1953.15   MARKWARD, WILLIAM BRADLEY. "A Study of the Phoenix Theatre in Drury Lane, 1617-1638." Ph.D. dissertation, University of Birmingham, 683 pp.

      Examines the Phoenix (or Cockpit) Playhouse in Drury Lane 1617-1638, with particular stress on the staging of the plays. The six main chapters treat the history of the playhouse, the evidence presented by the plays acted there, the structure of the stage, the use of auditory and visual effects, and the audience. Markward concludes that the Phonix stage was divided in the Adams manner into an outer stage, an inner stage, and an upper stage. Properties, sound effects, costumes, and even make-up were frequently used to create realistic effects. The dates of the study reflect the initial adaptation of the cockpit into a theatre and the death of the building's leaseholder and manager, Christopher Beeston.

1953.16   McCULLEN, JOSEPH T., Jr. "The Use of Parlor and Tavern Games in Elizabethan and Early Tudor Drama." *MLQ* 14 (March): 7-14.

      A survey of the use of card games, dice, chess, backgammon, and so on, in the Elizabethan and Jacobean theatre. The use of games on stage became a convention used to promote dramatic action and provide variety. See also 1953.23.

1953.17   MEADLEY, T. D. "Attack on the Theatre (*circa* 1580-1680)." *LQHR* 178 (January): 36-41.

      A general discussion of government regulation and Puritan opposition.

*1953.18   MÖHRING, HANS. "Als Shakespeare zu uns kam. Shakespeare-Aufführungen englischer Komödianten in Deutschland." *Theater der Zeit* 8, no. 12 (December): 6-12.

      Cited in 1963.14.

1953.19   PROUTY, CHARLES TYLER. "An Early Elizabethan Play-House." *ShS* 6, 64-74.

      Discusses the Accounts of the Churchwardens of St. Bodolph without Aldersgate, which demonstrate that a playhouse was set up in Trinity Hall from 1557 to 1568, and apparently used by the provincial companies when performing in London. Prouty prints a plan and elevation of the building and suggests that a curtain hung from the gallery.

1953.20   ROTHWELL, WILLIAM FRANCIS, Jr, "Methods of Production in the English Theatre from 1550-1598." Ph.D. dissertation, Yale University, 496 pp.

      Examines the staging methods, stage picture, and physical conditions of the Elizabethan stage before 1598 in light of English medieval practices. First

Rothwell discusses the "courtly" theatre, defined as the court, the schools, and the private playhouses, finding precedents among the traditional mysteries, the civic pageants, and the masques for staging methods after 1550. The Italian influence was minimal. Next Rotbwell examines the public theatres, tracing the traditional staging methods employed to the stage of the processional mysteries, with a stage house (mansion) and forestage. He concludes that Elizabethan production methods are rooted in the medieval methods, not the Italian.

1953.21   SMITH, WARREN D. "The Elizabethan Stage and Shakespeare's Entrance Announcements." *SQ* 4 (Autumn): 405-10.
      Examines entrance announcements such as "Look where he comes," concluding that they served as a cue for actors already on the platform to move forward.

1953.22   _____. "Stage Business in Shakespeare's Dialogue." *SQ* 4 (Summer): 311-16.
      Examines the nearly 3000 directions for stage business in the dialogue (as opposed to the less than 300 marginal notations), concluding that such implied directions are actually descriptions for members of the audience who could not see the action on stage at the moment.

1953.23   SOLEM, DELMAR E. "Indoor Game Scenes in the Elizabethan Drama and the Problem of Their Staging." Ph.D. dissertation, Northwestern University, 362 pp.
      Examines, from the point of view of the modern director, the production problems inherent in game scenes as part of the value of visual elements in Elizabethan plays. The four main chapters treat chess, tables, dice, and cards. Solem concludes that these games were staged in a conjectural "inner stage" and that similar games may have been staged in widely divergent manners. A valuable glossary is included in an appendix. See also 1953.16.

1953.24   SOUTHERN, RICHARD. "Inigo Jones and *Florimène*." *TN* (April): 37-39.
      A brief note, including eight plates of Jones's designs for the masque performed by the French in the Great Hall at Whitehall, 1635. Southern discusses the shutters and relieves used in the performance.

1953.25   SPRAGUE, ARTHUR COLBY. *Shakespearian Players and Performances.* Cambridge: Harvard University Press, 222 pp.
      Despite the title this work begins with the Restoration.

1953.26   SUMMERSON, JOHN [NEWENHAM]. *Architecture in Britain, 1530-1830.* Pelican History of Art, no. 23. London and Baltimore: Penguin Books, pp. 61-67.
      The relevant section, Part Two, Chapter Seven, "Inigo Jones at the Court of James I," contains a general discussion of Jones's theatre designs. Reprinted: 1955.25; 1958.22; 1963.18; 1969.16; 1970.30.

1953.27   SWINNEY, DONALD H. "The Globe Playhouse at Hofstra College, I: Notes on Reconstruction." *ETJ* 5 (March): 1-5.

  Discusses the building of a full-sized replica of the Globe to the specifications of J. C. Adams (1942.1). Three sides of the octagon he envisaged were constructed, containing essentially seven separate stages. See also 1953.1.

1953.28   WALTON, CHARLES E. "The Impact of the Court Masque and the Blackfriars Theatre upon the Staging of the Elizabethan-Jacobean Drama." Ph.D. dissertation, University of Missouri, 198 pp.

  Examines the masque and masque-like dramas in relation to the indoor playhouses. Walton concludes that masques were inserted into plays to add interest, and that well-equipped playhouses were required. "If these plays were produced even with a slight attention to the required staging, the drama of the period could not have been without its spectacular moments."

1953.29   WOODFILL, WALTER L. *Musicians in English Society from Elizabeth to Charles I.* Princeton: Princeton University Press, pp. 29-30, 41, 56-58, 65-66, 188, 236-37.

  Brief mentions of the relationship between musicians and actors and playhouses.

1954

1954.1   ANON. "A Model Elizabethan Playhouse." *Listener* 51 (29 April): 727.

  Describes Southern's model, with quotations from Southern. He used the Swan drawing as a basis, and decorated with paint. See also 1954.26.

1954.2   ARMSTRONG, WILLIAM A. "Shakespeare and the Acting of Edward Alleyn." *ShS* 7: 82-89.

  Attempts to assess the validity of the interpretations of passages in and 2 Henry IV that might be critical of Alleyn's acting by relating them to contemporary references. Armstrong concludes that recent disparagement of Alleyn's acting is not justified and that he should be considered on a par with Burbage, as he was in his own day.

1954.3   ASHE, DORA JEAN. "The Non-Shakespearean Bad Quartos as Provincial Acting Versions." *RenP* 1: 57-62.

  Examines the twelve non-Shakespearean bad quartos not previously studied by Greg. Ashe discusses the indications of prompt-book intent and the signs of provincial adaptation.

1954.4   BRYANT, JOSEPH ALLEN, Jr. "Shakespeare's Falstaff and the Mantle of Dick   Tarlton." *SP* 51 (April): 149-62.

  Discusses the character of Falstaff in the context of the Elizabethan clown, exemplified by Richard Tarlton. Bryant suggests that the role was shaped by

Shakespeare's desire to make use of the clown's antics in support of the play rather than in opposition to it, as was often the case.

1954.5   CUTTS, JOHN P. "Jacobean Masque and Stage Music." *M&L* 35 (July): 185-200.
        Discusses a manuscript held in the British Library, previously examined by Lawrence (1922.51, containing music used for various Jacobean masques. The bulk of the piece consists of a listing of the contents of the manuscript and commentary (including Cutts's differences with Lawrence) on each item.

1954.6   DeBANKE, CECILE. *Shakespearean Stage Production: Then and Now.* London: Hutchinson & Co., pp. 312.
        Reprint of 1953.4.

1954.7   EMPSON, WILLIAM. "The Elizabethan Stage." *TLS* (10 December): 801.
        A letter to the editor, challenging Hotson's conclusions in 1954.14. Empson suggests that the foreign spectator might have been mistaken in his description, and that the "eight partitions" cited by Hotson might well have provided the usual tiring house facade.

1954.8   FLETCHER, IFAN KYRLE. "Italian Comedians in England in the Seventeenth Century." *TN* 8 (July): 86-91.
        Covers the period 1620-1700. The only visit recorded prior to 1642 was that of Francis Nicolini, 18 February 1630.

1954.9   FOAKES, R. A. "The Player's Passion: Same Notes on Elizabethan Psychology and Acting." *E&S*, n.s. 7: 62-77.
        Steers a middle course through the seas of "natural" and "formal" acting styles, advocating "a range of acting capable of greater extremes of passion, of much action which would now seem forced or grotesque, but realistic within a framework of 'reality' that coincides to a large extent with ours." Foakes bases his discussion on Elizabethan psychology. See Index under Acting--Style.

1954.10   GREG, W[ALTER] W[ILSON]. "*Twelfth Night.*" *TLS* (31 December): 853.
        Points out in a letter to the editor that 1599/1600 was a leap year, not 1600/01 as Hotson says in 1954.14.

1954.11   HODGES, C[YRIL] WALTER. "New Light on Old Playhouses: Notes on Some Research by Richard Southern and Leslie Hotson." *ShStage*, no, 5   (June): 41-44.
        Discusses Southern's model of an Elizabethan playhouse (1954.26) and Hotson's discovery of an engraving showing the Curtain Playhouse and its external staircases (1954.15).

1954.12   HOPPE, HARRY R. "George Jolly at Bruges, 1648." *RES* n.s. 5 (July) :265-68.

   A brief note revealing further evidence of Jolly's pre-Restoration continental touring.

1954.13   HOSLEY, RICHARD. "The Use of the Upper Stage in Romeo and Juliet." *SQ* 5 (Autumn): 371-79.

   A paper read at the Southeastern Renaissance Conference at Duke University, April 1954. Hosley argues that the two balcony scenes (II.ii. and III.v. 1-68) were played on the upper level. He suggests that three other scenes (I1I.v. 69-242; IV.iii; IV.v.) sometimes thought to be played in this area were played on the platform.

1954.14   HOTSON, [JOHN] LESLIE. *The First Night of Twelfth Night*. London: Rupert Hart-Davis, 256 pp.

   An attempt at a reconstruction of the first performance of Shakespeare's comedy at Whitehall, 6 January 1600/01. Central to this discussion is the third chapter, "Shakespeare's Arena Stage," which parallels Hotson's other arguments about the four-sided nature of Elizabethan staging, with mansions scattered about the stage serving for doors, areas above, and discovery spaces (see 1953.11; 1959.9). Hotson also prints three documents, in Italian and German, that help lead him to his conclusions.

1954.15   ____. "'This Wooden 0': Shakespeare's Curtain Theatre Identified." *Times* (London), (26 March): 7, 14.

   Announces the discovery of an engraving of a view of London that shows the Curtain playhouse. As was the drawing, the engraving was found in the Library of the University of Utrecht. Hotson prints the engraving, with an enlargement of the area containing the playhouse, along with two photographs of Southern's model of an Elizabethan public theatre. See also 1954.26.

1954.16   MATTINGLY, ALTHEA SMITH. "The Playing Time and Manner of Delivery of Shakespeare's Plays in the Elizabethan Theatre." *SpMon* 21 (March): 29-38.

   Examines the texts of plays for evidence to support the "two hours traffic of our stage" and other similar statements about playing time. Line count is one indication; another is audience expectation. Mattingly examines both in detail, as well as what she calls "efficient elocution" and the possibility of cutting for perfomance. She concludes that the plays were normally cut to 2300 lines, and that a rate more rapid than that used in the modern theatre was employed. See also 1932.5-6; 1933.3.

1954.17   McCABE, JOHN CHARLES. "A Study of the Blackfriars Theatre, 1608-1642. Ph.D. dissertation, University of Birmingham, 330 pp.

   Attempts to bring together the facts fundamental to a thorough knowledge of the Blackfriars Pleyhouse from 1608 to 1642. The eight chapters examine the history of the theatre under the child companies and the King's Men; the plays presented there; the dimensions of the playhouse; the main platform and the tiring house facade; the use of large and small properties and scenic units; the use of costume, music, song, dance, and lighting; the audience of the theatre; and the staging of a typical Blackfriars play by the King's Men. McCabe concludes that the Farrar-Martin is substantially correct--with a platform stage the full width of a rectangular hall; a curtained recess or "inner stage," the curtain of which is split in the middle; two obliquely set side doors; an upper curtained stage level, complete with two angled window stages; and two rows of galleries. McCabe places the theatre in a conjectural "middle" story of the building rather than in the Parliament Chamber on the top floor. See also Index under Blackfriars Playhouse--Reconstructions.

1954.18   MILES, BERNARD. "Elizabethan Acting." *TLS* (2 April): 217.
          Cites a bill addressed to Cardinal Wollsey now held in the Public Record Office to confirm Joseph's assertion (in 1951.18) that Elizabethan acting was founded on the art of rhetoric and thus was formal in style.

1954.19   MONTGOMERY, ROY F. "A Fair House Built on Another Man's Ground." *SQ* 5 (Spring): 207-8.
          Identifies an allusion in *Merry Wives of Windsor* to the situation of the Theatre in 1598, "a fair house built on another man's ground."

1954.20   ROBERTSON, JEAN, and GORDON, D. J. "A Calendar of Dramatic Records in the Books of the Livery Companies of London 1485-1640." *MSC* 3: 37-204.
          The relevant section covers the Lord Mayor's Shows from 1535 to 1640 and miscellaneous records from 1485 to 1639. The contributions of ten of the twelve "Great" Livery Companies are calendared, the records of the other two having been destroyed in the Great Fire of 1666.

1954.21   ROSENBERG, MARVIN. "Elizabethan Actors: Men or Marionettes?" *PMLA* 69 (September): 915-27.
          An attack on the "formalist" school of Elizabethan acting in favor of the "naturalist" school. See also Index under Acting--Style. Reprinted: 1968.3.

1954.22   _____. "Public Night Performances in Shakespeare's Time." *TN* 8 (April): 44-45.
          A brief note, drawing attention to evidence for night performances in Heywood's *Apology for Actors*. See also Lawrence (1912.16; 1915.15) and Graves (1913.7; 1917.6).

1954.23   ROSENFELD, SYBIL. "Dramatic Companies in the Provinces in the Sixteenth and Seventeenth Centuries." *TN* 8 (April): 55-58.
          Summaries of some players' visits to seven provincial towns not noted in Murray (1910.15), Chambers (1923.2), or Bentley (1941.1).

1954.24   SAUNDERS, J. W. "Vaulting the Rails." *ShS* 7: 69-81.
         Examines the evidence for movement of actors from the platform into the
yard and back (as in medieval plays). The monument scene in *Antony and
Cleopatra* would be simplified to the hoisting of the body from the yard to
the stage. Other similar uses would be made of these two areas in *Pericles* (the
barge); *Romeo and Juliet* (the orchard wall); *1 Henry IV* (Orleans); *Coriolanus*
(the trenches); and others.

1954.25   SISSON, CHARLES J[ASPER]. "The Red Bull Company and the
         Importunate Widow." *ShS* 7: 57-68.
         Discusses the depositions in the Chancery suit of Worth v. Baskervile,
discovered by Sisson in the Public Record Office. The witnesses were almost all
members of the Red Bull company, and their testimony reveals a number of
important biographical and theatrical details. The "Importunate Widow" of the
title is Susan Browne Baskervile, widow first of Robert Browne of the Boar's
Head and later of Thomas Greene of the Red Bull. She was responsible, with
James Baskervile, her third husband, for the tangle of litigation that tied up Queen
Anne's Men for many years.

1954.26   SOUTHERN, RICHARD. "An Elizabethan Playhouse: A New Model
         Reconstruction." *Britain Today* 216 (April): 28-31.
         Describes the model of a generalized Elizabethan playhouse he made in
1954, with photographs. The model is sixteen-sided, with a tiring house facade
based on the Swan drawing, with hangings added between the two doors.

1954.27   TRACE, ARTHUR STORREY, Jr. "The Continuity of Opposition to the
         Theater in England from Gosson to Collier." Ph.D. dissertation, Stanford
         University, 376 pp.
         Examines opponents of the stage such as Gosson, Stubbes, Rainolds, and
Prynne, and links their arguments both with earlier arguments of the Church
Fathers and with the later arguments of Collier and his Anglican allies. See also
Index under Puritan Opposition to the Stage.

1955

1955.1   BRILEY, JOHN. "Of Stake and Stage." *ShS* 8: 106-08.
         A brief note presenting Alleyn's Petition to Lord Cranfield (1622) and An
Account of Expenses at the Bear Garden, 1615-1621, both bearing on the
economics of animal baiting.

1955.2   BYRNE, M[URIEL] St. CLARE. "Twelfth Night 'In the Round.'" *TN* 9
         (January): 46-52.
         Discusses 1954.14 and its arena staging concept. Byrne disagrees with
Hotson's interpretation of key passages, but finds "the preliminary research . . .
outstanding."

1955.3   CUTTS, JOHN P. "Some Jaeobean and Caroline Dramatic Lyrics." *N&Q*, n.s. 2 (March): 106-09.
Points out how the study of musical settings of dramatic lyrics can enhance the study of the lyrics alone. As examples Cutts cites extant music for songs from *The Rival Friends*, *Duchess of Malfi*, *The Tragedy of Brennorald*, and *Wild Goose Chase*.

1955.4   EWSON, WILLIAM. "The Elizabethan Stage." *Literary Guide* 70 (March): 12-14.
"To keep to the essentials, [Shakespeare] had an inner stage and a balcony, both with curtains to open and shut, but did most of the acting on an apron-stage." Empson also argues for the alternation theory, and he dismisses the Swan as pictured by DeWitt as "a speculation . . . which soon failed." His main thrust is toward the importance of the balcony, and he is prepared to prove that "both the blinding of Gloucester and the scolding by Hamlet of his mother in her bedroom" were staged there, although he offers no evidence for either contention here.

1955.5   FUSILLO, ROBERT JAMES. "Tents on Bosworth Field." *SQ* 6 (Spring): 193-94.
A brief note suggesting that no physical tents need be present on stage in Act V of Richard 111, but that doorways were localized by entrance and exit to serve as tents. The multiple staging of the mysteries and at court are offered as precedent.

*1955.6   GERSTNER-HIRZEL, ARTHUR. "The Economy of Action and Word in Shakespeare's Plays." Ph.D, dissertation, University of Basel.
Abstracted in 1955.7.

1955.7   ____. "Stagicraft and Poetry." *JDSG* 91: 196-211.
Abstract of 1955.6. Gerstner-Hirzel is concerned with the gestures implied in Shakespeare's lines, and he draws examples from several plays. He finds the histories have an average of 23 gestures per 1000 lines; the comedies, 40; the tragedies, 55; and the romances, 45.

1955.8   HOPPE, HARRY R. "English Acting Companies at the Court of Brussels in the Seventeenth Century." *RES*, n.s. 6 (January): 26-33.
Based on three surviving account books of the royal court at Brussels, covering entertainment from 1612 to 1618 and 1647 to 1652. Hoppe reveals some new information on English actors on the continent and their itineraries.

1955.9   HOTSON, [JOHN] LESLIE. "The Elizabethan Stage." *TLS* (7 January): 9.
Announces that he is working on a book an the subject of "Shakespeare's Arena." See also 1953.11; 1959.9.

1955.10   ____. *The First Night of Twelfth Night*. London: Rupert Hart-Davis, 256 pp.
Reprint of 1954.14.

1955.11   INGRAM, REGINALD WILLIAM. "Dramatic Use of Music in English
        Drama, 1603-1640." Ph.D. dissertation, University of London, 373 pp.
                Discusses music in the theatre in terms of instrumentation; musicians and
        composers; theatrical connections; special use of music in the private theatres
        (with particular reference to Marston); the tendency to use music for emotional
        effects in Shakespeare and Fletcher; and the use of songs and dances outside of
        masques. Three appendixes include discussions of the use of entre-act music;
        music at the Globe and Blackfriars after 1608; and a listing of dances used, song
        tunes performed, and instruments used. Ingram concludes by tracing three
        stages in the development of the dramatic use of music.

1955.12   JOSEPH, BERTRAM. "The Elizabethan Stage and Acting." In *The Age of
        Shakespeare*. Edited by Boris Ford. Pelican Guide to English Literature, no. 2.
        Aylesbury and London: Pelican Books, pp. 147-61.
                An exploration of audience expectations and how the actors met them,
        areuing for a formal acting style. Joseph includes a very brief summary of theories
        of the Elizabethan stage. Reprinted: 1956.19; 1961.15; 1962.10; 1975.19.

1955.13   _____. "The Elizabethan Stage and the Art of Elizabethan Drama." *JDSG* 91:
        145-60.
                Argues that the conventions of the original performance must be
        understood if we are to understand the drama. Specifically, Joseph discusses the
        use of conventional gesture in modern productions of Shakespeare.

1955.14   LANGER, LAWRENCE. "Letter to the Editor." *ShN* 5 (April): 11.
                Responds to Hotson in 1954.14, suggesting that Shakespeare could not
        have written the play in a few days, that with the Queen in the audience true arena
        staging would not have been possible, and that Orsino's name could have
        been a late change to flatter the real Orsino.

*1955.15   MÜLLER-BELLINGHUSEN, ANTON. "Die Wortkulisse bei Shakespeare."
        Ph.D. dissertation, University of Freiburg, 327 pp.
                Partially published: 1955.16.

1955.16   _____. "Die Wortkulisse bei Shakespeare." *JDSG* 91: 182-95.
                Partial publication of 1955.15. Müller-Bellinghausen examines
        Shakespeare's use of words to set the scene and his representation of the verbal
        scene on the actual stage.

*1955.17   NORBERG, LARS. "Shakespearetidens Teater." *Borås Tidning* 29: 10-?.
                Cited in 1963.14; the title of this Danish publication translates as "Theatre
        of Shakespeare's Time."

1955.18   POKORNÝ, JAROSLAV. *Shakespearova doba a divadlo [Shakespeare's Time and Theatre]*. Prague: Orbis, 199 pp.
>   A general discussion of the period, with particular emphasis on the Globe and the Chamberlain'slKing's Men. In Slovak.

1955.19   RACE, SIDNEY. "The First Night of *Twelfth Night*." *N&Q*, n.s. 2 (February): 52-55.
>   Responds to Hotson (1954.14), questioning many of his conclusions.

1955.20   ROSENFELD, SYBIL M. *Foreign Theatrical Companies in Great Britain in the 17th and 18th Centuries*. Pamplet no. 4. London: Society for Theatre Research, p. 1.
>   A chronological listing of the visits of foreign companies. Only four are listed prior to the Restoration; a French group in 1629; an Italian company in 1630; and French and Spanish organizations in 1635. Reprinted: 1962.17.

1955.21   ROTHWELL, WILLIAM F. "Decentralized Staging." *ShN* 5 (April): 11.
>   Responds to Hotson's theory of arena staging (1953.11), suggesting that a variety of different actor-audience relationships might have been used at different times.

1955.22   SAUNDERS, J. W. "The Elizabethan Theatre." *TLS* (11 November): 680.
>   Responds to Hotson (1953.11) and his conjectures about arena staging in the Elizabethan theatre.

1955.23   [SMET, ROBERT de.] *Le thèâtre Elizabéthain*. Collections Lebèque & Nationale, no. 114. Brussels: Office de Publicité, pp. 7-23.
>   Written under the pseudonym Romain Sanvic. The relevant section is the first chapter, which discusses the Elizabethan theatre in general terms. Smet discusses public and private playhouses and methods of presentations. The remainder of the volume concentrates on literary matters, despite the title.

1955.24   STAMM, RUDOLF. "Dramenforschung." *JDSG* 91: 121-35.
>   Differentiates between literary and theatrical research.

1955.25   SUMMERSON, JOHN [NEWENHAM]. *Architecture in Britain*, 1530-1830. 2d ed. Pelican History of Art, no. 23. Harmondsworth: Penguin Books, pp. 61-67. Reprint of 1953.26.

1955.26   WHITE, ANNE TERRY. *Will Shakespeare and the Globe Theatre*. Illustrated by C[yril] Walter odges. Eau Claire, Wisconsin: E. M. Hale: New York: Random House, 182 pp.
>   A juvenile treatment, strongly romanticized and of little historical value. Hodges's illustrations are interesting, but do not compare with those in 1964.15, his more sophisticated juvenile work.

1955.27   WILSON, F[RANK] P[ERCY]. "Court Payments for Plays: 1610-1611, 1612-1613, 1616-1617." *BLR* 5 (October): 217-21.
>   Minor corrections to Chambers (1923.2) and Bentley (1941.1) from the Rawlinson Manuscripts held in the Bodleian Library. Wilson cites six entries from the manuscripts.

1955.28   _____. "The Elizabethan Theatre." *Neophil* 39 (Winter): 40-58.
>   Originally a lecture at the University of Amsterdam. Wilson begins with a discussion of some theatres of the period, then considers problems of staging, and concludes with notes on audiences and acting. The original form dictated a general rather than specific work. Reprinted: 1955.29.

1955.29   _____. *The Elizabethan Theatre*. Groningen: J. B. Wolters, 21 pp.
>   Reprint of 1955.28.

1956

1956.1   ADAMS, JOHN CRANFORD. "Shakespeare's Use of the Upper Stage in *Romeo and Juliet*, III.v." *SQ* 97 (Spring): 145-52.
>   Responds to Hosley (1954.13), arguing for the use of window~stages and a curtained upper stage for the second balcony scene.

*1956.2   ANON. *The Site of the Office of the Times, 1276-1956*. London: privately printed.
>   Cited in 1963.14. The Blackfriars Playhouse was built on this site.

1956.3   BECKERMAN, BERNARD. "The Production of Shakespeare's Plays at the Globe Playhouse, 1599-1609." Ph.D. dissertation, Columbia University, 466 pp.
>   Published as 1962.2.

1956.4   BENTLEY, GERALD EADES. *The Jacobean and Caroline Stage*. Vols. 3-5. Oxford: Clarendon Press, 1456 pp.
>   A continuation of 1941.1, concluded in 1968.2. These volumes examine plays and playwrights, and Bentley tries to include "all plays, masques, shows, and dramatic entertainments which were written between 1616 . . . and the closing of the theatres in 1642," Playwrights are listed verse. in alphabetical order, with anonymous plays considered at the end of volume 5. A brief bibliography and a biography for each writer precedes the consideration of the plays, also in alphabetical order under each playwright. For each play Bentley gives the date of first production, the dates of all editions, and a chronological listing of all relevant seventeenth-century records. Bentley sees his primary task as "the setting of these plays in their theatrical context."

1956.5   BLAND, D. S. "The Barriers: Guildhall Library MS 4160." *GuildMisc* 1, no. 6 (February): 7-14.

An edition of the manuscript of the text of the "barriers" performed at the ceremony creating Arthur Prince of Wales, 4 November 1604. "Barriers" is a formal combat, on foot, between contestants who fight across a horizontal pole (the "barrier") hung with decorated cloths. It "lies on the very frontier of literature and the theatre," since it combines elements of the joust and the masque.

1956.6   BORDINAT, PHILIP. "A New Site for the Salisbury Court Theatrc." *N&Q*, n.s. 3 (February): 51-52.

From 1952.2. Bordinat challenges Bell's location of the playhouse (in 1912.7) by reference to the indenture relative to the leasing of the property in 1629 and two seventeenth-century maps. He locates the theatre in Water Lane (now Whitefriars Street), just south of Tudor Street. See also Brownstein, 1977.3.

1956.7   CARTER, JOEL JACKSON. "English Dramatic Music to the Seventeenth Century and Its Availability for Modern Production." Ph.D. dissertation, Stanford University, 565 pp.

Discusses the origins and development of the varying types of dramatic music in England before Shakespeare. The role of music in the development of Elizabethan drama, in particular, is seen as important. Eighteen illustrative examples of dramatic music from before 1600 are reproduced.

1956.8   CUTTS, JOHN P. "An Unpublished Contemporary Setting of a Shakespeare Song." *ShS* 9: 86-89.

Music, probably composed by Robert Johnson, for a song in *Winter's Tale* ("Get you hence, for I must go"), preserved in a manuscript held in the New York Public Library. From another manuscript an incomplete setting (scored for bass and two trebles) provides a previously unknown second verse.

1956.9   _____. "Le rôle de la musique dans les masques de Ben Jonson et notament dans *Oberon* (1610-1611)." In *Les fêtes de la Renaissance.* Vol. 1. Edited by Jean Jacquot. Paris: CNRS, pp. 285-303.

Examines music in Jonson's Maaque of Queenes (1609/10) and (1610/11). Cutts discusses the payment of the musicians and the composition of the music, as well as the structure of the masques. He also prints music by Robert Johnson and Alfonso Ferrabosco. Reprinted: 1973.2.

1956.10 DODDS, MADELAIN HOPE. "The First Night of *Twelfth Night*." *N&Q*, n.s. 3 (February): 57-59.

Examines the manuscript on which Hotson based his book (1954.14), questioning several of his conclusions.

1956.11   PELVER, CHARES STANLEY. "William Shakespeare and Robert Armin His Fool: A Working Partnership." Ph.D. dissertation, University of Michigan, 352 pp.

Examines the extent to which Shakespeare's fools were influenced by the writings and comic line of Armin. Felver suggests that Shakespeare drew heavily on Armin's works in creating an essentially new comic character; that the motley coat as costume was a joint development; and that a good deal of Shakespeare's fool-lore, including the name Touchstone, came from Armin's work. Partially published: 1961.10.

1956.12   GORDON, D. J. "Le Masque Mémorable de Chapman." In *Les fêtes de la Renaissance*. Vol. 1. Edited by Jean Jacquot. Paris: CNRS, pp. 305-17.

Discusses the masque Chapman composed for the marriage of Elisabeth, only daughter of James I, from a literary point of view. Reprinted: 1973.8.

1956.13   GREG, W[ALTER] W[ILSON]. "Fragments from Henslowe's Diary." *MSC* 4: 27-32.

Facsimiles of five pieces removed from the diary, containing various signatures, with commentary. See also 1938.5; 1940.1.

1956.14   HARRISON, G[EORGE] B[AGSHAWE]. *Elizabethan Plays and Players*. Ann Arbor: University of Michigan Press, Ann Arbor Books, 309 pp.

Includes parts of 1923.14. greatly expanded. Harrison follows a roughly chronological path, going from the building of the Theatre and the influence of Lyly to separate chapters examining the Lord Admiral's Men, Lord Chamberlain's Men, the Globe, the boy players, and the war of the theatres.

1956.15   HOLMES, MARTIN. "A New Theory about the Swan Drawing." *TN* (April): 80-83.

Suggests that the drawing represents a rehearsal, with actors and not audience members shown in the upper stage.

1956.16   HOSLEY, RICHARD. "More about 'Tents' on Basworth Field." *SQ* 7 (Summer): 458-59.

Comments on Fusillo's suggestion (1955.5) that the tents in *Richard III* might have been represented by the stage doors, and draws attention to a similar possibility in *3 Henry VI*.

1956.17   JACQUOT, JEAN, ed. *Les fêtes de la Renaissance*. Vol. 1. Paris: CNRS, pp. 259-317.

The relevant section contains essays dealing with English pageants and masques. Includes 1956.9, 12, 28, 33-34. Argues that the visual history of Shakespearean production influences our reading of the plays.

1956.18   JEWKES, WILFRED THOMAS. "Act Division in Elizabethan Plays, 1583-1616." Ph.D. dissertation, University of Wisconsin, 387 pp.
        Published: 1958.12.

1956.19   JOSEPH, BERTRAM. "The Elizabethan Stage and Acting." In *The Age of Shakespeare*. Edited by Boris Ford. A Guide to English Literature, no. 2. Harmondsworth: Penguin Books, pp. 147-61.
        Reprint of 1955.12.

1956.20   KLEIN, DAVID. "Elizabethan Acting." *PMLA* 71 (March): 280-82.
        A brief note, with additional examples supporting Rosenberg's argument in 1954.21.

1956.21   LAIRD, DAVID CONNOR. "The Inserted Masque in Elizabethan and Jacobean Drama." Ph.D. dissertation, University of Wisconsin, 196 pp.
        Primarily a literary study. The only theatrical element examined (and that briefly) is the spectacular, or scenic. Laird claims that inserted entertainment were used in the tragedies of the Inns of Court and the public theatres, and in early romantic comedy "to bring to drama the scenic display of rival court masques and disguisings."

1956.22   LANE, ROBERT P[HILLIPS]. "A Study of the Repertory of Queen Elizabeth's Company, 1583-1593." Ph.D. dissertation, the University of North Carolina, 326 pp.
        Examines, in five chapters, the personnel of the company, the plays of Robert Wilson, chronicle plays in the repertory, the plays of Robert Greene, and three miscellaneous plays of the repertory. Lane concludes that there was no structural complexity, but that there was a major contribution to the development of comedy by this company.

1956.23   MANIFOLD, JOHN STREETER. *The Music in English Drama from Shakespeare to Purcell*. London: Rockliff, pp. 2-105.
        The relevant section is the first nine chapters, dealing with music in Shakespeare's theatre. Manifold examines the plays of the period for uses of music, instruments called for, and effects of music.

1956.24   MERCHANT, W[ILLIAM] M[OELWYN]. "Visual Elements in Shakespeare Studies." *JDSG* 92: 280-90.
        Argues that the visual history of Shakespearean production influences our reading of the plays.

1956.25   NAGLER, A[LOIS] M. "Shakespeare's Arena Demolished." *ShN* (6 February): 7.
        Briefly replied to Hotson's claims in 1954.14 that *Twelfth Night* was played in the round by citing another Italian source that uses similar language to mean that the audience was on three sides instead of four.

1956.26   PALME, PER. *Triumph of Peace: A Study of the Whitehall Banqueting House*. Stockholrm: Almqvist & Wiksell, 328 pp.

Published version of an Upsala Ph.D. dissertation. Palme examines Inigo Jones's banqueting house in Whitehall. He begins with a simple chronicle of events, proceeds to the use of the hall for banquets, masques, and otherwise, and then embarks on a conjectural reconstruction, beginning with the present building and moving backwards to Jones's preliminary plan, held in the Worcester College, Oxford, library. Reprinted: 1957.12.

1956.27   REYNOLDS, GEORGE F[ULLMER]. "*Hamlet* at the Globe." *ShS* 9: 49-53.

Discusses changing perceptions of the original staging of *Hamlet*, with special concern for the use of the so-called "inner stage." Reynolds sets up a possible staging scheme that requires only a small curtained space and the bringing on and off of stage properties as needed.

1956.28   ROBERTSON, JEAN. "Rapports de poète et de l'artiste dans la préparation des cortèges du Lord Maire (Londres 1553-1640)." In *Les fêtes de la Renaissance*. Vol. 1. Edited by Jean Jacquot. Paris: CNRS, pp 265-78.

Examines the Lord Mayor's pageants, based on the archives and printed booklets of the corporations of the City of London. Robertson focuses on the relationships between modeller, carver, composer, artist, dyer, poet, and architect, especially payments (both single and group). Middleton, Jonson, Monday, and Jones are singled out. Robertson, Jacquot, Yates, and others discuss the ambiguity of Elizabethan technical vocabulary in a brief postcript. Reprinted: 1973.22.

1956.29   SCHANZER, ERNEST. "Thomas Platter's Observations an the Elizabethan Stage." *N&Q*, n.s. 3 (November): 465-67.

Literal translations of Platter's comments on the stage, with commentary. Chambers's translation in 1923.2 is unreliable, and Williams's standard edition (1937.9) is "somewhat freer than seems needful in view of the minute scrutiny these few passages will continue to receive."

1956.30   SCHNEIDERMAN, ROBERT IVAN. "Elizabethan Legerdemain, and Its Employment in the Drama, 1576-1642." Ph.D. dissertation, Northwestern University, 274 pp.

Attempts to give a clear picture of the legerdemain of the period--its potential value to the playwright, its psychological bases, its relation to physical staging--and an exposé of its methods. Specific effects Schneiderman discusses include appearances, disappearances, levitation, and scenes of violence involving mutilation. Since principles of legerdemain have not changed considerably since the Elizabethan period, their methods are often effective in modern productions.

1956.31 SMITH, IRWIN. "'Gates' on Shakespeare's Stage." *SQ* 7 (Spring): 159-76.
Examines gate scenes in several Shakespeare plays, arguing for the existence of property gates set up in the inner stage.

1956.32 _____. *Shakespeare's Globe Playhouse: A Modern Reconstruction in Text and Line Drawings*. New York: Charles Scribner's Sons. 240 pp.
Based on the J. C. Adams reconstruction of the Globe (1942.1), this work contains photographs of the model that Smith and Adams built and detailed drawings based on that model. The first thirteen chapters discuss Adams's reconstruction in detail, examining some of his evidence, with a few minor modifications. The final chapter contains fifteen scale drawings. Smith's only personal contribution (aside from the drawings) is the use of material drawn from his study of Tudor construction (see 1952.18).

1956.33 STEVENS, DENIS. "Pièces de théâtre et 'pageants' a l'epoque des Tudor." In *Les fêtes de la Renaissance*. Vol. 1. Edited by Jean Jacquot. Paris: CNRS, pp. 259-64.
Examines the role of music in plays, masques, and other pageantry, especially the work of composers William Cornish and John Redford. Primarily concerned with the reign of Henry VIII. Reprinted: 1973.29.

1956.34 WICKHAM, GLYNNE. "Contribution de Ben Jonson et de Dekker aux fêtes du couronment de Jacques Ier." In *Les fêtes de la Renaissance*. Vol. 1. Edited by Jean Jacquot. Paris: CNRS, pp. 279-83.
Examines Jonson's, Dekker's, and Middleton's contributions to James's royal entry into London for his coronation. Seven tableaux or pageants, much more uniform than earlier ones, covered the entire length of the city, from London Bridge to Temple Bar. Dekker apparently was in overall control, and he and Webster composed odes while Jonson and Middleton wrote the tableaux scenarii. During the postponement because of the plague, costs nearly doubled from the estimated £400 to £784. Reprinted: 1973.32.

1956.35 WILSON, F[RANK] P[ERCY]. "More Records from the Remembrancia of the City of London." *MSC* 4: 55-65.
Additions to 1907.5, from 1613 to 1616, bearing on the Whitefriars and Rosseter's Porter's Hall.

1957

1957.1 ARMSTRONG, WILLIAM A. "'Canopy' in Elizabethan Theatre Terminology." *N&Q*, n.s. 4 (October): 433-34.
Differentiates between the uses of "canopy" to mean a curtained discovery space and the awning covering a chair of state.

1957.2   BRIDGES-ADAMS, W[ILLIAM]. *The Irrestible Theatre*. Vol. I, From the
Conquest to the Cornonwealth. London: Sacker & Warburg; Cleveland: World
Publishing Co., pp. 79-392.
    The section on the Elizabethan period in a comprehensive history of
British theatre and drama. Bridges-Adams includes chapters on the Master of the
Revels, the boy companies, the adult companies, the playhouses, the audience,
acting styles, management, and the masque, as well as chapters on the major
playwrights, the Puritan opposition to the stage, and types of drama.

1957.3   CHALLEN, W. H. "Sir George Buck, Kt., Master of the Revels." *N&Q*, n.s. 4
(July): 290-92.
    Adds a few non-theatrical details to the biography of the early
seventeenth-century Master of the Revels. Continued in 1957.4.

1957.4   _____. "Sir George Buck, Kt., Master of the Revels." *N&Q*, n.s. 4 (August):
324-27.
    Continuation of 1957.3.

1957.5   CUTTS, JOHN P. "Music for Shakespeare's Company, the King's Men." 2 vols.
Ph.D. dissertation, University of Birmingham.
    Published as 1959.4.

1957.6   FLATTER, RICHARD. "Who Wrote the Hecate-Scene?" *JDSG* 93: 196-210.
    Argues that Shakespeare, rather than Middleton, wrote the scene. This is
the beginning of a controversy with Cutts. See 1958.6; 1959.5; 1960.5, 7.

1957.7   FLECKNOE, RICHARD. "A Short Discourse of the English Stage." In *Critical
Essays of the Seventeenth Century*. Vol. 2. Edited by 3. E. Spingarn.
Bloomington: Indiana University Press. pp. 91-96.
    Reprint of 1664.1

1957.8   HOSLEY, RICHARD. "The Gallery over the Stage in the Public Playhouse of
Shakespeare's Time." *SQ* 8 (Winter): 15-31.
    Examines the pictorial evidence of the Swan drawing and the stage
directions from a variety of plays to find out what they tell us about the acting
area above. Hosley concludes that "the gallery over the stage in the public
playhouse of Shakespeare's time functioned primarily as a Lord's room, and only
secondarily . . .as a raised production area; and that during such periods it
exercised both functions simultaneously."

1957.9   _____. "Shakespeare's Use of a Gallery over the Stage." *ShS* 10:77-89.
    Assumes that Shakespeare's plays were "designed for production in a
theatre having a gallery over the stage essentially similar to the Lord's room
shown in the Swan drawing," and then discusses how such an acting area would
have been used. Eighteen of Shakespeare's plays make no use of such an area. an
additional twelve use it only once. All together, Shakespeare uses this space only

thirty-five times in his plays. Generally, a secondary action aloft is introduced in support of an original action on the platform below. Hosley also examines and rejects J. C. Adams's assertions about the upper acting area's use as the location of interior above scenes.

1957.10   KERR, S. PAWELL. "The Constable Kept an Account." *N&Q*, n.s. 4 (April): 167-70.
     Among the gifts lavished on the Court by the Spanish in 1604 were "4780 reales" to "boatman, musicians, and players. . ." Halliwell-Phillips claimed that the King's Men performed for the Spanish at Somerset House and that he had found a Royal Order for such a periormance. Unfortunately, the order is now lost, and the Constable's account book sheds little light on the matter.

1957.11   MAIN, WILLIAM W. "Dramaturgical Norms in Elizabethan Repertory." *SP* 54 (April): 128-48.
     Surveys the norms in plot structure in Elizabethan plays from 1598 to 1602. There is little here of theatrical interest, although this item is included in *NCBEL*, col. 1395.

1957.12   PALME, PER. *Triumph of Peace: A Study of the Whitehall Banqueting House*. London: Thames & Hudson, 328 pp.
     Reprint of 1957.26.

1957.13   PATTERSON, REMINGTON P[ERRIGO]. "Philip Henslowe and the Rose Theatre." Ph.D. dissertation, Yale University, 348 pp.
     Examines the life of Henslowe as theatrical landlord and manager and the history of his Rose Playhouse on the Bankside. Includes transcriptions of unpublished (at the time) manuscripts from the Dulwich collection as documentation. No attempt is made to reconstruct the playhouse or to discuss methods of staging employed at the Rose. The Diary is used extensively, as are all of the Dulwich manuscripts.

1957.14   ROSENFELD, SYBIL. "Unpublished Stage Documents." *TN* 11 (April): 92-96.
     Includes the Salisbury Court petition (c. 1652) of Elizabeth Heton, William Wintersall, and William Jones that shows this playhouse was converted from a barn at a cost of £800.

1957.15   TEAGARDEN, JACK E. "Reaction to the Professional Actor in Elizabethan London." Ph.D. dissertation, University of Florida, 189 pp.
     Examines polemics, apologetics, drama, and popular writing 1590-1640 in order to determine the social status of Elizabethan actors. In general, reaction was predictable in terms of the individual bias of the reactor. Consequently, prose writers and playwrights used actors as characters to good effect.

1957.16   WATSON, GEORGE, ed. *The Cambridge Bibliography of English Literature.* Vol. 5 *Supplement: A. D. 600-1900.* Cambridge: University Press, pp. 244-46.
        Supplement to 1940.2. All relevant items have been included in this bibliography. See also 1974.25.

*1957.17   WILLIAMS, S. H. "The Lord Mayor's Shows from Peele to Settle: A Study of Literary Content, Organisation, and Methods of Production." Ph.D. dissertation, University of London.
        Cited in 1963.14.

1958

1958.1   ARMSTRONG, W[ILLIAM] A. *The Elizabethan Private Theatres: Facts and Problems.* Pamphlet no. 6. London: Society for Theatre Research, 17 pp.
        Revised text of a paper read before the Society in March 1957. Armstrong applies the principles used by Isaacs on the Blackfriars (see 1933.4) to the other private theatres. He examines some 150 plays written for the private theatres and published before the Restoration, but does not attempt to limit the evidence to a particular theatre or to use only texts dependent on prompt copy He concludes that "the general design of . . . [the private theatre] stage, complete with platform, stage doors, inner stage, upper stage, and windows, shows that it had obvious structural affinities with open air theatres like the Globe." At the same time, however, the "scenic methods [of the Private playhouses] were more various than those of any other English theatre of the period." Armstrong cites simultaneous, fixed, successive, and movable painted scenery as being used in the private theatres.

1958.2   BERNHEIMER, RICHARD. "Another Globe Theatre." *SQ* 9 (Spring): 19-29.
        An examination of the theatre pictured in Fludd, also examined by Yates (1966.28, 1967.17) and Shapiro (1966.20). Bernheimer describes the building and suggests that it was a remodelled tennis court, standing in Germany and providing space for touring English actors.

1958.3   BOLTON, JANET. "A Historical Study of English Theories and Precepts of Vocal and Gestural Expressiveness from Stephen Hawes to John Bulwer: 1509-1644." Ph.D. dissertation, University of Southern California, 401 pp.
        Examines characteristic English Renaissance theories and precepts of pronunciation relevant to the acting of the period. Balton discusses descriptions of the speech mechanism in Elizabethan scientific literature, the psychology of humours, physiognomy, grammars and prosodies, literary and dramatic criticism, pulpit delivery, and rhetoric, concluding that "standards of vocal and gestural communication are established by contemporary social ideals." The same might be said of the relative naturalness of acting, although Bolton does not make the connection.

1958.4   BRETT-EVANS, DAVID. "Der *Sommernachstraum* in Deutschland 1600-1650." *ZDP* 77: 317-83.

Discusses German adaptations of *Midsummer Night's Dream* during the first half of the seventeenth century, including performances by English players.

1958.5   BRILEY, JOHN. "Edward Alleyn and Henslowe's Will." *SQ* 29 (Autumn): 321-30.

Sheds much additional light an the issue of the division of Henslowe's property through revealing the contents of newly discovered court documents. In all there were seven cases in three courts concerning Henslowe's widow, his nephew, and Edward Alleyn (his son-in-law), end all were not settled until the three principals were dead. Briley finds the estate to have been larger, and that it was shared much more widely, than have previously been supposed.

1958.6   CUTTS, JOHN P. "Who Wrote the Hecate-Scene?" *JDSG* 94: 200-02.

Responds to Flatter (1957.6), arguing that Middleton may have written the scene since two of his songs are included in the First Folio version of *Macbeth*. Cutts agrees with Lawrence (1920.20) that three additional witches were introduced to sing and dance. See also the rest of the controversy: 1959.5; 1960.5, 7.

1958.7   ECCLES, MARK. "Martin Peerson and the Blackfriars." *ShS* 11: 100-106.

Examines Peerson's role as sharer in the Revels company during the early Jacobean period, with information drawn from various suits held in the Public Record Office. Peerson, who was a musician, might have composed music for the company or trained the boys' voices.

1958.8   ELLIS-FERMOR, UNA M. "The Jacobean Stage." In *The Jacobean Drama: An Interpretation*. 4th ed. London: Methuen, pp. 273-83.

Reprint of 1936.8.

1958.9   FEIL, J. P. "Dramatic References from the Scudemore Papers." ShS 11: 107-16.

Cites all dramatic references from the family papers of the Scudemores of Hereford from 1610 to 1638. A total of fourteen plays and masques are mentioned, all but one of which were performed. Five performances were attended by the Queen and one by the King.

1958.10   GOLDSTEIN, LEONARD. "On the Transition from Formal to Naturalistic Acting in the Elizabethan and Post-Elizabethan Theatre." *BNTPL* 62 (July): 330-49.

Examines the social and cultural conditions of the period and their relevance to the drama and acting. Goldstein argues that "the drama down to the time of Shakespeare was . . . essentially didactic" and that "the acting consonant with this type of drama was formal." There was n gradual change, however, and by the Jacobean period "the destructive individualism of the Court emerged. Here the isolated individual was representative and the acting depicted the disintegration of that individual. The acting became psychological and that meant naturalistic." See also Index under Acting--Style.

1958.11   HOSLEY, RICHARD. "An Elizabethan Tiring-House Facade." *SQ* 9 (Autumn): 588.
        A brief note with a photograph of a setting designed by Richard Southern for the 1958 season of the Bankside Players. There is a practicable Lord's room above and two sets of double doors flanking a nine foot wide "inner stage" below.

1958.12   JEWKES, WILFRED THOMAS. *Act Division in Elizabethan and Jacobean Plays, 1583-1616*. Hamden, Conn.: Shoe String Press, 374 pp.
        Published version of 1956.12. Examines 237 plays written between 1583 and 1616, in first and other relevant editions, with an eye toward act divisions and reasons for them. The plays written for the private theatres were divided almost without exception. The plays of the university wits were also apparently divided, although division did not always survive the playhouse into print. The public theatre plays, 1590-1607, were apparently not divided, although this practice changed after 1607.

1958.13   MITHAL, H. S. D. "'Will, My Lord of Leicester's Jesting Player.'" *N&Q*, n.s. 5 (October): 427-29.
        Examines a reference in a letter of Sir Philip Sidney from Utrecht, 24 March 1586, suggesting that rather than Willl Kempe, Robert Wilson might have been referred to. See Bruce (1844.1) for an earlier discussion; see also Bald (1959.3) for a response, and Mithal's rebuttal (1960.13).

1958.14   NAGLER, A[LOIS] M. *Shakespeare's Stage*. Translated by Ralph Manheim. New Haven and London: Yale University Press, 117 pp.
        Not an attempt to reconstruct the Globe or Blackfriars, which Nagler considers impossible, but rather to reconstruct an ideal type of Elizabethan theatre. Richly anecdotal, the study examines possibilities for all familiar elements of the stage: the doors, the platform, the discovery space, the upper stage, and the traps. Nagler imaginatively reconstructs the staging of *Romeo and Juliet* at the Globe and at Blackfriars, and he discusses costumes, management, and actors and acting, concluding with a composite portrait of a typical audience member.

1958.15   PARROTT, THOMAS MARC, and BELL, ROBERT HAMILTON. *A Short View of the Elizabethan Drama, Together with Some Account of Its Principal Playwrights and the Conditions Under Which It Was Produced*. New York: Charles Scribner's Sons, pp.45-62.
        Reprint of 1943,9, with an updated and expanded bibliography.

*1958.16   QUINN, SEABURY GRANDIN, Jr. "Ideological Spectacle: Theories of Staging Methods." Ph.D. dissertation, Yale University, 172 pp.
        Cited in 1963.14.

1958.17   RACE, SYDNEY. "Simon Formen's 'Bocke of Plaies' Examined." *N&Q*, n.s. 5 (January): 9-14.

1958.18   REESE, M. M. *Shakespeare: His World and His Work*. London: Edward Arnold & Co., pp. 97-344, 562-63.

      The relevant section is Part III, "The Elizabethan Stage." Reese devotes a chapter each to Elizabethan London, the theatres, tho players, the plays and playwrights, and the audience, as well as an appendix to Shakespeare's company. He follows J. C. Adams (1942.1) in most details of playhouse reconstruction, and in fact uses secondary sources exclusively throughout. Abstracted in Hebrew in 1965.13

*1958.19   RICKERT, ROBERT TURNHAM. "A Study of Henslowe's Diary." Ph.D. dissertation, University of Birmingham.

      Unlocatable. Cited in *DEAL*, p. 478. The only known copies are missing from the University of Birmingham Library and the Shakespeare Institute Library. See also Riekert and Foakes's edition of the diary (1961.13).

1958.20   RUSSELL, DOUGLAS A. "Shakespearean Costume: Contemporary or Fancy Dress." *ETJ* 10 (May): 105-12.

      Discusses Elizabethan costume conventions in light of what is known of stage decoration and masque costuming. While of some historical interest, this piece is intended more for the modern costumer than the historian.

1958.21   SMITH, IRWIN. "Ariel as Ceres." *SQ* 9 (Autumn): 430-32.

      Suggests that the masque was a late insertion into *Tempest*, and that the boy actor who played Ariel was forced to change costume and also undertake Ceres.

1958.22   SUMMERSON, JOHN [NEWENHAM]. *Architecture in Britain, 1530-1830*. 3d ed. Pelican History of Art, no. 23. Harmondsworth: Penguin Books, pp. 61-67. Reprint of 1953.26.

1958.23   TAYLOR, DICK, Jr. "The Masque and the Lance: The Earl of Pembroke in Jacobean Court Entertainments." *Tulane Studies in English* 8: 21-53.

      Discusses the involvement in the court masques and tilting of William Herbert, third Earl of Pembroke, before he became Lord Chamberlain in 1615. Pembroke was involved in both the Jonson-Daniel and Jonson-Jones disputes. He participated in the major masques of the early Jacobean years but ended his participation upon taking up the Chamberlain's staff. Argues that the notes on *Richard II, Winter's Tale, Cymbeline,* and *Macbeth* are Collier forgeries.

1958.24   WRIGHT, LOUIS B. *Shakespeare's Theatre and the Dramatic Tradition*. Washington: Folger Shakespeare Library, 36 pp.

      A brief pamphlet that treats the medieval antecedents of the Elizabethan theatre as well s the history of physical theatres in that period. Seventeen pages of plates are appended. Reprinted: 1961.23; 1963.22; 1966.26; 1969.22; 1972.34; 1979.34.

1959

1959.1   ALTON, R. E., ed. "The Academic Drama in Oxford: Extracts from the Records of Four Colleges." *MSC* 5: 29-95.
>   Records of expenses connected with dramatic entertainments between 1480 and 1650 at New College, Magdalen College, Christ Church, and St. John's College, with commentary.

1959.2   ARMSTRONG, WILLIAM A. "The Audience of the Elizabethan Private Theatres." *RES*, n.s. 10 (July): 234-49.
>   Examines contemporary plays, poems, and pamphlets for information about the audience of the private theatres as a group from 1575 to 1642. Armstrong concludes that audiences were mainly draw form the parts of London adjacent to the playhouses, that the social constitution of the audience was like the Restoration audience rather than the public theatre audience, and that a certain level of decorum was maintained. Reprinted: 1968.3.

1959.3   BALD, R[OBERT] C[ECIL]. "'Will, My Lord of Leicester's Jesting Player. '" *N&Q*, n.s. 6 (March): 112.
>   Responds to 1950.13, with the information (apparently unknown to Mithal) that Kempe was indeed with Sidney in November 1585, and that Wilson was as well. See Mithal's response, 1960.13.

1959.4   CUTTS, JOHN P. *La musique de scéne de la troupe de Shakespeare: The King's Men sous le regne de Jacques Ier*. Paris: CNRS, 199 pp.
>   Published version of 1957.5. Examines the music of eighty-eight plays of the King's Men in a critical introduction to an edition of over fifty stage songs and instrumental compositions. Cutts also considers music in interludes, postludes, and choruses, as well as the status of the actor-musician. He discusses the use of vocal and instrumental music on the stage in some detail, as well as the instrumentation required for the plays.

1959.5   FLATTER, RICHARD. "Hecate, 'The Other Three Witches,' and Their Songs." *JDSG* 95: 225-37.
>   Replies to Cutts (1958.6), who had responded to his 1957.6. Flatter here denies the existence of the second set of three witches, arguing that the First Folio stage direction which names them was simply an error. See also 1960.5, 7.

1959.6   GREG, WALTER W[ILSON]. "Copyright in Unauthorized Texts." In *Elizabethan and Jacobean Studies Presented to Frank Percy Wilson in Honor of his Seventieth Birthday*. Edited by Herbert Davis and Helen Gardner. Oxford: Clarendon Press, pp. 62-64.

A brief note throwing light on one problem of non-dramatic publication copyright in 1631. Included because of listing in *NCBEL* 1, col. 1384.

1959.7   HODGES, C[YRIL] WALTER. "The Lantern of Taste." *ShS* 12: 8-14.

Examines how changing tastes affect reconstructions of Elizabethan playhouses, using Tieck's and Godfrey's reconstructions of the Fortune as examples. Hodges discusses what he calls "antiquarian revival," "Timbered Cottage revival," "Cinema, the Experimental Movement and Flow of Action," and "an ornamental baroque reaction against former primitivism."

1959.8   HOSLEY, RICHARD. "The Discovery Space in Shakespeare's Globe." *ShS* 12: 35-46.

Published version of a paper read at the International Shakespeare Conference at Stratford-upon-Avon, 20 September 1957. Hosley proposes that discoveries at the first Globe were effected by opening a door or by drawing a curtain hung up in front of one of two or three doorways. He uses as evidence only those thirty plays definitely performed at this theatre from 1599 to 1608, when the King's Men began to use the Blackfriars. Only nine require discoveries, and seven require only one each. The hangings often referred to could be used to effect discoveries, Hosley declares, "but discovery was not their chief raison d'ètre." Reprinted: 1968.3.

1959.9   HOTSON, [JOHN] LESLIE. *Shakespeare's Wooden O*. New York: Macmillan, 335 pp.

A somewhat curious volume, following Hotson's 1954.14 in ascribing arena (or in-the-round) production as the norm in Elizabethan staging. Hotson uses Middleton's *A Game at Chess* to describe his arena-Globe, with entrances made through traps into portable curtained booths set about the stage in the medieval manner. The basis for this conjecture is the uncontested arena staging employed in earlier pageants. Hotson closes by identifying the Fortune and the Curtain on a ca. 1600 map of London.

1959.10   JOSEPH, BERTRAM. *The Tragic Actor*. London: Routledge & Kegan Paul; New York: Theatre Arts Books, pp. 1-27.

The relevant section is the first chapter, "The Age of Shakespeare." Joseph reviews the naturallformal debate, reversing his previous position by coming down on a middle ground, concluding that "the style of the acting expressed the style of the work, eliciting in performance the essential spirit of the play." He cites a variety of contemporary sources, especially as regards the rhetorical theory of the time, and he compares Burbage and Alleyn.

1959.11   KERNODLE, GEORGE R "The Open Stage: Elizabethan or Existential?" *ShS* 12: 1-7.

    Argues that Shakespeare's stage "was not a blank open platform, on which a lonely soul was spotlighted in an empty, insubstantial universe." Rather, our open stage is a reflection of our age, as Shakespeare's was of his. "Let us not forget," says Kernodle, "that the open stage was once used as part of a vision of man's central place in a cosmos of dignity and order."

1959.12   KINDERMANN, HEINZ. *Theatergeschichte Europas*. Vol. 3. Salzburg: Otto Müller, pp. 42-159.

    The relevant section of a comprehensive history. Kindermann discusses the playhouses, playwrights, actors, clowns, costumes, masques, government regulations, and audience of the period. He reviews various reconstructions of theatres, as well as the designs of Inigo Jones.

1959.13   KIRSCHBAUM, LEO. "The Copyright of Elizabethan Plays." *Library*, 5th ser. 14 (December): 231-50.

    Originally a paper read before The Bibliographical Society, 15 October 1957. The copyright of an Elizabethan play belonged to the stationer, not the playwright, and a second license was required before publication.

1959.14   LACY, ROBIN THURLOW. "An Encyclopedia of Stenographers, 534 B.C. to 1900 A.D." Ph.D. dissertation, University of Denver, 267 pp.

    Entries are included on Robert Peake, William Lyzarde, Inigo Jones, Nicholas Lanier, and John Webb.

1959.15   MERCHANT, W[ILLIAM] M[OELMIN]. *Shakespeare and the Artist*. London: Oxford University Press, pp. 1-19.

    The relevant section is the first chapter, "The Elizabethan Theatre and the Visual Arts." Merchant briefly summarizes the state of architectural scholarship, reprinting three of Hodges's plates (of the Theatre, the second Globe, and the Fortune).

1959.16   MILLER, WILLIAM E. "*Periaktoi* in the Old Blackfriars." *MLN* 74 (January): 1-3.

    Notes the reference to "the motion of late yeares to be seene in the blackfriers" in Abraham Fleming's translation of Vergil's *Eclogues* and *Georgics* of 1589. Miller interprets this as revolving motion, as in *periaktoi*. See also 1964.29.

17   MILLS, L. J. "The Acting in University Comedy of Early Seventeenth-Century England." In *Studies in the English Renaissance Drama in Memory of Karl Julius Holzknecht*. Edited by Josephine W. Bennet, Oscar Cargill, and Vernon Hall, Jr. New York: New York University Press, pp. 212-30.

    Draws evidence primarily from the plays performed at Oxford and Cambridge concerning the acting style employed. Mills simply points the way for a more thorough study, using representative examples to show the apparent exuberance of University acting of plays with comic scenes.

1959.18   NICOLL, ALLARDYCE. "'Passing Over the Stage.'" *ShS* 12: 47-55.
        Part of a presidential lecture delivered to the Society for Theatre Research on 30 April 1958. Nicoll argues that "passing over the stage" meant that actors enter in the yard and then walk onto and over the platform.

1959.19   PAFTORD, J. H. P. "Simon Forman's 'Bocke of Plaies.'" *RES*, n.s. 10 (July): 289-91.
        A brief note arguing for the authenticity of this document, based on the testimony of W. H. Black, who transcribed it for Collier in 1832.

1959.20   MODES, ERNEST LLOYD. "The Staging of Elizabethan Plays at the Rose Theatre, 1592-1603." Pb.D. dissertation, University of Kentucky. 316 pp.
        Published as 1976.21.

1959.21   RIEWALD, J. G. "Some Later Elizabethan and Early Stuart Actors and Musicians." *ES* 40 (February): 33-41.
        New information and commentary on sixteen actors and musicians, discovered by Riewald on the continent. Useful additions to Chambers (1923.2), Nungezer (1929.12), and Bentley (1941.1).

1959.22   ROBERTSON, JEAN, ed. "A Calendar of Dramatic Records in the Books of the London Cloth-Workers' Company." *MSC* 5: 1-16.
        Addenda to 1954.4, with entries from 1544 to 1634.

1959.23   ROTHWELL, W[ILLIAM] F[RANCIS]. "Was There a Typical Elizabethan Stage?" *Sh S* 12: 15-21.
        Examines the playhouses before 1598, permanent and temporary, and the different production methods utilized, using the new information obtained to answer the title's question in the negative.

1959.24   SELTZER, DANIEL. "Elizabethan Acting in *Othello*." *SQ* 10 (Spring): 201-10.
        Discusses the acting style for this play, based both on internal and external evidence. Stage directions implicit in the dialogue and comments in other sources indicate that relatively realistic business was used.

1959.25   SOUTHERN, RICHARD. "On Reconstructing a Practicable Elizabethan Playhouse." *ShS* 12: 22-34.
        Attempts "to estimate how far our present knowledge allows us to reconstruct a 'typical' Elizabethan playhouse sufficiently authentic to permit practical study of production." Using primarily the Fortune and Hope contracts and the Swan drawing, Southern comes up with a sixteen-sided polygonal structure 92 feet wide, with a stage 43 feet wide. There are the usual three

galleries (with standing space behind two rows of seats in the uppermost). The tiring house facade has two doors with curtains between, obscuring "a small discovery space," and a balcony running from side to side.

1959.26   STAMM, RUDOLF. "Elizabethan Stage-Practice and the Transmutation of Source Material by the Dramatists." *ShS* 12: 64-70.
        Argues that "the comparison between a play and its source renders us particularly sensitive to all those features in it that characterize it as a text intended for a certain type of stage performance." *Antony and Cleopatra* is the primary example cited. Stamm also stresses the importance of discovering implied stage directions embedded in the dialogue.

1959.27   STONE, LAWRENCE, ed. "Companies of Players Entertained by the Earl of Cumberland and Lord Clifford, 1607-39." *MSC* 5: 17-28.
        Extracts from the manuscripts of the Clifford family, with commentary. Most entries concern payments given to players. There are frequent mentions of company names and number of plays given as well as dates and amounts.

1959.28   STYAN, J. L. "The Actor at the Foot of Shakespeare's Platform." *ShS* 12: 56-63.
        Examines the actor's use of the depth of the Elizabethan stage in order to vary the type of contact with the audience. Styan finds six usual situations when the playwright sends the actor downstage: 1) the actor introduces himself and establishes an emotional relationship with the spectator; 2) the actor points out another character and establishes the relationship between them; 3) a character coments on a scene without himself leaving it; 4) the audience must distinguish some characters from the rest; 5) the audience temporarily collaborates in a deceit because of the revelation of a secret; and 6) the playwright suggests contrasting values of sincerity between characters. Styan draws examples from several plays by Shakespeare and others.

1959.29   WICKHAM, GLYNNE. *Early English Stages 1300-1660.* Vol. 1, *1300-1576.* London: Routledge and Kegan Paul; New York: Columbia University Press, 428 pp.
        The first of a projected five-volume work attempting "to trace the history of English stagecraft from its beginnings to the advent of the proscenium-arched scenic theatres that became public property shortly after the Restoration of the Monarchy in 1660." This volume establishes the background that the Elizabethans later built on. The three books that compose it treat open air entertainments of the middle ages, indoor entertainments of the same period, and dramatic theory and practice to 1576. Two more volumes had been published (1963.20 and 1972.32) at the time of initial publication of this book.

1960.1   AUERBACH, LAWRENCE. "The Use of Time in Plays of Four Periods of the Drama." Ph.D. dissertation, University of Wisconsin, 362 pp.
  The periods considered are classical, Elizabethan, realistic, and postrealistic. In each section Auerbach considers the physical stage, the audience, the critics and theorists, and the plays. Essentially he examines the relative advantages of observing the unity of time and its implications.

1960.2   BRADBROOK, M[URIEL] C. "Drama as Offering: *The Princely Pleasures* at Kenelworth." *Rice Institute Pamphlets* 46: 57-70
  Discusses what we know of Elizabethan country welcomes and the first text of a court show to survive. Elizabeth visited the Earl of Leicester from 9 to 28 July 1575, and the Earl is said to have spent over £1000 per day. Two accounts survive, one by George Gascoigne, who devised some of the outdoor shows, and Laneham's *Letter*. Bradbrook claims that the great historical drama of the Elizabethan age was born out of these personal offerings to Elizabeth.

1960.3   BURTON, E. J. *The British Theatre: Its Repertory and Practice, 1100-1900 A.D.*   London: Herbert Jenkins, pp. 59-138.
  Emphasizes presenting period plays today, but includes historical information. The relevant section includes chapters on Interludes, Renaissance drama, Elizabethan theatre, dance and decoration, Shakespeare, and the later Elizabethans.

1960.4   CAIRNCROSS, A. S. "Pembroke's Men and Some Shakespearian Piracies." *SQ* 11 (Summer): 335-49.
  Suggests that four of the earlier Shakespeare quartos-- *2 Henry VI, 3 Henry VI, Richard 111, Romeo and Juliet*-- were memorial reconstructions made by the same group of actors, members of Pembroke's company, when their group disbanded in 1593.

1960.5   CUTTS, JOHN P. "'Speak--Demand--We'll Answer' : Hecat(e) and 'the other three witches.'" *JDSG* 96:173-76.
  Responds to Flatter, 1959.5, reiterating his argument in 1958.6 for the presence of six witches plus Hecate instead of only three in *Macbeth*, and for the placement of the "Come away' song (1II.v.) before Hecate's exit. <u>See also</u> 1957.6; 1960.7.

1960.6   EDWARDS, H. R. L. "'Atorno, Atorno.'" *TLS* (10 June): 369.
  Responds to tiotson (1954.14). painting out an inconsistency in Hotson's use of "round."

1960.7   FLATTER, RICHARD. "Professor Platter's Reply." *JPSG* 96: 192-93.
  Replies to Cutts (1960.51, in the form of a letter suggesting an end to the controversy over the "other three witches" in *Macbeth*.

1960.8   FOAKES, R. A. "The Significance of Henslowe's *Diary*." *PP* 3, no. 4: 214-22.
          A modified version of a lecture given at Bratislava in November 1959. Foakes discusses in general terms the classes of evidence for Elizabethan stage conditions provided by the diary.

1960.9   GURR, A[NDREW] J. "DeWitt's Sketch of the Swan." *N&Q*, n.s. 7 (September): 328.
          Argues that what appear to be supports for the stage in the Swan drawing are actually the hangings around the stage that have been partially drawn open.

1960.10   HOLMES, MARTIN R. *Shakespeare's Public: The Touchstone of His Genius.* London: John Murray, 237 pp.
          Essentially a critical commentary on the plays, within the cultural context of the period. The audience serves as a point of reference for literary criticism rather than the central feature of the investigation. Reprinted with corrections: 1964.16.

1960.11   HOSLEY, RICHARD. "Was There a Music Room in Shakespeare's Globe?" *ShS* 13: 113-23.
          Examines the evidence for the upper curtained music room in Elizabethan theatres in general and at the first Globe in particular. Hosley limits his "internal" evidence to the thirty extant plays performed at that playhouse 1599-1608. These are with one exception unanimous in designating off-stage music at the first Globe as "within," which indicates the first level of the tiring house rather than the second or third, as J. C. Adams proposed (<u>see</u> 1942.1). Hosley concludes that "there was probably not a music-room over the stage at the First Globe before 1609."

1960.12   M[ARDER], L[OUIS]. "Hotson's Jack-in-the-Box Staging." *ShN* 10 (December): 44-45.
          Responds to Hotson (1959.9), arguing against his location of the tiring house beneath the stage.

1960.13   MITHAL, H. S. D. "'Mr. Kemp, called Don Gulielmo.'" *N&Q*, n.s. 7 (January): 6-8.
          Replies to Bald's response (1959.3) to his earlier note (1958.13) by examining the context of a letter cited by Bald and suggesting that it was not Will Kempe the actor who was referred to but perhaps a priest with the same name.

1960.14   PUTZEL, ROSAMUND. "Structural Patterns in the Repertory of the Child Actors through 1591." Ph.D. dissertation, University of North Carolina, 238 pp.
          Essentially a literary study of plays written for the boy companies at Paul's, Eton, Westminster, and elsewhere before 1591. Putzel concludes "that basic structural patterns changed and multiplied enormously . . . that continuity

was maintained in traditional English songs and comic themes, and there was a strong predilection on the part of later audiences for subject matter from classical narratives and mythology."

1960.15   RIEWALD, J. G. "New Light on the English Actors in the Netherlands, c. 1590-c. 1660." *ES*, 41, no. 2 (April): 65-92.

        Examines the English strolling players on the continent. Almost all began their tours in the Netherlands, many joining with native actors. Riewald's discussion is chronological, based upon newly discovered documents in city and national archives.

1960.16   SAUNDERS, J. W. "Staging at the Globe, 1599-1613," *SQ* 11 (Autumn): 401-25.

        Attempts to "explore a way out of the present position of scholarly stalemate by outlining certain principles . . . and then applying them to a reexamination of the basic problems." Saunders's principles are: I) the plays of one theatre at a time should be investigated; 2) deductions from staging necessities inferred from the action of the play rather than textual references should be made; 3) different solutions to staging problems are not necessarily mutually exclusive, and similar scenes may have been staged differently at different times; and 4) the design of the playhouse happened less by choice than by accumulated tradition. Saunders concludes that in addition to two doorways, there were two "wing" entrances to the Globe stage; that action above took place in two bay window side stages; that the areas underneath these bays (called "lower bays") were used for concealment; and that arras were hung across the back wall for discoveries. Reprinted: 1968.3.

1960.17   SHIRLEY, FRANCES ANN. "Shakespeare's Use of Off-Stage Sound." Ph.D. dissertation, Bryn Mawr College, 257 pp.

        Published as 1963.13.

1960.18   SISSON, C[HARLES] J[ASPER]. "The Laws of Elizabethan Copyright: The Stationer's View." *Library*, 5th ser. 15 (March): 8-20.

        Examines the problem of Elizabethan copyright in the light of evidence provided by Thomas Dawson, twice master of the Stationers' Company. Of theatrical interest because of the problems of using published plays to determine staging practices.

1960.19   _____. "The Theatres and the Companies." In *A Companion to Shakespeare Studies*. Edited by Harley Granville-Barker and G[eorge] B[agshawe] Harrison. New York: Doubleday, Anchor Books, pp. 9-43.

        Reprint of 1934,11.

1960.20   SOUTHERN, RICHARD. "The Mystery of the Elizabethan Stage." *Listener* 63 (24 March): 533-35.
        Text of a BBC radio program. The "mystery" of the title is what the stage looked like, and Southern reviews the possibilities in light of the theories of Lawrence, Hotson, and Hosley.

1961

1961.1   ADAMS, JOHN CRANFORD. *The Globe Playhouse: Its Design and Equipment.* 2d ed. New York: Barnes & Noble, 435 pp.
        Second edition of 1942.1. Revises the section an early maps and views; adds photographs of his model of the Globe and an analysis of the staging of *King Lear*. Reprinted: 1964.1.

1961.2   ARMSTRONG, WILLIAM A. "The Enigmatic Elizabethan Stage." *English* 13 (Autumn): 216-20.
        Brief "state of the art" survey, focusing on the staging of indoor scenes and, in particular, the use of the term "canopy." Armstrong suggests the use of a projecting curtained space for these scenes, and for discoveries in general, although his evidence is drawn from a variety of times and theatres. See also 1957.1.

1961.3   BRADBROOK, M[URIEL] C. "'Silk? Satin? Kersey? Rags?'--The Choristers' Theater under Elizabeth and James." *SEL* 1 (Spring): 53-64.
        Argues that the choristers' theatres declined as the common players flourished, because the boys "could not compete with the power and range of the masterpieces of ripeness and judgment that were written for the popular stages." They were "a decaying relic of the older nobility faced with a new and flourishing estate." <u>See also</u> 1961.4; 1962.4.

1961.4   BRADBROOK, MURIEL C. "The Status Seekers: Society and the Common Player in the Reign of Elizabeth I." *HLQ* 24 (February): 111-24.
        Originally a paper read 11 July 1959 at a Huntington Library Seminar. Bradbrook examines the rise in status of the conwon players in England in the sixteenth century through the pretense of serving some great Lord.

1961.5   COOK, DAVID, ed. "Dramatic Records in the Declared Accounts of the Treasury of the Chamber, 1550-1642." *MSC* 6:l-175.
        Includes records of payments to players and for "apparellings," and biographical notes, with several appendixes detailing references to entertainments in various other documents.

1961.6   DAVID, RICHARD. "Shakespeare and the Players." *PBA* 47: 139-59.
        The annual Shakespeare Lecture before the British Academy, read 19 April 1961. David examines what we know of Shakespeare's acting company,

based primarily on Baldwin (1927.1) and Joseph (1951.18). He discusses casting, the boy actors, rehearsals, and playwriting.

1961.7   DAWSON, GILES E. "Strolling Players in Kent." *ORRD* 5: 7-12.
While Dawson concentrates here on the fifteenth century, he also covers sixteenth-century records. This is but a brief report on his research. See also 1965.6.

1961.8   EGGAR, KATHARINE E. "The Blackfriars Plays and Their Music: 1576-1610." *PMLA* 87: 57-68.
A paper delivered before the Royal Music Association, 16 March 1961. Eggar examines the origin, maintenance, and disappearance of the boy companies playing at Blackfriars during the period. She traces the involvement of the Earl of Oxford, William Hunnis, Richard Farrant, Henry Evans, Nathaniel Giles, George Peele, John Mundy, and Sebastian Westcote in the first Blackfriars, and touches on the second.

1961.9   ELLIS-FERMOR, UNA M. "The Jacobean Stage." In *The Jacobean Drama: An Interpretation*. 4th ed. London: Methuen, pp. 273-83.
Reprint of 1936.8.

1961.10   FELVER, CHARLES S[TANLEY]. *Robert Armin, Shakespeare's Fool: A Biographical Essay*. Kent State University Bulletin 49, no. 1: Research Series, no. 5. Kent: Rent State University, 82 pp.
Partial publication of 1956.11

1961.11   FOAKES, R. A. "The Profession of Playwright." In *Early Shakespeare*. Stratford-Upon-Avon Studies, no. 3. London: Edward Arnold, pp. 11-33.
Examines theatrical conditions in general rather than, as the title suggests, the profession of playwright. Foakes includes in his discussion the theatres, companies, finance, repertories, and acting.

1961.12   ____, and RICKERT, R[OBERT] T[URNAM]. "An Elizabethan Stage Drawing?" *ShS* 13: 111-12.
Reproduces a sketch from Henslowe's papers that might be meant to represent a stage.

1961.13   HENSLOWE, PHILIP. *Henslowe's Diary*. Edited by R. A. Foakes and R[obert] T[urnam] Rickert. Cambridge: University Press, 426 pp.
A new edition based on fresh transcripts of all available material. A fifty-nine-page introduction is followed by the text of the diary, which is in turn followed by three indexes and a glossary. This has become the definitive edition. See also 1790.1; 1045.3; 1904.7; 1907.15; 1908.11; 1977.87.

1961.14   IVES, E. W. "Tom Skelton--A Seventeenth-Century Jester." *ShS* 13: 90-105.
Examines the costume of the fool, based on evidence presented in two contemporary paintinge of Tom Skelton. Patterned motley or patchwork seems to have been the uniform of the fool, and it was faithfully recreated on the stage.

1961.15   JOSEPH, BERTRAM. "The Elizabethan Stage and Acting." In *The Age of Shakespeare*. Edited by Boris Ford. London: Cassell, pp. 139-53.
Reprint of 1955.12.

1961.16   _____. "The Elizabethan Stage and Acting." In *The Age of Shakespeare*. Edited by Boris Ford. Pelican Guide to English Literature, no. 2. London: Pelican Books, pp. 139-53.
Reprint of 1955.12.

1961.17   MacKICHAN, L. A. L. "The Elizabethan Stage." *TLS* (6 October): 672.
Provides support for Hotson's theory of arena staging (see 1959.9) from Milton's *Samson Agonistes*.

1961.18   PATERSON, MORTON. "The Stagecraft of the Revels Office during the Reign of Elizabeth." In *Studies in the Elizabethan Theatre*. Edited by Charles T. Prouty. Hamden, Conn.: Shoe String Press, pp. 1-52.
Organizes and presents the information from the Revels documents relevant to stage practice, based primarily on Feuillerat (1908.6) and Chambers (1923.2).

1961.19   PEET, ALICE LIDA. "The History and Development of Simultaneous Scenery in the West from the Middle Ages to the Modern United States." Ph.D. dissertation, University of Wisconsin, 393 pp.
Despite the time frame implied in the title, this work does not examine the Elizabethan period.

1961.20   PROUTY, CHARLES T., ed. *Studies in the Elizabethan Theatre*. Hamden, Conn.: Shoe String Press, 198 pp.
Contains a brief introduction and a twelve-page bibliography (all relevant items of which have been incorporated into this one) as well as three essays (1961.18, 22, 25).

1961.21   ROSS, LAWRENCE J. "The Use of a 'Fit-Up' Booth in *Othello*." *SQ* 12 (Autumn): 359-70.
Examines the possible use of a portable curtained booth for the staging of *Othello*, particularly the last scene. Evidence for the presence of this structure is found in Iago's line in V.i. ("stand behind this bulk") and in the beginning of I.iii. with a discovery. Ross sees the booth as a structure of variously modifiable neutrality.

1961.22   SARLOS, ROBERT K. "Development and Operation of the First Blackfriars Theatre." In *Studies in the Elizabethan Theatre*. Edited by Charles T. Prouty. Hamden, Conn.: Shoe String Press, pp. 137-78.

      An attempt to summarize all that is known about the first Blackfriars, primarily from Feuillerat (1910.8; 1912.6; 1913.3), Wallace (1912.23), and Hillebrand (1926.6).

1961.23   SOUTHERN, RICHARD. *The Seven Ages of the Theatre*. New York: Hill & Wang, pp. 155-214.

      The relevant section is the fourth, "The Organized Examines the use of discovery space and the acting Stage." This is more a thumb-nail sketch than a fully area developed historical investigation, with quite a different purpose. Southern wishes to examine the evolution of the forms theatre has taken throughout the world, with an eye toward "the establishment of a body of information upon which the planning of new theatres can proceed with understanding." Consequently, there is a good deal of cross-cultural comparison, which is the work's greatest strength. For example, the Elizabethan stage is compared to the classical Chinese, the Noh, the Teatro Olimpico, the classical Indian, and the comnmedia dell'arte stages.

1961.24   STEVENS, JOHN E. *Music and Poetry in the Early Tudor Court*. Lincoln: University of Nebraska Press; London: Methuen, pp. 233-64.

      The relevant section is Chapter 11, "Music in Ceremonies, Entertainments, and Plays." Stevens touches on early Elizabethan court drama.

1961.25   STINSON, JAEIES. "Reconstruction of Elizabethan Public Play- houses." In *Studies in the Elizabethan Theatre*. Ed. by Charles T. Prouty. Aamden, Conn.: Shoe String Press, pp. 53-136.

      A summary of major reconstructions, including those by Hodges, Southern, Tieck, Archer and Godfrey, Chambers, Brodmeier, Albright, Corbin, Smith, Nicoll, Kernodle, Forrest, J. Q. Adams, J. C. Adams, and Hotson. A brief appendix lists thirty-two commonly reproduced maps and views of London, and twelve plates give visualizations of the reconstructions described. Stinson evaluates as well as describes each reconstruction. He finds Hodges's "the most careful and conservative attempt yet made."

1961.26   UNGERER, GUSTAV. "An Unrecorded Elizabethan Performance of *Titus Andronicus*." *ShS* 14: 102-9.

      Prints an eyewitness account (written in French) of a pre-1596 performance of the play at a private house in Rutland. The letter is included in the Anthony Bacon Papers preserved in Lambeth Place Library. The private performance was presented by an unknown professional company, perhaps the Lord Admiral's Men or the Lord Chamberlain's Men.

1961.27   WEINER, A[LBERT] B. "Elizabethan Interior and Aloft Scenes: A
Speculative Essay." *ThS* 2: 15-34.
        Examines the use of the discovery space and the acting area above, and
speculates that a solid but hinged and folding pavillion would solve the problems
of staging such scenes. Such a structure would be appropriate for scenes on the
walls and scenes calling for tents as well. The Swan drawing does not show this
pavilion because it is folded up and invisible against the tiring house facade.

1961.28   WRIGHT, LOUIS B. *Shakespeare's Theatre and the Dramatic Tradition.*
Washington: Folger Shakespeare Library, 36 pp.
        Reprint of 1958.24.

1962

1962.1   BALL, ROMA. "The Choir-Boy Actors of St. Paul's Cathedral." *ESRS* 10, no.
4 (June): 5-16.
        Based on an M.A. thesis at Kansas State Teachers College, Emporia, and
partially presented at the 1961 meeting of the Central Renaissance Society. Ball
traces several of the boys through their future careers, finding that seven became
distinguished musicians while only two (or possibly three) became actors.

1962.2   BECKERMAN, BERNARD. *Shakespeare at the Globe, 1599-1609.* New
York: Macmillan, 254 pp.
        Published version of 1956.3. Examines fifteen Shakespearean and
fourteen non-Shakespearean plays first produced at the Globe during the years
that the Chamberlain's/King's Men played only at that theatre. The five major
chapters treat the repertory, the dramaturgy, the stage, the acting, and the staging,
and a brief sixth chapter defines the style. Beckerman concludes that the style of
production at the Globe was "chiefly characterized.by its reconciliation of the
contradictory demands of convention and reality," defining the style as "at once,
ceremonial, romantic, and epic." He examines each part of the Globe stage (doors,
upper area, pillars, third door or enclosed space) carefully and thoroughly.

1962.3   BRADBROOK, M[URIEL] C. *Elizabethan Stage Conditions: A Study of Their
Place in the Interpretation of Shakespeare's Plays.* Hamden, Conn.: Archon, 149
pp.
        Reprint of 1932.2.

1962.4   ____. *The Rise of the Common Player: A Study of Actor and Society in
Shakespeare's England.* Cambridge: Harvard University Press, 326 pp.
        Explores "the social envelope within which [the Elizabethan plays] were
made." Bradbrook contends that actors were a new and experimental social group,
and that the opposition they met is a classic example of the force of unexamined
assumptions and social prejudice. The only new discovery revealed is a letter,
previously reprinted but without indication of authorship, that Bradbrook ascribes
to one of the Earl of Leicester's Men. The letter, as the only remaining literary

production from this first great Elizabethan acting company, thus becomes a document of importance to the theatre historian.

1962.5   CHILDS, HUBERT E. "On the Elizabethan Staging of *Hamlet*." *SQ* 13 (Autumn): 463-74.
> Not a historical piece, but an examination of the play as staged at Ashland, Oregon, in 1961.

1962.6   GOUSSEFF, JAMES WILLIAM. "The Staging of Prologues in Tudor and Stuart Plays." Ph.D. dissertation, Northwestern University, 609 pp.
> Investigates costume, makeup, properties employed, and staging of prologues. The prologue speaker's performance is traced "from the soundings which heralded his entrance to the bows which were the precursors of his exit," including choice of entrance and exit doors, contact with the audience, various forms of salutation, probable position on stage, and the nature of movement and gesture.

1962.7   HOOK, LUCYLE. "The Curtain." *SQ* 13 (Autumn): 499-504.
> Reveals discovery of a document bearing on this playhouse in The Calendar of Treasury Books that may establish its location and indicate that it still stood in 1690. Hook includes a complete review of the information available on the Curtain, with the suggestion that Collier's account of the end of the playhouses might be fictitious.

1962.8   JONES, ELDRED D. "The Physical Representation of African Characters on the English Stage during the 16th and 17th Centuries." *TN* 17 (Autumn): 17-21.
> Discusses the use of makeup, wigs, and costumes to portray black characters.

1962.9   JONES, MARION, and WICKHAM, GLYNNE. "Stage Furnishings of George Chapman's *The Tragedy of Charles, Duke of Biron*." *TN* 16 (Summer): 113-17.
> Discusses the possibility that the 1608 performance and printed play were based on a 1602 version referred to in Henslowe's diary. If this was the case, a scaffold and bar would both have been necessary for its staging.

1962.10   JOSEPH, BERTRAM. "The Elizabethan Stage and Acting." In *The Age of Shakespeare*. Edited by Boris Ford. Pelican Guide to English Literature, no. 2. Baltimore: Penguin Books, pp. 147-61.
> Reprint of 1955.12.

1962.11   KLEIN, DAVID. "Did Shakespeare Produce His Own Plays?" *MLN* 57 (October): 556-60.
> Differs with Hart, who claimed there was no direct evidence to support the theory that Shakespeare produced his own plays. Klein cites Johannes Rhenanus, a German visitor who claims to have witnessed a rehearsal; a Nashe play; Dekker's *Satiromastix*; Jonson's *Cynthia's Revels*; Bishop Hall's

Virgidermiarum; and a variety of other plays by Marston, Shirley, Munday, Middleton and Rowley, Massinger, and Jonson as evidence that the playwright normally directed his own work.

1962.12   LENNEP, WILLIAM Van. "The Death of the Red Bull." *TN* 216 (Summer): 126-34.
        Concerns the playhouse after the Restoration.

1962.13   McMANAWAY, JAMES G. "Notes an Two Pre-Restoration Stage Curtains." *PQ* 341 (January): 270-74.
        Examines the possibility that the front curtains shown in two largely ignored illustrations from the middle of the seventeenth century might help clarify staging practices in the court masques. Reprinted: 1969.8

1962.14   McNEIR, WALDO F. "The Staging of the Dover Cliff Scene in *King Lear*." In *Studies in English Renaissance Literature*. Edited by Waldo F. McNeir. Louisiana State University Studies, Humanities Series, no. 12. Baton Rouge: Louisiana State University Press, pp. 87-104.
        Originally a lecture at the University of Oregon, 1961. Suggests the use of a portable curtained booth, with a seven or eight foot jump, for Gloucester's Dover cliff scene.

1962.15   REYNOLDS, GEORGE F[ULLMER]. "Two Conventions of the Open Stage (as Illustrated in *King Lear*?)." *PQ* 41 (January): 82-95.
        Examines the possible use of curtains in front of a central doorway and continuous open staging for *King Lear*, with emphasis on the change of Location indicated by a character's immediate re-entry through a different doorway than the one used for the exit.

1962.16   RIFFE, NANCY LEE. "Shakespeare's Stage: A Bibliography." *ShN* 12 (November):   40.
        An unannotated list of books and articles on the physical stage from 1940 to 1962. All relevant entries have been incorporated into this bibliography.

1962.17   ROSENFELD, SYBIL. *Foreign Theatrical Companies in Great Britain in the Seventeenth and Eighteenth Centuries*. Pamphlet Series, no. 1. London: Society for Theatre Research, p. 1.
        Reprint of 1955.20.

1962.18   SMITH, HAL H. "Some Principles of Elizabethan Stage Costume." *JWCI* 25 (June): 240-57.
        A reevaluation of Elizabethan costuming practice, concluding that such plays as Troilus and Cressida were costumed in the classical manner as the Renaissance understood it. Evidence from the plays and emblem books is considered in the light of the Peachum illustration for *Titus Andronicus* and Platter's commentary.

1962.19   STAMM, RUDOLPH. "Dichtung und Theater in Shakespeares Werk." *JDSG* 90: 7-23.

A paper presented 22 February 1962 in Basel. Stamm argues for consideration of the theatrical--both in terms of staging and acting style—in the interpretation of Shakespeare.

1962.20   STOLZENBACH, CONRAD. "A Critical Acting Edition of *Antonio and Mellida* by John Marston (1602)." Ph.D. dissertation, University of Michigan, 258 pp.

Includes in the first section a history of the Children of Paul's, the company for which the play was written, and

1962.21   WAITH, EUGENE M. "The Staging of Bartholomew Fair." *SEL* 2 (Spring): 181-96.

A reconstruction of the original production at the Hope, 31 October 1614, based on information in the text and from the records of the Court performance the following day. Waith assigns the Hope two doorways (since it was supposedly similar to the Swan) and assumes the use of canvas-covered booths, as in the Court performance. Since three entrances are required, the arras must have covered the entire tiring house facade, with entrances through the middle and at either end. The booths were portable, being set up and taken down as needed.

1962.22   WEINER, ALBERT B. "Two Tents in Richard III?" *SQ* 13 (Summer): 258-60.

Responds to Fusillo (1955.5) and Hosley (1956.16), arguing for the presence of one tent on the stage, pitched by Richard's men at his command, and used by Richmond as his tent when Richard exits. The argument is based on stage directions in the First Folio.

1962.23   WICKLAND, ERIC. *Elizabethan Players in Sweden, 1591-92: Facts and Problems*. Stockholm: Almqvist & Wiksell, 199 pp.

Examines the English company at Nyköping in Sweden 1591-92. Previously believed to have been composed exclusively of musicians, this company may also have included actors. The recruiting, passage, and performance of the group is carefully scrutinized. Wickland cautiously concludes that the question is still open. See 1971.18.

1963

1963.1   BANKS, HOWARD MILTON. "A Historical Survey of the Mise-en-Scene Employed in Shakespearean Productions from the Elizabethan Period to the Present." Ph.D. dissertation, University of Southern California, 821 pp.

The relevant section is the first chapter, which surveys the nature of the Elizabethan playhouse and stage, concluding that "the data concerning the Globe public playhouse structure revealed a composite picture only of the physical characteristics attributable to any public playhouse of the day, Basically, there were Elizabethan playhouses with certain similarities, employing acting areas, balconies, windows, and doors which were common to all."

1963.2   BENTLEY, G[ERALD] E[ADES]. "Lenten Performances in the Jacobean and Caroline Theaters." In *Essays on Shakespeare and the Elizabethan Drama in Honor of Gordon Craig.* Edited by Richard Hosley. London: Routledge & Kegan Paul, pp. 351-59.
   A preliminary examination of evidence concerning Lenten performances (later published in more complete form as an appendix to 1968.2). Bentley concludes that the London theatres produced "a reduced number of plays, as well as variety turns, four days a week during the first five and a half weeks of Lent."

1963.3   FLECKNOE, RICHARD. "A Short Discourse of the English Stage." In *Critical Essays of the Seventeenth Century,* Vol. 2. Edited by J. E. Spingarn. Bloomington: Indiana University Press, pp. 91-96.
   Reprint of 1664.1.

1963.4   FOAKES, R. A. "Henslowe and the Theatre of the 1590s." *Renaissance Drama: A Report on Research Opportunities* 6: 4-6.
   Delineates some of the shortcomings of Greg's work on the Henslowe diary and papers (1904.7; 1907.15; 1900.11) as part of the rationale of his own edition (with Rickert, 1961.13). Ultimately, Foakes sees a need for a comprehensive history of the stage in the volatile 1590s. See in this regard 1964.31.

*1963.5   GURR, ANDREW J. "Elizabethan Acting and Shakespeare's Compnny." Ph.D. dissertation, Cambridge University.
   Cited in *DEAL,* p. 535.

1963.6   GURR, A[NDREW J.] 3. "Who Strutted and Bellowed?" *ShS* 16: 95-102.
   Examines the two distinct kinds of acting among the adult companies in the early seventeenth century, in response to Armstrong (1954.2). Gurr cites five references to Tamburlaine's violence to support his claim for exaggeration in the Red Bull style put forward by Alleyn.

1963.7   HARRIS, ANTHONY J. "William Poel's Elizabeth Stage: The First Experiment." *TN* 17 (Summer): 111-15.
   Describes the apron-stage model of the Fortune that Poel used in his 1893 production of *Measure for Measure.*

1963.8   HOSLEY, RICHARD. "An Approach to the Elizabethan Stage." *Renaissance Drama: A Report on Research Opportunities* 6: 72-78.
   Puts forward Hosley's theory of the use of stage doors for discovery spaces by drawing open the hangings in Elizabethan stage, reconciling their differences. No evidence is presented here, but the reader is referred to Hosley's "forthcoming book, *Elizabethan Playhouse Stages.*" While this work has not yet

appeared, it promises to be a major contribution to the field when it does. See Index, under Hosley, for his many articles.

1963.9   ____. "The Staging of Desdemona's Bed." *SQ* 14 (Winter): 57-65.
> Responds to Ross (1961.21), suggesting that the bed used in V.ii. was thrust out, not discovered. Hosley examines the staging of bed scenes in all plays written far the Chamberlain's/King's Men 1595-1642. Twenty-three uses of this property are catalogued, and in sixteen it is stated or implied that the bed is not brought on stage; in five, there is no evidencc that the bed was discovered; and in the other two there is no evidence for the use of a portable booth.

1963.10   JOSEPH, STEPHEN. *The Story of the Playhouse in England.* London: Barrie & Rockliff, pp. 42-74.
> The relevant section is chapters two through four, "First Stages," "Shakespeare and Company," and "Jonson v. Jones." Joseph summarizes what is known of the playhouses and production practices, and the presentation of masques. This is a secondary study aimed at a general or perhaps a school audience.

1963.11   KING, THOMAS JAMES. "Production of Plays at the Phoenix, 1617-42." Ph.D. dissertation, Columbia University, 261 pp.
> Examines textual evidence concerning staging methods employed at one of the most important private playhouses, the Phoenix in Drury Lane. King selects the thirty-two plays from the Phoenix repertory whose title-page claim of Phoenix production can be verified in an external historical markings related to prompt copy. Each text is examined for evidence of staging practices. King then divides the plays into two groups, depending upon staging requirements. The plays of the first group require nothing more than two doors and a platform for their staging, while the plays of the second group require an area above, hangings, a discovery space, or some combination of these elements. King suggests that the needs of the plays of the second group could be met if a portable curtained booth were set on the stage or if the playhouse possessed a gallery that could be used to suspend the hangings in front of a doorway. The first chapter traces the history of the playhouse, and appendices deal with music, dancing, and effects. See also 1965.9; 1971.10.

1963.12   REYNOLDS, GEORGE F[ULLMER]. "The Return of the Open Stage." *In Essays on Shakespeare and Elizabethan Drama in Honor of Gordon Craig.* Edited by Richard Hosley. London: Routledge & Kegan Paul, pp. 361-68.
> Reviews differing views of the Elizabethan stage, from the alternation theory to J. C. Adams to Richard Hosley, including practical reconstructions for production purposes.

1963.13   SHIRLEY, FRANCES ANN. *Shakespeare's Use of Off-Stage Sounds*. Lincoln: University of Nebraska Press, 258 pp.

Published version of 1960.17. Shirley discusses both the use and production of off-stage sounds, concentrating on *Julius Caesar, Hamlet*, and *Macbeth*. In an appendix she lists all such sounds she finds necessary in Shakespeare.

1963.14   SMITH, GORDON ROSS. *A Classified Shakespeare Bibliography, 1936-1958*. University Park: Pennsylvania State University Press, pp. 294-300.

A comprehensive but minimally annotated bibliography of scholarship for the years listed, continuing 1937.3. All relevant items have been incorporated into this bibliography.

1963.15   SOUTHERN, RICHARD. "The Contribution of the Interludes to Elizabethan Staging." In *Essays in Shakespeare an6 Elizabethan Drama in Honor of Gordon Craig*. Edited by Richard Hosley. London: Routledge & Kegan Paul, pp. 3-14.

Suggests that the groundwork for the Elizabethan drama was laid down in the interludes of the sixteenth century, that the interludes could be played on a portable booth-stage as well as before a hall screen, and that the hall screen and the booth-stage might have served as the prototype of the tiring facade.

*1963.16   SUGA, YASUO. *The Shakespearean Theatre and Stage*. Kyoto: Apollonsha. Cited in 1974.18.

1963.17   _____. "Theatre Ways, the Elizabethan and the Japanese." *ShStud* (Tokyo) 2: 1-9.

Compares Elizabethan stage conventions with their counterparts on the Kabuki and Noh stages. Suga discusses the stage-keepers, the open stage, and symbolic properties.

1963.18   SUMMERSON, JOHN [NEWENHAM]. *Architecture in Britain, 1530-1830*. 4th ed. Pelican History of Art, no. 23. Baltimore: Penguin Books, pp. 61-67. Reprint of 1953.26.

1963.19   UNWIN, GEORGE. *The Guilds and Companies of London*. 4th ed. London: Frank Cass & Co., 397 pp. Reprint of 1909.29.

1963.20   WICKHAM, GLYNNE. *Early English Stages 1300-1660*. Vol. 2, Pt. 1, *1576-1660*. New York: Columbia University Press, 408 pp.

The second of a projected five-volume work, intended to apply the information gathered in the first volume (1959.29) to the rise of the commercial theatre in London. The Tudor Interlude is seen as "the crucible in which a predominantly amateur and religious drama came to be translated into a predominantly professional and secular one." The two books that compose the volume deal with the regulation of the theatrc and the emblematic tradition, which

Wickham sees as central. The volume closes with a detailed description of the Swan, DeWitt's sketch of which Wickham accepts at face value. See also 1972.32.

1963.21   WILSON, F[RANK] P[ERCY]. "Lambarde, the Bel Savage and the Theatre." *N&Q*, n.s. 10 (March): 92-93.
   Points out that the reference to the Bel Savage Inn used as a playhouse in the 1576 edition of *Perambulation of Kent* is one of the earliest allusions to the use of the inn for that purpose. The second edition (1596) includes a reference to the Theatre.

1963.22   WRIGHT, LOUIS B. *Shakespeare's Theatre and the Dramatic Tradition.* Washington: Folger Shakespeare Library, 36 pp.
   Reprint of 1958.24.

1964

1964.1   ADAMS, JOHN CMNFORD. *The Globe Playhouse: Its Design and Equipment.* 2d ed. New York: Barnes & Noble, 435 pp.
   Reprint of 1961.1.

1964.2   ANGLO, SYDNEY. "La salle de banquet et le théâtre construits a Greenwich pour les fêtes franco-anglaises de 1527." In *Le lieu théâtral à la Renaissance.* Edited by Jean Jacquot. Paris: CNRS, pp. 273-88.
   Discusses the tradition of constructing provisional banqueting halls and theatres to house festivities held on occasions of diplomatic triumphs on the continent and in England during the sixteenth century. Specifically, Anglo examines the 1515 banqueting house in Greenwich and the 1520 banqueting house in Calais, both of which lead up to the 1527 Greenwich structure. This last is exceedingly well documented, and Anglo describes the festivities in detail, including construction practices, payments, dimensions, decor and ornamentation, and use. See also second edition (1968.1) and Hosley (1979.15).

1964.3   ARMSTRONG, WILLIAM A. "Actors and Theatres." *ShS* 17: 191-204.
   A general treatment of these two topics for a volume dealing with Elizabethan life. Armstrong examines acting styles, favoring the "naturalistic"; simultaneous and changeable painted scenery; and such staging devices as bowers, tents, thrones, and canopies.

1964.4   BERGERON, DAVID MOORE. "Allegory in English Pageantry 1558-1625." Ph.D. dissertation, Vanderbilt University, 303 pp.
   Published, much revised and expanded, as 1971.3. See also Index, under Bergeron, for his many articles on the subject.

1964.5   BEST, MICHAEL R. "The Development of Ideas and Techniques in the Drama of John Lyly: A Critical Study." Ph.D. dissertation, University of Adelaide, pp. 31-112.

       The relevant section is Chapters II and III, "The Stage" and "The Plays in Production." Best argues far "a method of production which . . . gives to the plays a tautness of action, and even of symbolism, of which we would otherwise be unaware." He describes this method in his more accessible 1960.8.

1964.6   BRADBROOK, M[URIEL] C. "Shakespeare and the Elizabethan Theatre." *English Language and Literature* (Korea) 15: 3-34.

       Text of a lecture presented to the Shakespeare Society of Korea, 6 April 1964, Seoul National University. Bradbrook here examines performances in the public and private playhouses, focusing on *Richard III*, which she sees as typical of public theatre plays, with spectacle, color, and a firmly established leading part; *King Lear*; and *Tempest,* which shows strong influence of the form of the court masque.

1964.7   BROWNSTEIN, OSCAR LEE. "Stake and Stage: The Baiting Ring and the Public Playhouse in Elizabethan England." Ph.D. dissertation, University of Iowa, 460 pp.

       Examines the theory that the general form of the Elizabethan public playhouse derives from amphitheatres for the baiting of bulls and bears. Brownstein first discusses the history of organized baiting, then examines the evidence for the existence of amphitheatres for baiting predating the erection of the Theatre in 1576. He finds that the first public playhouse in fact predated the first baiting amphitheatre by seven years, so "the theory that baiting amphitheatres preceded the Elizabethan playhouse is wholly untenable." See Index, under Brownstein, for several articles on this and similar subjects.

1964.8   DAWSON, GILES E. "London's Bull-Baiting and Bear-Baiting Arena in 1562." *SQ* 15 (Winter): 97-101.

       The account of Venetian merchant Alessandro Maguo of his trip to England in 1562 furnishes a detailed description of bull and bear baiting. Darrson correlates this information with the surviving illustrations of the baiting rings.

1964.9   DOWNER, ALAN S. "Prolegomena to a Study of Elizabethan Acting." *MuK* 10: 625-36.

       Argues against arbitrarily defining Elizabethan acting in terms of "formal" or "natural." Instead, Downer suggests an eclectic approach, based on what we know the actor thought he was supposed to be doing. Ho cites a number of contemporary sources, and concludes that the acting style was "not unrelated to other aesthetic manifestations of the Renaissance, in dance, in painting, in architecture, in poetic imagery, and in music." The actor's purpose was "the metaphorical or emblematic enriching of the texture of the dramatic situation."

1964.10   ELLIS-FERMOR, UNA M. "The Jacobean Stage." In *The Jacobean Drama: An Interpretation*. Vintage History and Criticism of Literature, Music, and Art, no. 261. New York: Vintage Books, pp. 273-63.
            Reprint of 1936.8.

1964.11   FISCHER, SIDNEY. *The Theatre, the Curtain, and the Globe*. Montreal: McGill University Library, 15 pp.
            Cast in the form of a letter to one Richard (presumably, Hosley), dated 26 February 1963. Fischer prints three "contemporary and hitherto unrecognized views of the *Theatre*, the *Curtain*, & the (second) *Globe* playhouse": the Utrecht view (pre-1597) showing the Theatre and Curtain; and the Hollar view (1667) after the Greet Fire showing the Globe. Fischer establishes the point of view of each drawing and coordinates what is known about location from other sources.

*1964.12   FRENCH, JOSEPH NATHAN. "The Staging of Magical Effects in Elizabethan and Jacobean Drama." Ph.D. dissertation, University of Birmingham, 342 pp.
            Cited in *DEAL*, Supplement 1, p. 194.

1964.13   HARBAGE, ALFRED. *Annals of English Drama, 975-1700*. Revised by Samuel Schoenbaum. London: Methuen, 321 pp.
            Revised edition of 1940.7.

1964.14   _____. "Shakespearean Staging." *ShN* 14 (April-May): 31.
            Essentially a review of the literature, from the discovery of the Swan drawing in 1888 through Wickham, 1963.20.

1964.15   HODGES, C[YRIL] WALTER. *Shakespeare's Theatre*. London: Oxford University Press, 103 pp.
            An introduction to the Elizabethan theatre for a juvenile audience, tracing the medieval origins as well as presenting typical production elements at the Globe. While of course there is no scholarly apparatus, this volume is one of the best introductions to the field available, and the scope is very wide far so simple and brief a book. The illustrations are from an Encyclopedia Britannica filmstrip that Hodges made on the subject.

1964.16   HOLMES, MARTIN R. *Shakespeare's Public: The Touchstone of His Genius*. London: John Murray, 237 pp.
            Reprint, with corrections, of 1960.10.

1964.17   HOSLEY, BICHARD. "The Origins of the Shakespearian Playhouse." *SQ* 15 (Spring): 29-39.
            Examines specifically the hall screen and the animal-baiting houses as contributors to the origin of the Elizabethan theatres. The baiting houses--open to the sky, built in a large number of bays, two stories, with an unpaved pit, flying flags--apparently furnished a model for the building (but see Brownstein, 1964.7),

while the hall screen--two doors below, gallery above--furnished a model for the tiring house facade.

1964.18 _____. "Reconstitution du théâtre du Swan." In *Le lieu théâtral à la Renaissance*. Edited by Jean Jacquot. Paris: CNRS. pp. 295-316.
A reconstruction of the Swan, based on the DeWitt sketch. See 1975.15 for a similar reconstruction in English. See also second edition, 1968.18.

1964.19 ___. "The Shakespearean Theatre." *ShN* 214 (April-May): 32-33.
A brief assessment of the state of scholarship in the field, through the pointing out of eight "landmarks" in the development of our understanding.

1964.20 _____. "Shakespearian Stage Curtains: Then and Now." *CE* 25 (April): 488-92.
An examination of the Elizabethan stage curtains used for discoveries. Hosley claims that production techniques were essentially the same at all times in all Elizabethan theatres and that very few plays require discoveries. Regular stage doors were used for them, with a curtain hung up in front and drawn open. The "inner stage" curtain combines this function with the modern proscenium curtain.

1964.21 _____. "The Staging of the Monument Scenes in Antony and Cleopatra." *Library Chronicle* (University of Pennsylvania) 30 (Spring): 62-71.
Conjectural reconstruction of two scenes. Hosley contends that the tiring house gallery represented the monument and that Antony was carried in in a chair and hoisted aloft to Cleopatra with a winch. He cites a Rose play and the Revels Accounts for substantiation of the possibility. The second monument scene, says Hosley, was played on the platform. See 1945.1.

1964.22 JACQUOT, JEAN. "Le théâtre élisabéthain," in "Les types de lieu théâtral et leurs transformations." In *Le lieu théâtral à la Renaissance*. Edited by Jean Jacquot. Paris: CNRS, pp. 491-96.
Discusses the approaches of Hosley and Southern to the problems of the Elizabethan stage, as apposed to those of Adams and Smith, with a clear preference for the former. See also second edition, 1968.22.

1964.23 JAMIESON, MICHAEL. "Shakespeare's Celibate Stage." In *Papers Mainly Shakespearian*. Edited by G. I. Duthie. Aberdeen University Studies, no. 147. Edinburgh: Oliver & Boyd, pp. 21-39.
"A slightly revised version of a term paper written several years ago for Professor G. E. Bentley's graduate course on Shakespeare (English 525) at Princeton University." Jamieson examines Shakespeare's accommodation to the use of boy actors in three plays, arguing that the boys were highly trained, assured, and valuable, and that while female parts are limited in number and, frequently, length, there was no limitation imposed on the playwright by lack of ability or verisimilitude. Reprinted: 1.968.3.

*1964.24   JOHNSTON, ELIZABETH CARRINGTON. "The English Masque and the French Court Ballet, 1581-1640." Ph.D. dissertation, Harvard University. Cited in *ADDT*, p. 49.

1964.25   JOSEPH, B[ERTRAM] L. *Elizabethan Acting*. 2d ed. London: Oxford University Press, 115 pp.
    Second edition of 1951.8. The new edition deletes the account of the part rhetoric played in the scheme of humanist learning and considers the intervening twelve years of scholarship. The picture of Elizabethan acting presented is essentially unchanged, but Joseph takes pains to point out that he does not sit exclusively in the "formalist" school.

1964.26   LAVER, JAMES. "Costumes in Shakespeare's Plays." *MuE* 10: 275-81.
    A historical survey, touching on the Elizabethan period only briefly.

1964.27   LEECH, CLIFFORD, [E. J.] "The Acting of Malarlowe and Shakespeare." *ColQ* 13, no. 1 (Summer): 25-46.
    Originally one of the George Fullmer Reynolds Memorial Lectures for 1964. Leech discusses the formal requirements of Marlowe's plays and the increasingly realistic demands of Shakespeare's later work, primarily from the point of view of the modern actor.

1964.28   LYONS, CLIFFORD P. "The Trysting Scenes in Troilus and Cressida." In *Shakespearean Essays*. Edited by Alwin Thaler and Noman Sanders. Knoxville: University of Tennessee Press, pp. 105-20.
    Discusses the divided grouping of III.i., with Pandarus moving between two groups on stage, and the Troilus-Cressida trysting scene, with Pandarus acting as go-between and dumb-show director. Somewhat interesting for its conjectural reconstruction of implied stage directions.

1964.29   MEHL, DIETER. *Die Pantomime im Drama der Shakesearzeit*. Schriftenreihe der deutschen Shakespeare-Gessellschaft-West, n.s. 10. Heidelberg: Quelle & Meyer, 160 pp.
    Published version of a 1960 Munich Ph.D. dissertation. See 1966.13 for translation.

1964.30   MILLER, WILLIAM E. "*Periaktoi*: Around Again." *SQ* 15 (Winter): 61-65.
    Replies to Hotson's questioning (in 1959.9) of his consideration of the use of *periaktoi* at the first Blackfriars (see 1959.16).

1964.31   RICKERT, R[OBERT] T. "That Wonderful Year--1596." *RenP 1963*, pp. 53-62.
    A paper presented at the Southeastern Renaissance Conference, 1963. Rickert examines information available to Chambers (1923.2) about the Lord Admiral's Men and the Lord Chamberlain's Men in 1596, challenging Chambers's

assertion that the year was a smooth one for both companies. He concludes that, in fact, 1596 was the most difficult year for both companies from 1594 to 1603. An interesting speculation that Rickert puts forward is that Henslowe deliberately split his company in order to hold the Swan against the Chamberlain's Men.

1964.32   SMITH, IRWIN. *Shakespeare's Blackfriars Playhouse: Its History and Its Design.* New York: New York University Press, 577 pp.

An attempt at both a comprehensive history of the precinct and the playhouse and a complete reconstruction of the theatre based on the plays that were presented there. The first twelve chapters deal with the history and the last four with the reconstruction. In addition Smith prints forty-six documents in an appendix and includes twenty-five drawings and eight photographic plates. While the historical part of the study takes better than half the volume, it is the reconstruction that is generally known. Smith follows the lead of Cranford Adams (1942.1) in this work, as he did in his similar book on the Globe (1952.18). His Blackfriars Playhouse is complete with inner above, oblique side doors with windows above, a third level, an inner below, and three galleries for spectators. See Index, under Blackfriars Playhouse--Reconstructions, for other approaches.

1964.33   SOUTHERN, RICHARD. "Current Controversies about the Elizabethan Stage." *World Theatre* 13 (Summer): 74-80.

Discusses the state of "some slight and comparatively genial controversy over a number of minor points" of the architecture of the Elizabethan stage. The Swan drawing and its lack of an "inner stage" is the major controversy, and Southern here sums up both sides of the case. A facing column French translation is a standard feature of this journal.

1964.34   _____. "Les interludes au temps des Tudor." In *Le lieu théâtral a la Renaissance.* Edited by Jean Jacquot. Paris: CNRS, pp. 289-94.

Examines the evolution of the complex Tudor Interlude from roughly 1500 to 1580. Southern here emphasizes the development of the physical aspects of the performance. He describes the typical Great Hall in detail, including the dais, the screen, and the buttery. See also 1973.26; second edition, 1968.37.

1964.35   THORNBERRY, RICHARD THAYER. "Shakespeare and the Blackfriars Tradition." Ph.D. dissertation, Ohio State University, 339 pp.

Attempts to determine whether Shakespeare's last five plays exhibit features attributable to the taste of the Blackfriars audience and whether he wrote them for that playhouse, for the Globe, or for both. Thornberry concludes that *Cymbeline* and *Henry VIII* were written exclusively for the Globe; that *Winter's Tale, Tempest,* and *Two Noble Kinsmen* were written for both playhouses; and that the interests of the Blackfriars audience exerted a limited but definite influence on four of Shakespeare's last five plays.

1964.36   TURNER, ROBERT Y. "Significant Doubling Of Roles in *Henry VI, Part Two*." *Library Chronicle* (University of Pennsylvania) 30 (Spring): 77-84.

        Argues that two actors in *2 Henry VI* "doubled roles of consistent moral significance." The actor who played Richard of York doubled as Jack Cade, and the actor who played Humphrey doubled as Lord Say and as Alexander Iden.

1964.37   WICKHAM, GLYNNE. "Emblème et image: Quelques remarques sur la manière de figurer et de représenter le lieu sur la scène snglaise au XVIᵉ siècle." In *Le lieu théâtral à la Renaissance*. Edited by Jean Jacquot. Paris: CNRS, pp. 317-22.

        Discusses the emblematic nature of Elizabethan spectacle in the sixteenth and early seventeenth centuries; based on 1963.20. See also second edition, 1968.38.

1964.38   _____. "Exeunt to the Cave: Notes on the Staging of Marlowe's Plays." *TDR* 8, no. 4 (Summer): 184-94.

        Examines the stage directions of Marlowe's plays for evidence of their original staging. Wickham finds no evidence for a trap, but ample evidence for an upper acting space, although it is not often used. Large properties (which Wickham calls "emblems") were frequently used. Reprinted: 1969.18.

1965

1965.1   ADAMS, BARRY 8. "Doubling in Bale's King Johan." *SP* (April): 111-20.

        Discusses the eight of fourteen roles marked for doubling by three actors in the only surviving text of the play and speculates that the remaining roles would also have been doubled; therefore, the entire interlude could have been played by six actors.

1965.2   ANGUS, WILLIAM. "Acting Shakespeare." *SQ* 72 (January): 312- 1

        Discusses both Shakespearean acting now and in the Renaissance, coming down firmly on the side of the "natural" school. Angus also offers a brief summary of approaches through the years to acting Shakespeare.

1965.3   ANIKST, A[LEKSANDR ABRAMOVICH]. *Teatr èpokhi Shekspira [Theatre of Shakespeare's Time.]* Moscow: Uskysstbo, 328 pp.

        A comprehensive survey of English theatre in the period, based on secondary sources. The fifteen Chapters examine the playhouses, actors, business practices, government regulation, companies, repertories, staging, costume practices, clowns, music, and Puritan opposition.

1965.4   BENTLEY, GERALD EADES. "Theatrical Conditions and Shakespeare's Plays." *SROI* 1: 21-24.

        Argues for approaching Shakespeare's plays "as products designed for Elizabethan theatres."

1965.5   CHARNEY, MAURICE. "*Hamlet* without Words." *ELR* 32 (December): 457-77.

> A paper read at the Eleventh Annual Shakespeare Conference, Stratford-upon-Avon, 1964. Charney discusses indications for sound effects, music, costumes, and properties in both the dialogue and stage directions.

1965.6   DAWSON, GILES E., ed. "Records of Plays and Players in Kent 1450-1642." *MSC* 7: 1-211.

> Entries in the records of thirteen towns in Kent recording visits by players or companies during the years indicated. Dawson also includes records of other entertainers, such as minstrels and jugglers. Most entries record payments made.

1965.7   DOLAN de AVILA, WANDA. "La vida y teatro de William Shakespeare." *Humanitas* 18: 209-20.

> Text of a paper presented at a conference celebrating the 400th anniversary of Shakespeare's birth, held at the National University of Tucumàn in Argentina. Approximately the last half presents a general summary (from secondary sources) of theatrical conditions of the period.

1965.8   ELLIS-FERMOR, UNA M. "The Jacobean Stage." In *The Jacobean Drama: An Interpretation*. 5th ed. London: Methuen, pp 273-83.

> Reprint of 1936.8.

1965.9   KING, T[HOMAS] J[AMES]. "The Staging of Plays at the Phoenix in Drury Lane, 1617-42." *TN* 19 (Summer): 146-66.

> Abstracted from King's Ph.D. dissertation (1963.11) and comes to the same conclusions. One difference, however, is that only thirty of the thirty-two plays first examined are included.

1965.10   LANGHANS, EDWARD A. "A Picture of the Salisbury Court Theatre." *TN* 19 (Spring): 100-101.

> Speculates that the Lea and Glynne 1706 map of London might by some unknown mistake show a picture of the playhouse destroyed some forty years earlier. The theatre shown, however, appears to be a rectangular three-story open air building rather than the enclosed building converted from a barn that the Salisury Court is known to have been.

1965.11   LOWER, CHARLES BRUCE. "Editorial Principles and Practices for Indicating Significant Elizabethan Staging in a Reader's Edition of Shakespeare." Ph.D. dissertation, University of North Carolina. 542 pp.

> Since "Shakespeare's stagecraft is essential to his artistry," Lower first establishes a consensus about the characteristics of the stage and then suggests the editorial implications of each technique of stagecraft. Specifically, he suggests printing Shakespeare's plays without act division or location designation, without speech-prefixes for some minor characters, and with detailed stage directions indicating stage groupings and essential movement.

1965.12   McMILLIN, HARVEY SCOTT, Jr. "The Staging of Elizabethan Plays at the
Rose Theatre." Ph.D. dissertation, Stanford University, 163 pp.
        Discusses staging techniques at the Rose, based on thirty-six printed plays
and manuscript plots (eleven of which "almost certainly reflect playing conditions
at the Rose alone"). McMillin finds that the Rose looked much like the Swan
drawing, with the addition of a larger central doorway "capable of
accommodating mass entrances, introducing large properties onto the platform,
and revealing occasional discoveries." There was apparently a trap, "heavens" and
its flying machinery, and a long gallery at the second level. Simultaneous settings
were also utilized. McMillin concludes that "drama performed within the stage
conditions of the Rose creates a world of potential moral order, organized by
openly theatrical conventions in which both actor and spectator participate."
See also Rhodes (1959.20; 1976.21).

1965.13   REESE, M. M. "The Elizabethan Playhouse." In *ha-'Olam ha-shekspiri [The
Shakespearean World]*. Edited by Murray Roston. Tel Aviv: Am Hassefer, pp.
59-76.
        A general survey of public and private theatres and audiences. Reese
focuses on the Globe. See 1958.18 for a discussion in English of the same
material.

1965.14   TATARKIEWICZ, N. "Theatrics: The Science of Entertainment from the
12th to the 17th Century." *JHI* 26 (April-June): 263-72.
        Traces the idea of a science of entertainment from Hugh of St. Victor
through John Henry Alsted. There is nothing here of specifically theatrical
interest. Included because of listing in *NCBEL* 1, col. 1393.

1965.15   WREN, ROBERT MERIWETHER. "The Blackfriars Theatre and Its
Repertory, 1600-1608." Ph.D. dissertation, Princeton University, 515 pp.
        Investigates the accommodations made by playwrights to the theatre,
actors, and theatrical conditions of the Blackfriars company 1600-1608. First
Wren discusses the management of the company, then he establishes the repertory
of twenty plays written for the Blackfriars during this period. The heart of the
study is the analysis of the plays, revealing a main playing space with five entries
and distinct playing areas, "architectonically defined." There was apparently a
"correspondence of literary technique to the age and relative maturity of the
actors, and to the peculiar talents of the leading actor, Nathan Field."

1966

1966.1   BARTHOLOMEUSZ, DENNIS STEPHEN. "*Macbeth* and the Actors: A
Critical Study of Players' Interpretations of the Roles of Macbeth and Lady
Macbeth on the English Stage from 1611 to the Present." Ph.D, dissertation,
University of London, pp. 1-40.
        Published as 1969.1.

1966.2   BAUR-HEINHOLD, MARGARETE. *Theater des Barock: Festliches Bühnenspiel im 17. und 18. Jahrhundert.* Munich: G. D. W. Callwey, pp. 117-19.
Barely three pages of the volume are given to "Shakespearbühne," linking it to the medieval tradition and comparing it with Spanish corrales.

1966.3   BECKERMAN, BERNARD. *Shakespeare at the Globe, 1599-1609.* New York: Collier Books, 254 pp.
Reprint of 1962.2.

1966.4   BERRY, HERBERT. "The Stage and Boxes at Blackfriars." *SP* 63 (April): 163-86.
Discloses discovery of a document at the Public Record Office that bears on the most important of the private playhouses. A newsletter from John Pory to Viscount Scudmore dated 4 February 1632 contains details of a brawl at Blackfriars that provides evidence that the boxes were contiguous to the stage and stood level with it, and that audience members stood on the stage. Berry speculates that boxes might have been at the back, rather than at the sides, of the stage.

1966.5   CUTTS, JOHN P. "New Findings with Regard to the 1624 Protection List." *ShS* 19: 101-07.
Attempts to reassess identifications of musicians in the 1624 List, to provide evidence for further identifications, and to explore the possibility of a permanent theatre orchestra. Seven of the twenty-four people mentioned in the Protection List "can definitely be identified as musicians," and a potential band of eleven musicians is inferred.

1966.6   FUSILLO, ROBERT J. "The Staging of Battle Scenes on the Shakespearean Stage." Ph.D. dissertation, University of Birmingham, 530 pp.
Examines the staging of battle scenes in publicly performed plays in the Elizabethan theatre, 1576-1642. During the first forty years of this period over one-third of all extant plays include such scenes, requiring "warlike conflict between two opposing forces of some size." This thesis brings together all available evidence from the plays (in reliable editions) and contemporary reports and analyzes the convention as a whole and its component parts. Six major chapters focus on the preliminaries to battle, the stage directions, the beginnings of battle, on-stage fighting, other on-stage activity, and the ends of battles. Fusillo concludes that, although usually most of a battle takes place off-stage with only highlights and climaxes shown on-stage, "constant attempts were made to improve and increase the realistic appearance and depiction of battles, probably in an attempt to adjust to the changing substance of drama." The prominence of battle scenes decreased as the plays became lass romantic after the turn of the seventeenth century.

1966.7   GREG, WALTER WILSON. *Collected Papers*. Edited by J. C. Maxwell.
      Oxford: Clarendon Press, pp. 1-28, 95-109, 226-38.
            Reprints 1900.2; 1923.6; 1931.9.

1966.8   GURR, ANDREW J. "Elizabethan Action." *SP* 63 (April): 144-56.
             Examines the evolution of "playing" into "acting" from 1550 to 1650.
Gurr compares the "action" of the orator as outlined in the rhetorical treatises of
the period with the "feigned imitation" of the players, and he traces the linguistic
changes accompanying the improvement in acting (at least in repute) around
1600.

1966.9   H[ODGES], C[YRIL] W[ALTER]. "Playhouse Structure." In *Readers
Encyclopedia of Shakespeare*. Edited by Oscar J. Campbell and Edward C. Quinn.
New York: Thomas Y. Crowell, pp. 636-43.
             Aimed at the general reader. Hodges presents a balanced summary of what
is known of the public and private playhouses, concentrating on recent theories of
reconstruction, including Adams (1942.1), Hotson (1959.9), and himself (1953.9).
The *Encyclopedia* also includes brief anonymous articles on a number of
theatrical matters: acting; acting companies; the Globe, Theatre, Curtain, Fortune,
Swan, Blackfriars, Salisbury Court, Phoenix, Cockpit-in-Court, Boar's Head, and
Hope Playhouses; Revels Accounts and Revels Office; the Burbages, Edward
Alleyn, Philip Henslowe; and so on.

1966.10   HUNT, J. A. "Staging by the Paul's Boys in the Seventeenth Century." Ph.D.
dissertation, University of Birmingham, 581 pp.
             Examines the plays associated with the Children of Paul's during the years
1600-1606 for what they tell us about the physical aspects of the theatre and the
company's production resources and techniques. The four chapters deal with the
history and operation of the company, the repertory performed by them and the
state of their published and manuscript plays, the stage and tiring house facade,
and the production resources available to the company (such as properties,
costumes, lighting, music, and special effects). Hunt concludes that, while the
location of the theatre remains obscure, the plays written for it presume the
availability of what he calls "the more basic elements of the seventeenth century
stage": three doors; a large enough platform to hold twenty actors and a standing
prop; a trap, probably without a mechanical lifting device; acting space above,
including a window for interiors and a balcony for exteriors; one discovery space
(a permanent projecting structure); and two other possibly curtained spaces
flanking the center space. Few elaborate properties were used, but music and
elaborate costumes were important parts of performance at this playhouse.

1966.11   KING, T[HOMAS] J[AMES]. "Review Article: Irwin Smith, *Shakespeare's
Blackfriars Playhouse*." *RenD* 9: 291-309.
             Included because the review contains a close analysis of the staging
requirements of fourteen King's Men plays whose texts carry markings related to
prompt copy and for which records of performance exist. King, following the

pattern he set in his previous work on the Phoenix (1963.11; 1965.9), sets forth the minimal stage features necessary for production of the plays he considers, including two stage doors, a trap, several large properties, an acting area above, and hangings. Discoveries, he says, could be effected by opening the hangings in front of an unused doorway, or by the use of a portable curtained booth. King's review of Smith (1.964.32) concludes: "only by a detailed analysis of the available historical and bibliographical evidence concerning each play can we gain a clear understanding of how this important body of dramatic literature was first staged." <u>See also</u> Hosley (1975.16).

1966.12   KOPECKÝ, JAN. "Shakespeare's Forgotten Theatre: A Contribution to the Problems of the Theatre Today." In *Charles University on Shakespeare*. Edited by Zdenek Stríbrný and Jamelia Ēmmerová. Prague: Charles University, pp. 93-113.
        A paper read at the Shakespeare Conference of Charles University, 23-24 April 1964. Kopeck5 argues that "Shakespeare's work implies the theory of his practices," and that by studying the plays we can see the theory in action. In particular, the theatrical scenes from the plays can tell us a good deal about Shakespeare's theatrical conditions.

1966.13   MEHL, DIETER. *The Elizabethan Dumb Show: The History of a Dramatic Convention*. Cambridge: Harvard University Press, 207 pp.
        Translation of 1964.29. Mehl traces the sources of the dumb show and then examines selected plays to show the uses to which the convention could be put.

1966.14   MORGAN, EDMUND S. "Puritan Hostility to the Theatre." *PAPS* 110, no. 5 (27 October): 340-47.
        A paper read before the American Philosophical Society, 22 April 1966. Morgan traces the hostility toward the theatre from 1579 to the end of the seventeenth century, and later. He ascribes it at least partly to the competition furnished by the theatres to the churches.

1966.15   PRESLEY, HORTON EDWARD. "'Showes, Mighty Showes': A Study of the Relationship of the Jones-Jonson Controversy to the Rise of Illusionistic Staging in the Seventeenth-Century British Drama." Ph.D. dissertation, University of Kansas, 308 pp.
        Examines the Jonson-Jones quarrel with regard to the increasing audience demand for spectacle. Chapter Five in particular discusses the state of both the demand and the spectacle when Jones began his work in the early seventeenth century, while Chapters Six and Seven document his designs for masques and plays and trace his influence on the public stage later in the century.

1966.16   RIBNER, IRVING. *Tudor and Stuart Drama*. Goldentree Bibliographies in Language and Literature. Northbrook, Ill.: A. H. M. Publishing, pp 5-10.

Selective unannotated bibliography, with emphasis on major works since 1920. Ribner lists 116 entries in the relevant section, "Dramatic Companies, Theatres, Conditions of Performance." All relevant entries have been incorporated into this bibliography. See second edition, 1978.22.

1966.17   RICHER, BODO L. O. "Recent Studies on Renaissance Scenography." *RenN* 19 (Winter): 344-58.

Essentially a lengthy review article, commenting on Jacquot's collection of essays (see 1964.2, 18, 22, 34, 37).

1966.18   SCHAAR, CLAES. "'They hang him in the arbor.'" *ES* 47 (February): 27-28.

Proposes the transposing of the two stage directions "They hang him in the arbor" and "They stab him" in *Spanish Tragedy* as more likely to reflect Kyd's intentions. See also 1966.21.

1966.19   SELTZER, DANIEL. "The Staging of the Last Plays." In *The Later Shakespeare*. Stratford-on-Avon Studies, no. 8. London: Edward Arnold, pp. 127-66.

Examines the last six of Shakespeare's plays with special reference to the techniques of the actors and the use of spectacle and music. Seltzer uses stage directions, both explicit and implicit, to recreate stage business, voice, blocking, and what he calls "address." He concludes that "the acting techniques . . . reveal an art conservative in its uses of the pest, yet thoroughly capable of a wide range of flexible stage movements, small details of business, modulation of facial expression and address, and stage moves. . . . Always the intention was to represent realistically the motion of the mind and the very shape of nature."

1966.20   SHAPIRO, I. A. "Robert Fludd's Stage-Illustration." *ShSt* 2: 192-209.

Takes issue with Yates's identification of the illustration as the Globe (in 1966.28), arguing instead for the Blackfriars. See also 1958.2; 1967.1; 1967.17.

1966.21   SMITH, JAMES L. "'They hang him in the arbor': A Defense of the Accepted Text." *ES* 47 (October): 372-73.

Defends the traditsal order of the stage directions "They hang him in the arbor" and "They stab him" in *Spanish Tragedy* on the basis of an imaginative visualization of the scene. Schaar, who proposed the transposition (see 1966.18). replies briefly.

1966.22   SOMERSET, JOHN ALAN BEAUFORT. "The Comic Turn in English Drama, 1470-1616." Ph.D. dissertation, University of Birmingham, 839 pp.

Focuses primarily on the development of the low comic scene through the interaction of the actors and the playwright. While primarily literary in orientation, Somerset does examine the improvisations of the clowns and direct audience address that are of theatrical interest. Also helpful is his tracing of the Elizabethan clown from the medieval vice.

1966.23   SOMERSET, J[OHN] A[LAN] B[EAUFORT]. "William Poel's First Full Platform Stage." *TN* 21 (Spring): 118-21.
        Discusses Poel's use of a full platform stage in 1927 for his production of Rowley's *When You See Me, You Know Me*.

1966.24   SPRAGUE, ARTHUR COLBY. *The Doubling of Parts in Shakespeare's Plays*. London: Society for Theatre Research, 35 pp.
        Primarily concerned uritl, the later stage history of doubling rather than with doubling in Shakespeare's day. Only the last three pages examine Elizabethan practice, and that generally.

1966.25   WHALLY, JOYCE I. "The Swan Theatre in the Sixteenth Century." *TN* 20 (Winter): 73.
        Transcribes the text of the Swan drawing, and prints photographs of both the drawing and the text.

1966.26   WRIGHT, LOUIS B. *Shakespeare's Theatre and the Dramatic Tradition*. Washington: Folger Shakespeare Library, 36 pp.
        Reprint of 1958.24.

1966.27   WRIGHT, W. S. "Edward Alleyn, Actor and Benefactor, 1566-1626." *TN* 20 (Summer): 155-60.
        A reappraisal of Alleyn's life, based on the holdings of the Dulwich College Library. See Index, under Alleyn, for earlier and more complete treatments.

1966.28   YATES, FRANCES. "New Light on the Globe Theatre." *NYRB* 6. no. 9 (26 May): 16-77
        Excerpted from a chapter of her *The Art of Memory*, and containing the same information on Fludd's 1619 *Ars Memoria*. Fludd printed illustrations of several "memory theatres," one of which looks rather like our typical idea of an Elizabethan playhouse, with two doorways, a gated discovery space, and an upper gallery. Yates suggests that it may shed light on the structure of the Globe. See also 1966.20; 1967.1, 17; 1958.2.

1967

1967.1   BERRY, HERBERT. "Dr. Fludd's Engravings and Their Beholders." *ShSt* 3: 11-21.
        Argues against the illustrations in Fludd's *Ars Memoriae* as being of English theatres, responding to Yates (1966.28) and Shapiro (1966.20). See also Yates's reply (1967.17) and Bernheimer (1958.2).

1967.2   HAWLEY, JAMES ABGRIFFITH. "Inigo Jones and the New English Stagecraft." Ph.D. dissertation, Ohio State University, 154 pp.

"An examination of the total staging contributions of the masques reached through an analysis of Inigo Jones's precise methods of staging." Hawley identifies definite periods of design style in Jones, from the early scaffold stage displaying large units in a shuttered enclosed area, to the later "full shutter nest" with flat wings. While some of this change in style can be traced to the development of the later masques, much of it occurred because of Jones's experimentation with continental devices.

1967.3   HOSLEY, RICHARD. "Elizabethan Theatres and Audiences." *RORD* 10: 9-16.

Text of a paper read at the 1966 MLA convention. Hosley here examines the size of the audience at both public (2500-3000) and private (about 720) playhouses and the influences exerted on the plays by these two classes of theatre. He also discusses the use of entre-act music in the private playhouses.

1967.4   KIRSCH, ARTHUR C. "*Cymbeline* and Coterie Dramaturgy." *ELH* 34 (September): 285-306.

Assumes *Cymbeline* was written for the particular audience of the Blackfriars and examines the text for evidence of how Shakespeare catered to this coterie. Deliberate self-consciousness, in the style of Fletcher and Marston, is one way. Another is the use of the tragicomic form. Still another is the conspicuousness of the workings of Providence. Kirsch sees the influence of the private theatre audience as important.

1967.5   KLEIN, DAVID. "Time Allotted for an Elizabethan Performance." *SQ* 18 (Autumn): 434-38.

Responds to Hart (1932.6), arguing for a presentation time of more than two hours.

1967.6   MATSON, MARSHALL NYVALL. "A Critical Edition of *The Wisdom of Doctor Dodypoll* (1600) with a Study of *Dodypoll*'s Place in the Repertory of Paul's Boys." Ph.D, dissertation, Northwestern university, 359 pp.

A critical old-spelling edition of the play, with a study of the Paul's repertory "with particular attention to the revival of boys' theatrical activities in late 1599 and *Dodypoll*'s part in that revival." An appendix examines staging and music.

1967.7   MULLIN, DONALD C. "An Observation on the Origin of the Elizabethan Theatre." *ETJ* 19 (October): 322-26.

Discusses the state of theories of the origin of the Elizabethan public theatres and rejects the idea of generation from inn-yards and baiting rings. Mullin sees a more direct classical influence, particularly from Roman arenas.

1967.8   REYNOLDS, GEORGE F[ULLMER]. *On Shakespeare's Stage*. Edited by Richard K. Knaub. Boulder: University of Colorado Press, 109 pp.

       Texts of four lectures at Stratford-upon-Avon, July 1954. Reynolds first examines the available evidence (pictorial and textual) concerning Shakespeare's stage, and then applies the evidence to two critical questions: the nature of the rear stage, and the use of the main platform. Reynolds also considers the use of scene boards to localize entrances and exits. He returns to his stress of the primacy of the platform, and reiterates his theory of the portable curtained booth. See also Index, under Reynolds, for more of his more original and well-known contributions.

1967.9   ROWAN, D. F. "The 'Swan' Revisited." *RORD* 10: 33-48.

       Text of a paper read at the 1966 MLA convention. Rowan reviews the state of scholarship on the Swan drawing, focusing on the debate over the lack of an "inner stage." He also discusses the only play known to have been produced at the Swan, *The Chaste Maid of Cheapside*, and concludes that the play could have been staged at the Swan as DeWitt drew it.

1967.10   SHAPIRO, MICHAEL. "The Plays Acted by the Children of Paul's, 1599-1607." Ph.D. dissertation, Columbia University, 398 pp.

       Expanded version published: 1977.32.

1967.11   SHAW, JOHN. "The Staging of Parody and Parallels in *1 Henry IV*." *ShS* 20: 61-73.

       Examines Prince Hal's interviews with Falstaff posing as the king and with the real king, and contemporary attitudes toward parody, to show that the scenes are meant to be similarly staged in order to reinforce the parallels. Shaw then examines two other scenes, the Hotspur-Kate interview and the Francis-Hal scene in the tavern, asserting that parallel staging will bring out a strong parallel in structure and meaning.

1967.12   SMITH, IRWIN. "Their Exits and Reentrances." *SQ* 18 (Winter): 7-16.

       Examines exits by characters at the end of one scene and immediate reentrances at the beginning of the next in Shakespeare. Smith discusses the sixteen possible violations of the so-called "Law of Reentry," and concludes that none of them, in fact, is a violation. This, to Smith, is evidence of a lack of act intermissions in the public playhouses.

1967.13   STYAN, J. L. *Shakespeare's Stagecraft*. Cambridge: University Press, 244 pp.

       Intended as a guide to exploration of Shakespeare's stage practices. The three parts review scholarship on the Elizabethan stage and acting conventions and discuss Shakespeare's visual and aural craft from the point of view of the director and actor. The main point is that "the requirement of Shakespearian scholarship . . . is first to be able to read the texts through the eyes of an Elizabethan actor." This is precisely what Styan attempts here.

1967.14   TAYLOR, ALISON. *The Story of the English Stage.* Oxford: Pergamon Press, pp. 20-33.

     A general treatment for an adolescent audience, complete with study questions at the end of each chapter. The relevant section is Chapter Three, "The Elizabethan Theatre." Taylor discusses the playhouse (reprinting the Swan drawing), the companies and actors, and production practices.

1967.15   WICKHAM, GLYNNE. "The Cockpit Reconstructed." *NTM* 7 (Spring): 26-36.

     A correlation of the information in the Accounts of the Office of Works with the Inigo Jones design for the Cockpit- in-Court allows Wickham to reconstruct that playhouse down to fine details. The date of the theatre's opening is set at 1630, rather than 1632, and the familiar design of the playhouse is discussed in terms of the records of its construction.

1967.16   WREN, ROBERT M. "The Five-Entry Stage at Blackfriars." *TP* 8, no. 3: 130-38.

     Based on Wren's Ph.D. dissertation (1965.15). Discusses plays presented by the Children of the Chapel at Blackfriars, 1600-1608. Wren concludes that "the Blackfriars theatre had a five-entry, architectonically-segmented facade stage, markedly unlike the Swan drawing or any reconstruction based on the Swan." He proposes the Amsterdam Schouwburg as a model, suggesting that it might be thought related to the Blackfriars. See also Hosley (1975.15) and King (1966.11).

1967.17   YATES, FRANCES A. "The Stage in Robert Fludd's Memory System." *ShSt* 3: 138-66.

     Replies to Shapiro (1966.20), answering his objections to her identification of the illustration in *Ars Memoriae* as the Globe and refuting his identification of it as the Blackfriars. See also Berry (1967.1) and Bernheim (1958.2).

1968

1968.1   ANGLO, SYDNEY. "La salle de banquet et le théâtre construits a Greenwich pour les fêtes franco-anglais de 1527." In *Le lieu théâtral à la Renaissance.* 2d ed. Edited by Jean Jacquot. Paris: CNRS, pp. 273-88.
     Reprint of 1964.2.

1968.2   BENTLEY, GERALD EADES. *The Jacobean and Caroline Stage.* Vols. 6-7. Oxford: Clarendon Press, 699 pp.

     The final volumes of Bentley's reference work, begun in 1941.1 and continued in 1956.4. Volume 6 deals with the theatres of the period 1616-42, and volume 7 contains appendices to volume 6 and an analytical index to all seven volumes. As in earlier volumes, the treatment of the playhouses in volume 6 is primarily documentary. That is, Bentley has presented all available documentary evidence for each theatre and has briefly weighed the conflicting hypotheses that have been put forward about each, but he has refrained from drawing any conclusions of his own. While there are entries for eight private theatres, sixteen public theatres, four court theatres, and two projected theatres, naturally not all are discussed in detail. For example, the entries on the first Blackfriars and the Theatre merely refer the reader to Chambers (1923.2) and J. 9. Adams (1917.3). The most space is devoted to the second Blackfriars, the Phoenix, the Salisbury Court, the second Fortune, and the second Globe. Each entry begins with a brief bibliography (up to 1962) and then presents all available evidence. The appendices in volume 7 include discussions of Sunday and Lenten performances and "Annals of Jacobean and Caroline Theatrical Affairs," perhaps the most valuable section of the entire series since it lays out all the material in chronological order. These seven volumes are without question the most important work in the field to date.

1968.3 _____, ed. *The Seventeenth-Century Stage: A Collection of Critical Essays*. Patterns of Literary Criticism, no. 6. Chicago: University of Chicago Press, 287 pp.

Reprints of 1926.12; 1927.18, 23; 1953.2; 1954.21; 1958.8; 1960.16; 1961.4; 1964.23. Also contains 1968.31, as well as an introduction by the editor and four seventeenth-century commentaries. These include selections from *The Gull's Horn Book* and *An Apology for Actors*, the Induction to *Bartholomew Fair*, and the Praeludium for *The Careless Shepherdess*. Bentley's Introduction lucidly describes the methods and history of scholarship in the field.

1968.4 BERGERON, DAVID M. "The Christmas Family: Artificers in English Civic Pageantry." *ELH* 35, no. 3 (September): 354-64.

Discusses the contributions Gerard Christmas and his two sons made to civic pageantry, illuminating the relationship between poet and architect in the process. The Christmases worked with Middleton, Dekker, and Heywood on the mayoral shows, and were frequent1y commended far their work. The role of artificer increased significantly during their tenure.

1968.5 _____. "The Emblematic Nature of English Civic Pageantry." *RenD*, n.s. 1: 167-90.

Some preliminary suggestions about the connection between emblems and civic pageantry, 1558-1640. Bergeron establishes that "the method of the emblem and the pageant is fundamentally the same," and while no direct link can be established, he argues for mutual inspiration.

1968.6 _____. "Harrison, Jonson and Dekker: The Magnificent Entertainment for King James (1604)." *JWCI* 31: 445-48.

A note on James's royal entry into London on 15 March 160314. Stephen Harrison designed and built the triumphal arches, while Jonson, Dekker, and Middleton collaborated on the text. There are inconsistencies, however, between Harrison's drawings and the textual descriptions, and Bergeron tentatively suggests that Harrison is more accurate.

1968.7   _____, "Prince Henry and English Civic Pageantry." *TSL* 13: 109-16.
           Discusses the relation of the Prince of Wales to the pageantry of the early
Stuart era. Bergeron traces the homage paid to Henry in Royal Entries and Lord
Mayor's Shows from 1610 until 1624, some fourteen years after the Prince's
death.

1968.8   BEST, MICHAEL R. "The Staging and Production of the Plays of John Lyly."
           TR 9, no. 2: 104-17.
           Based on Best's Ph.D. dissertation, 1964.5. He assumes that the first
Blackfriars, the stages at Court, and the stage at Paul's were "substantially the
same in structure," and then uses Lyly's plays to reconstruct them. Best finds
that a stage with two entrances from off-stage and with two houses set in
opposition across the stage would have been sufficient for the staging of Lyly's
plays.

1968.9   BRADBROOK, M[URIEL] C. *Elizabethan Stage Conditions: A Study of Their
           Place in the Interpretation of Shakespeare's Plays*. Cambridge: University Press,
           149 pp.
           Reprint of 1932.2.

1968.10   DEMADRE, ANTOINE. "Un témoin: Thomas Nashe." In *Dramaturgie et
           société: Rapports entre l'oeuvre théâtrale, son interpretation et son public aux
           XVIe et XVIIe siècles*. Vol. 2. Edited by Jean Jacquot. Paris: CNRS, pp. 577-88.
           Nashe's writings bear witness to changing theatrical conditions in late
sixteenth-century London. His works shed light on dates, places, attributions,
aspects and opponents of the theatre, and, representatively on a "University Wit in
a changing theatre and on an "author-victim" who lived in poverty and
persecution and who died miserably.

1968.11   DUCKLES, VINCENT. "The Music for the Lyrics in Early Seventeenth-
           Century English Drama: A Bibliography of Primary Sources." In *Music in English
           Renaissance Drama*. Edited by John H. Long. Lexington: University of Kentucky
           Press, pp. 117-60.
           Lists manuscript sources, modern editions, and period editions of music
for the songs in plays of the period. The list is broken down by playwright and
play.

1968.12   FREEHAFER, JOHN. "Brome, Suckling, and Davenant's Theater Project of
           1639." *TSLL* 10 (Fall): 367-84.
           Identifies Brome's *Court Beggar* as the banned play presented at the
Cockpit in 1640 and relates it to Brome's opposition to Davenant's project for
bringing the innovations of the court into the public theatres. Freehafer explores
the details of the Brome-Davenant rivalry and the plan for the projected
playhouse, and concludes that Davenant's Duke's Theatre of 1661 was the
realization of that plan.

1968.13 ____. "*The Italian Night Piece* and Suckling's *Aglaura*." *JEGP* 67 (Spring): 249-65.

Identifies *The Italian Night Piece* with Suckling's *Aglaura*, and asserts it was acted by the King's Men at Blackfriars and later in a new version with changeable scenery from a masque at court.

1968.14 GAIR, W. R. "Le Compagnie des Enfants de St. Paul, Londres (1559 à 1606)." In *Dramaturgie et société. Rapports entre l'oeuvre théâtrale, son interprétation et son public aux XVIe et XVIIe siècles.* Vol. 2. Edited by Jean Jacquot. Paris: CNRS, pp. 655-74.

Examines the theatre operated by the Children of Paul's and this company's role in the "War of the Theatres." Originally, St. Paul's Boys had a refined, aristocratic image, catering to those wanting to savor the entertainment played at court. External and internal pressures, however, caused the clientele and repertory to change from elite to sensation-seekers, from amateurs' aristocratic literary activities to a collection of scandals. Gair claims that St. Paul's failed as an amateur theatre because it became too popular.

1968.15 HAAKER, ANN. "The Plague, the Theater, and the Poet." *RenD*, n.s. 1: 283-306.

Discusses two 1640 documents which reveal a good deal about the relationship between the Salisbury Court Playhouse and its resident dramatist, Richard Brome. The first is a complaint filed by the actors and owners of Queen Henrietta's Men, and the second is Brome's reply. Much of the conflict concerns the closing of the theatres for the plague outbursts of 1636-37. Haaker also prints C. W. Wallace's transcripts of both documents in full.

1968.16 HODGES, C[YRIL] WALTER. *The Globe Restored.* 2d ed. New York: Coward-McCann, 177 pp.

Revised and enlarged edition of 1953.9. There are additional illustrations, already one of the work's greatest strengths, and a new chapter offering a conjectural reconstruction of the Globe that Hodges thought best to leave out of the first version.

1968.17 HOSLEY, RICHARD. "The Origins of the So-Called Elizabethan Multiple Stage." *TDP*, 12, no. 2 (Winter): 28-50.

Originally a paper read at the November 1966 meeting of the American Society for Theatre Research. Hosley examines the derivation of the component parts of the multiple stage proposed by J. C. Adams (1942.1) and others. He first lists the "external" evidence (the pictures) for the Elizabethan stage and then examines the obliquely set doors, the traps, the inner stage, the upper stage, and the music room, all common elements in reconstructions. He concludes that these elements were introduced by reasoning backwards from post-Restoration practices.

1968.18 ____. "Reconstitution du théâtre du Swan." In *Le lieu théâtral à la Renaissance*. 2d ed. Edited by Jean Jacquot. Paris: CMRS, pp. 295-316.
Reprint of 1964.17.

1968.19 INGRAM, R[EGINALD] W[ILLIAM]. "Patterns of Music and Action in Fletcherian Drama." In *Music in Engish Renaissance Drama*. Edited by John H. Long. Lexington: University of Kentucky Press, pp. 75-94.
Discusses the use of music for mood heightening in several of Fletcher's plays. Ingram argues that in Fletcher "music was a homogeneous part of the dramatic context."

1968.20 JACQUOT, JEAN, ed. *Dramaturgie et société: Rapports entre l'oeuvre théâtrale, son interpretation et public aux XVIe et XVIIe siècles*. Vol. 2. Paris: CNRS, pp. 525-888.
The relevant section examines England, including five essays of theatrical rather than literary interest: 1968.10, 14, 21, 24, 32.

1968.21 JACQUOT, JEAN. "Le répertorie des compagnies d'enfants à Londres (1660-1610): Essai d'interprétation socio-dramatique." In *Dramaturgie et société: Rapports entre l'oeuvre théâtrale. son interprétation et son public aux XVIe et XVIIe siècles*. Vol. 2. Edited by Jean Jacquot. Paris: CNRS, pp. 729-82.
Examines the repertories of the Children of Paul's and the Children of the Chapel and attempts by comparing common characteristics to pinpoint their creative influence. Histrio-Mastix gives us an idea of the children's companies' authors' view of society, of themselves, and of their audience. Jacquot views audience taste as leading to the development of tragicomedy and, eventually, comedy of manners.

1968.22 ____. "Les théâtres élisabéthain," in "Les types de lieu théâtral et leurs transformations." In *Le lieu théâtral à la Renaissance*. 2d ed. Edited by Jean Jacquot. Paris: CNRS, pp. 291-96.
Reprint of 1964.21.

1968.23 JENSEN, EJNER J. "The Style of the Boy Actors." *CompD* 2 (Summer): 100-14.
Argues for a natural style of acting in the children's companies, similar to the style employed by the adult actors.

1968.24 LECOCQ, LOUIS. "Le théâtre de Blackfriars de 1596 2 1606." *Dramaturgie et société:Rapports entre l'oeuvre théâtrale. son interprétation et son public aux XVIe et XVIIe siècles*. Vol. 2. Edited by Jean Jacquot. Paris: CNRS, pp. 675-704.
Examines the theatre building, the actors, the repertory, and the audience of the second Blackfriars under the Children. Lecocq summarizes the dealings of the Burbages with Henry Evans and the Children of the Queen's Revels from a variety of secondary sources.

1968.25   LONG, JOHN H., ed. *Music in English Renaissance Drama*. Lexington:
University of Kentucky Press, 104 pp.
Includes 1968.11, 19.

1968.26   McCMILLIN, [HARVEY] SCOTT. "Jonson's Early Entertainments: New
Information from Hatfield House." *RenD*, n.s. 1: 153-66
Discusses newly discovered documents bearing on four of Jonson's early
entertainments far the Earl of Salisbury, 1606-1609. McMillin includes
information about the actors, Inigo Jones's collaboration, payments to Jonson and
Jones, and the staging and costumes employed. Both Edward Alleyn and Nathan
Field were involved. The documents do not contain the texts of the
entertainments.

1968.27   NOSWORTHY, J. M. "Dornackes and Colysenes in Henslowe's Diary."
N&Q, n.s. 15 (July) :2 47-48.
Suggests that "dornackes" in the diary means '"dornick," a fabric used for
hangings, and that "colysenes" means "cullisance," a corruption of "cognizance."

1968.28   ORGEL, STEPHEN. "To Make Boards to Speak: Inigo Jones's Stage and the
Jonsonian Masque." *RenD*, n.s. 1: 121-52.
Considers the "interaction between the inventions of the poet and of the
designer," concentrating on the period 1610-18. Orgel sees both as moving toward
a significant redefinition of the form of the masque, which "in great measure
determined the course of English drama for the next three hundred years."

1968.29   PETIT, J. B. "'This Wooden O': Théâtre et signs dans les choeurs de Henry."
EA 21 (July-September): 268-92.
Examines the six speeches of the Chorus in for what they tell us about the
means of presentation in the Elizabethan playhouse. Petit argues that Shakespeare
dismissed the limitations of the theatre by the act of calling attention to them.

1968.30   RICHARDS, KENNETH R. "Changeable Scenery for Plays on the Caroline
Stage." *TN* 23 (Autumn): 6-20.
Reexamines the case for the use of changeable scenery on the stage of the
Caroline private playhouses. Richards identifies only twelve plays "for which
there is good evidence that they were performed with changeable painted
scenery," and all twelve were presented at court or in a private residence. He
concludes that there is little reason to believe that changeable painted scenery was
used in the playhouses.

1968.31   RINGLER, W[ILLIAM] A. "The Number of Actors in Shakespeare's Early
Plays." In *The Seventeenth Century Stage*. Edited by G[erald] E[adesl] Bentlev.
Patterns of Literary Criticism, no. 6. Chicago: University of Chicago Press, pp.
110-36.
Examines the plays Shakespeare wrote for the Lord Chamberlain's Men to
determine the number of actors available in that troupe. Eighteen pre-Globe plays

are examined, and through the creation of scene-by-scene charts and doubling schemes (the charts for *Julius Caesar* are printed) Ringler finds that sixteen actors represents the usual size of this company. Finally, the doubling in *Love's Labour's Lost* and *Midsummer Night's Dream* is examined for what it can tell us about Shakespeare's original productions.

1968.32 SALINGAR, L. G.; HARRISON, GERALD; and COCHRANE, BRUCE. "Les comédiens et leur public en Angleterre de 1520 à 1640." In *Dramaturgie et société: Rapports entre l'oeuvre théâtrale. son interprétation et son public aux XVIe et XVIIe siècles*. Vol. 2. Edited by Jean Jacquot. Paris: CNRS, pp. 525-76.

A comprehensive, statistical treatment of the vitality, development, and downfall of the dramatic arts during the Elizabethan age. The authors examine audience demand, intellectual quality of the public, the social composition of the audience, and the economics of the theatre. The tables and statistics focus attention on development during the period. Most information is secondary, drawn from Harbage and Schoenbaum (1964.13). Murray (1910.15), Chambers (1923.3), Bentley (1941.1; 1956.4; 1968.2), and Wickham (1959.29: 1963.20; 1972.32).

1968.33 SCHANZER, ERNEST. "Hercules and His Load." *RES*, n.s. 19 (February): 51-53.

A brief note suggesting that George Steevens, not Edmond Malone, was the first to state that the sign of the Globe Playhouse was a picture of Hercules carrying the globe.

1968.34 SCOUTEN, E. H. "Some Assumptions behind Accounts of the Elizabethan Stage." In *On Stage and Off: Eight Essays on English Literature*. Edited by John W. Ehrstine and Emmet Langdon Avery. Pullman: Washington State University Press, pp. 4-11.

A paper presented at the University of Toronto, 9 November 1967. Scouten uses Morse Peckham's theory of constructs to discover the unstated assumptions underlying standard histories of the Elizabethan stage, particularly Chambers (1923.2). The mast important assumption is evolution: there has been a gradual development in complexity, and the Elizabethan stage falls between the medieval and the Restoration. Scouten also attacks "the myth of the innyards" and the division of Shakespeare's texts into acts and scenes.

1968.35 SHAPIRO, MICHAEL. "Music and Song in Plays Acted by Children's Companies during the English Renaissance." *CM* 7: 97-110.

Examines the songs of the boy companies. Shapiro identifies four types of songs (complaints, servant songs, pastoral and supernatural songs, and religious songs) and discusses the use of instrumental music. One of his purposes "is to invite musicologists to collaborate with literary scholars in investigating music and sang and their uses in non-Shakespearean drama of the English Renaissance."

1968.36   SLOVER, GEORGE W. "The Elizabethan Playhouse and the Tradition of
Liturgical Stage Structure." Ph.D. dissertation, Indiana University, 448 pp.
Discusses the idea of "stage and theater structure as symbolic form," with
the Elizabethan stage in the tradition of the Greek, Roman, and medieval stages.
"The stage of the Elizabethan playhouse is . . . an emblem . . . [belonging] to the
emblem family representing *state*." Slover sees the Elizabethan stage as appearing
in the transition from "Medieval" to "Modern." The supplanting of it by the
picture-frame stage is part of the same transition.

1968.37   SOUTHERN, RICHARD. "Les interludes au temps des Tudor." In *Le lieu
théâtral à la Renaissance*. 2d ed. Edited by Jean Jacquot. Paris: CNRS, pp. 284-
94.
Reprint of 1964.34.

1968.38   WICKAM, GLYNNE. "Emblème et image: Quelques remarques sur la
manière de figurer et de représénter le lieu sur la scene anglaise au XVIe siéclé."
In *Le lieu théâtral à la Renaissance*. 2d ed. Edited by Jean Jacquot. Paris: CNRS,
pp 317-22.
Reprint of 1964.36.

1968.39   ZUCKER, DAVID HARD. "Stage and Image in the Plays of Christopher
Marlowe." Ph.D. dissertation, University of Syracuse, 231 pp.
Published as 1972.35.

1969

1969.1   BARTHOLOMEUSZ, DENNIS [STEPHEN]. *"Macbeth" and the Players*.
Cambridge: University Press, pp. 1-13.
Published version of 1966.1. The relevant section deals with *Macbeth* at
the Globe. Simon Forman's description of a performance in 1611 is the basis for
initial speculation that Macbeth first enters on horseback and that Banquo's
ghost is sitting in Macbeth's chair after Macbeth drinks his health. The final part
of the treatment involves less specific information, primarily about the acting of
Richard Burbage.

1969.2   BOURGY, VICTOR. *Le bouffon sur la scéne anglaise au XVIe siéclé (c. 1495-
1594)*. Paris: OCDL; Lille: University of Lille, pp. 354-445.
A University of Lille Ph.D. dissertation. Bourgy examines all aspects of
the clown or buffoon in English drama in the sixteenth century, including the
contributions of the actors, especially Tarlton, in Chapter Five. Reprinted: 1975.3.

1969.3   DEWEY, NICHOLAS. "The Academic Drama of the Early Stuart Period
(1603-1642): A Checklist of Secondary Sources." *RORD* 12: 33-42.
Divided into two sections: general criticism and scholarship, and
bibliography and chronology. This checklist contains a total of 110 items, some of

theatrical interest, sporadically annotated. All relevant items have been incorporated into this bibliography.

1969.4   ELLIS-FERMOR, UMA M. "The Jacobean Stage." In *The Jacobean Drama: An Interpretation*. London: Methuen, pp. 273-83.
        Reprint of 1936.8.

1969.5   GREG, W[ALTER] W[ILSON]. *Documents from the Elizabethan Playhouse: Stage Plots: Actors' Parts: Prompt Books*. 2 vols. Oxford: Clarendon Press, 432 pp.
        Reprint of 1931.9.

1969.6   KAHRL, STANLEY J., ed. "Records of Plays and Players in Lincolnshire 1300-1585." *MSC* 9: 1-108.
        Entries from the records of fourteen towns in Lincolnshire, regarding payment made to players and companies from 1300 to 1585. Very few entries are from the relevant period.

1969.7   MARKLAND, MURRAY F. "Two Italian Glimpses of the English Theatre." *TR* 10, no. 1: 32-36.
        Examines two manuscripts from the Biblioteca Riccardiana in Florence for what they tell us about English theatre in the seventeenth and eighteenth centuries. The relevant document, MS Ricc. 1493, is the diary of the travels of Guilio de Medici inEngland. He arrived in London on 7 July 1621 and on 23 July he went to a play, apparently about Henry VIII. Markland suspects there are many such untranslated documents in Italian archives.

1969.8   McMANAWAY, JAMES G. *Studies in Shakespeare, Bibliography, and Theater*. Edited by Richard Hosley, Arthur C. Kirsch, and John W. Velz. New York: Shakespeare Association of America, pp. 215-22.
        Contains a reprint of 1962.13 as well as many other McManaway essays not directly relevant to Elizabethan theatre.

1969.9   RIBNER, IRVING. "Elizabethan Theatres and Theatre Companies." In *William Shakespeare: An Introduction to His Life, Times,and Theatre*. Waltham, Mass.: Blaisdell Publishing Co., pp. 130-61.
        A general discussion summarizing the work of scholars in the field. The chapter includes subdivisions discussing medieval spectacle and staging, the rise of professional companies, the innyards, the public playhouse, the children's companies, productions at Blackfriars, Elizabethan acting, and the audience.

1969.10   ROWAN, D. F. "A Neglected Jones/Webb Theatre Project: Barber-Surgeons Hall Writ Large." *NTM* 9, no. 3 (Summer): 6-15.
        Tentatively identifies the Inigo Jones drawing held at Worcester College, Oxford, as the designs for Barber-Surgeons Hall. Rowan also points out the similarity of the drawing to Hosley's reconstruction of the second Blackfriars (see

1970.13). For Rowan's later thoughts on the drawing, see 1970.27; for another view, see 1977.25.

1969.11   SCHUMAN, SAMUEL. "Emblems and the English Renaissance Drama: A Checklist." *ORRD* 12: 43-56.
       Contains a total of 116 items, some of theatrical interest, sporadically annotated. All relevant items have been incorporated into this bibliography.

1969.12   SHAPIRO, MICHAEL, "Children's Troupes: Dramatic Illusion and Acting Style." *CompD* 3 (Spring): 42-53.
       Examines devices used by playwrights of the boy companies to draw attention to the actors as children. Shapiro finds four most commonly used: adults alongside children, bawdry, self-reference, and inductions. These are most often found in comedies. The style used by the boys varied, depending on the type of play. It was frequently formal, but at times, especially in the city comedies, could be natural.

1969.13   SJÖGREN, GUNNAR. "Thomas Bull and Other 'English Instrumentalists' in Denmark in the 1580s." *ShS* 22: 119-24.
       A new study of the Spanish documents previously drawn on by Bolte (1888.2) and Ravn (1906.9), establishing that one of the "English Instrumentalists," John Bull, was beheaded for murder in 1586.

1969.14   SOENS, ADOLPH E. "Tybalt's Spanish Fencing in Romeo and Juliet." *SQ* 20 (Spring): 121-27.
       Argues that Tybalt's fencing style is Spanish, not French or Italian. Soens then considers implications for the staging of the fights with Mercutio and Romeo. See also 1927.23.

1969.15   SPRINCHORN, EVERT. "'Wrapt in a Canapie.'" *TN* 24 (Autumn): 36-37.
       Suggest that canopy and arras were not in fact interchangeable terms, as they are often thought. See also 1957.1; 1964.3.

1969.16   SUMMERSON, JOHN [NEWENHAM]. *Architecture in Britain*, 1530-1830. Pelican History of Art, no. 23. Harmondsworth: Penguin Books, pp. 61-67.
       Reprint of 1953.26.

1969.17   WICKHAM, GLYNNE. "Notes on Inigo Jones' Designs for the Cockpit-in-Court." In *Shakespeare's Dramatic Heritage: Collected Studies in Mediaeval, Tudor, and Shakespearean Drama*. London: Routledge & Kegan Paul; New York: Barnes & Noble, pp. 151-62.
       Reprint of 1967.15.

1969.18 _____. "Notes on the Staging of Marlowe's Plays." In *Shakespeare's Dramatic Heritage: Collected Studies in Mediaeval, Tudor, and Shakespearean Drama.* London: Routledge & Kegan Paul; New York: Barnes & Noble, pp. 121-31.
   Reprint of 1964.38.

1969.19 _____. "Shakespeare's Stage." In *Shakespeare's Dramatic Heritage: Collected Studies in Mediaeval, Tudor, and Shakespearean Drama.* London: Routledge & Kegan Paul; New York: Barnes & Noble, pp. 132-50.
   A general discussion of the Elizabethan playhouse, with emphasis on the Swan drawing, the actors for whom the plays were written, and their use of large properties or "scenic emblems" which enabled them to perform virtually anywhere.

1969.20 _____. "The Stuart Mask." In *Shakespeare's Dramatic Heritage: Collected Studies in Mediaeval, Tudor, and Shakespearean Drama.* London: Routledge & Kegan Paul; New York: Barnes & Noble, pp. 103-17.
   An attempt "to distill the essence . . . of Masks of the Jacobean and Caroline period, relating the blossom itself to the roots from which it sprang and to the seed which it left against the future." Wickham sees the masque as a turning point, translating the English theatre from "one of suggestion, visual and poetic, into one of verisimilitude, realistic and prosaic." The masques grew out of the resolve of the privileged elite to assert its privilege, regardless of cost, and should not be judged by strictly literary standards.

1969.21 WREN, ROBERT M. "Salisbury and the Blackfriars Theatre." *TN* 23 (Spring): 103- 09.
   Discusses the role of the Earl of Salisbury in the affairs of the Blackfriars Playhouse, and demonstrates that he was clearly satirized on the stage of that theatre.

1969.22 WRIGHT, LOUIS B. *Shakespeare's Theatre and the Dramatic Tradition.* Washington: Folger Shakespeare Library, 36 pp.
   Reprint of 1958.24.

1969.23 YATES, FRANCES A. *The Theatre of the World.* Chicago: University of Chicago Press, 186 pp.
   Based on the chapter in her *Art of Memory* (see 1966.27) that argues that the stage illustration in Robert Fludd's *Ars Memoriae* can throw light on Shakespeare's Globe Playhouse. Primarily centered on John Dee and Fludd as representatives of Renaissance philosophy in England, particularly with regard to the influence of Vitruvius, this work does not attempt to present a full reconstruction of the Globe. The most that is offered is a new approach to the ground plan of the building and its stage. Yates sees the public theatres of London as "adaptations of the ancient theatre made within the sphere of the popular Vitruyianism generated by the Dee movement." The ground plan she offers consists of a circle inscribed within a hexagon (based on the largely discredited

evidence of Mrs. Thrale, friend of Dr. Johnson, who claimed to have seen the foundations of the Globe) with a smaller circle inside that, determined by the intersections of four equilateral triangles inscribed within the larger circle.

*1969.24   YOM, SUK-KEE. "Shakespearean Stage." In *An Introduction to Shakespeare*. Seoul (Korea): n.p., pp. 170-92.
        Cited in 1974.18.

1970

1970.1   ARNOTT, JAMES FULLARTON, and ROBINSON, JOHN WILLIAM. *English Theatrical Literature, 1559-1900: A Bibliography; Incorporating Robert W. Lowe's "A Bibliographival Account of English Theatrical Literature," 1888.* London: Society for Theatre Research. 486 pp.
        Includes 1888.9. The dates in the title refer not to events of theatrical history, but to the date of publication of the work included. In all there are 4506 entries, encompassing all phases of English, Irish, and Scottish theatre. Relevant entries are to be found throughout. The author, short-title, and place of publication indexes are drama useful, but a subject index would have been mare useful still.

1970.2   BERGERON, DAVID M. "Charles 1's Royal Entries into London." *GuildMisc* 3, no. 2 (June): 91-97.
        Examines the planned and aborted entries of Charles into a London in 1626, 1633, and 1641. The records demonstrate clearly the involvement of the city government, Aldermen and Council., and livery companies in the preparations, as well as the expenses and methods of financing used.

1970.3   _____. "The Elizabethan Lord Mayor's Show." *SEL* 10 (Spring): 269-86.
        Traces the development of the Lord Mayor's Show in the sixteenth century from a simple procession to complex and sophisticated plays concentrating on history, mythology, and moral allegory. Particularly important is the pageant written by Peck. One measure of the development of the farm is the cost, which went from £151 in 1561 to £747 in 1602.

1970.4   BERRY, HERBERT. "The Playhouse in the Boar's Head Inn, Whitechapel." In *The Elizabethan Theatre, II*. Edited by David Galloway. Toronto: Macmillan; Hamden, Conn.: Archon, pp. 45-73.
        The first of two articles on the Boar's Head (see also 1973.1), which Berry calls "one of the more successful Elizabethan playhouses," based on documents discovered by Sisson (see1972.29) and supplemented by Hotson (1959.9) and Berry himself. Berry untangles the complicated litigation surrounding the Boar's Head, and a picture emerges of an inn located just outside the London city limits converted into a permanent playhouse. The major figures in the theatre's history were Oliver Woodliffe, who leased the building in 1594; Richard Samwell, who subleased from Woodliffe; John Mags, a contractor who was to expand the upper galleries; Frances Langley, builder of the Swan who was

looking for a new investment, and Robert Browne, head of the acting company involved at the Boar's Head.

1970.5 DeMOLEN, RICHARD LEE. "Richard Mulcaster: An Elizabethan Savant." Ph.D. dissertation, University of Michigan, 319 pp.

The relevant section is the fourth chapter, where DeMolen discusses Mulcaster's use of literary and theatrical forms. He claims that "Mulcaster employed pageantry, poetry and drama for hortatory and didactic reasons as well as for purposes of flattery and persuasion." DeMolen sees the revival of the acting company at St. Paul's as Mulcaster's responsibility. See also 1972.6; 1974.10.

1970.6 DODD, KENNETH M. "Another Elizabethan Theatre in the Round." *SQ* 21 (Spring): 125-56.

Discusses the "Game Place" in Suffolk, described in a 1581 manuscript, as a circular stone retaining wall filled with earth and was related to the medieval method of staging rather than the Elizabethan.

1970.7 FOAKES, R. A. "Tragedy of the Children's Theatres after 1600: A Challenge to the Adult Stage." In *The Elizabethan Theatre, II*. Edited by David Galloway. Toronto: Macmillan; Handen, Conn.: Archon, pp. 37-59.

Suggests that Harbage's "rival traditions" (see 1952.8) need reexamination. The impact of the revival of the children's companies in 1600 was very great, and the adult companies had to take over the style and techniques of the boys in order to compote. Thus the children's companies and their playwrights had a strong influence on the drama and theatre of the seventeenth century.

1970.8 GALLOWAY, DAVID, ed. *The Elizabethan Theatre, [I]*. Toronto: Macmillan; Hamden, Conn.: Archon, 130 pp.

"Papers given at the International Conference on Elizabethan Theatre held at the University of Waterloo, Ontario, in July 1968." Contains 1970.4, 13, 25, 29, 31, as well as an introduction by the editor and two other non-theatrical articles.

1970.9 _____, ed. *The Elizabethan Theatre, II*. Hamden, Conn.: Archon, 148 pp.

"Papers delivered at the Second International Conference on Elizabethan Theatre held at the University of Waterloo, Ontario, in July 1969." Contains 1970.7, 10-20, 27, as well as other nontheatrical papers and an introduction by the editor.

1970.10 GURR, ANDREW [J]. *The Shakespearean Stage*. Cambridge: University Press, 192 pp.

Primarily a summary of Bentley (1941.1; 1956.4; 1968.2), Chambers (1923.2), and other such works. According to Gurr this work "should be read as a preliminary, outlining study of the background circumstances out of which the plays first appeared." He includes chapters on the companies, actors, playhouses, staging, and audience.

1970.11   HART, ALFRED. "Play Abridgement: The Length of Elizabethan and Jacobean Plays, Time Allotted for the Representation of Elizabethan and Jacobean Plays, Acting Versions of Elizabethan and Jacobean Plays." In *Shakespeare and the Homilies, and Other Pieces of Research in the Elizabethan Drama*. New York: Octagon, pp. 77-1.53
        Reprint of 1934.3, which in turn reprints 1932.5-6; 1934.2.

1970.12   HODGES, C[YRIL] WALTER. *Shakespeare and the Players.* 2d ed. New York: Coward-McCann, 110 pp
        Second edition of 1949.6. Retains the original illustrations but adds a few new ones, and makes a few minor additions to the text. The most important addition is an appendix of eleven extracts from theatrical documents of the period.

1970.13   HOSLEY, RICHARD. "A Reconstruction of the Second Blackfriars." In *The Elizabethan Theatre [I]*. Edited by David Gallowav. Toronto: Macmillan: Hamden, Conn.: Archon, p. 74-88.
        Conjectural reconstruction of Shakespeare's private playhouse, based on the size of the hall, the influence of the hall screen, and analogues in the Fortune contract. Hosley locates the theatre in the upper Parliament Chamber, places the stage at one end, and endows it with three doorways in the tiring house facade, three upper acting spaces (one above each doorway), and three galleries. The acting area on the stage is assumed to be 29 feet wide (with a gallery at stage level on either side) and 18½ feet deep to the tiring house facade. No information from the plays staged at the Blackfriars is here considered (but see his 1975.15). Illustrations of Hosley's conjectures are provided by Richard Southern. See also Index, under Blackfriars Playhouse--Reconstructions, for alternative conjectures.

1970.14   HUBBARD, BARBARA. "The Boar's Head Redefined." M.A. thesis, University of Iowa, 185 pp.
        Reexamines the available evidence concerning this inn-yard playhouse, including location, structure, history, and theatrical activities. Hubbard includes transcriptions of published and unpublished documents of the Boar's Head and sections of several contemporary maps and views. While only a master's thesis, this work is as comprehensive as many doctoral dissertations.

1970.15   INGRAM, WILLIAM. "The Playhouse at Newington Butts: A New Proposal." *SQ* 21 (Autumn): 385-90.
        Following up a reference in a 1955 London County Council Survey of London, Ingram was led to a series of documents that suggest that this playhouse was built by actor Jerome Savage: that it may have preceded Burbage's Theatre; that Savage's company, Warwick's Men, played at Newington Butts without incident from 1576 to 1580; and that the Earl of Oxford's Men took over in the latter year. Further, Ingram suggests that Henslowe never had a proprietary interest in this playhouse, it being managed by Peter Hunninghorn until 1595 and Paul Buck until 1597, at which time it was dismantled.

1970.16   JENSEN, EJNER J. "A New Allusion to the Sign of the Globe Theater." *SQ* 21 (Winter): 95-97.

> Points out a possible allusion to the Globe sign in the Introduction to Marston's *Antonio and Mellida*.

1970.17   JOHNSON, ROBERT CARL. "Audience Involvement in the Tudor Interludes." *TN* 24 (Spring): 101-10.

> Discusses the interplay between actors and audience in the Interludes, relevant because of the parallel to the Elizabethan actor-audience relationship.

1970.18   LAVIN, J. A. "The Elizabethan Theatre and the Inductive Method." In *The Elizabethan Theatre, II*. Edited by David Galloway. Toronto: Macmillan; Camden, Conn.: Archon, pp. 74-86.

> An attack on the inductive method--"extracting general laws from particular instances"--in the study of Eliza- bethan theatre history. Lavin takes J. C. Adams, Irwin Smith, T. W. Baldwin, and Bertram Joseph in particular to task, although even such contemporary luminaries as Richard Hosley are prone to inductive reasoning errors. Lavin concludes that "attempts to generalize about Elizabethan theatres, acting, dramatic companies, and theatrical texts are at the best naive, and at the worst positively misleading."

1970.19   LENNAM, TREVOR. "The Children of Paul's, 1551-1582." In *The Elizabethan Theatre, II*. Edited by David Galloway. Toronto: Macmillan; Camdon, Conn.: Archon, pp. 20-36.

> Examines the career of Sebastian Westcott sod discusses the repertory and composition of his company of boys. While "the precise location of the Paul's playhouse remains obscure," Lennam examines and rejects several sites and suggests two new possibilities. See also 1975.22.

1970.20   MARKER, LISA-LONE. "Nature and Decorum in the Theory of Elizabethan Acting." In *The Elizabethan Theatre, II*. Edited by David Galloway. Toronto: Macmillan; Camden, Conn.: Archon, pp. 87-107.

> A broad view of Elizabethan acting techniques. Marker sees a more homogeneous style than many other writers on the subject, one that changed little over the years and was deeply rooted in past practice. Contemporary rhetoricians are examined for their contributions.

1970.21   McKENZIE, D. F. "A Cambridge Playhouse of 1638." *RenD*, n.s. 3: 263-72.

> Discusses the building constructed for the performance of plays at Queen's College in 1638, based on later drawings of the building and contemporary records. McKenzie finds that the playhouse apparently shares many features with the Cockpit-in-Court and that the tiring house facade corresponds with the Swan drawing.

1970.22   MULLIN, Donald C. *The Development of the Playhouse: A Survey of Theatre Architecture from the Renaissance to the Present.* Berkeley and Los Angeles: University of California Press, pp. 32-42.

      The relevant section is Chapter III, "The Triumph of Albion." Mullin presents a general summary of the playhouses of the period, illustrated with contemporary and modern drawings. He discusses how various have used stage directions and allusions to postulate certain physical features of the stage without endorsing those methods. Mullin concludes with a discussion of staging in the court masques.

1970.23   PINCISS, G. M. "The Queen's Men, 1583-1592." *ThS* 11 (May): 50-65.

      Examines the provincial and London records of this unusually large group of twelve men drawn from the other companies. They were clearly the most important adult company during the later 1580s, but were soon eclipsed by the Lord Chamberlain's Men.

1970.24   RIDDELL, JAMES A, "Some Actors in Ben Jonson's Plays." *ShSt* 5: 285-98.

      Discusses the names of actors written in a copy of the 1616 Jonson folio, apparently with the parts distributed as they were between 1610 and 1615. Riddell concludes that while the ascription of actors to roles in the seventeenth-century hand is possible, it cannot be proven or disproven with the available evidence.

1970.25   ROWAN, D. F. "The Cockpit-in-Court." In *The Elizabethan Theatre [I].* Edited by David Galloway. Toronto: Macmillan; Hamden, Conn.: Archon, pp. 89-102.

      Examines the Inigo Jones drawings for this theatre held at Worcester College, Oxford, concluding that this was "an actual Elizabethan theatre which was not . . . a classical 'coterie' theatre for elegant amateurs, but was, in fact, a traditional 'popular' theatre for experienced professionals, which only happened to be located at Court." . Rowan examines the staging of The Lost Lady in detail. See also Wickham (1967.15) and Star (1972.30; 1974.23) on this theatre.

1970.26   _____. "A Neglected Jones/Webb Theatre Project: Barber-Surgeon's Hall Writ Large." *ShS* 23: 125-29.

      Abridged from 1969.10.

1970.27   _____. "A Neglected Jones/Webb Theatre Project, Part II: A Theatrical Missing Link." In *The Elizabethan Theatre, II.* Edited by David Gallowav. Toronto: Macmillan: Hamden, Conn.: Archon, pp. 60-73.

      Reexamines his earlier identification of the Inigo Jones drawings of the unidentified private playhouse with the Barber-Surgeon's Hall. Instead, Rowan now see these drawings as a "missing link" between the two best pieces of evidence we have of the Elizabethan theatre: the Swan drawing and the Cockpit-in-Court drawings. There was apparently a continuous tradition in theatre architecture from the 1590s to the 1630s.

1970.28   SHAPIRO, MICHAEL. "Three Notes on the Theatre at Paul's c. 1569-c. 1607." *TN* 24 (Summer): 147-53.

        Notes on the location, auditorium, and admission price of the theatre at Paul's. Based on Shapiro's Ph.D. dissertation, 1967.6.

1970.29   SPENCER, T. J. B. "Shakespeare: The Elizabethan Theatre-Poet." In *The Elizabethan Theatre [1]*. Edited by David Gallowav. Toronto: Macmillan: Hamden, Conn.: Archon, pp. 1-20.

        Examines the divergent courses of Shakespearean production and criticism, revealing "artistic connections between stage and dramatic form."

1970.30   SUMMERSON, JOHN [NEWENHAM]. *Architecture in Britain,1530-1830.* Pelican History of Art, no. 23. Harmondsworth: Penguin Books, pp. 61-67.

        Reprint of 1953.26.

1970.31   WICKHAM, GLYNNE. "The Privy Council Order of 1597 for the Destruction of All London's Theatres." In *The Elizabethan Theatre, II.* Edited by David Galloway. Toronto: Macmillan; Hamden, Conn.: Archon, pp. 21-44.

        Explains why the order was never carried out and suggests that the Privy Council never intended it to be. Wickham points out that since the public and private companies to prepare for Court performances, theatres were held to be rehearsal halls for the various companies to prepare for court performances. Information on those performances might yield valuable information on performances in the public and private playhouses.

<u>1971</u>

1971.1   BECKERMAN, BERNARD. "Philip Henslowe." In *The Actor-Manager in England and America: Players in a Perilous Game.* Princeton: Princeton University Press, pp. 19-62.

        Examines the various roles (banker, impresario, entrepeneur, etc.) played by Henslowe in the theatrical life of the period. Beckerman breaks Henslowe's career into four phases (1592-1596, 1597-1604, 1604-1611, and 1611-1616 and discusses each with emphasis on the first (the Rose period) and fourth (the Hope period). He concludes by distinguishing the historical meaning of Henslowe's position as manager from his personal styleWhile historically he represents "the manager of the future at an early stage of development," we must recognize the prosaic qualities of his style.

1971.2   BENTLEY, GERALD EADES. *The Profession of Dramatist in Shakespeare's Time: 1590-1642.* Princeton: Princeton University Press, 329 pp.

        "An explication of the normal working environment circumscribing the activities of those literary artists who were making their living by writing for the London theatres" from the time of Shakespeare to the closing of the playhouses. Bentley examines relations with the company, pay, working conditions, contractual obligations, status, regulation and censorship, collaboration, revision, and publication. The final chapter, where Bentley traces the publication patterns of eleven playwrights, is particularly important. See also J. Q. Adams (1932.1).

1971.3   BERGERON, DAVID M. *English Civic Pageantry: 1558-1642*. London: Edward Arnold; Columbia: University of South Carolina Press. 325 no.
    Expanded published version of 1964.4, incorporating the findings of several of his published articles, including treatment of pageants, including progresses, royal entries, and Lord Mayor's shows. This is the most complete work in the area of pageantry yet produced.

1971.4   BROWNSTEIN, O[SCAR] L. "A Record of London Inn-Playhouses c. 1565-1580." *SQ* 22 (Winter): 17-24.
    Examines "The Register of the Masters of Defense" (MS Sloane 2530 in the British Library) for references to early playhouses. "It is," says Brownstein, "the only systematic account of activities of any kind at four of the earliest Elizabethan playhouses during thc period of the origin of these playhouses." Apparently the only distinction made between the innyard theatres of the city (the Bull, the Bell-Savage, the Cross Keys, the Bell, the Boar's Read) and the suburban playhouses (the Theatre, the Newington Butts, the Swan) was their location, not their facilities. Brownstein also suggests that the Bell-Savage Inn contained a public theatre that pre-dated Burbage's Theatre.

1971.5   _____. "The Saracen's Head, Islington: A Pre-Elizabethan Inn Playhouse." *TN* 24 (Winter): 68-72.
    Discusses what is known about the management, location, and activities at the inn, where it is known theatrical performances were given as earlv as 1557. Brownstein opens and closes with a plea for additional research into the innyard playhouses.

1971.6   FREEHAFER, JOHN. "Inigo Jones's Scenery for *The Cid*." *TN* 24 (Spring): 84-92.
    Argues that Simpson and Bell's Inigo Jones design no. 361, frequently thought to represent the first scene of *The Queen of Aragon*, actually was designed for *The Cid* in 1639.

1971.7   HOSLEY, RICHARD. "Three Kinds of Outdoor Theatre before Shakespeare." *ThS* 12 (May): 1-33.
    Examines the place-and-scaffolds theatre, the pageant wagons, and the booth stages of the middle ages. The last is relevant, since most scholars believe that the Elizabethan playhouses were influenced by the booth stage. Unfortunately, Hosley sheds little light on the issue here.

1971.8   HUDSON, KATHERINE. *The Story of the Elizabethan Boy-Actors*. Illustrated by Robert Micklewright. London: Oxford University Press, 90 pp.

A popular treatment intended for a juvenile audience. Hudson begins with the middle ages and traces the Children of Paul's and the Children of the Chapel through the seventeenth century.

1971.9   INGRAM, WILLIAM. "The Closing of the Theatres in 1597: A Dissenting View." *MP* 69 (November): 105-15.

Ingram reviews the *Isle of Dogs* incident and speculates that the performance took place after the decision of 28 July to close the playhouses. Sir Robert Cecil took advantage of the incident to break Francis Langley, already in trouble with the Crown over a stolen diamond. Documentary evidence from the Public Record Office and the collection of the Marquis of Salisbury substantiate the case. See also 1970.31.

1971.10   KING, T[HOMAS] J[AMES]. *Shakespearean Staging, 1599-1642*. Cambridge: Harvard University Press, 163 pp.

A "systematic survey of theatrical requirements for 276 plays first performed by professional actors in the period between the Autumn of 1599 . . . and 2 September 1642." King's primary aim is to find positive correlations between the internal evidence of the texts of the plays presented during this period and the external evidence as provided by surviving illustrations. He makes no attempt to deal with the plays by playhouse of presentation. King presents the evidence in order of increasing complexity: subsequent chapters treat entrances, areas above, hangings and discoveries, and traps. He also includes an imaginative reconstruction of the staging *Twelfht Night* at the Middle Temple and a review of the major scholarship in the field since 1940. King concludes that all the plays he examines could with minor adjustments have been staged upon any of the nine stages represented in the surviving illustrations. See also 1971.11; 1972.17.

1971.11   _____. "Shakespearean Staging, 1599-1642." *SRO* 5-6: 30-35.

Summarizes conclusions from 1971.10, with suggestions for further research.

1971.12   KOHLER, RICHARD CHARLES. "The Fortune Contract and Vitruvian Symmetry." *ShSt* 6: 311-26.

As a test of Yates's ideas on the use of Vitruvian principles in the Elizabethan theatre (see 1969.23), Kahler compares her ground plan of the Globe to the Fortune contract and the Swan drawing, and estimates the sizes of the Fortune, Swan. Rose, and Globe. He concludes that there is exact correspondence between two of the measurements found in the Fortune contract and the Vitruvian scheme, and that there is no conflict with any other data. Consequently, Roman influence on the Elizabethan theatre is quite possible.

1971.13   ORDISH, T. FAIRMAN. *Early London Theatres--In the Fields*. London: White Lion Publishers, 316 pp.
>   Reprint of 1894.4, with a new Foreword by Hodges.

1971.14   SHAPIRO, MICHAEL. "*Le prince d'amour* and the Resumption of Playing at Paul's." *N&Q*, n.s. 18 (January): 14-16.
>   Suggests that the Children of Paul's resumed playing by the fall of 1597 instead of 1599-1600 as previously thought.

1971.15   _____. "What We Know about the Children's Troupes and Their Plays." *SRO* 5-6: 36-45.
>   A review of the literature on and state of knowledge of the boy companies.

1971.16   SKURA, MERIDETH ANNE. "Shakespeare's Clowns." Ph.D. dissertation, Yale University, 231 pp.
>   A literary study of little theatrical or historical interest.

1971.17   WHITTY, JOHN CHRISTOPHER. "The Lord Admiral's Men, 1594-1600: What the Actor Did." Ph.D. dissertation, University of Iowa, 356 pp.
>   Examines a body of eleven plays produced by a single company in a limited period of time to find out what instructions to the actors are contained in the texts. Using this information and other historical records, Whitty has described as completely as possible what the actors who first appeared in these plays actually did physically and vocally. This is an attempt to deal with "the substance rather than the style of Elizabethan acting." The most important contribution of this work is the development of a system far script analysis, codifying the hit-and-miss intuitive methods of most historians. The major conclusion is that "physical modes of behavior creating visual effects formed a considerable part of the actor's craft." The bulk of the work consists of four appendixes containing tables of cues and various verifications.

1971.18   WIKLAND, ERIC. *Elizabethan Players in Sweden, 1591-92*. Translated by Patrick Hort. 2d ed., revised and enlarged. Stockholm: Almqvist & Wiksell, 281 pp.
>   Revised edition of 1962.23. Additional material extends the coverage to 1594 and 1617, and Wikland prints additional illustretions.

<u>1972</u>

1972.1   BAKER, Sir RICHARD. *Theatrum Redivivum, or The Theatre Vindicated*. New York: Johnson Reprint Corp., 141 pp.
>   Reprint of the 1662 edition, with an introduction by Peter Davison.

1972.2   BALE, JOHN, and LODGE, THOMAS. "The Epistle Exhortatory of an English Christian" and "Reply to Gosson." New York: Johnson Reprint Corp., 124 pp.

   Renrints of the 1544 and 1579-80 editions, with introductions by Peter Davison.

1972.3   CHETTLE, HENRY, and RANKINS, WILI.IAM. *"Kind Heart's Dream" and "Mirror of Monsters."* New York: Johnson Reprint Corp., 246 pp.

   Reprints of the 1587 and 1592 editions, with introductions by Peter Davison.

1972.4   CRASHAW, WILLIAM. *Sermon Preached at the Cross, February 14, 1607.* New York: Johnson Reprint Corp., 188 pp.

   Reprint of the 1608 edition, with an introduction by Peter Davison.

1972.5   DAVISON, PETER, ed. *Critics and Apologists of the English Theatre: A Selection of Seventeenth-Century Pamphlets in Facsimile.* New York: Johnson Reprint Corp., 107 pp.

   Reprints of six printed tents and one manuscript dealing with the attack and defense of the English stage. Included are *The Actors' Remonstrance*, 1643; the forged *Mr. William Prynne, His Defence of Stage Plays*, 1649; *The Players Petition to Parliament*, 1643; A *Short Treatise Against Stage-Plays*, 1625; *The Stage-Players' Complaint*, 1641; and *Testimonies of Pagans, of Infidels, of Christian Fathers, on the Nature and Tendency of Theatrical Amusements*, 1819. The editor includes a brief introduction to each selection.

1972.6   DeMOLEN, RICHARD L. "Richard Mulcaster and the Elizabethan Theatre." *ThS* 13 (May): 28-41.

   Examines the role Mulcaster played as Headmaster of the Merchant Taylor's School from 1561 to 1585, and of St. Paul's, 1596 to 1608. While he may have written some plays, he almost certainly adapted some to suit his young actors, and he was responsible for the revival of the boy companies in 1600. DeMolen also claims that Shakespeare modeled Holofernes in Love's Labour's Lost on Mulcaster.

1972.7   FEATHER, JOHN. "Robert Armin and the Chamberlain's Men." *N&Q*, n.s. 19 (December): 448-50.

   Examines Armin's movement from Lord Chandos's Men to the Lord Chamberlain's company, suggesting that the transfer took place in 1598 rather than 1599.

1972.8   FEILDE, JOHN, and W., T. *"A Godly Exhortation by Ocassion of the Late Judgement of God Showed at Paris-Garden, the Thirteenth Day of January"* and *"A Sermon Preached at Paul's Cross, 3 November 1577."* New York: Johnson Reprint Corp., 160 pp.
     Reprints of the 1583 and 1578 editions, with introductions by Peter Davison.

1972.9   FENTON, GEORGE. *Form of Christian Policy Gathered Out of French.* New York: Johnson Reprint Corp., 142 pp.
     Reprint of the 1574 edition, with an introduction by Peter Davison.

1972.10   GOSSON, STEPHEN. *Plays Confuted in Five Actions.* New York: Johnson Reprint Corp., 128 pp.
     Reprint of the 1582 edition, with an introduction by Peter Davison.

1972.11   HABICHT, WERNER. "Tree Properties and Tree Scenes in Elizabethan Theater." *RenD*, n.s. 4: 69-92.
     An attempt "to point out the use to which a constantly recurring type of property was put in an important phase of the history of the theater." Habicht discusses the emblematic and literary uses of trees, not their use as a property in actual stage practice.

1972.12   HAMMER, GAEL WARREN. "The Staging of Elizabethan Plays in the Private Theatres, 1632-1642." Ph.D. dissertation, University of Iowa, 194 pp.
     Examines the staging of plays at the Blackfriars, Phoenix, and Salisbury Court Playhouses during the last ten years of their legitimate existence, with special reference to the possible use of painted perspective scenery. He establishes a group of "place-realism" plays that might have used such scenery during this period, and infers from internal evidence in Nabbes's Microcosmus what it might have been like. Hammer also attempts to determine the structural features of the playhouse stages, using the method of script analysis proposed by Whitty (1971.17). He concludes that the three playhouses were similar in structure and staging methods.

1972.13   HEYWOOD, THOMAS, and G[REENE], J[OHN]. *"An Apology for Actors"* and *"A Refutation of the Apology for Actors."* New York: Johnson Reprint Corp., 144 pp.
     Reprints of the 1612 and 1615 editions, with introductions by J. W. Binns.

1972.14   HOSLEY, RICHARD. "The Interpretation of Pictorial Evidence for Theatrical Design." *RORD* 13-14: 123-25.
     Summary of a paper presented at the 1969 MLA convention. Hosley discusses distortion of scale in a painting of a 1615 pageant wagon, distortion of point of view in the Swan drawing, and distortion of shape in Hollar's "Long Bird's Eye View of London."

1972.15   INGRAM, WILLIAM. "'Neere the Playe House': The Swan   Theatre and Community Blight." *RenD*, n.s. 4: 53-68.

   A detailed examination of the charge that the Swan was the cause of the decline of the neighborhood in which it was located. Ingram shows how Frances Langley's "neglectful and exploitive attitudes" were responsible for the bad reputation of his playhouse and how that reputation improved considerably when Hugh Browker, "a respected member of the community," took over.

1972.16   KINCAID, A. N. "A Revels Office Scrap Deciphered." *N&Q*, n.s. 19 (December): 461-63.

   Reexamines one of Sir George Buc's Revels Office entries, changing the name from Bald's reading. An unknown play, *Cupid's Festival*, was approved 18 December 1614, and held at the Revels Office for "Dwarf Bob" the actor, also unknown.

1972.17   KING, T[HOMAS] J[AMES]. "The Stage in the Time of Shakespeare: A Survey of Major Scholarship." *RenD*, n.s. 4: 199-235.

   Reprinted in part from 1971.10. King reviews major scholarship by nineteen writers "to show how the failure of some scholars to apply consistent criteria for the evaluation of evidence has led to widely divergent and sometimes mutually contradictory theories." Includes reviews of Albright, Thorndike, Chambers, Lawrence, Greg, Reynolds, J. C. Adams, Kernodle, Southern, Hodges, Hotson, Harbage, Irwin Smith, Hosley, Nagler, Beckerman, Wickham, Yates, and Gurr in a roughly chronological treatment. See Index, under each writer, for specific references.

1972.18   MANNING, THOMAS JOHN. "Staging of Plays at Christ Church, Oxford: 1582-1592." Ph.D. dissertation, University of Michigan, 223 pp.

   Examines three plays by William Gager performed at Christ Church, Oxford, 1582-92, in order to reconstruct the staging practices employed. Essentially medieval techniques of simultaneous staging were apparently used. One mansion was equipped with curtains for a discovery, and there was an upper acting space available.

1972.19   McMILLIN, [HARVEY] SCOTT. "Casting for Pembroke's Men: The *Henry VI* Quartos and *The Taming of a Shrew*." 23 (Spring): 141-59.

   Examines three reported or "bad" quartos to see what they tell us about the casting of Pembroke's Men. McMillin concludes that a company of eleven actors could double all parts in these plays, assisted by four boys in female parts and five hired men for walk-ons. He also speculates on the origin and membership of the company.

1972.20   MONTANUS, JOANNES FERRARIUS. *Work Touching the Good Ordering of a Common Weal*. Translated by William Bauande. New York: Johnson Reprint Corp., 88 pp.

   Reprint of the 1559 edition, with an introduction by Peter Davison.

1972.21   NAOGERGUS, THOMAS. *Popish Kingdom; or, Reign of Antichrist Written in Latin Verse*. Translated by R. Googe. New York: Johnson Reprint Corp., 124 pp.

        Reprint of the 1570 edition, with an introduction by Peter Davison.

1972.22   PRYNNE, WILLIAM. *Histrio-Mastix: The Player's Scourge, or, Actor's Tragedy*. 2 vols. New York: Johnson Reprint Corp. 1006 pp.

        Reprint of the 1633 edition, with an introduction by Peter Davison.

1972.23   RAINOLDS, JOHN. *The Overthrow of Stage-Plays*. New York: Johnson Reprint Corp., 190 pp.

        Reprint of the 1599 edition, with an introduction by W. Binns.

1972.24   ROWAN, D. P. "The English Playhouse: 1595-1630." *RenD*, n.s. 4: 37-51.

        Argues for considering both "public" and "private" theatres together, and restricts the time frame in this examination to the limitations imposed by the Swan drawin and the Inigo Jones design for the Cockpit-in-Court. Rowan views the unidentified Jones drawings held at Worcester College, Oxford, as "a theatrical missing-link between the Swan and the Cockpit-in-Court." It is now, he says, possible to discuss the physical features of the Elizabethan playhouse stage with some assurance. See also 1970.27.

1972.25   _____. "The Tiring-House Wall and the Galleries in the Second Blackfriars: Two Points in Dispute." *TN* 26 (Spring): 101-04.

        Rowan differs with Hosley (1970.13) in placing the tiring house wall at the end of the sixty-six-foot Parliament Chamber and in surrounding the pit with three galleries.

1972.26   SALOMON, BROWNELL. "Visual and Aural Signs in the Performed English Renaissance Play." *RenD*, n.s. 5: 143-69.

        Defines "sign" as a sensory datum explicitly demanded by the playwright's text that assumes interpretative relevance, and discusses that concept (from semiotics) in selected plays. Specifically, Salomon discusses language, vocal tone, gesture, movement, makeup, costume, hand properties, the decor, lighting, music, and sound effects. He concludes that "thematically relevant details can be organized so they will mare effectively demonstrate how or to what extent theatre poets have realized dramatic meaning in phenomenal terms, in a total, histrionic frame."

1972.27   SALVIANUS and EUTHEO [pseuds.]. *Second and Third Blast of Retreat from Plays and Theatres*. New York: Johnson Reprint Corp., 142 pp.

        Reprint of the 1580 edition, with an introduction by Peter Davison.

1972.28 SIMMONS, J. L. "Elizabethan Stage Practice and Marlowe's *The Jew of Malta*." *RenD*, n.s. 4: 93-104.

Examines the staging of one scene of the play for what it tells us of the playhouse. Simmons contends that the supposedly dead body of Barabas was thrown from the stage into the yard, reentering from a trap. Similarly, Calymath and his Turks enter into the yard and assault the stage from the front.

1972.29 SISSON, C[HARLES] J[ASPER]. *The Boar's Head Theatre: An Inn-Yard Theatre of the Elizabethan Age.* Edited by Stanley Wells. London and Boston: Routledge & Kegan Paul, 100 pp.

Posthumous cumulation of Sisson's previous work on the Boar's Head (see 1936.21; 1954.25), edited by his student and friend. The four chapters examine the inn-yard theatres in general, the George Inn in Whitechapel, the history of the Boar's Head, and the legal battle for control of the theatre. Sisson makes the important point that the inn was given over entirely to the presentation of plays, with no other business conducted. The work is based on a series of documents discovered by Sisson in the Public Record Office, rediscovered more recently by Berry (see 1970.4; 1973.1).

1972.30 STAR, L[EONIE] R[ACHEL]. "A Note on the Use of Scenery at the Cockpit-in-Court." *TN* 26 (Spring): 89-91.

Suggests the use of "backcloths" rather than changeable painted scenery behind three of the five doorways at the Cockpit-in-Court. Based on research leading to her Ph.D. dissertation (1974.21). See also Freehafer (1971.6), against whom she argues, and his answer (1973.6).

1972.31 STUBBES, PHILIP. *The Anatomy of Abuses.* New York: Johnson Reprint Corp., 120 pp.

Reprint of the 1583 edition, with an introduction by Peter Davison.

1972.32 WICKHAM, GLYNNE. *Early English Stages, 1300-1660.* Vol. 2, Pt. 2, *1576-1660.* London: Routledge & Kegan Paul; New York: Columbia University Press, 266 pp.

The third of a projected five-volume work, following 1959.29 and 1963.20. Wickham here treats the development from multi-purpose gamehouses to single-purpose theatres. He examines the inns used as playhouses as well as public and private theatres built specifically for the purpose. While the many excellent drawings and photographs lend an air of authority, many statements made here are conjectural. Nonetheless, Wickham explores a great many intriguing possibilities, and when the evidence from the plays is added, as is promised for a subsequent volume, Early English Stages may well end up as one of the most comprehensive contributions to the field.

1972.33   WRIGHT, JAMES, and FLECKNOE, RICILARD. *"Historia Histrionica"*
and *"A Short Discourse of the English Stage Appended to Love's Kingdom."* New
York: Johnson Reprint Corp., 46 pp.
Reprints of 1664.1 and 1699.1, with introductions by Peter Davison.

1972.34   WRIGHT, LOUIS B. *Shakespeare's Theatre and the Dramatic Tradition.*
Washington: Folger Shakespeare Library, 36 pp.
Reprint of 1958.24.

1972.35   ZUCKER, DAVID WARD. *Stage and Image in the Plays of Christopher
Marlowe.* Salzburg Studies in English Literature, no. 7. Salzburg: Institut fur
englische Sprache und Literatur, Universitat Salzburg, pp. 10-15, passim.
Published version of 1968.39. As part of a literary study of Marlowe,
Zucker (drawing entirely on secondary sources) discusses the stage he wrote for.
The remainder of the study examines visual iconography in the plays.

1973

1973.1   BERRY, HERBERT. "The Boar's Head Again." In *The Elizabethan Theatre,
III.* Edited by David Galloway. Toronto: Macmillan; Hamden, Conn.: Archon, pp.
33-65.
Continuation of 1970.4. Berry traces the major figures in the Boar's Head
from 1562 to 1621 and uses the Ogilby and Morgan 1676 map of London, several
subsequent maps and surveys, and various legal documents to discover more
about the property and playhouse.

1973.2   CUTTS, JOHN P. "Le rôle de la musique dans le masques de Ben Jonson et
notament dens Oberon (1610-1611)." In *Les fêtes de la Renaissance.* Vol. 1.
Edited by Jean Jacquot. Paris: CNRS, pp. 285-303.
Reprint of 1956.9.

1973.3   DOEBLER, JOHN. "A Lost Paragraph in the Revels Constitution." *SQ* 24
(Summer): 333-34.
Transcribes this important document, held at the Folger Shakespeare
Library. Kempe (1836.1), and all subsequent transcriptions based on Kempe
including that by Chambers (1923.2), leave out the third paragraph. See also
1974.11.

1973.4   EVANS, G. BLAKEMORE. "An Elizabethan Theatrical Stocklist.'" *HLB* 21
(July): 254-70.
An attempt to establish the provenance of the folio leaf held by the
Houghton Library, to determine its connection with Edward Alleyn, and to
examine its influence on the study of Elizabethan theatre history. The leaf
contains a price stock list of costumes and properties and a notation of estate
accounts and rents. While not part of Henslowe's diary, as had been suspected, the
list was in Alleyn's possession, as his handwriting attests. Evans suggests that the

list represents costumes and properties assembled by John Alleyn, Edward's brother, and sold to some acting group, perhaps for provincial touring.

1973.5 FLECKNOE, RICHARD. "A Short Discourse of the English Stage." In *Love's Kingdom*. New York: Garland, pp. 99-109.
Reprint of 1664.1, with a preface by Arthur Freeman.

1973.6 FREEHAFER, JOHN. "Perspective Scenery and the Caroline Playhouses." *TN* 27 (Spring): 98-113.
Examines the influence of Italian perspective scenery and theatre building on the Caroline work of Inigo Jones. Freehafer argues against Star (1972.30) and King (1965.9, 1971.10), claiming changeable perspective scenery was used at the Cockpit-in-Court for several productions, at the Phoenix at least for *Hannibal and Scipio,* and at the Salisbury Court for *Microcosmus*. He also accepts Wickham's conjecture (in 1972.32) that the Inigo Jones drawings held at Worcester College were designs for the Salisbury Court Playhouse, lending credence to the possible use of scenery there. But <u>see</u> 1977.25.

1973.7 GALLOWAY, DAVID, ed. *The Elizabethan Theatre, III*. Toronto: Macmillan; Hamden, Conn.: Archon, 149 pp.
Contains three essays of theatrical interest (1973.1, 14, 15) and five others, as well as an introduction by the editor. The theme of the volume, as of the conference whose papers it publishes (Third International Conference on Elizabethan Theatre, University of Waterloo, Ontario, July 1970), is "Theatre and Society."

1973.8 GORDON, D. J. "Le Masque Mimorable de Chapman." In *Les fêtes de la Renaissance*. Vol. 2. Edited by Jean Jacquot. Paris: CNRS, pp. 305-17.
Reprint of 1956.12.

1973.9 GOSSETT, SUZANNE. "Drama in the English College, Rome, 1591- 1660." *ELR* 3 (Winter): 60-93.
Identifies eleven specific productions, 1612-1648, including an English play, *The New Moon*, 1633. After 1634 a removable stage with changeable scenery was used; before that date the plays were performed "in the tradition of the Elizabethan manner," but Gossett is not more specific.

1973.10 HARRIS, JOHN; ORGEL, STEPHEN; and STRONG, ROY, eds. *The King's Arcadia: Inigo Jones and the Stuart Court*. London: Arts Council of Great Britain, 232 pp.
Catalogue of the exhibition in the Whitehall Banqueting Hall, 12 July-2 September 1973. Composed of three parts: "Jones in the Making," "The British Vitruvius," and "The King's Arcadia." Parts II and III deal with the theatre architecture and the masque designs. The many illustrations are the work's greatest strength. <u>See also</u> 1973.21.

1973.11   HODGES, C[YRIL] WALTER. *Shakespeare's Second Globe: The Missing Monument*. London: Oxford University Press, 100 pp.

        A reconstruction of the Second Globe, erected on the same site after the first playhouse by that name burned. Hodges bases his conjectures on the preliminary sketch and subsequent etching of Wenceslaus Hollar of 1647 ("The Long View of London"). An important second chapter clearly establishes the credibility of the source, and Hodges goes on to solve problems of proportion, size, the superstructure, and the interior. He proposes a sixteen-sided building, 92 feet in diameter, with three galleries, eleven, ten, and nine feet high respectively. He omits pillars supporting the "Heavens," which in this reconstruction are open to view. The size of the stage here (43' x 27'6") is taken from the Fortune contract. The tiring house facade contains two doors and a built-in projecting booth in front of a larger center door that could be fitted with hangings and used for discoveries. The booth also provides an acting area above, as does the open gallery behind it, with openings above the side doors. Despite the fact that no use is made of the plays known to have been staged at the Second Globe, and that Hodges had by 1980 modified some of his conclusions (regarding the number of sides and the diameter of the playhouse, the use of pillars to support the heavens, and the type of flying machinery available), this is perhaps the most authoritative reconstruction of the Globe to date.

1973.12   HOSLEY, RICHARD. "Three Renaissance English Indoor Playhouses." *ELR* 3 (Winter): 166-82.

        Distinguishes five classes of hall screen (with one, two, or three doors), with detailed descriptions of the screens of the Hampton Court Great Hall, the Trinity Hall of St. Bodolph-without-Aldersgate, and the unidentified hall pictured on *The Wits* frontispiece. The five-class descriptive model enables Hosley to depict the playhouses set up in these halls.

1973.13   JACQUOT, JEAN, ed. *Les fêtes de la Renaissance*. Vol. 1. Paris: CNRS, pp. 259-317.

        Reprint of 1956.17, including 1956.9, 12, 28, 33-34.

1973.14   KING, T[HOMAS] J[AMES]. "Shakespearean Staging, 1599-1642." In *The Elizabethan Theatre, III*. Edited by David Galloway. Toronto: Macmillan; Hamden, Conn.: Archon, pp. 1-13.

        A report on the content of King's book (1971.10).

1973.15   LAVIN, J. A. "Shakespeare and the Second Blackfriars." In *The Elizabethan Theatre, III*. Edited by David Galloway. Toronto: Macmillan; Hamden, Conn.: Archon, pp. 66-81.

        Argues against the theory, put forth most persuasively by Bentley (1948.1). that Shakespeare's craft was strongly influenced by the acquisition of the Blackfriars Playhouse by his company. Further, Lavin "assert[s] categorically that there is not a shred of evidence to show that the dramaturgy of Elizabethan playwrights was materially affected by the physical arrangement of the public playhouses."

1973.16 LEACROFT, RICHARD. *The Development of the English Playhouse*. Ithaca:
   Cornell University Press, pp. 25-77.
      The relevant section surveys the development of the Elizabethan stage.
   Leacroft provides scale-drawing reconstructions of the Swan and the second
   Globe (which he gives four doors and a door-sized discovery space, each of
   which has a corresponding curtained balcony above it). A separate chapter
   considers the staging of the masques. He also considers (and provides scale-
   drawing reconstructions of) the Cockpit-in-Court and the unidentified playhouse,
   both designed by Inigo Jones.

1973.17 LELL, GORDON. "'Ganymede' on the Elizabethan Stage: Homosexual
   Implications of the Use of Boy-Actors." *Anglia* (Moorehead, Minn.) 1 (Spring): 5-
   15.
      Argues that "Elizabethans were not completely naive concerning
   suggestions of homosexuality," and that Shakespeare and the other dramatists
   regularly exploited the irony of a boy impersonating a woman.

1973.18 MacKINTOSH, IAIN. "Inigo Jones--Theatre Architect." *TABS* 31, no. 3
   (September): 99-105.
      An attempt to draw attention to Jones as the architect of theatres other than
   the masquing houses, one of which--the Banqueting House--still exists.
   Mackintosh discusses the Jones drawings of the Cockpit-in-Court and the
   unidentified private playhouse at length. He suggests that the latter drawings are
   of the Phoenix in Drury Lane, and that it was intended as a flexible theatre--to be
   used both for Elizabethan staging and for the use of changeable scenery. See also
   Orrell (1977.25).

1973.19 MEAGHER, JOHN C. "The Lord Mayor's Show of 1590." *ELR* 3 (Winter):
   94-104.
      An edition of the British Library copy of the text with commentary.

1973.20 O'DONNELL, C. PATRICK, Jr. "The Repertory of the Jacobean King's
   Company." Ph.D. dissertation, Princeton University, 413 pp.
      Investigates Philip Henslowe's valuable records of the finances of the Lord
   Admiral's Men and applies the findings to the King's Men, with attention to the
   special circumstances of that group. The heart of the study is the third chapter, an
   annotated bibliography of plays from the King's company's repertory containing
   the documentation for the conclusions reached in the previous chapter.

1973.21 ORGEL, STEPHEN, and STRONG, ROY. *Inigo Jones: The Theatre of the
   Stuart Court.* 2 vols. Berkeley: University of California Press, 843 pp.
      The first volume contains four chapters of text (on the poetics of spectacle,
   the mechanism of Platonism, the arts of design, and Platonic politics), and a
   catalogue of Jones's masques from 1605 to 1631, text and designs of which were

reproduced primarily from the collection of the Duke of Devonshire. The second volume continues the catalogue to 1640. Orgel and Strong see Jones as "the most important single person in the arts in seventeenth-century England" and attempt to view his work from a variety of perspectives. This is a seminal work essential to an understanding of the Stuart masques.

1973.22   ROBERTSON, JEAN. "Rapports de poète et de l'artiste dans le préparation des cortèges du Lord Maire (Londres 1553-1640)." In *Les fêtes de la Renaissance*. Vol. 1. Edited by Jean Jacquot. Paris: CNRS, pp. 265-78.
   Reprint of 1956.28.

1973.23   SCHOENHERR, DOUGLAS EDGAR. "The Pageant of the People: A Study of Queen Elizabeth I's Royal Entries." Ph.D. dissertation, Yale University, 209 pp.
   Examines the Elizabethan royal entries from the point of view of the roles into which the Queen was cast in the various pageants. Schoenherr reconstructs the five Coronation pageants and the two most important provincial entries from contemporary descriptions. English pageantry in the sixteenth century is seen as extremely traditional and conservative, adapting types introduced over a century earlier to new uses.

1973.24   SCRAGG, LEAH. "Macbeth on Horseback." *ShS* 26: 81-88.
   Discusses the implications of Simon Forman's "Bocke of Plaies" for the original staging of *Macbeth*. Scraggs differs with Bartholomeusz (1969.1) on the possible use of a horse, contending that Forman's description cannot be taken literally.

1973.25   SNYDER, FREDERICK E. "Composition des fêtes et cortèges d'apparat élisabéthains." *RHT* 25: 244-56.
   Discusses the city and country royal entries, festivals, and processions early in Elizabeth's reign. The reasons for these include reinforcement of the idea of reciprocity between Queen and subjects, affirmation of the queen's new rites, and filling the royal treasury. All theatrical elements were located outdoors, in front of monuments and on specially built stages. A major purpose of such entertainments was to satisfy public taste for amusement and spectacle.

1973.26   SOUTHERN, RICHARD. *The Staging of Plays Before Shakespeare*. New York: Theatre Arts Books, pp. 399-595.
   The relevant sections are Parts Three and Four, dealing with the rise of the stage from the interludes and the building of the Theatre. Southern deals comprehensively with the development of staging practices from 1466 to 1589. He clearly delineates the differences in the traditions of the travelling professional Interlude players performing in private halls and those of the Inns of Court, the Universities, and the Court performances. The general conclusion, that the building of the Theatre and the other professional playhouses was strongly influenced by the experiences of the Interluders playing before hall screens, cannot be doubted.

1973.27   SPINUCCI, PIETRO. *Teatro elisabettiano, teatro di stato: La polemica dei puritani inglesi contro il teatro nei secc. XVI e XVII.* Pubblicazioni dell'istituto di lingua e letteratura inglese e di letteratura anglo-americana, no. 2. Florence: Leo S. Olschki, pp. 61-91.

   The relevant section is Chapter Three, on the political control of the Elizabethan and Jacobean theatre.

1973.28   STEVENS, DAVID. "A Study of Christopher Beeston and the Phoenix or Cockpit Theatre." Ph.D. dissertation, Bowling Green University, 326 pp.

   An attempt to find out as much as possible about the management, repertory, staging practices, and audience of the Phoenix, from an examination of extant records and the body of ninety-one plays produced at this playhouse. Stevens concludes that the stage had three doorways and an upper gallery; that discoveries could be effected by drawing a curtain that had been hung up in front of the center door; that Christopher Beeston, the playhouse manager until his death in 1637, was particularly sophisticated in his business practices; that appropriate costumes, properties, and music were used for virtually all of the plays staged at this playhouse; and that the audience of the Phoenix was sophisticated and demanding.

1973.29   STEVENS, DENIS. "Pièces de théâtre at 'pageants' a l'epoque des Tudor." In *Les fêtes de la Renaissance.* Vol. I. Edited by Jean Jacquot. Paris: CNRS, pp. 259-64.

   Reprint of 1956.33.

1973.30   WERTHEIM, ALBERT. "James Shirley and the Caroline Masques of Ben Jonson." *TN* 27 (Summer): 157-61.

   Discusses the picture of the Jonsonian masque in Shirley's *Love's Cruelty,* suggesting that it gives us a good sense of what the Jonson-Jones masques must have been like.

1973.31   WHITMARSH-KNIGHT, DAVID. "The Second Blackfriars: The Globe Indoors." *TN* 27 (Spring): 94-97.

   Clarifies his differences with Hosley (1970.13) and Smith (1964.22), arguing that there was no substantial difference between the Globe and the Second Blackfriars in size or symmetry.

1973.32   WICKHAM, GLYNNE. "Contributions de Ben Jonson et de Dekker aux fêtes du couronnement de Jacques Ier." In *Les fêtes de la Renaissance.* Vol. 1. Edited by Jean Jacquot. Paris: CNRS, pp. 279-83.

   Reprint of 1956.34.

1973.33   YARROW, DAVID ALEXANDER. "A Stage History of Shakespeare's *Romeo and Juliet* in London, 1597 to 1800." Ph.D. dissertation, University of New Brunswick, 244 pp.

     Since there is almost no evidence concerning the staging of this play before the Restoration, most of the study falls beyond the scope of the present listing.

1974

1974.1   ANON. "Theatre and Play Productionin Shakespeare's Time." In *The New Century Shakespeare Handbook*. Edited by Sandra Clark. Englewood Cliffs, NJ: Prentice-Hall, pp. 18-42.

     A survey (for the general reader) of the playhouse, the stage and stagecraft, the audience, and the actors and companies.

1974.2   ASTINGTON, JOHN HAROLD. "The Staging of the Beaumont and Fletcher Collaborations, 1606-1616." Ph.D. dissertation, University of Toronto, 253 pp.

     Examines nine collaborations, in relation to the theatres and companies associated with their initial performances. It is assumed that Beaumont and Fletcher wrote particularly for private playhouses and that this was of help to the King's Men when they began playing at Blackfriars in 1609. Astington examines the acting style associated with boy and adult companies and concentrates on the uses made of the various physical features of the stage by the dramatists. He concludes that they write with a strong sense of the play as a piece of physical action and that there were probably no differences in presentation between the adult and boy companies.

1974.3   BINNS, J. W. "Women or Transvestites on the Elizabethan Stage? An Oxford Controversy." *SCJ* 5 (October): 95-120.

     Discusses the controversy among Rainolds, Gager, and Alberico Gentili over "stage transvestitism." Rainolds and Gentili corresponded in Latin, and Binns translates several sections and comments on them. Essentially, Gentili argues that the law of Deuteronomy prohibiting the wearing of women's garments by men should not be taken literally in the case of the theatre.

1974.4   BLISSETT, WILLIAM. "Your Majesty Is Welcome to a Fair." In *The Elizabethan Theatre, IV*. Edited by G[eorgel] R. Hibbard. Toronto: Macmillan; Hamden, Conn.: Archon, pp. 80-105.

     Examines the court performance of Bartholomew Fair in 1614.

1974.5   CAVANO, JANET M. JEFFREY. "*Macbeth*: The Book of the Play and the King's Men: A Study of the Stage-Copy in Production and Performance." Ph.D. dissertation, University of North Carolina, 497 pp.

     Since the First Folio text of *Macbeth* was almost certainly set in type from the prompt-book, careful study of it can help us understand in what ways it could serve as a guide to the company in production and performance. Cavano finds no support far such common assertions as "A stage-copy should be precise" or "the book-keeper adapts the author's manuscript for performance." Staging notations are incomplete, and entrance and exit notations inconsistent.

1974.6   COOK, ANN JENNALIE. "The Audience of Shakespeare's Plays: A Reconsideration." *ShSt* 7: 283-305.
Reexamines Harbage's hypothesis (in 1941.4) that the working class formed the majority of Shakespeare's audience. Cook first arrives at a definition of the working class at the time, and concludes that they did not form a majority of the population of London. Next she examines the admissions structure, concluding that it was not especially designed for the working class. Ultimately, she concludes that the working class did not form the majority of Shakespeare's audience.

1974.7   COPE, JACKSON I. "Marlowe's *Dido* and the Titillating Children." *ELR* 4 (Autumn): 315-25.
Discusses the compatibility of declamation and farce. Cope sees the success of the play as "dependent upon a cast . . . of child actors."

1974.8   CROSSLEY, D. W. "Ralph Hogge's Ironworks Accounts, 1576-1581." *Sussex Archaeological Collections* 112: 48-79.
Discusses the material from Henslowe's diary from before Henslowe began to use it. Crossley transcribed the accounts and comments on them. See also 1977.8.

1974.9   CUTTS, JOHN P. "An Entertainment for Queen Elizabeth, 1591." *SMC* 4, no. 3: 554-60.
A paper presented at the Fourth Conference on Medieval Studies, 13-15 March 1968, Western Michigan University. Cutts examines the question of authorship, rejecting Nicholas Breton and supporting John Lyly. His major contribution here concerns the "consort of six musicians provided by the Lord of Hertford to entertain her Majesty." Cutts argues for John Johnson's authorship of two songs and his participation in the Elvetham Entertainment.

1974.10   DeMOLEN, RICHARD L. "Richard Mulcaster and Elizabethan Pageantry." *SEL* 14 (Spring): 209-21.
Examines Mulcaster's use of pageantry. He participated in all three types: royal entries, Lord Mayor's pageants, and royal progresses. Mulcaster wrote pageants "for purposes of flattery and amusement and as a device for persuasion," according to DeMolen. Based in part on 1970.5.

1974.11   DOEBLER, JOHN. "A Lost Paragraph in the Revels Constitution." *SQ* 25 (Spring): 286-87.
Reprint of 1973.3, with corrected lineation and line references.

1974.12   DOLLERUP, CAY. "Danish Costume on the Elizabethan Stage." *RES*, n.s. 25 (February): 53-58.
>   Suggests that "pludderhoser," a low hat with an ostrich feather, and gold chains around the neck were the typical costume indications of Danes on the Elizabethan stage.

1974.13   DOLMAN, ROBERT CHRISTOPHER SIBSON. "Formal Implications of Staging in the Elizabethan Metatheatre." Ph.D. dissertation, Johns Hopkins University, 287 pp.
>   Examines Elizabethan assumptions about the mimetic nature of the stage as a metaphor for life. Of greatest theatrical interest is the discussion of emblematic staging conventions before 1590 and the end of that tradition with the installation of flying thrones in the Rose and Swan about 1595.

1974.14   EDMOND, MARY. "Pembroke's Men." *RES*, n.s. 25 (May): 129-36.
>   Based on the discovery of Simon Jewell's will, and illuminates Pembroke's Men. Especially interesting is the suggestion that Ben Jonson began his career as a hired man with this group in 1592, a suggestion here supported by overlooked entries about Jonson in the records of the Tilers' and the Bricklayers' Company. See also 1976.16.

1974.15   GEORGE, DAVID. "Early Cast Lists for Two Beaumont and Fletcher Plays." *TN* 28 (Winter): 9-11.
>   Discusses apparent cast lists for *Philaster* and *Maid's Tragedy*, dating from ca. 1640 and ca. 1660, held in the Folger Shakespeare Library. The lists are written in quarto editions of the plays included in a scrapbook possibly assembled by Halliwell-Phillipps.

1974.16   HIBBARD, G[EORGE] R., ed. *The Elizabethan Theatre, IV*. Toronto: Macmillan; Hamden, Conn.: Archon, 175 pp.
>   "Papers given at the Fourth International Conference on Elizabethan Theatre held at the University of Waterloo, Ontario in July 1972." This volume focuses on Ben Jonson, and only one paper--1974.4--is of theatrical interest.

1974.17   KERNAN, A. B. "This Goodly Frame, the Stage: The Interior Theatre of Imagination in English Renaissance Drama." *SQ* 25 (Winter): 1-5.
>   Originally a paper presented st the meeting of the Shakespeare Association of America, March 1973. Kernan is concerned not with the physical theatre building but with theatrical metaphors in the plays.

1974.18   KOLIN, PHILIP C., and WYATT, R. O., II. "A Bibliography of Scholarship on the Elizabethan Stage since Chambers." *RORD* 15-16: 33-59.
>   Contains a total of 361 items, unannotated but including reviews of relevant items. They "included only those works which deal with the stage as s material object of empirical investigation." The listing is alphabetical. All relevant entries have been incorporated into this bibliography.

1974.19   McKERROW, RONALD B[RUNLEES]. "The Elizabethan Printer and Dramatic Manuscripts." In *Ronald Brunlees McKerrow: A Selection of His Essays*. Compiled by John Philip Immroth. Great Bibliographers Series, no. 1. Metuchen, N.J.: Scarecrow Press, pp 139-58.
　　　　　Reprint of 1931.12.

1974.20   MORSEBERGER, ROBERT E. *Swordplay and the Elizabethan and Jacobean Stage*. Jacobean Drama Studies, no. 37. Salzburg: Instirut für englische Sprache un Literatur. Universität Salzburg, 129 pp.
　　　　　After three chapters of background on styles of fencing, Morseberger examines fencing methods used in the theatres, the swordplay of actors and the techniques of Elizabethan fencing, the performance of stage fights, and the duel in *Hamlet*.

1974.21   PINCISS, G. M. "Shakespeare, Her Majesties Players, and Pembroke's Men." *ShS* 27: 129-36.
　　　　　Examines the evidence for Shakespeare's association with the Queen's Men, 1583-92, which comes from the close interconnection he had with at least four plays from the repertory of that company. Pinciss then discusses the rise of Pembroke's Men as a division of the Queen's company, with Shakespeare following the split section in 1593, and then moving on to the Chamberlain's Men in 1594.

1974.22   SHAW, JOHN. "'In Every Corner of the Stage': *Antony and Cleopatra*. IV, iii." *ShSt* 7: 227-32.
　　　　　Examines the implications of the stage direction of the title. Shakespeare appears to have been influenced by the book of Revelation, and he used the emblematic tradition to clarify his point.

1974.23   STAR, LEONIE RACHEL. "The Staging of Plays at the Cockpit-in-Court." Ph.D. dissertation, University of New Brunswick, 228 pp.
　　　　　Attempts to examine and evaluate all available evidence concerning the Cockpit-in-Court from 1630, when it was remodeled by Inigo Jones, until the closing of the theatres in 1642. Twenty-six extant plays were performed there, and Star examines them for evidence of staging at this theatre. She finds "no essential difference between the mounting of plays at court, and in the professional 'public' and 'private' theatres of the time." She does, however, consider some of Jones's designs in relation to the Cockpit-in-Court.

1974.24   VISWANATHAN, S. "The Seating of Andrea's Ghost and Revenge in *The Spanish Tragedy*." *ThS* 15 (November): 171-76.
　　　　　Suggests that the two Inductor-Presenter-Chorus characters were seated in the gallery rather than at opposite sides of the stage as has sometimes been supposed. The suggestion is partly based on the theories of Yates (1969.23).

1974.25　WATSON, GEORGE, ed. *The New Cambridge Bibliography of English Literature*. Vol. 1, *600-1660*, Cambridge: University Press, columns 1379-1400.

　　　　As in the CBEL (1940.2), the relevant section is Parts II and III of the Renaissance Drama listings. The earlier volume and its Supplement (1957.16) are brought up to date. All new relevant items are included in this bibliography.

1974.26　WEIXLMANN, JOSEPH. "How the Romans Were Beat Back to Their Trenches: An Historical Note on Corialanus, I. iv." *N&Q*, n.s. 20 (April): 133-34.

　　　　Suggests (following Saunders, 1954.24) that the Roman soldiers jumped off the stage but that the officers made their retreat through a stage door.

1975

1975.1　BARKER, KATHLEEN M.D. "An Early Seventeenth Century Provincial Playhouse." *TN* 29 (Spring-Summer): 81-84.

　　　　Discusses a privately-owned playhouse in Bristol from some time after 1598 until 1619. The lease of the property, payment records in the Hospital School Treasurer's Book, and the owner's will all attest to its existence, as does the patent for the only licensed provincial company.

1975.2　BERGERON, DAVID M. "Civic Pageants and Historical Drama." *JMRS* 5 (Spring): 89-105.

　　　　Argues that the "city pageants constitute a genre of history play and should be considered a part of the development of historical drama." Bergeron links the city pageant with the medieval mysteries, both in content and iconography.

1975.3　BOURGY, VICTOR. *Le bouffon sur la scéne anglaise au XVIe siècle (c. 1495-1594)*. Lille: University of Lille, 544 pp.

　　　　Reprint of 1969.2.

1975.4　BRADBROOK, MURIEL C. "The Triple Bond: Audience, Actors, Author in the Elizabethan Playhouse." In *The Triple Bond: Plays, Mainly Shakespearean, in Performance*. Edited by Joseph G. Price. London and University Park: Pennsylvania State University Press, pp. 50-69.

　　　　Discusses the relationship between actors, audience, and playwright in the sixteenth century. She concludes that "the relationship of actors to audience moved from the customary to the contractual. The actors' role became increasingly interpretative, that of the audience differentiated, while in certain kinds of play the author acquired independent status."

1975.5　BÜCHLER, KLAUS. "Explizite und implizite Bühnen- und Spielen-weisungen in Shakespeares *Tempest*." *JDSh* 1975, pp. 174-78.

　　　　Examines The Tempest for cues for actors implicit in the dialogue as well as explicitly stated in stage directions. Büchler finds several detailed descriptions of appearance and behavior.

1975.6   CHARNEY, MAURICE. "The Children's Plays in Performance." *RORD* 18: 19-24.

   Examines differences in effect on the audience of the children's plays, arguing that the boy companies had a "witty, musical, and very distanced style." Charney concludes that "the hard lines of distinction between the repertories of the children and the adult companies need to be reexamined."

1975.7   COGHILL, NEVILL. "*Macbeth* at the Globe, 1606-1616(?): Three Questions." In *The Triple Bond: Plays, Mainly Shakespearean, in Performance*. Edited by Joseph G. Price. London and University Park: Pennsylvania State University Press, pp. 223-39.

   Discusses the questions of the witches' flying, Malcolm's army entering into the yard before passing over the stage, and the loss of part of one scene.

1975.8   COLDEWEY, JOHN C. "The Last Rise and Final Demise of Essex Town Drama." *MLQ* 36 (September): 239-60.

   An assessment of the influences affecting town drama in the county of Essex in the first two decades of Elizabeth's reign. While there was Puritan opposition, Coldewey feels that, at least in Essex, local drama died out as much from the Vestiarian controversy as from church objections, simply because of material convenience.

1975.9   CRAIK, T. W. "The Reconstruction of Stage Action from Early Dramatic Texts." In *The Elizabethan Theatre, V*. Edited by G[eorge] R. Hibbard. Toronto: Macmillan; Hamden, Connm.: Archon, pp. 76-91.

   Looks at the evidence of the original text and stage directions for what they can tell us about stane action. Peele's *David and Bethsabe*, Kyd's *Spanish Tragedy*, Marlowe's *Doctor Faustus*, *The Jew of Malta*, and *Richard II* serve as examples. Craik considers various staging problems.

1975.10   DESSEN, ALAN C. "Two Falls and a Trap: Shakespeare and the Spectacle of Realism." *ELR* 5 (Autumn): 291-307.

   Argues for "a mixed mode of presentation not limited to the tenets of realism." Dessen specifically discusses the stage falls in *Titus Andronicus* and *King Lear* as he feels Shakespeare intended they be played.

1975.11   ETHERIDGE, CHARLES LARIMORE. "The Image of Truth: The Evidence of a Natural Style of Acting in the Elizabethan Theatre c. 1600." Ph.D. dissertation, Cornell University, 253 pp.

   Attempts to establish the distinguishing characteristics of the professional actor in Shakespeare's London. "Formal" and "natural" are the alternative styles considered, with no new historical information introduced. Etheridge examines material specifically related to the professional players at the close of the sixteenth century. The players' sequence in *Hamlet* is the central piece of evidence. He finds that the material he examines can be read at face value, without dismissing or reinterpreting any of it, and that it clearly points toward the use of a "natural" style. See Index under Acting--Style.

1975.12   EWBANK, INGA-STINA. "'What words, what looks, what wonders?': Language and Spectacle in the Theatre of George Peele." In *The Elizabethan Theatre, V*. Edited by G[eorge] R. Hibbard. Toronto: Macmillen; Hamden, Conn.: Archon, pp. 124-54.

        Argues that Peele's achievement has been underrated because too much attention has been paid to his use of language and not enough to his use of theatrical spectacle. Peele's main purpose was to create a sense of wonder in the audience, as he did in his pageants. *David and Bethsabe* is seen as "a link between the Mysteries and Shakespeare's last plays ."

1975.13   GREBANIER, BERNARD. *Then Came Each Actor: Shakearearean Actors, Great and Otherwise, Including Players and Princes, Rogues, Vagabonds and Actors Motley, from Will Kempe to Olivier and Gielgud and After*. New York: David McKay, pp. 15-24.

        The relevant section is Chapter Two, "In Shakespeare's Day." Grebanier discusses Richard Burbage and a few other members of the Chamberlain's/King's Men in general terms.

1975.14   HIBBARD, G[EORGE] R., ed. *The Elizabethan Theatre, V*. Toronto: Macmillan; Hamden, Conn.: Archon, 158 pp.

        "Papers given at the Fifth International Conference on Elizabethan Theatre held at the University of Waterloo, Ontario, in July 1973." Contains 1975.9, 12, 26, as well as other papers concerned with the medieval period and an introduction by the editor.

1975.15   HOSLEY, RICHARD. "The Playhouses." In *Revels of Drama in English*. Vol. 3, *1576-1613*. Edited by Clifford [E. J.] Leech and T. W. Craik. London: Methuen, pp. 119-236.

        Discusses the playhouses generally and includes detailed reconstructions of the Swan, the first Globe, and the second Blackfriars. The Swan reconstruction is made on the basis of the well-known sketch and the Fortune contract, and is complete down to fine architectural details. It is based on Hosley's earlier 1964.18. The Globe reconstruction is based in the internal evidence of twenty-nine plays produced at this playhouse 1599-1608 and the assumption of similarity between the first Globe and the Swan. The second Blackfriars reconstruction is based on both internal and external evidence, and it differs from the Swan and Globe primarily in size, capacity, and the existence of a third stage door. Twenty plays performed at Blackfriars 1600-1608 are used in the reconstruction. Hosley concludes by defining the "upper station" and the "discovery space" as parasitic uses of the boxes intended for spectators or musicians and the entries to the stage. In his view, the day of the "upper stage" and "inner stage" is over.

1975.16 _____ . "The Second Globe." *TN* 29 (Autumn): 140-45.
Essentially an extended review of Hodges (1973.11). Hosley questions the theory of the postless superstructure and rejects Hodges's open ceiling. The diameter of the building and its number of sides are also subject to varying interpretations.

1975.17 JENSEN, EJNER J. "The Boy Actors: Plays and Playing." *RORD* 18: 5-12.
Discusses repertories and performances, with emphasis on the techniques of the playwrights.

1975.18 JOSEPH, BERTRAM. "The Elizabethan Stage and Acting." In *The Age of Shakespeare*. Edited by Boris Ford. The Pelican Guide to English Literature, no. 2. Harmondsworth and Baltimore: Penguin Books, pp. 147-61.
Reprint of 1955.12.

1975.19 KING, T[HOMAS] J[AMES] . "*Hannibal and Scipio* (1637): How The Places Sometimes Changed."' *TN* 29 (Winter): 20-22.
Responds to Freehafer (1973.6), showing how Nabbes altered accounts in Livy, thus "changing the places," rather than requiring the use of scenery.

1975.20 LATTER, D. A. "Sight-Lines in a Conjectural Reconstruction of an Elizabethan Playhouse." *ShS* 28: 125-35.
A generalized reconstruction of a typical public playhouse, with twelve sides end a diameter of 90 feet. Most dimensions correspond to the Fortune or Hope contract. Latter attempts to maximize the audience size, especially in the higher-priced areas, with consideration of sightlines as his primary criterion. While Latter argues against an inner stage, he considers the arrangement of the tiring house facade only briefly.

1975.21 LEGGATT, ALEXANDER. "Companies and Actors." In *Revels History of Drama in English*. Vol. 3, *1576-1613*. Edited by Clifford [E. J.] Leech and T. W. Craik. London: Methuen, pp. 95-118.
Focuses on the Admiral's Men with Edward Alleyn and the Chamberlain's Men with Richard Burbage, but Leggatt also considers clowns Tarlton and Kempe and the boy companies. He discusses methods of rehearsal and performance and the style of acting employed, taking a middle-of-the-road approach to the formal versus natural debate.

1975.22 LENNAM, TREVOR [N. S.]. *Sebastian Westcott, the Children of Paul's, and "The Marriage of Wit and Science."* Toronto and Buffalo: University of Toronto Press, pp. 5-80.
The relevant section is the first half, "Sebastian Westcott and the Children of Paul's," containing chapters on Westcott's life and his relationship with the boy company. Includes slightly expanded reprint of 1.970.19.

*1975.23   MERZLAK, ANTHONY GEORGE. "A Theatrical History of *Macbeth*, 1606-1853." Ph.D. dissertation, Harvard University.
> Cited in Comprehensive Dissertation Index, 1975 Supplement 5: 301.

1975.24   ORGEL, STEPHEN. *The Illusion of Power: Political Theater in the English Renaissance.* Berkeley: University of California Press, 95 pp.
> An extension and development of certain ideas in his Inigo Jones (1973.21). Deals with theatre at court; specifically, the three chapters treat theatres and audiences, royal spectacle, and the role of the King. Orgel's thesis is that the marvels of the new stagecraft, imported from Italy by Inigo Jones, are the supreme examples of Renaissance kingship.

*1975.25   OZAKI, MAKOTO. "Puritans and the Stage in Elizabethan Period." *AnRS* (Kyoto, Japan) 26, no. 1: 64-79.
> Cited in *1976 PMLA International Bibliography* 1, entry 3066. In Japanese.

1975.26   ROWAN, D. F. "The Staging of *The Spanish Tragedy*." In *The Elizabethan Theatre, V*. Edited by G[eorge] R. Hibbard. Toronto: Macmillan; Hamden, Conn.: Archon, pp. 112-23.
> Questions about staging are answered by a return to the original stage directions. Rowan concludes that the Ghost and Revenge sit on the main stage (see 1974.24) and that the "arbour" is possibly the most important element used in the staging of the play.

1975.27   SALGĀDO, GĀMINI. *Eyewitnesses of Shakespeare: First Hand Accounts of Performances, 1590-1890*. New York: Harper & Row--Barnes & Noble Import Division, pp. 15-65.
> Compilation of records of Shakespeare's plays in performance. The material in Part 1 (1590-1700) is, of course, the least detailed, but it is nonetheless of interest since it brings together all extant contemporary accounts.

1975.28   SHAPIRO, MICHAEL. "Theatrical Perspectives of Children's Companies." *RORD* 18: 13-18.
> Examines "the unique qualities of the children's troupes and their plays," concentrating an "the atmosphere that surrounded performances." Shapiro discusses the audience's sensc of the theatrical occasion, its attitudes and behavior in the playhouse, and its awareness of the actors as actors

1975.29   SMITH, WARREN D. *Shakespeare's Playhouse Practice*. Hanover, N.H.: University Press of New England, 119 pp.
> Examines cues for actors and technicians in Shakespeare for hints on how the plays were staged. One conclusion that Smith reaches is that Shakespeare probably described in dialogue as much of the action as possible to help those

who might not have been able to see the stage clearly. Other sections examine his methods of bringing characters on and off stage. Based on smith's Ph.D. dissertation

1975.30   STAR, LEONIE [RACHEL]. "The Use of Bibliographical Methods in Studies of English Renaissance Staging." *Parergon* (Journal of the Australian and New Zealand Association for Medieval and Renaissance Studies) 12: 32-38.
      Reviews the state of bibliographical scholarship in theatre reconstruction, based on her Ph.D. dissertation (1974.23). Star follows the method proposed by Reynolds (1940.10) and refined by King (1965.9) but does not recognize the inherent contradiction in her work on the Cockpit-in-Court, all the plays of whose repertory were staged at other playhouses and thus present printed texts of doubtful value for the reconstructor.

1975.31   WILSON, F[RANK] P[ERCY], and HILL, R. F., eds. "Dramatic Records in the Declared Accounts of the Office of Works, 1560-1640." *MSC* 10: 1-59.
      Extracts from the Declared Accounts of the Office of Works, from its inception under Queen Elizabeth until 1640. All references regarding plays and masques and the preparations for their performances are included. Among these are the records for the construction of the Cockpit-in-Court (drawn upon by Wickham in 1967.15) and Inigo Jones's banqueting houses.

1976

1976.1   ADAMS, VICTOR. "When 'The Players' Came to Blandford." *Dorset Year Book (1975-76)*, pp. 25-30.
      The only relevant item appears in the first paragraph, noting that £11.7s.1d was earned for six performances at a race meeting in 1603.

*1976.2   AZZI VISENTINI, MARGRERITA. "Il teatro di Inigo Jones." *Comunita* 30: 273-93.
      Cited in *1976 MLA International Bibliography* 1, item 3789. In Italian.

1976.3   BERRY, HERBERT. "Americans in the Playhouses." *ShSt* 9: 31-44.
      Discusses the contributions of Americans (including Canadians) to the study of the Elizabethan playhouse. Berry breaks studies of the playhouse down into three periods: 1882-1923, dominated by the Germans and the alternation theory, closed by Chambers; 1923-1968, dominated by J. C. Adams and the inner below and upper stages, closed by Bentley; and 1968-present, dominated by tightly controlled evidence and single-playhouse studies.

1976.4   BERRY, HERBERT; BROWNSTEIN, OSCAR; HOSLEY, RICHARD; INGRAM, WILLIAM; and WICKHAM, GLYNNE. "Abstracts of Papers at the International Shakespeare Association Congress. The First Public Playhouse: The Theatre 1576-1976." *ShN* 36, no. 3 (May): 27.
      Abstracts of papers printed in 1979.4.

1976.5   BODDY, G. W. "Players of Interludes in North Yorkshire in the Early Seventeenth Century." *NYCROJ* 3: 95-130.

Examines Cholmley's Men, a North Yorkshire provincial company, and their leaders, Robert and Christopher Simpson. Boddy uses information from various lawsuits to discuss the players and their repertory. He is able to plot two of the company's tours.

1976.6   BRADBROOK, MURIEL C. *The Living Monument: Shakespeare and the Theatre of His Time.* Cambridge: University Press, 287 Pp.

Deals with the "sociology of theatre" (by which she means the relationship between actors and audience and its effect on plays and playwrights) rather than its "archaeology." Part One explores this topic, with emphasis on the development of Shakespeare's history plays and the early masques. Part Two examines the Jacobean Shakespeare, and Part Three returns to the masque, but in its new form. Perhaps best viewed as a companion piece to Bradbrook's *Rise of the Common Player* (1962.4).

1976.7   CARRÈRE, FÉLIX. "Vitruve et le théâtre Elisabéthain." In *De Shakespeare à T. S. Eliot: Melanges offerts à Henri Pluchère.* Edited by Marie-Jeanne Durry, et al. Etudes anglaises, no. 63. Paris: Didier, pp 11-18.

Examines the influence of Vitruvius on the Elizabethan theatre, emphasizing the microcosmic nature of the drama.

1976.8   CARSON, NEIL. "The Elizabethan Soliloquy: Direct Address or Monologue?" *TN* 30 (Winter): 12-18.

Discusses Heywood's *The Silver Age* as an example of the movement away from direct address to monologue, a more realistic form of speech.

1976.9   _____. "The Staircases of the Frame: New Light on the Structure of the Globe." *ShS* 29: 127-32.

Examines the drawing inxnslowe's diary, speculating that instead of having to do with the stage, as has been supposed, it instead illustrates the relationship of the staircase in the frame to the benches. Carson hypothesizes that this is a drawing of the Globe made to illustrate the Fortune contract. See also 1960.8.

1976.10   GRAVES, ROBERT BRUCE. "English Stage Lighting: 1576-1642." Ph.D. dissertation, Northwestern University, 380 pp.

Traces the contrasting traditions of sunlit and candle-lit plays, and estimates their effect. Graves assesses the quality and quantity of Elizabethan general lighting, drawing on extant documents, contracts, maps, and occasional references in the plays. The number and placement of windows and candles in private playhouses are inferred from ecclesiastical and Tudor architecture. The conventions of outdoor and indoor lighting are found to be similar, with an adequately lit stage without contrasts of light and dark. Graves concludes with an examination of a scene from *Duchess of Malfi* for its lighting requirements. <u>See</u> <u>also</u> 1978.13.

1976.11 HARBAGE, ALFRED. "Copper into Gold." In *English Renaissance Drama: Essays in Honor of Madeleine Doran and Marc Eccles*. Edited by Standish Henning, Robert Kimbrough, and Richard Knowles. Carbondale: Southern Illinois University Press; London and Amsterdam: Feffer & Simons, pp. 1-14.

Examines the decade of the 1570s, when the strolling players became resident companies. This in turn led to the development of professional playwrights for the first time, launching the Golden Age of English drama.

1976.12 HONIGMANN, E. A. J. "Re-Enter the Stage Direction: Shakespeare and Some Contemporaries." *ShS* 29: 117-25.

Discusses the placement of stage directions (including speech prefixes) in modern critical editions.

1976.13 HUNTER, G[EORGE] K. "Were There Act-Pauses on Shakespeare's Stage?" In *English Renaissance Drama: Essays in Honor of Madeleine Doran and Marc Eccles*. Edited by Standish Henning, Robert Kimbrough, and Richard Knowles. Carbondale: Southern Illinois University Press; London and Amsterdam: Feffer & Simons, pp. 15-35.

Reexamines the evidence for pauses between the acts, ultimately begging the historical question. Hunter then argues that pauses are often needed in production to reinforce meaning.

1976.14 KOLIN, PHILIP C. "An Annotated Bibliography of Scholarship on the Children's Companies and Their Theatres." *RORD* 19: 57-82.

Divided into three sections: Background Studies (68 items), Critical Studies (67 items), and Music Studies (32 items). Kolin surveys the scholarship since Hillebrand (1926.6), although a few earlier works are included. Relevant entries have been incorporated into this bibliography.

1976.15 LAMB, MARGARET A. "Shakespeare's *Antony and Cleopatra* on the English Stage." Ph,D. dissertation, New York University, 363 pp.

Examines major English productions from 1606-7 through 1973. While there is no direct evidence that the King's Men ever performed the play, an original production by that group is assumed, since "the play, with its wide-ranging action, is clearly suited to the neutral facade, swift speech and economical battles of Shakespeare's theatre."

1976.16 McMILLIN, [HARVEY] SCOTT. "Simon Jewell and the Queen's Men." *RES*, n.s. 27 (May): 174-77.

A note in response to 1974.3, suggesting that the Queen's Men, rather than Pembroke's, might have been the company referred to in Simon Jewell's will. McMillin further speculates that the "Johnson" referred to was not Ben but William, an early member of the Queen's Men.

1976.17   ORRELL, JOHN. "Inigo Jones and Amerigo Salvetti: A Note on the Later Masque Designs." *TN* 30 (Autumn): 109-14.

    Discusses the correspondence between Salvetti and the Duke of Florence from 1616, which includes commentary on masques and plays at court. Salvetti apparently furnished Jones with designs from Italy which Jones used in the late 1630s. See also 1979.23.

1976.l8   _____. "Productions at the Paved Court Theatre, Somerset House, 1632/3." *N&Q,* n.s. 24: 223-25.

    Reviews Reyher's arguments (in 1909.23) that the pastoral produced on 9 January was not repeated on 5 March, but that a masque was presented in the altered theatre instead. Newsletters of the time, the accounts of the Office of Works, and dispatches from the Florentine Resident in London are all cited in support.

1976.19   PALUMBO, RONALD 3. "From Melodrama to Burlesque: A Theatrical Gesture in Kyd, Shakespeare, and Marston." *ThS* 17 (November): 220-23.

    Examines the frequently used theatrical gesture of an actor throwing himself to the ground in grief or sorrow. Palumbo traces the evolution of the gesture from melodrama in Kyd's *Spanish Tragedy* to burlesque in Marston's *Antonio and Mellida*, by way of *Richard II* and *Romeo and Juliet*.

1976. 20   PENNINGER, FRIEDA ELAINE. *English Drama to 1660 (Excluding Shakespeare): A Guide to Information Sources*. American Literature, English Literature, and World Literature in English: Information Guides Series, no. 5. Detroit: Gale Research, pp. 175-86.

    Selected, annotated bibliography, with the relevant section Part I, Chapter 11, "Theatre and Stagecraft." Only thirty-seven books are included, to cover both medieval and Renaissance periods in England. All relevant entries have been incorporated into this bibliography.

1976.21   RHODES, ERNEST L. *Henslowe's Rose: The Stage and Staging*. Lexington. University Press of Kentucky, 286 pp.

    Revised, published version of 1959.20. Rhodes assumes, following Yates (1969.23), that the public theatres were based upon classical Vitruvian models. He also makes use of what he calls "the documents of the Rose," to be found among Henslowe's personal papers and diary. The study concludes that the stage of the Rose had five entrances, consisting of a central set of gates flanked by a pair of curtained discovery spaces, flanked in turn by a pair of doorways. That doorways could serve as either gates or discovery spaces appears not to have occurred to him. A "penthouse" with a window was located above the gates, and a gallery was available over both doors end discovery spaces. All elements of the stage were used to represent specific places. See also McMillin (1965.12) for different interpretations of the same evidence.

1976.22   SMITH, MARY E. "Staging Marlowe's *Dido Queene of Carthage*." *SEL* 16 (Spring): 177-90.

An imaginative recreation of the play as it might have been acted in the Elizabethan theatre, despite the fact that it may never have been so acted. Smith divides the acting area by a wall, running from the back of the stage to the front. This wall is an open, ornamental structure with a large functional gate allowing the action to pass freely from one side to the other. On one side is a pastoral setting, represented by an emblematic bush. On the other is Carthage, consisting of a palace and a banquet ball. This staging is supposed in an Elizabethan Great Hall, in front of a hall screen with two doorways. Smith also draws inferences about costume and spectacle from the text of the play.

1976.23   STAR, LEONIE [R]. "The Middle of the Yard, Part II: The Calculation of Stage Sizes for English Renaissance Playhouses." *TN* 30 (Spring-Summer): 65-69.

Continuation of 1976.24. Star argues that calculations of the size of the stage should be based on the six sizes we are sure of rather than on other considerations, and that permanent theatres always had spectators on three sides of the stage. Permanent stages were also always as wide or wider than they were deep. Thus, a working hypothesis for the stage size at the second Blackfriars would be 30 feet wide by 30 feet (at most) deep.

1976.24   STAR, L[EONIE] R. "The Middle of the Yard: A Second Inner Stage?" *TN* 30 (Winter): 5-9.

Discusses the phrase "the middle of the yard," from the Fortune contract, suggesting that it was not necessarily standard practice for stages to extend to that point. Continued as 1976.23.

1976.25   TWEEDIE, ELEANOR M. "'Action is Eloquence': The Staging of Thomas Kyd's *Spanish Tragedy*." *SEL* 16 (Spring): 223-39.

An imaginative recreation of the play in the theatre, concerned with what Tweedie calls "stage imagery": props, setting, and action. One of the most important things in the play is Kyd's use of repeated images; the audience is forced to make comparisons. Tweedie discusses the use of large properties in the play and concludes with a possible method of staging the play-within-a-play.

1977

1977.1   ADAMS, VICTOR J. "When the Players Came to Bridport." *Dorset Year Book (1977)*, pp. 61-66.

The relevant section is the first page, noting the appearance of a troupe of puppet-players, led by William Sands, in 1630. Sands and two members of the company got into a fight with the local Puritan preacher, and the group was ordered to quit the county.

1977.2   BENTLEY, G[ERALD] E[ADES]. "The Salisbury Court Theatre and Its Boy Players." *HLQ* 40 (February): 129-49.

Additional information about the Salisbury Court, its company, and one of the actors, from two suits in the Court of Requests in 1632, discovered and transcribed by Wallace in 1910 but never published. The dates of the lease of the building and its terms are verified, and a new estimate of the cost of conversions (£300) is made. The origins of the Revels Children as a boy company meant to supply the King's Men is clarified. Finally, the position of Stephen Hammerton, popular actor in the King's company, at Salisbury Court is clarified.

1977.3   BROWNSTEIN, OSCAR L. "New Light on the Salisbury Court Playhouse." *ETJ* 29 (May): 231-42.

Announces discovery of a document in the Guildhall Library that finally pinpoints the location of the playhouse and casts some light upon "the dimensions, the internal arrangements, end . . . the role of this last Caroline playhouse in the preservation of the theatrical traditions of the private playhouse during the Interregnum." Important conclusions in addition to the location of the playhouse include William Beeston's probable presentation of plays to "persons of honor" from 1652 onwards, and a correction of Hotson (1928.7) on the matter of raising the roof thirty feet when the playhouse was repaired in 1652. Brownstein argues that it was raised three feet instead, a more reasonable figure. He feels that the "thirty" was mistakenly copied from the line above.

1977.4   CARSON, NEIL. "Literary Management in the Lord Admiral's Company, 1596-1603." *ThR* 2, no. 3 (May): 186-97.

Examines the questions of play selection and alteration, based on a reconsideration of Henslowe's diary, Carson suggests that it was always the company, not Henslowe the financier, who commissioned plays, and that after 1599 the loose System of payment for scripts was reformed because of the company's financial difficulties. He identifies Robert Shaw, Thomas Downton, and Samuel Rowley as the primary policymakers among the shareholders, and speculates as to their reasons for failing to combine the functions of resident playwright and literary manager. Carson concludes with a statistical analysis of the authorization and purchase of plays by the company from 1597 to 1603.

1977.5   COLDEWEY, J[OHN] C. "Playing Companies at Aldeburgh, 1566-1635." *MSC* 9: 16-23.

Records of provincial plays and players at Aldeburgh, primarily from the Chamberlain's Accounts preserved in the East Suffolk Record Office, Ipswich. The accounts covering 1593-1623 have not survived, but except for those years all references to plays and players, mostly records of payment, are transcribed.

1977.6   COLDEWEY, JOHN C. "That Enterprising Property Player: Semi-Professional Drama in Sixteenth-Century England." *TN* 31 (Winter): 5-12.

Originally a paper presented at the Tenth Conference on Medieval Studies at Western Michigan University, May 1975. Coldewey examines the professional directors of London who worked with amateur actors in the provinces before 1576. Three of the four centers of local drama in sixteenth-century Essex used such "property players," as did other cities in Kent and Suffolk. His duties included finance as well as staging.

1977.7   CUMMINGS, I. A. "'Parte of a Play': A Possible Dramatic Fragment (c. 1550) from the Office of the Master of the Revels." *REEDN* 2: 2-15.
        An edition of a fragment front the office, with facsimiles and commentary. <u>See also</u> Proudfoot (1977.28).

1977.8   FOAKES, R. A., ed. *The Henslowe Papers*. 2 vols. London: Scolar Press; New York: British Book Centre, unpaged.
        Facsimiles of Henslowe's diary and the other theatrical papers held at Dulwich College. The first volume is the diary and associated papers and the second is MSS One and Two, the theatre papers and the Bear Garden papers af Henslawe and Alleyn.

1977.9   GALLOWAY, DAVID. "The 'Game Place' and 'House' at Great Yarmouth, 1493-1595." *TN* 31, no. 2 (Spring-Summer): 6-9.
        Discusses references in various records to a "game place" at Great Yarmouth, suggesting that it was not used mainly for staging plays.

1977.10   GEORGE, DAVID. "Pre-1642 Cast Lists and a New One for *The Maid's Tragedy*" *TN* 31, no. 3 (Autumn): 22-27.
        Reviews all known cast lists and adds one. George also draws attention to a prologue for Philaster "which sheds light on pre-Restoration actors for that play." The list is written in, and has been cropped so that only fragments remain, but George attempts identification of King's Men in the roles.

1977.11   KING, T[HOMAS] J[AMES]. "The King's Players at Stratford-upon-Avon, 1622." *TN* 31, no. 2 (Spring-Summer): 4-6.
        A brief note examining records of performances in Shakespeare's home town, suggesting that the company that visited in 1622 was a provincial troupe headed by Richard Errington rather than the London King's Men.

1977.12   KIPLING, GORDON. "Triumphal Drama: Form in English Civic Pageantry." *RenD*, n.s. 8: 37-56.
        Discusses the civic triumph in London in the sixteenth century, from a primarily literary point of view.

1977.13   LANCASHIRE, IAN. "Records of Drama and Minstrelsy in Nottinghamshire to 1642." *REEDN* 2: 15-28.
        Discusses the evidence for theatrical performances in Nottinghamshire to be found in various town records. Lancashire corrects Murray (1910.15) in several particulars, and adds one new provincial company to those known. He prints a "semi-dramatic fragment" from a private household in 1622 or 1623.

1977.14   LEVIN, MARTHA WASKO. "Patterns in the Comedies Staged at the Theater of Paul's Children and at Blackfriars 1599-1606." Ph.D. dissertation, University of Colorado, 200 pp.

Separates the comedies staged at the two theatres and examines them to determine the differences between the two groups. Levin finds a variety of petterns both between the companies and within their repertories, including the treatment of dance and song, the use of boy actors, the treatment of humanistic themes, and the emphasis given to satiric or city comedy.

1977.15   LIMON, JERZY. "Przypuszczalne zwiazki teatru gdanskiej 'Szkoły Fechtunku' z teatrem 'Fortune' w Londynie." *Pamiętnik Teatralny* 26, no. 1: 29-38.

Discusses the existence of a possible copy of the Fortune playhouse in Gdansk in thc seventeenth century. See 1979.18 for an article on the same subject in English.

1977.16   LINNELL, ROSEMARY. *The Curtain Playhouse*. London: privately printed by the Curtain Theatre, 64 pp.

Attempts "to bring together as much as possible of the known history of the Curtain" along with Elizabethan theatre in general to see if any additional conclusions may be drawn. Linnell reviews information about acting in general and the Curtain in particular, and then develops a conjectural reconstruction of the Curtain as an octagonal structure, forty feet or so high and only some forty feet wide. Differing entertainments could be set up in different arrangements in the twenty-foot interior. The reconstruction is based on a "View of the City of London from the North Toward the South," so identified by Hotson in 1950.

1977.17   METZ, G. HAROLD. "Stage History of *Titus Andronicus*." *SQ* 28 (Spring): 154-69.

The relevant section (I) lists recorded and unrecorded performances in England from 1594 to at least 1620.

1977.18   MILLS, A. D. "A Corpus Christi Play and Other Dramatic Activities in Sixteenth-Century Sherborne, Dorset." *MSC* 9: l-15.

Extracts from the Churchwardens' Accounts for Sherborne relating to the performance of a Corpus Christi play and interludes, to performances by touring companies, and to other matters apparently related to plays. Dates range from early sixteenth century to 1617.

1977.19   MULHOLLAND, P. A. "The Date of *The Roaring Girl*." *RES*, n.s. 28 (February): 18-31.

Redates the play 1611, based on the correction of a misdating of the incident on which it was based and several textual allusions. Mary Firth, alias Moll Cutpurse, the Roaring Girl, apparently appeared on the Fortune stage in early 1611. Mulholland also prints the corrected court record.

1977.20 MURAD, ORLENE. "The 'Theatre Letter' of Archduchess Maria Magdalena: A Report an the Activities of the English Comedians in Graz, Austria, in 1608." *Mosaic* 10 (Summer): 119-31.

 The complete text of the Letter in English translation, with commentary. The Archduchess refers by plot summary to several plays performed by the English actors in Graz. Reprinted: 1978.19.

1977.21 MURPHY, J. L., ed. "A Seventeenth-Century Play from the Essex Record Office." *MSC* 9: 30-51.

 The incomplete dramatic manuscript, probably written sometime during 1642, held in the Essex Record Office, Chelmsford. Murphy suggests, based on unspecified internal evidence "to be set forth elsewhere," that the author of the piece was John Tatham. A company of twelve, half of whom were boys, was required for performance.

1977.22 NOSWORTHY, J. M., ed. "An Elizabethan Jig from the National Library of Wales." *MSC* 9: 24-29.

 A previously overlooked Blizabethan farce jig, presumably from the end of the sixteenth century.

1977.23 ORBISON, TUCKER. "Research Opportunities at the Inns of Court." *RORD* 20: 27-33.

 Lists manuscripts held in the 1.ibraries of the Inns of Court, as well as the catalogues of those libraries, with suggestions for research.

1977.24 ORRELL, JOHN. "The Agent of Savoy at The Somerset Mssque." *RES*, n.s. 28 (August): 301-04.

 A description of Campion's Somerset Masque from the dispatch of the Agent of Savoy who attended its performance in 1613. Orrell prints the original Italian and provides a translation.

1977.25 _____. "Inigo Jones at the Cockpit." *ShS* 30: 157-68.

 Suggests that the Inigo Jones drawings of an unidentified indoor playhouse held in the Worcester College, Oxford, Library, are probably for the Phoenix, or Cockpit, in Drury Lane. Orrell bases his suggestion on a dating of the drawings by John Harris (see 1973,lO) and careful measurements of the actual drawings which reveal Vitruvian influences. There is also a possible connection between the Phoenix manager, Christopher Beeaton, and Jones. Finally, the designs for *The Siege of Rhodes* appear to fit the Jones drawing exactly, as do the rough sketches Jones made far an unknown production for "ye cockpitt" in 1639. See also 1973.18.

1977.26 PAFFORD, J. H. P. "Blandford Forum. Early Records of the Drama." *N&QSD* 30 (September): 283-87.

 Extracts from the Chamberlain's Accounts 1564-1752, recording payments to companies and players. The relevant extracts cover the years 1588 to 1621 and name several provincial companies including Lord Mounteagle's Men and Lord Stafford's Men. See also 1976.1.

1977.27   PRINDLE, RODERIC MARVIN. "Apes and Boys, Men and Monsters: The Aesthetics of Elizabethan Acting." Ph.D. dissertation, University of California at Berkeley, 1010 pp.

   Defines three principal modes of Elizabethan acting: the old, required by the plays of Marlowe, Kyd, and so on, practiced by men on the public stage and exemplified by Alleyn; the new, developed by Shakespeare and Burbage, practiced by men on the public stage; and the coterie, required by the plays of Marston, Jonson, and Chapman, and presented privately by boys aged ten to fifteen. Both specific techniques and audience expectations and response are examined as each mode of acting is discussed by itself and in relation to the other two. Prindle rejects the usual terms "natural" and "formal." He posits the formula of Heraclitus (God:man=man:ape/boy) as the pattern for the mutual relationship he finds, and the figure of Hercules is described as a major element in the aesthetic of Elizabethan meta-theatre. See Index under Acting--Style.

1977.28   PROUDFOOT, G.R., ed. "Five Dramatic Fragments from the Folger Shakespeare Library and the Henry E. Huntington Library." *MSC* 9: 52-75.

   The fifth fragment, described by Harbage as "'unique', ca. 1625," contains stage directions calling for flying machinery. It may have been an evening Christmas performance by children, put on by Andrew, seventh Lord Grey.

1977.29   RICHARDS, KENNETH. "A Sunday Play Performance at the Caroline Court." *N&Q*, n.s. 24 (December): 535.

   Notes a reference to a Sunday performance in 1633 in the autobiography of Richard Baxter, the divine.

1977.30   _____. "Theatre Audiences in Caroline and Early Restoration London: Continuity and Change." In *Das Theater und sein Publikum: Referate der Internationalen theaterwissenschaftlichen Dozentenkonferenzen in Venedig 1975 und Wien 1976.* Veröffentlichungen des Inst. für Publikumforschungen 5, SÖAW 327. Vienna: Österr. Akad. Wissenschaften, pp. 162-87.

   Compares the evidence regarding audience composition immediately before and after the Commonwealth to illustrate the audiences of both periods. Richards cites prologues, dedicatory epistles, and epilogues for much of his evidence. He concludes that "the interregnum was not a great divide, and that both continuity and change were as much features of the composition of theatre audiences as they were of organization, acting, and the dramatic repertory.

1977.31   SHADY, RAYMOND C. "The Stage History of Heywood's *Love's Mistress*." *ThS* 18, no. 2 (November): 86-95.

   Traces the stage history of Heywood's masque from its initial production in 1635 at the Phoenix through the end of the seventeenth century. Shady examines the possible use of three unidentified Inigo Jones designs for the second performance at Denmark House.

1977.32   SHAPIRO, MICHAEL. *Children of the Revels: The Boy Companies of Shakespeare's Time and Their Plays.* New York: Columbia University Press, 313 pp.

Greatly expanded published version of 1967.10: it is so much changed, however, as to be better described as inspired by 1967.10, Shapiro concentrates more on the plays than the companies, rendering his study of more interest to the student of dramatic literature than the theatre historian, but he does discuss the companies, the occasion, and the audience in three preliminary chapters, and he examines the "natural" vs. "formal" debate in relation to the boy actors. Three appendices discuss song and music in the children's plays and list court performances and repertories of the companies. The terminal date is 1613.

*1977.33   SHIBATA, TOSHIHIRO. "Elizabeth-cho no Kankyaku: Oboegaki." In *Shakespeare no Engekiteki Fudo.* Tokyo: Kenkyusha, pp. 97-112.

Cited in 1977 MLA International Bibliography 1, entry 2742. The title of the book translates as *Dramatic Climate of Shakespeare*; the subject of the relevant article is the Elizabethan audience. In Japanese.

1977.34   STEVENS, DAVID. "The Stagecraft of James Shirley." *ETJ* 29 (December): 493-516.

Examines the twenty-two plays of James Shirley staged at the Phoenix from 1625 to 1637, when Shirley left London for Ireland. "Shirley is of special interest because his plays abound with sophisticated use of the physical features of the Elizabethan playhouse stage and effective theatrical use of auditory and visual effects indicated by both dialogue and stage directions in the printed texts . . . . Shirley can thus serve as an exemplary resource for the study of Elizabethan staging techniques." Stevens concentrates more on the style and texture of a production at the Phoenix than on determining precisely what the physical structure of the stage was, although he clarifies his differences with King (1965.9). primarily over the existence of a third stage door.

1977.35   SUMMERSON, JOHN [NEWENHAM]. *Architecture in Britain, 1530-1830.* 6th ed. Pelican History of Art, no. 23. Harmondsworth and New York: Penguin Books, pp. 61-67.

Reprint of 1953.26.

<u>1978</u>

1978.1   BARTHOLOMEUSZ, DENNIS [STEPHEN]. *"Macbeth" and the Players.* Cambridge: University Press, pp. 1-13.

Reprint of 1969.1.

1978.2   BENTLEY, GERALD EADES. "The Troubles of a Caroline Acting Troupe: Prince Charles's Company ." *HLQ* 41 (May): 217-49.

    New information on the acting company, from a suit preserved in the Public Record Office, discovered by Wallace in about 1910 but never published. While never serious rivals of the King's Men, Prince Charles's company at least managed to stay together through the 1630s and early 1640s, which is a better record than most of their contemporaries had.

1978.3   BERGERON, DAVID M. "Elizabeth's Coronation Entry (1559): New Manuscript Evidence." *ELR* 8 (Winter): 3-8.

    Discusses evidence from the Loseley collection in the Folger Shakespeare Library that demonstrates that Elizabeth herself assisted in the preparations for her coronation entry by loaning costumes from the Revels Office.

1978.4   BILLINGTON, SANDRA. "Sixteenth-Century Drama in St. John's College, Cambridge." *RES*, n.s. 29 (February): l-10.

    Discusses the inventories of goods and furniture belonging to the College, including several bearing on theatrical performances. Costumes are most frequently mentioned. Billington suggests that two of Terence's comedies were among the plays performed.

1978.5   BLACKSTONE, MARY ANNA. "The Eighth Fairy: Stage Music and *A Midsummer Night's Dream* to 1880." Ph.D. dissertation, University of New Brunswick, 268 pp.

    The relevant section examines the use of music in the original text. Shakespeare used the music as a dramatic device unifying the plot, characterization, and theme of the play.

1978.6   BRADBROOK, M[URIEL] C. "Shakespeare and the Multiple Theatres of Jacobean London." In *The Elizabethan Theatre, VI.* Edited bv G[eorge] R. Hibbard. Toronto: Macmillan; Hamden, Conn.: Archon, pp. 88-104.

    Examines the relationship between the playwright and his audience, focusing on the influence of the court masque. Bradbrook claims that masques were a subject for irony in Jacobean plays rather than a direct influence.

1978.7   _____. *Shakespeare: The Poet in His World.* New York: Columbia University Press; London: Weidenfeld & Nicolson, pp. 91-201.

    The most relevant section is the second, "The World He Made," where Bradbrook examines Shakespeare's successful years with the Lord Chamberlain's/King's Men. She interweaves a wealth of historical and cultural material into her biographical narrative.

1978.8   DESSEN, ALAN C. "The Logic of Elizabethan Stage Violence: Some Alarums and Excursions for Modern Critics, Editors, and Directors." *RenD*, n.s. 9: 39-70.

    Discusses realistic duels and selectivity in battle scenes as well as what might be called "symbolic" violence. Dessen argues far an other than straightforwardly realistic approach to the staging of scenes of violence in Elizabethan plays.

1978.9   FORDYCE, RACHEL. *Caroline Drama: A Bibliographic History of Criticism.* Boston: G.K. Hall, pp. 157-70.

The relevant section, "Stage History," contains a total of fifty-five annotated entries: a few other relevant entries are scattered throughout the other sections. This is a highly selective listing, and at times the criteria for selection are difficult to discern. All relevant items have been incorporated into this bibliography.

1978.10   GAIR, [W.] REAVLEY. "Chorister-Actors at Paul's." *N&Q* ,n.s. 25 (October): 440-41.

Notes on the names of previously unknown Paul's choristers in the parish records of St. Gregory-by-Paul's. Gair also determines a range of ages for them from six to twelve.

1978.11   ____, "The Presentation of Plays at Second Paul's: The Early Phase (1599-1602)." In *The Elizabethan Theatre, VI.* Edited by G[eorge] R. Hibbard, Toronto: Macmillan; Hamden, Conn.: Archon, pp. 21-47.

Presents an account of the setting up of the second playhouse in 1599 and uses the plays presented there as evidence of staging methods employed. Gair finds that the playhouse had two doors on either side of a small stage (at least one of which contained or was near a grate); a third, larger door between them, sometimes curtained for discoveries; a trap, operated from below; an upper acting area the entire width of the stage, with one or two casements opening onto the stage. Gair also locates the playhouse and discusses *Antonio and Mellida* and *Antonio's Revenge* in more detail.

1978.12   GEORGE, DAVID. "Another Elizabethan Stage." *TN* 32, no. 2 (Spring-Summer): 63-67.

A sketch from a copy of the 1600 quarto of *2 Henry IV*, previously printed by Halliwell-Phillipps in 1861. George suggests that it is a diagram of the stage action at that point, made by the prompter, and thus gives us a possible diagram of the stage of the Globe. He further suggests that the sketch is upside down, which would give the stage of that playhouse two small side stages, perhaps for audience members.

1978.13   GRAVES, R[OBERT] B[RUCE]. "*The Duchess of Malfi* at the Globe and Blackfriars." *RenD*, n.s. 9: 193-209.

Examines the "dead man's hand" scene in relation to what is known of illumination at the King's Men's two playhouses. Graves suggests that the scene was not originally staged in a completely darkened auditorium at Blackfriars, since the audience reaction would be enhanced by enough light to see by. He further suggests that, at least in this one respect, staging methods in the public and private playhouses may not have been quite so divergent as has sometimes been thought. Based on 1976.10.

1978.14   HIBBARD, G[EORGE] R., ed. *The Elizabethan Theatre, VI.* Toronto: Macmillan; Hamden, Conn.: Archon, 161 pp.

"Papers given at the Sixth International Conference on Elizabethan Theatre held at the University of Waterloo, Ontario, in July 1975." Contains 1978.6, 11, 15, as well as other nontheatrical papers and an introduction by the editor.

1978.15   HOSLEY, RICHARD. "A Reconstruction of the Fortune Playhouse: Part I." In *The Elizabethan Theatre, VI.* Edited by G[eorge] R. Hibbard. Toronto: Macmillan; Hamden, Conn.: Archon, pp. 1-20.

Examines "some basic questions which have arisen in an attempt to reconstruct the first Fortune playhouse: depth of stage, height of tiring-house storeys, number and size of bays of the playhouse frame, location of yard entrances, and location of staircases." The remainder of the reconstruction is to be treated in Part II, to be published later. Hosley illustrates his conclusions with eleven line drawings. He argues for a ten-inch overhang on both second and third storeys, for a platform extending to the middle of the yard but only 25'10" deep rather than the 27'6" usually assumed, for twenty-four-bay construction, and for the entrances to the playhouse being located opposite the stage, thus placing the stage on the north end.

1978.16   INGRAM, WILLIAM. *A London Life in the Brazen Age: Frances Langley, 1548-1602.* Cambridge: Harvard University Press, 335 pp.

A biography of the theatrical entrepeneur, based largely on various historical. records examined by the author. Chapters seven through fifteen contain the details of Langley's theatrical affairs, which included the building and management of the Swan and the management of the Boar's Head. This is an apparently complete and well-documented study of a sometimes forgotten major theatrical figure. Ingram incorporates material from 1971.9 and 1972.15 into this work.

1978.17   MARDER, LOUIS. "The Henslowe Papers: 200 Years of Editing." *ShN* 28 (February): 2-3.

On the occasion of the publication of the facsimile edition (1977.8), the editor of the Newsletter briefly discusses the earlier editions, including those of Malone (1790.1; 1821.1). Collier (1841.1), Greg (1904.7; 1907.15; 1908.11), and Foakes and Rickert (1961.13).

1978.18   MOYNES, JON CRAIG. "The Reception of Elizabeth I at Norwich." Ph.D. dissertation, University of Toronto. 192 pp.

An edition of the two surviving accounts of the Queen's 1578 reception in Norwich, including the royal entry prepared by Bernard Garter and a series of outdoor entertainments conceived by Thomas Churchyard.

19   MURAD, ORLENE. *The English Comedians at the Habsburg Court in Graz. 1607-08.* Elizabethan and Renaissance Studies, no. 81. Salzburg: Institut für englische Sprache und Literatur, Universität Selzburg, 101 pp:

      Reprints 1977.20 and chronicles the eleven plays known to have been performed by ringlish actors in Graz, Austria, 1607-1608, based on letters and other documents.

1978.20   NEILL, MICHAEL. "'Wits most accomplished Senate': The Audience of the Caroline Private Theaters." *SEL* 18 (Spring): 341-60.

      A reevaluation of the previously labelled "decadent" audience of the pre-Commonwealth theatre. Neill asserts that, while there are different groups discernable in the audience, far more important than any one of them is the audience's sense of itself as a so-called "court of taste." The audience craved novelty but often preferred old plays to new. The rise of published dedications, epistles to the reader, prologues, and epilogues shows the concern of the theatres for the audiences. Neill concludes with a discussion of "wit," which he claims was the chief concern of the Caroline audience.

1978.21   PARRY, GRAHAM. "A New View of Bankside." *ShS* 31: 139-40.

      A sketch of the Bankside, including the Globe in rough outline, from one of Hollar's notebooks preserved in the John Rylands Library. It apparently dates from 1642-43, and is drawn from the point of view of the tower of St. Mary's Southwark. The roundness of the building and the double gable of the stage roof are substantiated.

1978.22   RIBNER, IRVING, and HUFFMAN, CLIFFORD CHALMERS. *Tudor and Stuart Drama.* 2d ed. Goldentree Bibliographies in Language and Literature. Arlington Heights, Ill.: A. H. M. Publishing Corp., pp. 6-12.

      Second edition of 1966.16, revised and enlarged.

1978.23   SMITH, DUNCAN BRUCE. "Shakespeare's Comic Cast: A Study of the Relationship between Actor and Character in the Early Comedies." Ph.D. dissertation, University of California at Berkeley, 317 pp.

      Examines four early comedies in order to determine the extent to which Shakespeare may have considered the stage personalities of the actors of his company as he created the characters. Smith concludes that while he took careful account of the composition of the company he did not treat all of the actors equally. The clowns especially were exploited in this manner.

1978.24   SMITH, M[ARY] E. "Personnel at the Second Blackfriars: Some Biographical Notes." *N&Q*, n.s. 25 (October): 441-44.

      Presents informatlon about the lives outside the theatre of Edward Kirkham, Thomas Kendall, and Henry Evans, all of whom were involved in the management of the boy company ousted by the King's Men.

1978.25   STAR, LEONIE [R.] "Inigo Jones and the Use of Scenery at the Cockpit-in-Court." *ThS* 19 (May): 35-48.

   Partly based on 1974.23, her Ph.D. dissertation. Star examines the possible use of painted perspective scenery at the Cockpit, particularly the possible use of scene designs by Inigo Jones in the Duke of Devonshire's collection. She concludes that Jones probably maintained the distinction between masques and plays, and that the Cockpit-in-Court was designed in the typical Elizabethan manner for professional acting companies who performed at Court. Consequently, painted perspective scenery was rarely, if ever, used.

1978.26   STREITBERGER, W. R. "On Edmond Tyllney's Biography." *RES*, n.s. 29 (February): 11-35.

   Attempts e more complete biography of the Elizabethan Master of the Revels, concentrating on the cross-pressures Tyllney faced from the Court, the City, and the Church.

1978.27   _____. "Renaissance Revels Documents, 1485-1642." *RORD* 21: 11-16.

   A brief history of the Office of the Revels and a listing of available documents, with commentary and references to discussions of the documents elsewhere.

1978.28   TEAGUE, FRANCES. "Ben Jonson's Stagecraft in *Epicoene*." *RenD*, n.s. 9: 175-92.

   Discusses Jonson's use of the various elements of the Whitefriars Playhouse (as described in Wickham, 1963.20). "Jonson tried to use peripheral stage areas or to exploit the theater's small size when he thought it might further the dramatic action or ensure that his audience would respond as he wanted then to." Teague also discusses the use of the child acting company and the use of songs in the play.

1978.29   VISSER, COLIN. "The Killigrew Folio: Private Playhouses and the Restoration Stage." *ThS* 19 (November): 119-38.

   Examines the Worcester College, Oxford, copy of the 1664 folio of Killigrew's plays annotated in his own hand. Visser shows that the plays originally meant for the private playhouses of pre-Commonwealth London could have been adapted easily for Restoration production. He uses the stage directions to establish two doors, a discovery space, an upper acting area, bay windows aver the doors, and traps in the private playhouse (probably Blackfriars) that these plays were written for. Killigrew's handwritten directions then yield information on how the plays were adapted for the scenic stage.

1978.30   WILLIAMS, PATRICK R. "Ben Jonson's Satiric Choreography." *RenD*, n.s. 9: 121-45.

   An attempt to find an approach to Jonson's plays that accounts for both their theatrical characteristics and for their satiric humor, one in terms of the other. Williams does so by contrasting the flexibility of the stage itself with the playwright's insistence on maintaining the unity of place. "Open" and "closed" compositions use the tiring house facade to create a variety of tensions on the stage.

1979

1979.1   ALSOP, J. D. "A Sunday Play Performance at the Jacobean Court." *N&Q*, n.s. 26 (October): 427.
       A brief note regarding a previously unnoticed reference to a Sunday performance (17 December 1615) before Queen Anne in the accounts of her receiver-general, held in the Public Record Office.

1979.2   BERRY, HERBERT. "A Handlist of Documents about the Theatre in Shoreditch." In *The First Public Playhouse: The Theatre In Shoredirch, 1576-1596*. Edited by Herbert Berry. Montreal: McGill-Queen's University Press. pp. 97-133.
       Catalogues the documents concerning the Theatre held in the Public Record Office, according to the four categories suggested by Chambers (1923.2). All previous transcriptions (Wallace, 1913.19; Stopes, 1913.15) are checked for accuracy, with discrepancies noted, although no new transcriptions are offered. Berry interprets the evidence held in the documents in 1979.3.

1979.3   _____. "Aspects of the Design and Use of the First Public Playhouse. In *The First Public Playhouse: The Theatre In Shoredirch, 1576-1596*. Edited by Herbert Berry. Montreal: McGill-Queen's University Press. pp. 30-45.
       Interprets the documentary evidence catalogued in 1979.2 Berry includes little new material, but he draws some new conclusions, particularly concerning the profitability of the playhouse. He suggests £190 per year us a reasonable guess at the housekeepers' profits.

1979.4   _____, ed. *The First Public Playhouse: The Theatre in Shoreditch, 1576-1598*. Montreal: McGill-Queen's University Press, 139 pp.
       Contains 1979.2-3, 8, 16-17, 33.

1979.5   BERRY, HERBERT; LIMON, JERZY; KING, T[HOMAS] J[AMES]; ORREL, JOHN; MOSLEY, RICHARD; and YOUNG, ALAN R. "The Public Playhouse: Architectural Problems." *ShN* 19 (May): 20.
       Abstracts of papers presented at the Shakespeare Association of America meeting in San Francisco, 13 April 1979. Berry reconstructed the Boar's Head (with drawings by Hodges); Limon discussed his 1979.18; King compared the superstructure of the second Globe with Herbert's House, York; Orrel discussed his 1979.25; Hosley discussed the ground plan of the Swan from 1975.15; and Young calculated sun dial configurations for London, "useful for calculating the amount of light and the angle of the sun's rays in the theatre."

1979.6   BOOTH, STEPHEN. "Speculations on Doubling in Shakespeare's Plays." In *Shakespeare: The Theatrical Dimension*. Edited by Philip C. McGuire and David A. Samuelson, AMS Studies in the Renaissance, no. 3. New York: AMS, pp. 103-31.

Speculates on unverified doubling for theatrical effect in *Midsummer Night's Dream, King Lear, Winter's Tale, Twelfth Night,* and *Cymbeline*. Booth's purpose is not to suggest historical practice but to stimulate contemporary experimentation in casting.

*1979.7   BOYLE, ROBERT RAYMOND. "The End of the Elizabethan Theatre: The Interaction of Cultural Conditions and Theatrical Productions in London 1632-1642." Ph.D. dissertation, New York University, 486 pp.

Cited in *DAI*, no. 11A: 5649.

1979.8   BROWNSTEIN, OSCAR [J.]. "Why Didn't Burbage Lease the Beargarden? A Conjecture in Comparative Architecture." In *The First Public Playhouse: The Theatre in Shoreditch, 1576-1598*. Edited by Herbert Berry. Montreal: McGill-Queen's University Press, pp. 81-96.

Questions the assumption that the form of the Elizabethan public playhouse was adapted from the animal-baiting rings. Brownstein shows that baiting rings were available and would have been cheaper to adapt. The question is, "if baiting arenas were so 'readily adaptable for stage plays, why didn't Burbage merely lease a beargarden?" Brownstein hypothesizes that playhouses and baiting rings accommodated their customers in fundamentally different ways, and that rather than being similar they were in fact quite different structures.

1979.9   CARSON, NEIL. "Production Finance at the Rose Theatre, 1596-98." *ThR*, n.s. 4, no. 3 (May): 172-83.

Examines daily income records from the Rose, from Henslowe's diary. Carson points out that the company borrowed from Henslowe only when low attendance or irregular playing schedules reduced their weekly income, and that their repayment was prompt. The players also regularly mounted new productions without resort to borrowing from the manager.

1979.10   CARTELLI, THOMAS PAUL. "Marlowe's Theater: The Limits of Possibility." Ph.D. dissertation, University of California at Santa Cruz, 419 pp.

Attempts to balance our critical estimate of Marlowe by establishing a theatrical perspective from which to view his major plays. While Cartelli does consider commercial questions, the physical layout of the playhouse, the use of the stage, and the nature of the audience, his study is essentially literary rather than theatrical in nature.

1979.11   CHARNEY, MAURICE. "Female Roles and the Children's Companies: Lyly's Pandora in *The Woman in the Moon*." *RORD* 22: 37-44.

Examines the seven separate roles Pandora plays, as well as Lyly's complete stage directions.

1979.12   CHILLINGTON, CAROL ANNE. "Philip Henslowe and his 'Diary.'" Ph.D. dissertation, University of Michigan, 294 pp.

      A comprehensive examination of Henslowe's life and diary, balancing the standard portrait with a picture of the courtier, landowner, magistrate, and churchwarden. The heart of the study analyzes the playhouse accounts in detail, both the daily receipts of 1592-97 and the loan and repayment accounts of 1597-1603. Chillington also discusses the players' performance schedules, especially the problems they faced when two companies amalgamated. The remainder of the study discusses the process of playwriting and collaboration in the public theatre. Chillington also transcribes Henslowe's will.

*1979.13   GEORGE, DAVID. "Records of Interest at the Lancashire Records Office." *REEDN* 2: 2-6.

      Cited in *1979 MLA International Bibliography 1*, entry 4735.

1979.14   GLENN, SUSAN MacDONALD. "The Designation of General Scene in English Dramatic Texts, 1500-1605." Ph.D. dissertation, University of Arizona, 133 pp.

      Examines the origins of designating scenes by tracing the use of scene-designations in continental and English texts, and explores rationales for the practice by analyzing the wording of such designations. Glenn argues that one reason for scene-designation is as an indication that the play in question observes the unity of place.

1979.15   HASLER, JÖRG. "The Serpent's Tongue: Shakespeare and the Actor." *ES* 60 (August): 389-401.

      Examines Shakespeare's plays for images of actors and acting (finding many) and traces of Shakespeare's acting experiences (finding a few). The main focus is literary, tracing the theatrical image of the audience hissing a poor performance.

1979.16   HOSLEY, RICHARD. "The Theatre and the Tradition of Playhouse Design." In *The First Public Playhouse: The Theatre in Shoreditch, 1576-1598*. Edited by Herbert Berry. Montreal: McGill-Queen's University Press, pp. 47-79.

      The first part of the essay relates what we know of the design of the building to what is known of later Elizabethan and Jacobean public playhouses. Hosley reminds us that the Theatre and the first and second Globes must have all been of the same size and shape, since the second Globe was built on the foundation of the first, and the first Globe was built with the timbers of the dismantled Theatre. The second part of the essay examines Henry VIII's Calais banqueting house (1520) as an antecedent of public playhouse design. This was a sixteen-sided structure 121 feet in diameter with three galleries; as Hosley says, it was "fairly close to our understanding of the . . . tradition of public-playhouse design."

1979.17 INGRAM, WILLIAM. "Henry Lanman's Curtain Playhouseas an 'Easer' to the Theatre, 1585-1592." In *The First Public Playhouse: The Theatre in Shoreditch, 1576-1598.* Edited by Herbert Berry. Montreal: McGill-Queen's University Press, pp. 17-28.

     Examines the profit-sharing arrangement James Burbage and Lanman entered into in 1585 and suggests that it was actually a sale, with Lanman settling for seven years' profits rather that the more usual fifteen. According to this theory, Burbage financed his later purchase of the Blackfriars by selling the Curtain to the players.

*1979.18 KNIGHT, W. NICHOLAS. "Comic Twins at the Inns of Court." *PMPA* 4: 74-82.

     Cited in *1979 MLA International Bibliography* 1, entry 4289.

1979.19 LIMON, JERZY. "Pictorial Evidence for a Possible Replica of the London Fortune Theatre in Gdansk." *ShS* 32: 189-99.

     Based on 1977.15. Liman discusses an engraving by a Dutch artist of a Gdansk theatre between 1664 and 1687. He cites stage directions from plays presented there in order to reconstruct staging practices, finding familiar Elizabethan usages such as doors, machinery, simple emblematic properties, and a trap. Limon suggests that some of the many English actors who played in the city had also played at the Fortune and provided information for a close copy of the playhouse in Gdansk. He concludes with a chronology of English performances there, 1600-1612. See also 1895.1.

1979.20 LINDLEY, DAVID. "Who Paid for Campion's *Lord Hay's Masque*?" *N&Q*, n.s. 26 (April): l44-45.

     Argues that the Earls of Exeter, Salisbury, and Suffolk footed the bills for the wedding masque of James Hay and Honors Denny on Twelfth Night, 1607, "as part of their political activity to gain the King's favour."

1979.21 MIRABELIA, BELLA MARYANNE. Part I, "Mute Rhetoric: Dance in Shakespeare and Marston;" Part II, "The Machine in the Garden: The Theme of Work in *Tess of the d'Urbervilles*;" Part III, "Art and Imitation in Edith Wharton's *The House of Mirth*." Ph.D. dissertation, Rutgers University, pp. 1-141.

     The first part considers dance as a literary convention and a dramatic device. Mirabella also examines the linkage between dance and disguise in *Love's Labour's Lost, Much Ado About Nothing,* and *Malcontent.*

1979.22 NIEMEYER, CHRISTIAN BERNARD. "Shakespeare and the Chamberlain's Men (1594-1603): A Reexamination of the Evidence." Ph.D. dissertation, Vanderbilt University, 469 pp.

     Reexamines the evidence for when and where Shakespeare's company acted between 1594 and 1603 and the evidence for the dates of eleven of his plays that certainly appeared during that time. Part One details the Chamberlain's Men's movements from their formation in 1594 from the Newington Btts to the Cross Keys to the Theatre to the Swan to the Globe. Niemeyer also documents the political and plague-related restrictions of acting as wells as the summer provincial tours of the company.

1979.23   ORRELL, JOHN. "Amerigo Salvetti and the London Court Theatre, 1616-1640." *ThS* 20 (May) :1-26.
Translation of parts of British Library Additional MS 27962, the diplomatic dispatches sent from London to Florence by Tuscan agents in the seventeenth century. The selections deal with the Court drama of the period. Orrell makes many additions to Bentley and The Calendar of State Papers Venetian. See 1976.17.

1979.24   _____. "Court Entertainment in the Sumer of 1614: The Detailed Works Accounts." *REEDN* 1: 1-9.
Fifteen extracts from a manuscript ledger giving accounts of work performed at Whitehall and Somerset House for various Court entertainments from April to August, with commentary.

1979.25   _____. "On the Construction of Elizabethan Theatres." *ShN* 29 (May): 20.
A brief note reporting results of his research into the ad triangulum and ad quadratum methods of laying out buildings. Orrell suggests hat Peter Street used these methods in building both the Globe and the Fortune, and he cites figures from the Fortune contract in support. A fuller treatment is to be published in *ShS*, presumably in the 1980 volume.

1979.26   _____. "The London Court Stage in the Savoy Correspondence, 1613-1675." *ThR*, n.s. 4, no. 2 (May): 79-93.
Extracts and translates passages on the English theatre from the correspondence of the Savoy agent in London during the dates indicated. All but one entry predates 1642. Five individuals, most importantly Giovanni Battiste Gabaleone, contributed to the correspondence.

1979.27   PHELPS, WAYNE H. "The Second Night of Davenant's *Salmacida Spolia*." *N&Q*, n.s. 26 (December): 512-13.
Pinpoints the date of the second performance of this masque as 18 February 1639/40, based on references in the Sidney Papers at Penshurst.

1979.28   SCHOENRAUM, S[AMUEL]. *Shakespeare: The Globe and the World*. New York and Oxford: Oxford University Press, 208 pp.
Prepared for the touring Folger Shakespeare Library exhibition of the same name. Includes general discussions of the Globe and the acting company.

1979.29   SHAW, CATHERINE M. *"Some Vanitie of Mine Art": The Masque in English Renaissance Drama*. 2 vols. Jacobean Drama Studies. no. 81. Salzbura: Institut für Anglistik und Amerikanistik, 580 pp.

        Primarily a literary study of the inserted masque, but Shaw includes discussions of staging possibilities throughout.

1979.30   SHOAP, JEFFREY. "The Children's Plays of Marston, Chapman and Middleton, 1600-1605." Ph.D. dissertation, University of Massachusetts, 286 pp.

        Essentially a literary study, but Shoap does briefly examine the effects of theatre design, child actors, and audience sophistication an the plays.

1979.31   SMEATH, FRANCES ANN. "Great Reckonings in Little Roams: Christopher Marlowe, Thomas Kyd, and Certain Circles of Association, 1583-1593." Ph.D. dissertation, Brigham Young University, 225 pp.

        Examines a group of documents arising out of the arrest of Kyd and the arrest of Marlowe for evidence about the acting company patron for whom the two dramatists worked.

1979.32   STEVENS, DAVID. "The Staging of Plays at the Salisbury Court Theatre, 1630-1642." *TJ* 31 (December): 511-25.

        Examines stage directions and textual allusions in twenty-five plays known to have been staged at this playhouse. Stevens concludes that the physical features necessary for the staging of these plays are "neither startling nor very different from what is known about the other private theatres." The tiring house facade probably resembled the Inigo Jones designs (held in the Worcester College Library and here reproduced) for the unknown private playhouse, with three doors below and an open gallery above, The center door, fitted with hangings, could serve as a discovery space.

1979.33   WICKHAM, GLYNNE. "'Heavens,' Machinery, and Pillars in the Theatre and Other Early Playhouses." In *The First Public Playhouse: The Theatre in Shoreditch,1576-1642*. Edited bv Herbert Berry. Montreal: McGill-Queen's University Press, pp. 1-15.

        Gathers the evidence regarding the existence of these elements in the early playhouses. Of the forty-five plays written for public performance from 1576 to 1591, only two seem to require pillars, and in each case the dialogue references could have been satisfied by the use of a standing prop. Similarly, no machinery for ascents and descents is even vaguely suggested in a play before 1595. Wickham suggests that Henslowe's modification of the Rose in the 1590s was for purposes of increased spectacle, which led to the incorporation of machinery and supporting posts in subsequent playhouses.

1979.34   WRIGHT, LOUIS B. *Shakespeare's Theatre and the Dramatic Tradition*. Washington: Folger Shakespeare Library, 36 pp.

        Reprint of 1958.24.

1979.35   YOUNG, ALAN R. "The Orientation of the Elizabethan Stage: 'That Glory to the Sober West.'" *TN* 33, no. 2 (Spring- Summer): 80-85.

Discusses the apparently conventional placement of the stage on the west side of Elizabethan theatre buildings. Young links the lighting problem to the orientation and offers three speculations: 1) the placement of the stage involved a preconceived iconography, derived from church architecture; 2) the placement resulted from Elizabethan interpretations of Vitruvian theory; and 3) protection from rain required artificial lighting.

Adams, Joseph Quincy, Jr., 1911.1;
        1912.1; 1917.1-3; 1919.1-2;
        1923.15; 1932.1; 1933.1; 1935.6;
        1940.1; 1946.1; 1961.25; 1968.2
Adams, Victor J., 1976.1; 1977.1
Albrecht, Alexander, 1883.1
Albright, Victor Emanuel, 1908.1;
        1909.1-2; 1911.1; 1913.1;
        1914.20; 1933.1; 1961.25:
        1972.17
Aldus, Paul John, 1951.2
Alleyn, Edward, 1841.1; 1843.1; 1877.1;
        1881.4; 1886.7; 1889.7; 1904.9;
        1907.15; 1916.5; 1919.1; 1927.7,
        17; 1929.12; 1939.1, 6; 1950.5;
        1952.9; 1954.2; 1955.1; 1958.5;
        1959.10; 1963.6; 1966.9, 27;
        1968.26; 1973.4; 1975.21
Alsop, J. D., 1979.1
Alternation Theory, 1900.2; 1907.4;
        1908.1; 1909.2; 1910.16;
        1913.17; 1914.20; 1916.16;
        1922.7; 1949.11; 1950.18;
        1955.4; 1963.12; 1976.7.
Alton, R. E., 1959.1
Amphitheatres, 1894.4; 1914.3-4;
        1949.8 1964.7
Anglo, Sydney, 1964.2; 1968.1
Angus, William, 1965.2
Anikst, Aleksandr Abramavich, 1965.3
Animals, 1927.20; 1932.8
Anon., 1870.1; 1887.1; 1902.1; 1909.3-
        4; 1910.1-2; 1911.2-3; 1914.1;
        1938.2; 1954.1; 1956.2; 1974.1
Archer, Thomas, 1893.1
Archer, William, 1888.1; 1907.1;
        1908.2-3; 1916.1; 1924.2;
        1950.1; 1961.25
Arkwright, Godfrey Edward Pellew,
        1909.6, 1914.2-4
Armin, Robert, 1927.6; 1952.12;
        1956.11; 1961.10; 1972.7
Amstrong, William A., 1954.2; 1957.1;
        1958.1; 1959.2; 1961.2; 1963.6;
        1964.3
Arnott, James Fullerton, 1970.1

Aronstein, Philip, 1910.3-4; 1925.1
Ashbee, A., 1872.2
Ashe, Dora Jean, 1954.3
Astington, John Harold, 1974.2
Aubrey, John, 1911.6
Audience, 1885.10; 1886.10; 1888.12;
        1892.1, 3; 1904.9; 1910.5;
        1911.4; 1913.13; 1914.6; 1916.8,
        15; 1920.4; 1921.15; 1923.17;
        1927.4, 15; 1930.6; 1934.14;
        1935.4, 18; 1936.8; 1941.5;
        1944.3; 1946.2; 1949.3; 1951.23;
        1953.15; 1954.16-17; 1955.12,
        28; 1957.2; 1958.14, 18; 1959.2,
        12; 1960.10; 1964.35; 1967.3-4;
        1968.21, 24, 32; 1969.9;
        1970.10, 17, 28; 1973.28;
        1974.1, 6; 1975.6, 24, 28;
        1976.6; 1977.30, 33; 1978.20
Auerbach, Lawrence, 1960.1
Avery, Emmet Langdon, 1968.34
Azzi Visentini, Margherita, 1976.2

Bachrsch, Alfred Gustav Herbert, 1949.1
Baesecke, Anna, 1935.2
Baiting Rings, 1964.7-8, 17;
        1967.7; 1973.16; 1979.7
Baker, Henry Barton, 1878.1; 1879.1;
        1881.1. 1889.1; 1904.2
Baker, Sir Richard, 1972.1
Balcony, See Upper Acting Area
Bald, Robert Cecil, 1943.2;
        1952.1; 1959.3; 1960.13
Baldwin, Thomas Whitfield,
        1926.1; 1927.1-2; 1930.8;
        1931.1, 8; 1961.6; 1970.18
Bale, John, 1972.2
Ball, Robert Hamilton, 1943.6;
        1958.15
Ball, Roma, 1962.1
Bang-Kaup, Willy, 1904.3, 8;
        1910.20
Banks, Howard Milton, 1963.1
Bankside, 1878.3; 1909.13;

1924.7; 1948.11; 1950.12
Barbetti, Emilio, 1946.2
Barker, Kathleen H. D., 1975.1
Barker, Rennie, 1949.2
Barrell, Charles Wisner, 1944.1-2
Barriers, 1956.5
Barry, Lodowick [Lordinge], 1912.1;
    1917.8; 1922.3
Bartholomeusz, Dennis Stephen,
    1966.1; 1969.1; 1973.24;
    1978.1
Baskervile, Susan Brown Greene,
    1885.2-3; 1954.25
Baskervill. Charles Read. 1911.4;
    1929.2; 9
Bateson, Frederick Wilse, 1940.2
Baty, Gaston, 1933.1
Bauande, William, 1972.20
Baur-Heinhold, Margarete, 1966.2
Baxter, Richard, 1977.29
Bayley, Arthur Rutter. 1915.1: 1517.4
Bear Garden, 1881.4; 1884.3; 1885.8,
    15; 1894.4; 1909.34; 1920.24;
    1950.12; 1955.1; 1979.8.
    See also Hope Playhouse
Beaumont, Francis, 1974.15
Beckermen, Bernard, 1953.1; 1956.3;
    1962.2; 1966.3; 1971.1;
    1977.17
Beckwith, Ada, 1929.3
Beeston, Christopher, 1953.15; 1973.28;
    1977.25
Beeston, William, 1849.4; 1911.6;
    1925.16; 1977.3 1956.6
Beeston's Boys, 1941.1
Bel Savage Inn, 1963.21; 1971.4
Bell, Charles Frances, 1924.10
Bell, Walter George, 1912.7; 1956.6
Bendishe, Sir Thomas, 1951.14
Bennet, Agnes, 1951.27
Bennett, Henry Stanley, 1944.3; 1969.1
Bentley, Gerald Eades, 1928.1-2;
    1929.4-7; 1930.1; 1938.3;
    1941.1; 1942.2; 1948.1;
    1951.30; 1954.23; 1955.27;
    1956.4; 1959.21; 1963.2;

1964.23; 1965.4; 1968.2-3,
    32; 1970.10; 1971.2; 1973.15;
    1976.3; 1977.2; 1978.2; 1979.23
Bereblock, John, 1905.1; 1914.6
Bergeron, David Moore, 1964.4;
    1968.4-7; 1970.2-3; 1971.3;
    1975.2; 1978.3
Bernheimer, Richard, 1958.2
Berry, Herbert, 1966.4; 1967.1;
    1970.4; 1972.29; 1973.1;
    1976.4; 1979.2-5, 8, 16-17,
    33
Best, Michael R., 1964.5, 1968.8
Bethel, Samuel Leslie, 1944.4;
    1948.2; 1950.2
Bibliographies, 1888.9; 1917.3;
    1923.8; 1929.12; 1931.6;
    1937.3; 1940.2; 1957.16;
    1961.20; 1962.16; 1963.14;
    1966.16; 1969.3, 11; 1970.1;
    1974.18, 25; 1976.14; 1978.9, 22
Billington, Sandra, 1978.4
Binns, J. W., 1972.13, 23; 1974.3
Binz, Gustav, 1899.1
Blackfriars Playhouse, 1870.1; 1874.2;
    1882.2; 1886.2, 4-6; 1888.5-7;
    1889.3; 1904.9; 1906.10;
    1907.20; 1908.18; 1909.24, 30;
    1910.12, 24; 1911.4: 1912.4:
    1913.3. 21: 1914.21; 1915.i, 13;
    1917.1; 1927.19; 1928.8, 15;
    1933.4; 1938.3; 1948.1; 1951.14;
    1953.28; 1954.17; 1955.11;
    1956.2; 1958.7, 14; 1964.32, 35;
    1965.15; 1966.4, 9. 11, 20;
    1967.16; 1968.2, 13, 24; 1969.9-
    10, 21; 1972.12, 25; 1973.31;
    1974,2; 1976.23; 1977.14;
    1978.24; 1979.17.
-First, 1910.8; 1911.13; 1912.6, 17, 23;
    1913.3; 1914.6; 1917.1; 1959.16;
    1961.8, 22; 1964.30, 32; 1968.8
-Reconstructions, 1921.5; 1954.17;
    1964.32; 1970.13; 1975.15
Blackstone, Mary Anna, 1978.5
Blagrave, Sir William, 1929.16

Blanch, William Harnett, 1877.1
Bland, D. S., 1956.5
Blissett, William, 1974.4
Boar's Head Playhouse, 1888.11;
    1936.21; 1966.9; 1970.5,
    14; 1971.4; 1972.29; 1973.1;
    1978.16; 1979.5
Boas, Frederick S., 1907.2; 1909.7;
    1914.5; 1925.2; 1933.2
Boas, Guy, 1937.1
Boddy, G.W. 1976.5
Bolte, Johannes, 1888.2; 1893.2; 1895.1;
    1900.1
Bolton, Janet, 1958.3
Booth, Stephen, 1979.6
Borcherdt, Hans Heinrich, 1926.2
Bordinat, Philip, 1952.2; 1956.6
Boswell, Eleanore, 1928.8; 1931.2
Boswell, James, 1821.1
Bourgy, Victor, 1969.2; 1975.3
Bowers, Robert H., 1948.3
Boyle, Robert Raymond, 1979.7
Bradbrook, Muriel Clara, 1932.2;
    1906.2; 1961.3-4; 1962.3-5;
    1964.6; 1968.9; 1975.4; 1976.6;
    1978.6-7
Bradner, Leicester, 1925.3
Braines, William Westmoreland, 1915.2;
    1917.5; 1921.1; 1923.11; 1924.3;
    1948.11
Brandl, Alois, 1904.4; 1936.5
Brawner, James Paul, 1942.3: 1943.3
Brayley, Edward Wedlake, 1826.1;
    1833.1
Brendon, Henry S., 1870.2
Brereton, John Le Gay, 1912.3; 1916.2;
    1920.1; 1948.4-5
Brett-Evans, David, 1958.4
Brettle, Robert Edward, 1927.3
Bridges-Adams, William, 1957.2
Briley, John, 1955.1; 1958.5
Bristol, 1847.3; 1936.7; 1975.1
Brock, James Wilson, 1950.3
Brodmeier, Cecil, 1904.3, 5, 8; 1907.4;
    1961.25
Bromberg, Murray, 1950.4; 1951.3

Brome, Richard, 1921.17; 1941.10;
    1950.6; 1968.12, 15
Brook, Donald, 1950.5
Brotanek, Rudolk, 1902.2
Browker, Hugh, 1972.15
Brown, Arthur, 1951.4; 1952.3
Brown, Ivor, 1936.6
Brown, John Russell, 1953.2
Browne, Robert, 1936.21; 1954.25;
    1970.4
Brownstein, Oscar Lee, 1964.7, 17;
    1971.4-5; 1976.4; 1977.3; 1979.8
Bruce, John, 1844.1; 1868.1
Bryant, Joseph Allen, Jr., 1954.4
Buc, Sir George, 1849.3; 1930.9;
    1933.3; 1957.3-4; 1972.16
Buchler, Klaus, 1970.5
Buck, Paul, 1975.5
Budde, Fritz, 1951.5
Bülow, Gottfried von, 1892.2
Burbage, Cuthbert, 1909.25;
    1913.15; 1914.21; 1968.24
Burbage, James, 1849.1; 1886.4;
    1887.1; 1909.26-27; 1910.19;
    1913.15, 19; 1914.21; 1915.5;
    1979.8, 17
Burbage, Richard; 1846.1; 1868.1;
    1904.9; 1909.25; 1913.15, 18;
    1914.21; 1916.5; 1927.9;
    1929.12; 1939.1, 6; 1946.3;
    1949.5; 1950.5; 1954.2;
    1959.10; 1966.9; 1968.24;
    1975.21
Burrell, John, 1947.1
Burton, E. J., 1960.3
Byrne, Muriel St. Clare, 1927.4, 1955.2

Cairncross, A. S., 1960.4
Calmour, Alfred Cecil. 1894.1
Cambridge University, 1923.20;
    1948.13; 1959.17; 1970.21;
    1978.4
Campbell, Lily Bess, 1921.2; 1923.1;
    1933.1; 1941.2

Campion, Thomas, 1977.24
Canopy, 1957.1; 1964.3; 1969.15
Capocci, Valentina, 1951.6
Cargill, Alexander, 1891.1; 1916.3-4
Cargill, Oscar, 1959.17
Carrère, Félix, 1976.7
Carson. Neil. 1976.8-9; 1977.4; 1979.9
Cartelli, Thomas Paul, 1979.10
Carter, Joel Jackson, 1956.7
Cartwright, William, 1929.8
Carwarden, Sir Thomas, 1836.1
Castle, Eduard, 1940.3
Cavano, Janet M. Jeffrey, 1974.5
Cecil, Sir Robert, 1971.9
Censorship, 1913.4; 1917.2; 1922.1;
    1971.2
Challen, W. H., 1957.3-4
Chalmers, George, 1797.1; 1799.1;
    1813.4; 1821.1; 1917.2
Chambers, Sir Edmund Kirchever,
    1906.1-2; 1907.3-5; 1908.4;
    1909.8-9; 1911.5-9; 1920.22;
    1921.3; 1923.2-3; 1924.2;
    1925.1, 4-5, 8, 10; 1926.8;
    1931.2-3, 13; 1933.1; 1934.16;
    1935.6; 1940.4; 1941.1; 1944.5-
    6; 1950.4; 1951.30; 1954.23;
    1955.27; 1956.29; 1959.21;
    1961.18, 25; 1964.31; 1968.2,
    32, 34; 1970.10; 1972.17;
    1973.3; 1974.18; 1976.3
Chambrun, Clara Longworth, 1946.3
Chapel Royal, 1872.1; 1892.4; 1900.3;
    1905.9; 1908.18; 1910.12, 20;
    1911.5; 1914.2; 1920.11; 1926.6;
    1960.14; 1967.16; 1968.21;
    1971.8
Chapman, George, 1901.1; 1977.27;
    1979.30
Chapman, Raymond, 1951.7
Charney. Maurice, 1965.5; 1975.6;
    1979.11
Chettle, Henry, 1849.2; 1972.3
Child, Harold M., 1910.5; 1919.3;
    1932.3; 1934.1; 1949.4; 1950.6

Children's Companies, 1901.2; 1904.10;
    1907.16; 1908.18; 1914.2, 18;
    1916.14; 1923.2; 1926.6; 1928.5;
    1929.11; 1934.10; 1941.9;
    1943.3; 1956.14; 1957.2;
    1960.14; 1961.3, 8; 1965.15;
    1968.23; 1969.9, 12; 1970.7;
    1971.8. 15; 1972.6; 1974.2, 7;
    1975.6, 18, 21, 28; 1976.14;
    1977.2, 12; 1978.24; 1979.30.
    See also the names of individual
    companies, such as such as
    Paul's Boys, King's Revels, etc.
Children of Paul's. See Paul's Boys
Children of the Chapel. See Chapel
    Royal
Childs, Herbert E., 1962.5
Chillington, Carol Anne, 1979.12
Cholmeley's Men, 1942.8
Christmas, Gerard, 1968.4
Clapham, Alfred W., 1912.4; 1917.1
Clark, Andrew, 1907.6-9; 1909.10
Clark, Sandra, 1974.1
Clinton-Baddeley, V. C., 1953.3
Cochrane, Bruce B., 1968.32
Cockpit-in-Court Playhouse, 1860.1;
    1925.14; 1951.22; 1966.9;
    1567.15; 1970.21, 25, 27;
    1972.24, 30; 1973.16, 18;
    1974.23; 1975.31; 1.978.25
Cockpit Playhouse. See Phoenix
    Playhouse
Coghill, Nevill, 1975.7
Cahn, Albert, 1886.1
Coldewey, John C., 1975.8; 1977.5-6
Collier, John Payne, 1831.1; 1841.1;
    1843.1; 1844.5; 1846.1; 1848.1;
    1849.1-2; 1861.1; 1875.1;
    1879.2; 1886.8; 1887.7; 1889.7;
    1891.2; 1904.7; 1912.2; 1917.3;
    1924.8; 1928.16; 1929.6;
    1950.15; 1958.17; 1959.19;
    1962.7; 1978.17
Collins, Churton, 1911.10
Collins, Fletcher, Jr., 1931.4

Commedia dell'Arte, 1908.17; 1912.19;
    1920.7, 22; 1922.1; 1926.13;
    1928.11; 1929.15; 1934.8;
    1961.23
Commonwealth, 1888.3; 1921.13;
    1923.10, 19; 1928.7; 1936.10
Companies, See Acting--Companies
Company Licenses, 1909.9; 1917.2
Conrad, Hermann, 1910.6
Cook, Ann Jennalie, 1974.6
Cook, David, 1961.5
Cooper, Charles William, 1931.5
Cope, Jackson I., 1974.7
Corbin, John, 1906.3; 1911.11; 1961.25
Costumes, 1903.2; 1911.22; 1916.11;
    1927.21; 1928.20; 1933.2;
    1936.17-18; 1938.6; 1952.4;
    1953.4, 15; 1954.17; 1958.20;
    1959.12; 1961.14; 1962.6, 8, 18;
    1964.26; 1965.3, 5; 1966.10;
    1968.26; 1972.27; 1973.4, 28;
    1974.12; 1976.22
Court Performances, 1906.1; 1909.8, 12;
    1910.10-11; 1912.24; 1913.6;
    1916.15; 1917.2; 1920.17, 29;
    1923.2; 1924.10; 1925.3, 17;
    1926.10; 1928.1; 1934.10;
    1937.8; 1941.1; 1945.2; 1950.7;
    1952.19; 1953.20; 1954.14;
    1955.27; 1956.26; 1961.24;
    1968.8; 1970.31; 1974.4;
    1975.31; 1976.18; 1977.32;
    1979.1, 23-24, 26
Cowling, George Herbert, 1913.2;
Craik, T. W., 1975.9, 15
Crane, Ralph, 1926.12
Crashaw, William, 1972.4
Creizenach, Wilhelm Michael Anton
    1889.2; 1903.1; 1916.5; 1923.4
Crosfield, Thomas, 1925.2
Cross Keys Inn, 1971.4; 1979.22
Crossley, D. W., 1974.8
Crouch, Jack Herbert, 1952.4
Crüger, Johannes, 1887.2
Crundell, H. W., 1936.7; 1937.2; 1941.3
Cullen, Charles, 1912.5

Cummings, L. A., 1977.7
Cunliffe, John William, 1911.2
Cunningham, Peter, 1842.11; 1845.1;
    1848.1; 1849.3-4; 1911.15-18,
    26-28; 1912.13-14, 20; 1913.8;
    1920.12-13, 26; 1922.8; 1924.9;
    1928.16
Curtain Playhouse, 1798.1; 1844.5;
    1885.6; 1894.4; 1904.9; 1928.10;
    1944.3; 1954.11, 15; 1959.9;
    1962.7; 1964.11; 1966.9;
    1977.16; 1979.17
Cutts, John P., 1920.20; 1954.5; 1955.3;
    1956.8-9; 1957.5; 1958.6;
    1959.4; 1960.7; 1966.5; 1973.2;
    1974.9

Dance, 1927.24; 1951.26; 1953.4;
    1954.17; 1955.11; 1963.11;
    1979.21
Daniel, Samuel, 1927.3; 1958.23
Danzig, 1895.1. See also Gdansk
Darlington, William Aubrey, 1949.5
David, Richard, 1061.6
Davies, William Robertson, 1938.4
Davis, John Lee, 1943
Davison, Peter, 1972.1-5, 8-10, 20-22,
    27, 31, 33
Dawson, Giles E., 1947.2; 1961.7;
    1964.8; 1965.6
DeBanke, Cécile, 1953.4; 1954.6
Dee, John, 1969.2 3
Dekker, Thomas, 1920.14
DeMolen, Richard Lee, 1970.5; 1972.6;
    1974.10
Denkinger, Emma Marshall, 1926.3
Denmark House, 1977.31
Dessen, Alan C., 1975.10; 1978.8
de Vere, Edward, Earl of Oxford,
    1944.1-2; 1961.8
Dewey, Nicholas, 1969.3
DeWitt, Johannes. See Swan
    Playhouse--DeWitt Sketch
Dickinson, Thomas H., 1916.6

Dickson, M. J., 1930.2

Discovery Space, 1891.2; 1903.6; 1904.3, 5, 8; 1907.4, 20; 1908.10; 1913.6; 1916.1, 5, 13, 16; 1918.1; 1921.5, 13; 1924.2, 12; 1927.5, 8, 13; 1928.6, 12; 1929.3; 1933.4; 1936.1; 1940.6, 10-11; 1942.1; 1945.1; 1948.6-7; 1949.3, 11; 1950.18; 1952.2, 11; 1953.8-9, 15, 23; 1954.14, 17; 1955.4; 1956.27, 31; 1957.1; 1958.1, 11, 14; 1959.8, 25; 1960.16; 1961.2, 21, 27; 1962.2, 15; 1963.1, 8, 11; 1964.20, 32-33; 1965.12; 1966.10-11; 1967.8-9; 1968.17; 1970.13; 1971.10; 1972.18; 1973.11, 15, 28; 1975.15; 1976.21; 1978.29; 1979.32

Disguises, 1902.2; 1916.15

Dobell, Bertram, 1901.1

Dodd, Kenneth M., 1970.6

Dodds, Madelain Hope, 1956.10

Dodsley, Robert, 1874.3; 1876.2

Doebler, John, 1973.3; 1974.11

Dolan de Avila, Wanda, 1965.7

Dollerup, Cay, 1974.11

Dolman, Robert Christopher Sibson, 1974.13

Dorset, 1977.18

Dowling, Margaret, 1930.3

Downer, Alan S., 1951.8; 1964.9

Downton, Thomas, 1977.4

Dramatic Criticism, 1903.7

Dramaticus, 1844.2; 1849.5

Drayton, Michael, 1922.3

Dryden, John, 1936.19

Duckles, Vincent, 1968.11

Duke of Devonshire, 1924.10

Duke of York's Men, 1849.9

Duke of Wurtemberg, Visits of, 1865.2

Dulwich College, 1841.1; 1877.1; 1881.4; 1889.7; 1904.6; 1907.15; 1927.7; 1952.9; 1957.13; 1966.27; 1977.8

Dumb Show, 1919.4; 1951.11, 24, 31: 1964.29; 1966.13

Dunmow, 1951.14

Dunwich, 1921.4

Durand, Walter Yale, 1902.3; 1905.1; 1908.5

Durry, Marie-Jeanne, 1976.7

Dwarf Bob, 1972.16

Ebisch, Walther, 1931.6; 1937.3

Eccles, Mark, 1933.3; 1958.7

Edinborough, Arnold, 1951.9

Edmond, Mary, 1974.14

Edwards, H. R. L., 1960.6

Edwards, Richard, 1902.3; 1908.5

Eggar, Katharine E., 1961.8

Ehrstine, John W., 1968.34

Eich, Louis M., 1939.1

Eliot, Samuel A,, Jr., 1939.2

Ellis, George, 1874.1

Ellis, Henry, 1798.1

Ellis-Fermor, Una M., 1936.8; 1947.3; 1953.5; 1958.8; 1961.9; 1964.10; 1965.8; 1969.4

Emmeroá, Jamelia, 1966.12

Empson, William, 1951.10; 1954.7; 1955.4

Engelen, Johannes, 1926.4

Errington, Richard, 1977.11

Essex, 1934.8-9; 1937.6; 1975.8; 1977.6, 21

Etheridge, Charles Larimore, Sr., 1975.11

Eutheo, 1972.27

Evans, G. Blakemore, 1973.4

Evans, Henry, 1961.8; 1968.24

Evans, M. Blakemore, 1923.5

Ewbank, Inga-Stina, 1975.12

Ewouts, Hans, 1950.7

Fairholt, Frederich William, 1843.2; 1845.4

Farrant, Richard, 1910.8; 1912.6; 1913.3; 1921.9; 1961.8
Farrar, J. H., 1924.6
Feather, John, 1972.7
Feil, J. P., 1958.9
Feilde, John, 1972.9
Feldman, Abraham Bronson, 1950.7; 1952.5; 1953.6
Felver, Charles Stanley, 1956.11; 1961.10
Fencing, 1974.20
Fenton, George, 1972.9
Ferrabasco, Alfonso, 1935.12; 1956.9
Feuillerat, Albert, 1908.6; 1910.7-8; 1911.13; 1912.6, 17; 1913.3; 1925.1; 1961.18, 22
Field, Nathaniel, 1849.2; 1904.9; 1914.19; 1926.1; 1933.5; 1965.15; 1968.26
Finance, 1886.6; 1904.9; 1907.14; 1909.30-32; 1910.4-5, 25; 1911.20; 1918.2-3; 1919.2, 19; 1920.27-30; 1921.8; 1927.2; 1934.6; 1935.4; 1.942.7; 1952.7; 1955.1; 1957.2; 1959.1: 1961.5; 1971.1-2; 1979.3, 9
Firth, Sir Charles Harding, 1888.3
Fischer, Walther, 1950.5
Fisher, Sidney, 1964.11
Fitzgibbon, H. Macauley, 1931.7
Flatter, Richard, 1920.20; 1951.11-12; 1953.7; 1957.6; 1950.6; 1959.5; 1960.5, 7
Fleay, Frederick Gard, 1881.2; 1882.1; 1834.1; 1887.7; 1890.1; 1908.16; 1912.2; 1929.6; 1950.4
Flecknoe, Richard, 1664.1; 1909.11; 1931.1.9; 1.957.7; 1963.3; 1972.33; 1973.5
Fletcher, Ifan Kyrle, 1954.8
Fletcher, John, 1974.15
Flood, William Henry Grattan, 1912.17; 1921.4
Fludd, Robert, 1958.2; 1966.20, 28; 1967.1, 17

Foakes, R. A,, 1954.9; 1960.8; 1961.11-13; 1963.4; 1970.7; 1977.8; 1978.17
Ford, Boris, 1955.12; 1956.19; 1961.15; 1962.10; 1975.19
Fordyce, Rachel, 1978.9
Forestier, Amédée, 1910.9; 1911.14
Forman, Simon, 1849.6; 1876.1; 1907.18; 1919.8; 1947.11; 1958.17; 1959.19; 1973.24
Forrest, G. Topham, 1921.1, 5; 1961.25
Fortune Playhouse, 1813.1; 1870.2, 4; 1882.2; 1886.7; 1889.7; 1.904.6, 9; 1906.8; 1907.1; 1908.2-3, 10-11; 1909.34; 1914.20; 1916.10; 1917.4, 7, 10; 1919.11; 1929.6; 1959.9, 15; 1966.9; 1971.12; 1977.15, 19; 1979.19, 25
-Contract, 1874.2; 1885.9; 1902.1; 1906.6; 1907.4; 1908.10; 1909.3; 1916.11; 1914.7; 1924.12; 1935.17; 1949.2; 1959.9; 1959.25; 1970.13; 1971.12; 1973.11; 1975.15, 20; 1976.9; 1976.24
-Reconstructions, 1908.10; 1911.2-3, 14; 1912.8; 1916.1; 1934.14; 1959.7; 1961.24; 1963.7; 1978.13
-Second, 1968.2
Fowell, Frank, 1913.4
Fredén, Gustav, 1928.4; 1939.3
Freehafer, John, 1968.12-13; 1971.6; 1972.30; 1973.6; 1975.17
Freeman, Arthur, 1973.5
Freeman, Sidney Lee, 1951.13
French, Joseph Nathan, 1964.12
Fronius, Clans, 1950.8
Fulman, William, 1933.8
Furniss, Warren Todd, 1952.6
Furnivall, Frederick J., 1878.2; 1882.2; 1904.6
Fusillo, Robert James, 1955.5; 1956.16, 22; 1966.6

G., G. N., 1908.7
Gabaleone, Giovanni Battiste, 1979.26
Gaedertz, Karl Theodor, 1888.1, 4. 10. 12
Gager, William, 1907.2; 1916.17-18; 1972.18; 1974.3
Gair, W. Reavley, 1968.14; 197.10-11
Galloway, David, 1970.4, 7-9, 13, 18-20, 25, 27, 29, 31; 1973.1, 7, 14-15; 1977.9
Gaw, Alllison, 1925,6-7; 1936.9
Gayton, Edmund, 1941.4
Gdansk, 1979.19; see also Danzig
Gentili, Alberico, 1974.3
George Inn, 1972.29
George, David, 1974.15; 1977.10; 1978.12; 1979.13
Gerstner-Hertzel, Arthur, 1055.6-7
Gildersleeve, Virginia Crocheron, 1908.8-9; 1943.5
Giles, Nathaniel, 1911.5; 1961.8
Gilson, Julius Parnell, 1925.15
Glenn, Susan MacDonald, 1979.14
Globe Playhouse,1849.1; 1858.1; 1870.1; 1874.2; 1878.3; 1882.2; 1884.3; 1885.9, 12; 1888.11; 1903.10; 1904.9; 1907.4, 20; 1909.30. 32; 1910.25; 1914.20-21; 1915.22; 1916.3, 10; 1921.1; 1928.8; 1935.1; 1938.3; 1942.1; 1944.3; 1948.6, 11; 1949.2, 15; 1950.7, 15; 1951.16, 29; 1952.18; 1955.11, 18; 1956.3, 14, 27; 1958.14; 1959.8-9; 1960.11, 16; 1961.2; 1963.1; 1964.15, 32, 35; 1965.13; 1966.9. 20. 28; 1968.16, 33; 1969.23; 1970.16; 1971.13; 1973.31; 1975.7, 15; 1976.9; 1978.12; 1979.16, 22, 25, 28
-Reconstructions, 1902.1; 1936.1-3; 1942.1; 1943.6; 1946.6; 1948.6; 1950.12; 1953.1, 9, 27; 1956.32; 1961.1, 24; 1962.2; 1968.16; 1975.15

-Second, 1933.11; 1952.14; 1959.15; 1964.11; 1968.2; 1973.11, 16; 1975.16; 1979.5, 16
-Site of, 1909.3-5, 13-14, 19-21, 32; 1910.2, 13; 1912.12-15, 17, 24-25; 1915.6-12, 14, 16-19, 23; 1921.1; 1923.11; 1924.3; 1948.11; 1950.15
Godfrey, Walter H., 1908.10; 1911.2-3; 1912.8; 1913.5; 1916.1; 1920.24; 1934.14; 1950.15; 1959.7; 1961 75
Goldstein, Leonnrd, 1958.10
Gollancz, Israel, 1916.2, 9
Gordon, D. J., 1.954.20; 1956.12; 1973.8
Gorelik, Mordechai, 1940.5; 1947.4
Gossett, Suzanne, 1973.9
Gosson, Stephen, 1908.19; 1910.26; 1942.6; 1954.27; 1972.10
Gousseff, James William, 1962.6
Government Regulation, 1908.7-9; 1910.3; 1916.15; 1923.2; 1939.5; 1943.5; 1953.17; 1959.12; 1963.20; 1965.3; 1971.2; 1973.27
Grabau, Carl, 1902.4
Grabo, Carl H., 1906.4-7; 1907.10-11
Granville-Barker, Harley, 1925.8; 1926.5; 1934.14; 1936.4-5, 10; 1960.19
Graves, Robert Bruce, 1976.10; 1978.13
Graves, Thornton Shirley, 1912.9-11; 1913.6-7; 1914.6-8; 1915.3-4,15; 1916.7; 1917.6; 1920.2-6;1921.6-7; 1922.1-2; 1925.9
Gray, Austin K., 1927.6
Gray, Cecil G., 1951.14-15
Gray, Henry David, 1919.4; 1920.7, 14; 1930.4; 1931.1, 8
Gray, Margaret Muriel, 1939.4
Great Yarmouth, 1977.9
Grebanier, Bernard, 1975.13
Green, Thomas, 1933.5
Greene, John, 1928.15; 1972.13
Greene, Thomas, 1885.2-3;

Greenslade, S. L., 1952.7
Greenstreet, James, 1885.1-4;
Greg, Sir Walter Wilson, 1900.2;1904.7;
        1907.15; 1908.4, 11; 1909.7, 9;
        1911.9; 1919.5-6, 10; 1920.8-10,
        15, 23; 1962.11; 1967.5; 1970.11
        1921.8 1923.6; 1924.4; 1925.1,
        10-12; 1927.7; 1928.5; 1929.3;
        1931.9; 1932.4; 1938.5; 1940.1,
        6; 1954.3, 10; 1956.13; 1959.6;
        1963.4; 1966.7; 1969.5; 1972.17;
        1978.17
Griffin, William James. 1939.5: 1943.5
Gurr, Andrew J., 1960.9; 1963.5-6;
        1966.8; 1970.10; 1972.17

Haaker, Ann, 1968.15
Habicht, Werner, 1972.11
Haines, C. M., 1925.13; 1927.8;
Hale, Edward Everett, Jr., 1903.2
Hall Screen, 1931.4; 1952.4; 1963.15;
        1964.17, 34; 1970.13; 1973.12,
        26; 1976.22
Hall, Samuel Carter, and Hall, Mrs.
        Samuel Carter, 1858.1; 1859.1;
        1867.1; 1869.1; 1877.2
Hall, Vernon, Jr., 1959.7
Halliwell-Phillipps, James Orchard,
        1843.1; 1844.3; 1849.6-7;1870.1,
        3; 1874.2; 1881.3; 1882.3;
        1884.2-3; 1885.5; 1886.3;
        1887.3-4; 1889.4, 6; 1890.2;
        1891.2; 1898.1; 1907.12; 1917.3;
        1943.2; 1957.10; 1974.15;
        1978.12
Hammer, Gael Warren, 1972.12
Hammerton, Stephen, 1977.2
Harbage, Alfred, 1936.11; 1939.6;
        1940.7; 1941.4; 1948.3; 1951.23;
        1952.8; 1953.8; 1964.13-14;
        1968.32; 1970.7; 1972.17;
        1974.6; 1976.11
Harris, Arthur J., 1963.7 1924.25
Harris, Charles, 1907.13-14

Harris, John, 1973.10; 1977.25
Harrison, George Bagshawe, 1886.2, 8;
        1888.5-8; 1889.3 1923.7, 14;
        1927.9; 1934.14; 1956.14;
        1960.19
Harrison, Gerald, 1968.32
Hart, Alfred, 1932.5-6; 1934.2-3;
        1962.11; 1967.5; 1970.11
Hartleb, Hans, 1934.4; 1936.12
Hasler, Jörg, 1979.15
Haslewood, Joseph, 1813.1-3; 1814.1;
        1837.1; 1845.2
Hawley, James Abgriffith, 1967.2
Hayward, Wayne Clinton, 1951.16
Hazlitt, William Carew, 1869.2; 1874.3
Hecht, Hans, 1929.13 0
Helmholtz-Phelan, Anna Augusta,
        1909.12
Heming's Players, 1847.3
Henning, Standish, 1976.11, 13
Henslowe, Philip, 1841.1; 1890.3;
        1904.7; 1907.15; 1908.11;
        1928.6, 12; 1927.7; 1929.8, 14;
        1950.4; 1952.9; 1957.13; 1958.5;
        1961.12; 1963.4; 1963.15;
        1964.17, 34; 1970.13; 1964.31;
        1966.9; 1970.15; 1973.12, 26;
        1976.22; 1971.1; 1973.20;
        1976.21; 1977.4, 8; 1978.17;
        1979.12, 33
-Diary, 1845.3; 1881.4; 1885.7; 1904.7,
        11; 1906.3, 7, 15; 1908.11;
        1921.8, 16; 1927.2; 1938.5;
        1940.1; 1957.13; 1960.8;
        1961.13; 1962.9; 1963.4;
        1968.27; 1973.20; 1974.8;
        1976.9. 11; 1977.4, 8; 1978.17;
        1979.9, 12
Herbert, J. F., 1844.4 1898.1; 1907.12;
        1917.3;
Herbert, Sir Henry, 1885.3; 1913.4;
        1917.2; 1923.15
Herbert, William, Third Earl of
        Pembroke, 1958.23
Hercules, 1977.27
Hereford, 1958.9

Herford, Charles Harold, 1923.8
Herz, Emil, 1903.3
Heywood, Thomas, 1972.13: 1977.31
Hibbard, George R., 1974.4, 16; 1975.9,
	12, 14, 26; 1978.6, 11, 14-15
Hill, R. F., 1975.31
Hillebrand, Harold Newcombe, 1914.9;
	1915.5; 1920.11; 1922.3; 1926.6;
	1927.3; 1961.22; 1976.14
Hind, Arthur Maygar, 1922.4
Hipwell, Daniel, 1892.1
Hodges, Cyril Walter, 1947.5; 1948.6;
	1949.6; 1950.9; 1951.17;
	1952.20; 1953.9-10; 1954.11;
	1955.26; 1959.15; 1961.25;
	1964.15; 1966.9; 1968.16;
	1970.12; 1971.13; 1972.17;
	1973.11; 1975.16; 1979.5
Hogge, Ralph, 1974.8
Hollar, Wenceslaus, 1922.4; 1933.11;
	1948.11; 1949.15; 1952.1;
	1964.11; 1972.14; 1973.11;
	1978.21
Holmes, Martin R., 1956.15; 1960.10;
	1964.16
Holzknecht, Karl J., 1923.9
Honeyman, John, 1927.12
Honigman, E. A. J., 1976.12
Hood, Eu. See Haslewood, Joseph
Hook, Lucyle, 1962.7
Hope Playhouse, 1813.3; 1882.2;
	1885.8, 15; 1894.4; 1904.9;
	1908.11; 1929.9; 1962.21;
	1966.9: 1971.1
-Contract, 1920.24; 1959.25; 1975.20
Hoppe, Harry R., 1949.7; 1954.12;
	1955.8
Hort, Patrick, 1971.18
Hosking, George Llewellyn, 1952.9
Hosley, Richard, 1952.10; 1954.13;
	1956.1, 16; 1957.8-9; 1958.11;
	1959.8; 1960.11, 20; 1962.22;
	1963.2, 8-9, 12, 15; 1964.11, 17-
	22; 1967.3; 1968.17-18; 1969.8,
	10; 1970.13, 18; 1971.7;
	1972.14, 17, 25; 1973.12, 31;

	1975.15; 1976.4; 1978.15;
	1979.5, 16
Hotson, John Leslie, 1923.10; 1928.7;
	1949.8; 1951.30; 1952.11-12, 15;
	1953.10-13; 1954.7. 10-11;
	1955.2, 9-10, 14, 19, 21-22;
	1956.10, 25; 1959.9; 1960.6, 12,
	20; 1961.17, 25; 1964.30;
	1966.9; 1970.4; 1972.17;
	1977.16
Howarth, Robert Guy, 1948.4-5
Hubbard, Barbara, 1970.14
Hubbard, George, 1909.4, 13; 1912.12;
	1915.6-12, 14, 17; 1923.11;
	1924.3
Hudson, Katherine, 1971.8
Huffman, Clifford Chalmers, 1978.22
Hugon, Cecile, 1916.5
Huminghorn, Peter, 1970.15
Hunnis, William, 1892.4; 1900.3;
	1910.8, 20; 1961.8
Hunt, J. A., 1966.10
Hunt, Richard William, 1947.11
Hunt, Theodore B., 1935.3
Hunter, George K., 1976.13
Hunter, Sir Mark, 1926.7; 1927.19;
	1928.8, 18

Imroth, John Phillip, 1974.19
Improvisation, 1903.2; 1908.17; 1922.1;
	1951.6
Ingleby, Clement Mansfield, 1861.1
Ingram, Reginald William, 1955.11;
	1968.19
Ingram, William, 1970.15; 1971.9;
	1972.15; 1976.4; 1978.16;
	1979.17
Inner Stage. See Discovery Space
Inns of Court, 1977.23; 1979.18
Innyards, 1905.1; 1906.5; 1913.6;
	1925.8; 1927.14; 1931.4; 1967.7;
	1968.34; 1969.9; 1971.4-5;
	1972.29, 32
Ipswich, 1931.3

Isaacs, Jacob, 1927.10-11; 1933.4;
    1958.1
Ives, E. W., 1961.14

Jackson, Henry, 1933.8
Jackson, Richard C., 1909.14; 1914.14
Jacquot, Jean, 1956.9, 12, 17, 28, 33-34;
    1964.2, 18, 22, 34, 37; 1966.17;
    1968.1, 10, 14, 18, 20-22, 24, 32,
    37-38; 1973.13
Jamieson, Michael, 1964.23
Jarvis, Royal Preston, 1908.12-13
Jenkins, Bernard, 1945.1
Jenkinson, Wilberforce, 1914.10
Jensen, Ejner J., 1968.23; 1970.16;
    1975.27
Jewell, Simon,1974.14; 1976.16
Jewkes, Wilford Thomas, 1956.19;
    1958.12
Jigs, 1908.12-13; 1919.7; 1927.14;
    1929.2, 9; 1952.22; 1977.22
Johnson, John, 1974.9
Johnson, Robert Carl, 1970.17
Johnston, Elizabeth Carrington, 1964.24
Jonas, Maurice, 1914.11; 1915.23;
    1917.7
Jones, Eldred D., 1962.8
Jones, Inigo, 1848.1; 1903.5; 1914.16;
    1916.15; 1924.4, 6, 10; 1925.5,
    14; 1937.7; 1946.4; 1952.19, 21;
    1953.24-26; 1958.23; 1959,12,
    14; 1966.15; 1967.2, 15;
    1968.26, 28; 1969.10; 1971.6;
    1972.24; 1973.10, 16, 18, 21, 30;
    1974.23; 1975.24, 31; 1976.2,
    17; 1977.25, 31; 1978.25
Jones, Marion, 1962.9
Jones, Tom, 1914.12
Jonson, Ben,1848.1; 1901.1; 1902.5;
    1921.8, 16-17; 1932.7; 1933.8;
    1934.5; 1941.10; 1942.2; 1951.6;
    1952.6; 1956.9; 1958.23;
    1966.15; 1968.26, 28; 1973.2,

    30; 1974.14, 16; 1977.27;
    1978.28, 30
Joseph, Bertram L., 1949.1; 1950.10;
    1951.18; 1854.18; 1955.12-13;
    1956.19; 1959.10; 1961.6, 15-16;
    1962.10; 1964.25; 1970.18;
    1975.18
Joseph, Stephen, 1963.10
Jouvet, Louis, 1936.13
Junius, Archduke Philip, 1892.2; 1902.6

K., L. L., 1914.13; 1914.14-15, 17;
    1915.12, 14
Kahrl, Stanley J., 1969.6
Keith, William Grant, 1914.16; 1925.14
Keller, Wolfgang, 1904.8
Kelly, Francis Michael, 1938.6
Kelly, William, 1855.1; 1865.1
Kempe, Alfred John, 1836.1
Kempe, Will, 1844.1; 1882.4; 1904.9;
    1906.9; 1926.13; 1927.6, 9;
    1930.4; 1931.1, 8; 1946.3;
    1950.5; 1958.13; 1959.3;
    1960.13; 1975.21
Kendall, Richard, 1925.2
Kent, 1961.7; 1.965.6; 1977.6
Kernan, A. B., 1974.17
Kernodle, George Riley, 1937.4; 1944.7;
    1959.11; 1961.25; 1972.17
Kerr, S. Parnell, 1957.10
Killigrew, Thomas, 1925.16; 1929.8;
    1978.29
Kimbrough, Robert, 1976.11, 13
Kincaid, A. N., 1972.16
Kindermann, Heniz, 1959.12
King James I, 1828.1
King, Thomas James, 1963.11; 1965.9;
    1966.11; 1971.10-11; 1972.17;
    1973.14; 1975.19, 30, 1977.11,
    34; 1979.5
King's Company (Restoration), 1929.8
King's Men, 1886.5; 1909.15, 31;1911.7;
    1920.17; 1921.4; 1926.12;
    1927.12, 19; 1928.1, 8; 1941.1;

1946.3; 1951.22; 1954.17;
1955.18; 1957.5, 10; 1958.18,
1959.4, 8; 1961.6; 1963.5;
1968.13; 1973.20; 1974.2, 5;
1975.13; 1976.15; 1977.2, 10-11;
1978.7
King's Revels, 1912.1; 1919.9; 1922.3;
1926.6; 1958.7; 1977.2
King's Theatre (Restoration), 1924.8
Kingland, Gertrude Southwick, 1923.12-
13
Kingsley, Charles, 1873.1; 1889.5
Kipling, Gordon, 1977.12
Kirke, John, 1924.7
Kirsch, Arthur C., 1967.4; 1969.8
Kirschbaum, Leo. 1949.9; 1959.13
Klein, David, 1956.20; 1962.11; 1967.5
Knight, W. Nicholas, 1979.18
Knowles, Richard, 1976.11, 13
Kohler, Richard Charles, 1971.12
Kolin, Philip C., 1974.18; 1976.14
Kopecký, Jan, 1966.12
Krempel, Daniel Spartakus, 1953.14
Kyd, Thomas, 1977.27; 1979.31

L., H., 1854.1
Lacy, John, 1931.5
Lacy, Robin Thurlow, 1959.14
Laird, David Connor, 1956.21
Lamb, Margaret A., 1976.15
Lamborne, Edrnund Arnold Greening,
1923.14
Lancashire, 1931.16; 1979.13
Lancashire, Ian, 1977.13
Landsdowne Manuscripts, 1908.4;
1947.8
Lane, Robert Phillips, 1956.22
Langhans, Edward A., 1965.10
Langner, Lawrence, 1955.15
Langley, Frances, 1970.4; 1971.9;
1972.25; 1978.16
Lanier, Nicholas, 1959.14
Lanman, Henry, 1979.17
Latter, D. A., 1975.20

Laver, James, 1964.26
Lavin, J.A., 1970.18; 1973.15
Law, Ernest Philip Alphonse, 1909.15;
1910.10-11; 1911.15-18, 26-28;
1912.13-14, 20: 1913.8; 1920.12-
13, 26
Lawrence, William John, 1902.5;
1903.4-6; 1905.2; 1908.14;
1909.16-17; 1910.6; 1911.19-20;
1912.15-18; 1913.7, 9-12;
1914.11; 1915.15; 1916.1, 8-10;
1917.4, 6, 8; 1918.1; 1919.6-11,
13, 19; 1920.8-10, 14-24; 1921.3,
9-11; 1922.5-6; 1923.15-17;
1924.4-9; 1927.12-14; 1928.8-
10, 19; 1929.9; 1930.5-7;
1931.10; 1932.7-9; 1933.5;
1934.5-7; 1935,5, 7, 13; 1936.3,
4, 10, 14-15; 1937.5; 1950.1;
1952.19; 1954.5; 1958.6;
1960.20; 1972.17
Lea, Kathleen Margarite, 1931.11;
1934.8
Leacroft, Richard, 1973.16
Lecoq, Louis, 1968.24
Lee, Sidney, 1909.15, 18; 1916.1, 14-15;
1950.1, 16-17
Leech, Clifford E. J., 1934.9; 1935.8-9;
1941.5; 1950.11; 1964.27;
1975.15, 21
Legerdemain, 1949.12; 1956.30. See
also Magic
Leggett, Alexander, 1975.21
Leicester's Men, 1844.1; 1906.9; 1911.8;
1943.2; 1962.4
Lell, Gordon, 1973.17
Lennam, Trevor N. S., 1970.19; 1975.22
Lennep, William Van, 1962.12
Levin, Martha Wusko, 1977.14
Levyveld, Toby Bookholz, 1951.19
Lewes, George Henry, 1936.16
Lewis, John Colby, 1940.8
Liebscher, Frieda Margot, 1920.25
Lighting, 1952.21; 1954.17; 1972.27;
1976.10; 1978.13
Limon, Jerzy, 1977.15; 1979.5, 19

Lincolnshire, 1969.6
Lindley, David, 1979.20
Linn, John Gaywood, 1951.20
Linnell, Rosemary, 1977.16
Linthicum, Marie Charming, 1936.17-18
Livery Companies, 1954.20; 1959.22
Livy, 1975.19
Lodge, Thomas, 1908.19; 1910.25;
    1931.14; 1933.7, 9; 1934.15;
    1972.2
Logeman, H., 1897.1
London, City of, 1931.13
Long. John H., 1951.21; 1968.11, 19. 25
Lord Admiral's Men. 1921.8; 1923.6-7;
    1925.11; 1927.1- 2, 7; 1928.14;
    1935.16; 1956.14; 1961.26;
    1964.31; 1971.17; 1973.20;
    1975.21; 1977.4
Lord Chamberlain, Office of, 1907.3;
    1911.7; 1931.2; 1951.22;
    1958.23
Lord Chamberlain's Men, 1887.14;
    1907.3; 1910.17; 1919.14;
    1923.7; 1928.14; 1930.6;
    1933.10; 1935.16; 1939.2;
    1944.2; 1946.3; 1955.18;
    1956.14; 1961.26; 1963.5;
    1964.31; 1968.31; 1970.23;
    1972.7; 1975.13, 21; 1978.7;
    1979.22, 28
Lord Chando's Men, 1972.7
Lord Mayor's Pageants, 1837.2; 1843.2;
    1845.4; 1848.2; 1909.29;
    1913.18; 1920.32; 1935.9;
    1951.33; 1954.20; 1956.28;
    1957.17; 1964.4; 1968.4-5, 7;
    1970.3; 1971.3; 1973.19;
    1974.10; 1975.2
Lord Mounteagle's Men, 1977.26
Lord Stafford's Men, 1977.26
Lord Strange's Men, 1925.11; 1931.16;
    1946.3
Lord's Room, 1908.15; 1957.8-9, 11.
    See also Upper Acting Area
Loseley Manuscripts, 1836.1; 1911.13;
    1912.6; 1917.1

Lounsbury, Thomas R., 1923.18
Lowe, Robert W., 1888.9; 1970.1
Lower, Charles Bruce, 1965.11
Lowin, John, 1946.3
Lüdeke, Henry, 1917.9; 1950.12
Lyly, John, 1929.16; 1964.5; 1968.8;
    1974.9; 1979.11
Lyons, Clifford P. 1964.28
Lyzarde, William, 1939.7; 1959.14

Maas, Hermann, 1901.2; 1907.16
McCabe, John Charles, 1954.17
McCalmon, George, 1946.4
McCullen, Joseph T., Jr., 1953.16
McDonnell, Michael F. J., 1909.22
McDowell, John M., 1945.2; 1948.7;
    1949.11
McGuire, Philip C., 1979.6
Machyn, Henry, 1848.2
MacKensie, D. F., 1970.21
McKerrow, Ronald B., 1931.12;
    1935.10; 1974.19
MacKichan, L. A. L., 1961.17
Mackintosh, Iain, 1973.18
McManaway, James G., 1951.22;
    1962.13; 1969.8
McMillin, Harvey Scott, Jr., 1965.12;
    1968.26; 1972.19; 1976.16
McNeir, Waldo F., 1941.4; 1962.14
Magic, 1927.22, 24; 1949.12; 1956.30;
    1964.12. See also Legerdemian
Maginnis, James P., 1911.2
Mags, John, 1970.4
Maguo, Alessandro, 1964.8
Main, William N., 1957.11
Maldon, 1907.6-9
Malone, Edmond, 1790.1-2; 1794.1;
    1799.2; 1800.1; 1813.4; 1821.1;
    1839.1; 1875.1; 1901.3; 1917.2-
    3; 1925.1, 18; 1950.15; 1968.33;
    1978.17
Manifold, John Streeter, 1956.23

Manly, John Matthews, 1910.12; 1919.12; 1932.10; 1934.10; 1949.10; 1950.13

Manning, Thomas John, 1972.18

Manningham, John, 1868.1

Mantzius, Karl, 1901.4; 1904.9; 1937.6

Marcham, Frank, 1925.15; 1926.8

Marder, Louis, 1960.12; 1978.17

Marker, Lisa-Lone, 1970.20

Markham, Gervase, 1910.21

Markland, Murray F., 1969.7

Markward, William Bradley 1953.15 1954.16

Marlowe, Christopher, 1951.6; 1964.27, 38; 1969.18, 39; 1972.28, 35; 1974.7; 1977.27; 1979.10, 31

Marshall, Wilhelm, 1928.11

Marston, John, 1977.27; 1979.21, 30

Martin, R. L., 1921.5

Martin, William, 1909.4, 19-21,28; 1910.13-14, 17; 1915.9, 16-19, 23

Martinelli, Drusiano, 1929.15

Masques, 1848.1; 1902.2; 1903.5; 1904.1; 1909.23; 1912.22-23; 1913.16; 1916.15; 1920.18; 19211.9; 1922.5; 1923.1; 1924.4, 10-11; 1925.17; 1926.10; 1934.14; 1935.9, 11-12; 1936.9; 1937.7-8; 1940.8; 1947.7-8; 1950.17; 1951.20; 1952.6, 19, 21; 1953.24, 28; 1954.5; 1956.12, 21, 33; 1957.2; 1958.9, 20-21, 23; 1959.12; 1962.13; 1964.6, 24; 1967.2; 1968.28; 1969.20; 1970.22; 1973.2, 16, 21, 30; 1975.31; 1976.6. 17-18; 1977.24, 28; 1978.6; 1979.20, 29

Massinger, Phillip, 1927.18

Mastr of the Revels, 1836.1; 1847.2; 1849.3; 1870.3; 1886.2; 1906.2; 1908.6, 9; 1910.7; 1913.4; 1916.15; 1917.2; 1919.9; 1925.15; 1926.8, 10; 1929.16; 1933.3; 1947.2; 1951.9; 1957.2-

4; 1961.18; 1966.9; 1972.16; 1973.3; 1974.11; 1978.27

Matson, Marshall Nydall, 1967.6

Mattingly, Althea Smith, 1954.16

Mead, Robert Smith, 1952.13

Meadley, T. D., 1953.17

Meagher, John C., 1973.19

Medici, Guilio de, 1969.7

Mehl, Dieter, 1964.29; 1966.13

Meissner, Johsnnes, 1884.4-5

Menius, Freidrlch, 1939.3; 1941.7

Mepham, William A., 1934.11-13; 1937.6

Merchant, William Moelwyn, 1956.24; 1959.15

Merzlak, Anthony George, 1975.23

Messalina Print, 1908.1; 1909.24; 1911.1; 1948.4

Metz, G. Harold, 1977.17

Meyer, C. F., 1902.6

Meymott, Joseph, 1887.8

Middle Temple, 1868.1; 1971.10

Middleton, Thomss, 1920.20

Mildmay, Sir Humphrey, 1938.3

Miles, Bernard, 1954.18

Miles, Theodore, 1942.4

Mill, Anna Jean, 1931.13

Miller, William E., 1959.16; 1964.30

Mills, A. D., 1977.18

Mills, L. J., 1959.17

Milton, John, 1961.17

Mirabella, Bella Maryanne, 1979.21

Mitchell, Lee, 1937.7; 1941.6; 1947.6; 1948.8; 1949.12

Mithal, H. S. D., 1958.13; 1959.3; 1960.13

Möhring, Hans, 1953.18

Mönkemeyer, Paul, 1905.3; 1933.1

Montanus, Joannes Ferrarius, 1972.20

Montgomery, Roy F., 1954.19

Moody, Dorothy Belle, 1938.7

Moore, John Robert, 1929.10

Morgan, Edmund S., 1966.14

Moritz, Landgraf, 1936.12

Morseberger, Robert E., 1974.20

Moryson, Fynes, 1904.4; 1907.14
Motter, Thomas Hubbard Vail, 1929.11
Moynes, Jon Craig, 1978.18
Mulcaster, Richard, 1909.22; 1943.3; 1970.5; 1972.6; 1974.10
Mulholland, P. A., 1977.19
Müller, C., 1910.14
Müller-Bellinghausen, Anton, 1955.15-16
Mullin, Donald C., 1967.7; 1970.22
Mumming, 1916.15
Munday, Anthony, 1849.2; 1928.17
Mundy, John, 1961.8
Murad, Orlene, 1977.20; 1978.18
Murphy, J. L., 1977.21
Murray, John Tucker, 1905.4; 1910.15; 1912.2; 1920.30; 1929.6; 1936.7; 1954.23; 1968.32
Musgrave, Sir William, 1925.19-20
Music, 1845.4; 1886.6; 1908.14; 1909.6; 1910.14; 1913.2; 1914.2; 1920.19; 1922.5; 1923.16; 1927.15, 24; 1929.10; 1931.7; 1933.4; 1935.4; 1947.7; 1950.3; 1951.21; 1952.22; 1953.29; 1954.5, 17; 1955.3, 11; 1956.7-9, 23, 33; 1957.5; 1958.7; 1959.4; 1960.11; 1961.8, 24; 1963.11; 1965.3, 5, 10; 1967.3, 6; 1968.11, 19, 25, 35; 1972.27; 1973.2, 28; 1974.9; 1976.14; 1978.5
Mutschmann, Heinrich, 1950.5

Nabbes, Thomas, 1975.19
Nagler, Alois M., 1956.25; 1958.14; 1972.17
Nairn, J. Arbuthnot, 1914.18
Naogeorgus, Thomas, 1972.21
Nashe, Thomas, 1968.10
Neill, Michael, 1978.20
Neundorff, Bernard, 1910.16

Newington Butts Playhouse, 1888.11; 1894.4; 1904.9; 1970.15; 1971.4; 1979.22
Newman, Philip P., 1888.11
Newport, Edward, 1951.14
Nichols, John, 1788.1; 1805.1; 1823.1; 1828.1; 1837.2; 1848.2
Nichols, John Gough, 1918.4
Nicholson, Brinsley, 1882.4; 1892.3
Nicolini, Francis, 1954.8
Nicoll, Allardyce, 1925.16; 1935.11; 1936.19; 1937.8; 1948.9-10: 1959.18; 1961.24
Niemeyer, Christian Bernard, 1979.22
Noble, Richard, 1927.15; 1928.6, 12
Noh, 1961.23
Norberg, Lars, 1955.17
Norman, William, 1914.19
Nosworthy, J. M., 1968.27; 1977.22
Nungezer, Edwin, 1927.16; 1929.12; 1959.21

O'Donnell, C. Patrick, Jr., 1973.20
Office of Works, 1975.31
Onions, Charles Talbut, 1916.1, 14-15; 1950.1, 16-17
Orbison, Tucker, 1977.21
Ordish, T. Fairman, 1885.6-10; 1886.4-8; 1887.5-7; 1894.2; 1899.2; 1908.16; 1971.13
Orgel, Stephen, 1968.28; 1973.10, 21; 1975.24
Orrell, John, 1976.17-18; 1977.24-25; 1979.23-26
Orsini, Napoleone, 1946.5
Ostler, William, 1933.5
Overall, H. C., 1878.2
Overall, William Henry, 1878.2
Oxford, Earl of. See de Vere, Edward, Earl of Oxford
Oxford University, 1907.2; 1909.7; 1933.8; 1948.13; 1959.1, 17; 1972.18; 1974.3
Oxford's Men, 1970.15

Ozaki, Makoto, 1975.25

Pafford, J. H. P., 1959.19; 1977.26
Paget, Alfred Henry, 1891.2-3
Palme, Per, 1956.26, 1957.12
Palmer, Prank, 1913.4
Palumbo, Ronald J., 1976.19
Paradise, N. Burton, 1931.14; 1933.9
Paris Garden. See Swan Playhouse
Parrott, Thomas Marc, 1943.6; 1958.15
Parry, Graham, 1978.21
Pascal, Ray, 1940.9; 1941.7
Patent Rolls, 1909.9
Paterson, Morton, 1961.18
Patterson, Remington Perrigo, 1957.13
Paul's Boys, 1814.1; 1889.6; 1912.7;
        1914.2; 1915.5; 1926.6; 1943.7;
        1951.4; 1952.3; 1960.4; 1962.1,
        20;1966.10; 1967.6, 10; 1968.14,
        21; 1970.10, 19; 1971.8, 14;
        1972.6; 1975.22; 1977.14;
        1978.10
Pavy, Salathiel [Salmon?], 1914.18;
        1942.2
Peake, Robert, 1959.14
Peckham, Morse, 1968.34
Peels, George, 1961.8
Peerson, Martin, 1958.7
Peet, Alice Lida, 1961.19
Pembroke's Men, 1911.28; 1921.8;
        1950.20; 1960.4; 1972.19;
        1974.14, 21; 1976.16
Penshurst, 1979.27
Penniman, Josiah Harmar, 1895.2;
        1897.2
Penninger, Frieda Elaine, 1976.20
Percy, Eustace, 1907.17
Percy, William, 1913.1; 1914.20
Periaktoi, 1959.16; 1964.30
Petit, J. B., 1968.29
Phelps, Wayne H., 1979.27
Phillips, Augustine, 1951.27
Phoenix Playhouse, 1860.1; 1882.2;
        1885.1-3; 1887.5; 1904.9;

1905.2; 1921.14; 1928.15;
        1938.3; 1953.15; 1963.11;
        1965.9; 1966.9; 1968.2; 1972.12;
        1973.18, 28; 1977.25, 31, 34
Pilch, Leo, 1911.21
Pinciss, G. M., 1970.23; 1974.21
Planche, James Robinson, 1848.1
Platter, Thomas, 1899.1; 1929.13,
        1937.9; 1956.29; 1962.18
Plomer, Henry R., 1906.8
Poel, William, 1913.14; 1916.11;
        1963.7; 1966.23
Pokorný, Jaroslav, 1955.18
Pollard, Alfred W., 1919.10, 13-16. 18.
        21-22
Pollock, Arthur, 1915.20; 1916.12
Porter, Charlotte, 1915.21-22; 1916.13
Powell, Wilford, 1892.2
Presley, Elorton Edward, 1966.15
Price, Joseph G., 1975.4, 7
Prince Charles's Men, 1849.9; 1978.2
Prindle, Roderic Marvin, 1977.27
Prior, Moody E., 1951.23
Private Playhouses, 1874.1; 1875.1;
        1908.14; 1912.17; 1916.10;
        1920.19; 1921.9, 15; 1923.2;
        1930.5; 1934.10; 1942.4; 1952.8:
        1953.20; 1955.23; 1958.12;
        1959.2; 1964.6; 1965.13; 1967.3-
        4; 1968.2, 30; 1972.24, 32;
        1978.29. See also the names
        of individual playhouses, such as
        Blackfriars, Phoenix, Salisbury
        Court, Whitefriars
Privy Council, 1907.17; 1911.9;
        1912.21; 1924.1; 1970.31;
        1971.9
Proudfoot,G. R., 1977.7, 28
Prouty, Charles Tyler, 1961.18, 20, 22,
        25
Provincial Companies, 1905.4; 1910.15;
        1920.20; 1922.11; 1941.13;
        1942.8; 1953.19; 1959.27;
        1961.7; 1965.6; 1975.1; 1977.4,
        11, 13, 21, 26

Provincial Tours, 1887.4; 1905.4;
        1909.10; 1919.10, 13-16, 21-22;
        1920.16, 30-31; 1922.11; 1927.7,
        24; 1931.15; 1933.10; 1936.7;
        1937.6; 1941.11, 13; 1953.3;
        1954.23; 1959.27; 1961.7;
        1965.6; 1973.4; 1976.11; 1977.6;
        1979.22
Prynne, William, 1910.26; 1912.5;
        1917.10; 1920.6; 1923.18;
        1928.8; 1928.19; 1943.4;
        1972.22
Public Record Office, 1889.3; 1909.16,
        18, 34; 1910.21-25; 1911.7, 29;
        1925.20; 1928.3, 7; 1929.14;
        1930.2; 1931.2; 1942.8; 1943.7;
        1954.18; 1958.7; 1966.4; 1971.9;
        1972.29; 1978.2; 1979.2
Purdom, C. B., 1950.14; 1951.24
Puritan Opposition to the Stage, 1873.1:
        1886.10; 1889.5; 1903.8-9;
        1907.2; 1908.9; 1910.26; 1912.5;
        1916.14, 17- 18; 1920.6; 1921.6;
        1923.18; 1930.10; 1931.14;
        1934.14; 1942.5-6; 1953.17;
        1954.27; 1957.2; 1965.3;
        1966.14; 1972.1-5, 8-10, 13, 20-
        23, 26, 31; 1975.8, 25
Putzel, Rosamund. 1960.14

Queen Anne's Men, 1849.9; 1947.9;
        1954.25
Queen Elizabeth, 1788.1; 1805.1;
        1838.1; 1912.22; 1974.8
Queen Elizabeth's Men, 1911.8; 1926.1;
        1939.4; 1956.22; 1970.23;
        1974.21; 1976.16
Queen Henrietta's Men, 1968.15
Queen Jane's Men, 1914.22
Queen Mary, 1905.9
Queen's Revels, 1912.2; 1926.6; 1927.3;
        1968.24
Quinn, Seabury Grandin, Jr., 1958.16

R., 1938.8
Race, Sydney, 1955.19; 1958.17
Rainolds, John, 1907.2; 1910.26;
        1916.17-18; 1954.27; 1972.23;
        1974.3
Raleigh, Walter A,, 1926.1, 14-15;
        1950.1, 16-17
Rankin, George, 1870.4
Rankins, William, 1910.26; 1972.3
Rannie, David Watson, 1926.9
Ravn, Vilhelm Carl, 1906.9
Rawlidge, Richard, 1920.6
Rear Stage. See Discovery Space
Reardon, James Purcell, 1847 .l; 1849.8
Red Bull Playhouse, 1885.1-4; 1886.8;
        1904.9; 1909.34; 1914.12, 19;
        1916.10; 1921.14; 1933.6;
        1940.10; 1942.7; 1954.25;
        1962.12; 1963.6; 1966.9
Reese, Georg Hermann, 1911.22
Reese, M. M., 1958.18; 1965.13
Remenbrancia, 1878.2; 1907.5; 1956.35
Rendle, William, 1878.3-4: 1885.9, 12-
        15; 1887.8; 1888.10-11; 1890.3;
        1909.3; 1910.13
Renwick, William Lindsay, 1935.12
Revels Accounts, 1842.1; 1909.12;
        1911.15-18, 26-28: 1912.13-14,
        20; 1913.8; 1920.12-13, 26;
        1922.8; 1924.9; 1925.20; 1930.9;
        1964.21; 1966.9
Revels Office. See Master of the
        Revels
Reyher, Paul, 1909.23
Reynolds, George Fullmer, 1905.5-8;
        1906.7; 1907.4, 18; 1908.16;
        1911.23; 1914.20; 1919.17;
        1920.1: 1930.8; 1933.6; 1940.10;
        1941.8; 1949.13-14; 1951.25;
        1953.9; 1956.27; 1962.15;
        1963.12; 1964.27; 1967.8;
        1972.17; 1975.30; 1977.14
Rhenanus, Johannes, 1931.10
Rhodes, Ernest Lloyd, 1959.20; 1976.21
Rhodes, R. Crornpton, 1921.12-13;
        1922.7

Ribner, Irving, 1966.16; 1969.9; 1978.22
Rice, John, 1913.18
Richards, Kenneth R., 1968.30; 1977.29-
    30
Richey, Dorothy, 1951.26
Richter, Bodo L. O., 1966.17
Rickert, Robert Turnham, 1958.19;
    1961.12-13; 1964.31; 1978.17
Riddell, James A., 1970.24
Riewald, J. G., 1959.21; 1960.15
Riffe, Nancy Lee, 1962.16
Rimbault, Edward Francis, 1846.2;
    1872.1; 1920.11
Ringler, William A., 1942.5-6; 1968.31
Roberts, J. R. H., 1950.15
Robertson, Jean, 1954.20; 1956.28;
    1959.22; 1973.22
Robinson, Richard, 1845.1
Rollins, Hyder E., 1921.14;
Rose Playhouse, 1813.3; 1885.7, 15;
    1888.11; 1894.4; 1903.10;
    1925.2; 1904.9; 1908.11;
    1910.17; 1914.20; 1924.8;
    1950.15; 1957.13; 1959.20;
    1964.21; 1965.12; 1971.1;
    1974.13; 1976.21; 1979.9, 13
Rosenberg, Marvin, 1954.21-22
Rosenfeld, Sybil M., 1954.21-22
Ross, Lawence J., 1961.21; 1963.9
Rosseter's Porter's Hall, 1956.35
Rothwell, William Francis, Jr., 1953.20;
    1955.21; 1959.23
Rowan, D. F., 1967.9-10; 1970.25-27;
    1972.24-25; 1975.26
Roxana Print, 1911.1; 1948.4 1960.16;
    1974.26
Royal Entries, 1902.5; 1918.4; 1951.33;
    1956.34; 1968.6-7; 1970.2;
    1971.3; 1973.23, 25; 1974.10;
    1975.24; 1978.3, 18
Royal Processions. 1788.1; 1805.1;
    1828.1; 1837.2; 1951.33; 1971.3;
    1973.25; 1975.24
Royal Progresses, 1788.1; 1805.1;
    1828.1; 1855.1; 1910.14;
    1911.12; 1924.6; 1934.6;

1951.33; 1953.12; 1960.2;
    1979.28 1971.3; 1973.25;
    1974.9; 1975.24; 1978.18
Russell, Douglas A., 1958.20 1937.3;
    1941.9
Rye, William Brenchley, 1865.2

Sabol, Andrew Joseph. 1947.7
Sack, Marie, 1928.13
St. Giles, Cripplegate, 1929.6
St. Paul's, Playhouse at, 1902.4;
    1909.17; 1915.5; 1962.20;
    1966.10; 1968.8, 14; 1970.19,
    28; 1971.13; 1978.11
Salgādo, Gāmini, 1975.27
Salingar, L. G., 1968.32
Salisbury, Earl of, 1969.21
Salisbury Court Playhouse, 1813.2;
    1849.4; 1882.2; 1887.6; 1904.9;
    1912.2; 1916.1; 1925.2; 1928.7;
    1929.8; 1923.19 1952.2;
    1956.12; 1957.14; 1965.10;
    1966.9; 1968.2, 15; 1972.12:
    1977.2-3; 1979.32
Salomon, Brownell, 1972.26
Salvetti, Amerigo, 1976.17; 1979.23
Salvianus, 1972.27
Sampson, George, 1935.13;
Samuelson, David A., 1979.6
Samwell, Richard, 1970.4
Sanders, Norman, 1964.28
Sands, William, 1977.1
Sanvic, Ramain. See Smet, Robert de
Saracen's Head Inn, 1971.5
Sarlos, Robert K., 1961.22
Saunders, F. R., 1952.14
Saunders, J. W., 1954.24; 1955.22;
    1960.16; 1974.26
Savage, Jerome, 1970.15
Savoy, Agent of, 1972.24; 1979.26
Schaar, Claes, 1966.18, 21 1974.10;
    1975.24; 1978.3, 18
Schanzer, Ernest, 1956.29; 1968.33

Schelling, Felix E., 1902.7; 1951.33; 1971.3; 1973.25;
Schless, Howard H., 1952.15
Schneiderman, Robert Ivan, 1956.30
Schoenbaum, Samuel, 1964.13; 1979.28
Schoenherr, Douglas Edgar, 1973.23
Schücking, Levin L., 1931.6; 1937.3; 1941.9
Schuman, Samuel, 1969.11
Scouten, E. R., 1968.34
Scragg, Leah, 1973.24
Seh, L. H., 1935.15
Seltzer, Daniel, 1959.24; 1966.19
Semper, I. J., 1952.16-17
Shady, Raymond C., 1977.31.
Shakespeare Association, 1927.17
Shakespeare, William, 1868.1; 1891.1; 1902.3; 1909.32; 1910.20-25; 1911.21; 1912.22; 1915.1, 13; 1916.11, 13-14; 1918.3;.1919.13-16, 21-22; 1920.18, 20, 22, 25, 28, 30-31; 1921.12-13; 1925.21; 1927.4-5, 8-11, 14-15, 17, 19; 1929.10; 1930.7-8; 1931.15- 16; 1932.8; 1933.8; 1934.7, 14; 1936.9-10, 14-20; 1940.3, 5-6; 1946.3; 1950.19-20; 1951.6, 14; 1953.7; 1961.11, 21, 26; 1964.6, 17, 19, 23, 26-28, 35-36; 1974.21-22, 25; 1977.27; 1978.7; 1979.6, 15, 21-22, 28
Shapiro, I. A., 1948.11; 1949.15; 1966.20; 1967.1, 17
Shapiro, Michael, 1967.10; 1968.35; 1969.12; 1970.28; 1971.14-15; 1975.28; 1977.32
Sharpe, Robert Boies, 1928.14; 1935.16
Sharpham, Edward, 1935.8
Shaw, Catherine M., 1979.29
Shaw. John. 1967.11: 1974.22
Shaw, Robert, 1977.4
Sherborne, 1953.3; 1977.18
Shibata, Toshihiko, 1977.33
Shield, H. A., 1951.27
Shirley, Frances Ann, 1960.17; 1963.13
Shirley, Henry, 1928.1: 1929.4

Shirley, James, 1944.8; 1973.30;1977.34
Shoap, Jeffrey, 1979.30
Shoreditch, 1978.1; 1979.2-4, 8, 16-17, 33
Sidney, Sir Philip, 1844.1; 1958.13; 1959.3; 1979.27
Simmons, J. L., 1972.28
Simpson, Percy, 1916.14-15; 1924.10; 1950.16-17
Simpson, William Sparrow, 1889.6
Simpson's Men, 1942.8
Sincklo, John, 1925.7
Sisson, Charles Jasper, 1921.15; 1927.18; 1929.14; 1933.7, 9; 1934.14; 1936.21; 1940.11; 1942.7-8; 1943.7; 1954.25; 1960.18-19; 1970.4; 1972.29
Sjögren, Gunnar, 1969.13
Skelton, Tom, 1961.14
Skemp, Arthur R., 1909.24
Skopnik, Giinter, 1938.9
Skura, Meridith Anne, 1971.17
Slover, George W., 1968.36
Sly, William, 1946.3
Small, George Wilson, 1935.17
Smeath, Frances Ann, 1979.31
Smet, Robert de, 1955.23
Smith, Duncan Bruce, 1978.23
Smith, G. C. Moore, 1923.20
Smith, Gordon Ross, 1963.14
Smith, Hal H., 1962.18
Smith, Irwin, 1951.28; 1952.18; 1956.31-32; 1958.21; 1961.25; 1964.22, 32; 1966.11; 1967.12; 1970.18; 1972.17; 1973.31
Smith, James L., 1966.21
Smith. Mary E., 1976.22; 1978.24
Smith, Milton, 1931.15
Smith, Warren D., 1948.12; 1951.29: 1953.21-22; 1975.29
Smith, William Henry, 1857.1
Smith, Winifred, 1908.17; 1912.19; 1929.15
Snyder, Frederick E., 1973.25
Soens, Adolph E., 1969.14
Solem, Delmar E., 1953.23

Somerset House. See Court Per-
      formances
Somerset, John Alan Beaufort, 1966.22-
      23
Sound Effects, 1924.5; 1927.14; 1945.3;
      1947.6; 1950.3; 1953.15;
      1960.17; 1963.13; 1965.5;
      1972.27
Southern, Richard, 1939.7; 1947.8;
      1952.19-20; 1953.24; 1954.1, 11,
      15, 26; 1958.11; 1959.25;
      1960.20; 1961.23, 25; 1963.15;
      1964.22, 33-34; 1968.37;
      1970.13; 1972.17; 1973.20
Southwark, 1878.3-4; 1903.10; 1933.11
Spencer, M. Lyle, 1911.25
Spencer, T. J. B., 1970.29
Spens, J., 1919.5, 18
Spinchorn, Evert, 1969.15
Spingarn, Joel Elias, 1909.12; 1957.7;
      1963.3
Spinucci, Pietro, 1973.27
Sprague, Arthur Colby, 1935.18; 1945.3;
      1953.25; 1966.24
Stage Directions, 1904.5; 1905.3;
      1907.10, 20; 1910.16; 1911.20-
      21; 1916.13; 1920.18, 25;
      1921.12-13; 1927.13, 18; 1930.7;
      1935.10; 1938.1, 7; 1940.5;
      1947.6; 1952.10; 1953.22;
      1959.26; 1962.22; 1964.28, 38;
      1965.5, 1.1; 1966.18, 21;
      1971.10; 1974.5, 22; 1975.5, 9,
      15; 1976.12
Staging, 1885.10; 1903.2; 1905.8;
      1906.3: 1907.1.8-20; 1909.12;
      1910.5; 1911.23; 1912.3, 16;
      1913.1; 1914.20; 1916.1, 6, 13,
      16; 1919.1.7; 1921.13; 1923.2;
      1927.1, 5, 8, 13-14, 21-22;
      1934.14; 1935.13; 1936.1, 9-10,
      15; 1938.1: 1940.6, 9-10; 1941,6-
      7; 1942.3; 1943.1; 1945.2;
      1947.8; 1948.6-7; 1950.18-19;
      1951.5, 10; 1952.2; 1954.3, 11,
      15, 28; 1954.17, 24; 1955.5, 28;

1956.27, 30-31; 1957.8, 14, 16;
      1959.8-9, 18, 20, 23, 26, 28;
      1960.16; 1961.1-2, 21, 27;
      1962.2, 5-6, 9, 14-15, 19, 21-22;
      1963.9, 11; 1964.12, 14, 21, 28,
      32, 38; 1965.3, 9, 11-12, 15;
      1966.6, 10-11, 19; 1967.6, 9, 11,
      16; 1968.8, 26; 1969.9, 14;
      1970.10, 13, 22, 25; 1971.10;
      1972.12, 18, 28-29; 1973.25, 28;
      1974.1, 13, 22-24, 26; 1975.7, 9-
      10, 15, 26, 29-30; 1076.22, 25;
      1977.14, 34; 1978.8, 11, 28-29;
      1979.32
Stamm, Rudolf, 1951.30; 1955.24;
      1959.26; 1962.19
Stamps, Alfred Edward, 1930.9
Star, Leonie Rachel, 1972.30; 1974.21;
      1975.30; 1976.23-24; 1978.25
Steele, Mary Susan, 1924.11; 1926.10-
      11
Steevens, George, 1968.33
Stevens, David, 1973.28; 1977.34;
      1979.32
Stevens, Denis, 1956.33, 1973.29
Stevens, John E., 1961.24
Stevenson, Allen H., 1944.8
Stewart, Alan, 1917.10
Stinson, James, 1961.25
Stolzenbach, Conrad, 1962.20
Stone, Lawrence, 1959.27
Stopes, Charlotte Carmichael, 1892.4;
      1900.3; 1905.9; 1907.19, 25-27;
      1910.17-20; 1911.26-28;
      1912.20-21; 1913.8, 15;
      1914.13,21-23; 1915.6, 16, 23;
      1920.12-13, 26; 1924.9; 1925.1;
      1931.12; 1979.2
Stratman, Carl J., 1948.13
Street, Peter, 1952.5, 18; 1979.25
Streitberger, W. R., 1978.27
Stribrný, Zdenek, 1966.12
Strong, Roy, 1973.10, 21
Strunk, William, Jr., 1917.11; 1920.3

Stubbes, Philip, 1847.1; 1849.8;
      1910.26; 1912.5; 1928.10;
      1954.27: 1972.31
Stunz, Arthur Nesbitt, 1939.8
Sturman, Betta, 1947.9
Styan, J. L., 1959.28; 1967.13
Suffolk, 1970.6; 1977.6
Suga, Yasuo, 1963.16-17
Sullivan, Mary, 1912.22; 1913.16
Summerson, Sir John Newenham,
      1953.26; 1955.25; 1958.22;
      1963.18; 1969.16; 1970.30;
      1977.35
Swan Playhouse, 1813.3; 1858.1;
      1885.11, 13-14; 1894.4; 1910.17;
      1911.29; 1912.10; 1913.13;
      1950.1.5; 1951.7; 1952.20;
      1962.7.1.; 1963.20; 1964.1.8, 31;
      1966.9, 25; 1967.9; 1968.18;
      1971.4, 12; 1972.15; 1973.16;
      1974.13; 1975.1.5; 1.978.1.6;
      1979.5, 22
-DeWitt Sketch, 1888.1.1, 4, 10, 12;
      1897.1; 1902.1; 1903.6; 1904.9;
      1906.6; 1907.20; 1908.1, 3, 10;
      1909.3; 1911.1; 1916.1-2;
      1920.1; 1922.7; 1924.2; 1931.4;
      1935.17; 1940.9; 1944.1; 1948.4,
      9; 1950.9, 18; 1951.7; 1952.1;
      1954.1, 15, 26; 1955.4; 1956.15;
      1957.8-9; 1959.25; 1960.9;
      1961.27; 1964.14, 18, 33;
      1965.12; 1967.9, 14, 19;
      1970.21, 27; 1 972.14, 24;
      1975.15
Swinney, Donald H., 1953.27
Symmes, Harold S., 1903.7
Symonds, E. M., 1928.15

T., S. A,, 1921.11
T., S. W., 1870.5
T.-D., G., 1925.17
Tannenbhaum, Samuel. A,, 1920.16;
      1929.3

Tarlton, Richard, 1844.3; 1.882.2;
      1904.9; 1920.21; 1937.5; 1938.2;
      1941.2; 1950.5; 1954.4; 1969.2;
      1975.21
Tarras. See Upper Acting Area
Tatararkiewicz, W., 1965.14
Tatham, John, 1977.21.
Taylor, Alison, 1967.14
Taylor, Dick Jr., 1958.23 1938.10;
      1963.19
Taylor, George C., 1930.1.0
Teagarden, Jack E., 1957.15
Teague, Frances, 1978.27
Teatro Olimpico, 1961.23
Thaler, Alwin, 1918.2-3; 1919.19;
      1920.27-30; 1921.8, 16-17;
      1922.9-11.; 1.931.16; 1932.13;
      1941.10-13; 1964.28
Theatre Playhouse, 1798.1; 1849.1
      1885.6, 1.1.; 1887.1; 1.894.4;
      1904.9: 1909.25-27; 1910.1.9;
      1913.15, 19; 1914.18, 21, 23;
      1915.2; 1916.1; 1917.5; 1928.10;
      1944.3; 1952.18; 1963.21;
      1964,7, 11; 1966.9; 1971.4;
      1973.26; 1979.2-4, 8, 16, 22, 33
Thompson, Elbert Nevius Sebring,
      1903.8-9
Thoresbie, William, 1951.14
Thornberry, Richard Thayer, 1964.35
Thorndike, Ashley Horace, 1913.17;
      1916.16; 1972.17
Tieck, Ludwig, L., 1917.9; 1959.7;
      1961.25
Tillotson, Geoffrey, 1933.8
Tilting, 1958.23
Tittman, Julius, 1880.1
Tomlins, Thomas Edlyne, 1844.5;
      1847.2; 1849.9
Trace, Arthur Storrey, Jr., 1954.27
Trafford, Sir Edmund, 1931.16
Trautmann, Karl, 1886.9; 1887.11-12
Tree, Herbert Beerbohm, 1909.19, 28
Trevel, William, 1930.2-3
Triebel, L. A., 1950.18
Turnor, Celeste, 1928.1.7

Turner, Olga, 1949.16
Turner, Robert Y., 1964.36
Tweedle, Eleanor M., 1976.25
Tylney, Edmund, 1847.2
Tyson, William, 1847.3

Ungerer, Gustav, 1961.26
Unwin, George, 1909.29; 1925.18;
    1938.10; 1963.19
Upper Acting Area, 1903.2; 1907.4, 20;
    1908.10, 15, 24; 1912.18;
    1916.1, 5, 13; 1921.5; 1922.7;
    1924.2, 12; 1927.5, 8; 1929.3;
    1933.4; 1935.5; 1936.1, 3, 5, 10,
    15; 1940.6; 1942.1; 1944.7;
    1948.6; 1949.3; 1951.10, 25;
    1952.2; 1953.9, 15; 1954.13-14,
    17; 1955.4, 1956.1, 15; 1957.8;
    1958.1, 14; 1959.25; 1960.16;
    1961.27; 1962.2, 14; 1963.1, 11;
    1964,32, 38; 1965.12; 1966.10-
    11; 1968.17; 1970.13, 16, 28;
    1975.15; 1976.21; 1978.29;
    1979.32. See also Lord's Room
Upper Stage. See Upper Acting Area
Ure, Peter, 1951.31 1.969.10

Variety Entertainments, 1927.20, 22-24;
    1928.21-22; 1931.1.7
Vatke, Theodor, 1886.10
Velz, John W., 1969.8
Venezky, Alice S., 1951.32-33
Vestiarian Controversy, 1975.8
Views of London, 1884.3; 1902.1;
    1922.4; 1924.3; 1933.10;
    1948.11; 1949.15; 1952.1;
    1954.15; 1961.25; 1964.10;
    1972.14; 1973.11; 1978.21
Visser, Colin, 1978.29
Viswanathan, S., 1974.24

W., T., 1972.8
Waith, Eugene M., 1962.2
Walker, Alice, 1.933.9; 1.934.15
Walker, John Anthony, 1952.21
Wallace, Charles William, 1849.4;
    1887.7; 1888.8; 1906.10-11;
    1908.18; 1909.5, 14, 18-19, 21,
    28, 30-34; 1910.1, 21-25; 1911.4,
    29; 1912.23; 1913.15, 18-19;
    1914.1, 8, 13, 17, 24-25;
    1915.14; 1925.1; 1961.22;
    1968.15l 1977.2; 1978.2; 1979.2
Waller, W. R., 1910.5, 12, 26; 1919.3,
    12, 20; 1932.3, 10, 12; 1934.1,
    10, 20; 1949.4, 10, 17; 1950.6,
    13, 21.
Walton, Charles E., 1953.28
War of the Theatres, 1896.2; 1897.2;
    1923.7; 1928.14; 1935.16;
    1952.8; 1956.14; 1968.2
Ward, A. W., 1910.5, 12, 26; 1919.3, 12,
    20; 1932.3, 10, 12; 1934.1, 10,
    20; 1949.4, 10, 17; 1950.6, 13,
    21
Ward, Bernard Mordaunt, 1929.16;
    1933.10
Warner, Sir George Frederic, 1881.4
Watkins, Ronald, 1946.6; 1947.10;
    1950.19
Watson, George, 1957.16; 1964.25
Webb, John, 1925.14; 1959.14; 1969.10
Wegener, Richard, 1907.20; 1909.24
Weiner, Albert B., 1961.27;
Weixlman, Joseph, 1974.26
Wells, Stanley, 1972.29
Wentersdorf, Karl, 1950.5, 20
Wertheim, Albert, 1973.30
Westcott, Sebastian, 1912.7; 1915.5;
    1943.3, 7; 1951.4; 1952.3;
    1961.8; 1970.19; 1975.22
Whalley, Joyce I., 1966.25
Whanslaw, Harry William, 1924.12
Wheatley, Henry B., 1888.12
White, Anne Terry, 1955.26
White, Beatrice, 1934.36
White, Eric Walter, 1952.22

Whitefriars Playhouse, 1813.2; 1849.4; 1887.7; 1888.8; 1912.1-2; 1922.3; 1930.2-3; 1935.6; 1956.35
Whitehall. See Court Performances
Whitmarsh-Knight, David, 1973.31
Whitty, John Christopher, 1971.17
Wickham, Glynne, 1956.34; 1959.29; 1962.9; 1963.20; 1964.14, 37-38; 1967.15; 1968.32, 38; 1969.17-20; 1970.31.; 1972.17, 32; 1973.32; 1976.4; 1978.28; 1979.33
Wikland, Eric, 1962.23; 1971.18
Wilkinson, Robert, 1825.1;
Williams, Clare, 1937.9
Williams, Iolo A,, 1933.11
Williams, Patrick R., 1978.30
Williams, S. H., 1957.17
Willoughby, Edwin Elliot, 1928.18
Wilson, Edward M., 1949.1.6
Wilson, Frank Percy, 1926.12; 1955.27-29; 1956.35; 1963.21; 1975.31
Wilson, Jack, 1846.2
Wilson, John Dover, 1908.19; 1919.10, 14-16, 20-22; 1920.16, 31; 1927.19; 1928.8, 19; 1932.12; 1934.17; 1947.11; 1948.14; 1949.17; 1950.21
Wilson, Robert, 1926.1; 1958.13; 1959.3
Wilson, William, 1919.1
Winninghof, Elisabeth, 1928. 20
Withington, Robert, 1913.20; 1918.4; 1920.32
Wits Frontispiece, 1911.1; 1973.12
Wood, D. T. B., 1925.19-20

Woodfill, Walter L. , 1953.29
Woodford, Thomas, 1922.3
Woodliffe, Oliver, 1970.4
Woolf, Artlur H. , 1903.1.0
Worcester's Men, 1849.7
Wren, Robert Meriwether, 1965.15; 1967.16; 1969.21.
Wright, George R., 1860.1; 1887.13
Wright, James, 1699.1; 1845.1; 1872.2: 1874.3: 1876.2: 1972.23
Wright, Louis Booker, 1926.13; 1927.20-24; 1928.20-21; 1931.17; 1938.24; 1961.28; 1963.22; 1966.26; 1969.22; 1972.34; 1979.34
Wright, Thomas, 1838.1
Wright, W. S., 1966.27
Wyatt, R. O., II, 1974.18
Wylie, Charles, 1875.1

Yarrow, David Alexander, 1973.33
Yates, Frances A., 1925.21; 1956.28; 1958.2; 1966.20, 28; 1967.1.. 17; 1969.23; 1971.12; 1972.1.7; 1974.24; 1976.21
Yoh, Suk-Kee, 1969.24
Yorkshire, 1942.8
Young, Alan R., 1979.5, 35
Young, Karl, 1916.17-18
Young, William, 1889.7

Zucker, David Hard, 1968.39, 1972.35

Printed in Great Britain
by Amazon.co.uk, Ltd.,
Marston Gate.